# AMERICAN GULAG

# AMERICAN GULAG

INSIDE U.S. IMMIGRATION PRISONS

**MARK DOW**

University of California Press   Berkeley   Los Angeles   London

University of California Press
Berkeley and Los Angeles, California

University of California Press, Ltd.
London, England

© 2004 by the Regents of the University of California

*Frontispiece:* A Pakistani and a Mexican detainee in a
holding cell at the Baltimore INS office, where they
were brought from Maryland's Wicomico County Jail,
2002. Photo: Steven Rubin.

Library of Congress Cataloging-in-Publication Data

Dow, Mark.
    American gulag : inside U.S. immigration prisons / Mark Dow.
        p.    cm.
    Includes bibliographical references and index.
    ISBN 0-520-23942-3 (cloth : alk. paper)
    1. United States—Emigration and immigration—Government
policy.    2. Immigrants—Government policy—United States.
3. Alien detention centers—United States.    4. Human rights—
United States.    5. Emigration and immigration law—United States.
I. Title: Inside U.S. immigration prisons.    II. Title.
JV6483.D69    2004
365'.4—dc22                                        2003026179


Manufactured in the United States of America

13    12    11    10    09    08    07    06    05    04
10    9    8    7    6    5    4    3    2    1

The paper used in this publication meets the
minimum requirements of ANSI/NISO Z39.48-1992
(R 1997) *(Permanence of Paper).*

*for the prisoners*

# CONTENTS

"She tells it so much better than I do," says the director of a human rights organization, introducing the woman with her on the church podium. The audience consists mostly of immigration advocates, along with a few journalists. "She's asked me to interview her rather than just tell her story."

The first question is about the young woman's reasons for leaving her country. The speaker explains quickly that the military kidnapped her older sister, then came looking for her brother and her. The narrative is so rote it sounds as if she were reading from a script. The interviewer asks about entering the United States. "I didn't know about the word 'asylum,'" she says. At the airport an INS official told her, "You African monkeys should go back to your country." She was taken to an INS detention center, where all the inmates were asylum seekers, and made to "bend down and cough" three times. She was menstruating at the time.

As she speaks, her long braids occasionally slip forward and she brushes them back from the microphone on the lectern. Sometimes the incidental details seem less about explaining anything to us than about orienting herself. On that first day in detention, for example, she was shackled to a Spanish-speaking detainee "at around twelve in the afternoon." She has said it all before, to me among many others, although earlier in the day we cut short an interview in her hotel room after several monosyllabic answers and long silences.

But it isn't all rehearsed. She is looking for the words again now. "I don't know how to say this," she says. "They took me as an animal, not a human being. . . . I promised myself whatever happens I will not cry." She means in detention. She is still talking about the first day. Standing there now on the church dais above us, she stifles a sob. She describes how the other detainees would comfort her. They made her bed for her. "They was like, 'I spent three months'" in detention already. The officer-in-charge was less understanding. "She was like, 'If you do not stop crying, I will send you to a real prison.'"

The interview format of the talk gives way to the young woman's stream of memory, though the interviewer stands at her side throughout. She begins to tell the part of her story that, quite possibly, every person in her audience already knows. It is the reason she has been invited. A photograph of her wearing a prison uniform appeared in a human rights group's world survey. In it the twenty-year-old looks like she is twelve. For another group's report, a famous film actress sketched the young woman through Plexiglas, holding a visiting room phone to her ear. In the drawing the actress wrote the young woman's first name, by which she was known throughout the immigrant advocacy community, and next to it her own encircled initials. A television actor from a cop show testified to Congress on behalf of the woman. The hearings on detention conditions had only mentioned asylum seekers because advocates thought the committee might be sympathetic at least to them.

The young woman recalls how certain of the women prisoners were summoned by their eight-digit alien numbers. They were being transferred to a "real prison." They started to cry. They were scared. They tried to call relatives and attorneys, but the phones had been turned off. The women were shackled and put in a van for the drive. "The whole truck was messed up" because there was no bathroom. At the prison they had to bend and cough and be searched again. Three times, just like before. This time she laughs when she tells it. Then she pauses a long time and says it was three o'clock in the morning.

From the holding cell, she tried to show her asylum application to one of the correctional officers. Maybe they didn't understand that these women were asylum seekers and not criminals, she thought. The guard wasn't interested. The young woman could hear other inmates screaming in the nearby maximum security unit. "I was so afraid . . . I was crying . . . so they had to move me to a small room." She was taken to the BAU, or Behavioral Adjustment Unit, known among inmates as the Bad Attitude Unit.

"They asked me to take off my uniform. . . . They asked me to take off my underwear and bra. . . . 'No, even if you are female, I cannot do that.'" So the correctional officers undressed her. She crawled "down [under] the bed just to hide [her] body." Other officers, wearing masks, came over and watched. The one she calls the "Captain" was "tall, big." "I was afraid to even look at him. . . . I don't know how to say this," she tells us, and her next words are absent from my notes. She is crying a lot now, and she stops to hug the woman who introduced her. She continues. Her voice is strong and often interrupted by her sobs. Not completely interrupted, because she seems to talk through the crying. She is poised and distraught.

"They asked me, do you feel like killing yourself?" Defiantly, maybe matter-of-factly, she told them that if she had wanted to kill herself, she would have stayed in her country. They asked if she was hearing voices. Then she felt a needle. They "injected me real hard, the way you can inject your own dog. . . . I started talking to God in my language." She says she asked God, "Do you know what's going on?"

There were five officers, three women and two men. The men were twisting her arms. "I promised myself even if they give me poison to drink not to say nothing. . . . [Then they] spread me out . . . both my legs and my hands. . . . They injected me once again." She remembers they cursed at her. They were watching her as they spread her legs. She turned her head away. She was shivering. Again, "[I was] talking to God in my language. . . . They threw a small something, like a rag, not even a blanket. I struggled to cover myself. . . . That was the last thing that happened when I was conscious."

When she woke up, she was dressed. "I didn't say nothing to them because I was afraid even to ask who dressed me up." Someone gave her a rosary. Medical personnel asked again if she wanted to kill herself and whether she was hearing voices. She told them she was hungry and dizzy, and then she was moved to the dorm. The other detained women wanted to know about the dog that the guards had had with them, but she had not even noticed the dog. She collapsed when the women told her about it. They picked her up. Then they bathed her and braided her hair.

Later she spoke to a minister who visited the prison. "Let me go and die in my own country," she says she told her. "I can't die in America."

She tells us, "I was so tired of myself. I couldn't believe that was me again." Then she stops and with a fully opened hand covers her face.

She was interviewed by a foreign television network about the experience she is describing to us, and then she was moved back to the INS detention center. She never really wanted to speak with the television reporter, but other inmates urged her to do it. Afterward, the Captain threatened them all, and they were afraid. "Who do you think you are?" they demanded of her. She mimics their threatening tone, and she starts crying again.

I had had a couple of beers with a group of attorneys before the program. Now, I don't take my notebook with me as I leave for the bathroom, but I can hear her voice in the hallway through the amplifier system that had been installed for spillover church services. When I return she is no longer talking about her prison experience, but she has more to say. It seems possible that she may talk for hours, not because she is long-winded, but because she is stranded and uncontained. And so we all sit there in the pews, maybe a hundred of us, watching her and listening. Later, quietly, a handful of attorneys and human rights workers tell me they feel the young woman should not have been put through this. An attorney working on the woman's asylum case is the most explicit. "I can't believe they let her do that . . . unless they think that the exploitation has a higher good, and I don't think it does." The attorney was not at the event. "I think it was prurient on their part," she says.

"After going through all of that," the young woman says to us, "even after winning asylum, I lost all the joy that was in me. I lost all the happiness that was in me. . . . Even when they asked me how old I was, I couldn't remember. They thought I was joking." "All the joy and happiness I knew were already gone," she repeats. When some of her fellow detainees were released, she "felt sorry for them." Sometimes "people say a hundred words" and she realizes she hasn't been listening. "I don't have a future anymore. I'm just dead. I'm not interested in anything. . . . Right now I'm seeing a doctor to let me forget about everything. . . . I think I will thank God if they won't ever do this to anybody else. . . . Sometimes I feel like a crazy person. . . . I don't want to go anywhere."

Then she says that she misses prison. We are far from the air of rehearsal in her opening words, yet she is speaking seamlessly, and that makes her revelation all the more unsettling. If she had not elaborated, if she had simply said it and moved on, I always would have thought I had misheard her.

"I felt like that was my home for the rest of my life," she says. "I have dreams of my friends in detention." They used to stay up through the night with her when she couldn't sleep. Now, on the outside, when she wakes up screaming they are not there to hold her. Sometimes when she tries to scream, no sound comes out. She is making involuntary choking sounds as she says this. She pauses. The interviewer comforts her a moment. The young woman tries to talk about the food in prison, about the windowless rooms. Then she lets go of the details. She talks about "giv[ing] up on God." She felt she was going to lose her temper with those who came to minister to her. She couldn't pray anymore. "They say the devil is with you. . . . I say I talked to God. . . . Let this be home . . . I will be here till he opens the door for me."

She was released from detention after a year and a half. She was granted political asylum. She says, "I felt I was leaving my family." She would say to her aunt, "I wish they would just send me back because I'm not used to this kind of life. . . . They messed up my life . . . I feel like I could go back . . . I feel like a newborn baby." Her voice is muffled now as she wipes her tears. "A place for suffering only, no joy . . . [I ask God,] please stop with me. Nobody else."

She has spoken for perhaps an hour. A man moderating the program says into another microphone, "You are a good woman and a child of God." He thanks her. There is hesitation, then a standing ovation. At a nearby hotel, there is a wine and cheese reception. Several human rights advocates take turns having their photo taken with her; I take out my notebook. Downstairs, outside the elevators, a television monitor is showing an excerpt from a documentary about detention. The young woman is on the screen. She is saying, "I won't cry. I'll never cry again."

# 1 | INVISIBILITY, INTIMIDATION, AND THE INS

The letter begins with elaborate politeness and without question marks:

> I must thank you for your kind understanding. How are you doing. How was your health. As for me, I am here by the grace of God. Monday at 2 o'clock in the morning I was upset by the action of officers who came in with batons in their hands and threatened the detainees to stay in their beds without moving a muscle and not to look and to close their eyes. Then they deported 34 Haitians who didn't even get to say a word to their friends because the officers would not let them talk. I am happy that you gave me that collection of Gaston. It is very entertaining to read about the adventures of Gaston. You may write my poem in the newspaper but without my name. Because I am afraid they will put me in a cold cell or even deport me to another prison. That is the reason I do not want you to use my name.

The Krome detention center of the U.S. Immigration and Naturalization Service is a sprawling complex at the edge of the Everglades, about thirty miles west of downtown Miami. In 1990, employed part-time by the Dade County public schools, I taught a high school equivalency class at Krome for a few months. One of my students wrote the letter from the detention center. Most of the contract teachers understood, I think, that our real job was not so much to teach anything as to help alleviate the boredom of long days in detention. I soon learned that we had another role and that I was a cog in the machine. Fellow teachers explained that our true role, as far as our employer was concerned, was to fill registration sheets with the names of detainees passing through the camp. Our employers could then use these numbers to apply for state funding, which they could direct to other programs.

The despair and frustration of the prisoners at Krome were unmistakable. In the afternoon glare, as I drove back toward Miami Beach from Krome, my mind's eye retained the image of large groups of mostly dark-skinned prisoners sitting around a yard or in a cement-block building in their bright orange uniforms—what my student referred to in his poem as his "uniform of contempt."[1] Before the hopelessness that pervaded Krome had dissipated, I would be back on familiar freeways, passing the usual strip malls and subdivisions; in an hour I would be home on the beach. I realized that Krome was invisible.

In fact, at the time, Krome was attracting local and national media attention for allegations that detention officers were mistreating detainees. The officers who ran the camp were immune to the effects of bad publicity. As one of them later told me, "We knew about the criticisms, but it wasn't something we really paid attention to. To tell you the truth, everybody in there felt untouchable. It was our world." But the Krome administrators— the Miami INS bureaucrats—were not completely immune to media and political pressure, and so the siege mentality so common to law enforcement was in full force. But I did not understand that yet.

The young Haitian student who wrote the letter told me that during a "shakedown" officers had confiscated his dictionary, photos, address book, receipts for money and a suitcase, a book entitled *Esperance sans illusions* (Hope without illusions), and a photocopy of a Belgian comic book featuring Gaston Lagaffe. The student was upset, so without thinking much about it, I walked from the men's dorm over to the administration building to speak with the officer-in-charge, Constance "Kathy" Weiss. When I started teaching at Krome, Weiss had told me that I should drop by if there was ever a problem.

Three weeks before I walked into Weiss's office the *Miami Herald* had run a lengthy front page feature: "Krome: Stories of despair. Beatings by guards among tales of horror"; "Humiliation, harassment, and suffering a part of everyday life, refugees report." The story, by Debbie Sontag, included a set of photos with vivid captions. One showed a Haitian man who alleged that a Krome guard beat him, threw him into isolation, then brought another officer to show off his handiwork. The second photo showed a Haitian couple. The man told Sontag that when he was detained, an officer forced him to wash his personal car; the woman alleged that guards regularly groped female prisoners' "breasts and buttocks." The third photo, above the other two, was probably the most important. It showed a white woman next to a crucifix. "What goes on at Krome is more horrible than anyone on the outside can imagine. But not much gets out because people don't put stock in what the families of detainees say," the woman told the *Herald*. She was identified in bold print as "Janine Todaro, Krome teacher."[2]

Todaro had been teaching at Krome for seven years, and out of what she described as her sense of Christian duty, she had decided to break her silence. In her interview with the *Herald*—which was denied access to Krome by Miami INS officials, another piece of the emerging pattern— and in statements she later gave to Miami's Haitian Refugee Center (HRC), Todaro emphasized her concerns about detained women and children. She could no longer bear to listen to the women's horror stories, she said. For years, female detainees had been telling her that guards regularly coerced sexual favors from them in exchange for promises of release. Todaro had also gone to a lot of trouble to find the birth certificates of detainees who claimed to be minors, so that the INS might move them to a juvenile facility. Years later, the INS acknowledged internally that something had to be done about the minors held at Krome—a practice that had become illegal.[3] My student had practiced his English one day by writing, "I am sixteen years old and I have two months twelve days at Krome. I write this poem to squeeze out my suffering."

It was only as I sat in Weiss's wood-paneled office that I began to realize what was happening. Weiss assured me that she too was disturbed that books were confiscated. More important, she let me know that my student had not been singled out; all of the detainees had had their belongings confiscated. Some things were probably in the property warehouse now, and some things would have been thrown away, Weiss explained. She told me that the order had come from the district director's office and that she was only complying with it. I couldn't have known Krome's property room and Weiss herself would become subjects of federal inquiries. A few years later INS officials reported that the detainees' property was not always returned to them when they were deported or released. Weiss would be removed from her position after she admitted to the Justice Department's watchdog agency, Office of the Inspector General (OIG), that she had organized transfers out of Krome to hoodwink a visiting congressional delegation about overcrowding at the camp; she admitted that detainees were "stashed out of sight for cosmetic purposes." But she would soon be returned to a position of authority.[4]

Miami remains a small town in its own way. I called the district director's office and spoke to Assistant District Director George Waldroup. He went into a rage, accused me of not having gone through proper channels, and said that I had probably given my students "contraband." Ten minutes later I received a call from my boss in the school system: "I understand that there was a situation this morning which you tried to handle yourself and that you went beyond your scope." She asked me not to speak to anyone until she got back to me. Later that day she called to say that she was concerned I might "add fuel to the fire" started by Janine Todaro's public allegations. She said she also was concerned about the future of the school program at Krome and added that a problem had been discovered regarding my teaching certification. Within days school officials discovered problems with my class enrollment as well, and my class was canceled.

Between the day of the "situation" and my dismissal, all Krome teachers were required to attend an orientation, at which Krome INS officer Anthony Rivera calmly explained that the media tend to distort what they are told because their only goal is to sell papers. Another day, an INS "recreation specialist" paid a visit to the teacher's office and informally suggested that we watch for suspicious activity. "I guess I'm asking you to be our spies," he said. Years before, a group of Cuban detainees had started a fire at the detention center. Now, because of an upcoming demonstration planned by Miami's Haitian community outside Krome's gates, administrators had decided to take precautions and confiscate what the district director called "combustibles." That's when my student, along with his four hundred fellow detainees, lost his possessions. But combustibles were dangerous for another reason too: a teacher who had noticed my students reading the newspaper one day warned me in a hushed voice that the guards didn't want detainees to see what was in it.

The demonstration at Krome took place in April 1990. A week or so later I heard a rumor in the teacher's office that Todaro was going to be fired because she had been seen by INS officials in a videotape they had made of the demonstration. Indeed, Todaro had written a letter to her church inviting fellow parishioners to join her in showing "concern for the detainees of all nationalities." I called Todaro to tell her about the rumor, and she laughed it off. Her class was canceled a few days later; officials said there was not enough security available for it. Todaro found this out when a guard at the Krome gatehouse stopped her as she drove in to work and handed her a letter from her boss in the school system.

I helped Todaro put together a statement about her experience for Miami's Haitian Refugee Center, and before long I was working as a staff member at its storefront legal assistance office. One of my jobs was to interview Krome detainees, but the INS refused to let me do so. Administrator Weiss, who had claimed earlier that my dismissal from teaching was between me and the school system and that it had absolutely nothing to do with the INS, now explained that I would not be permitted to enter Krome's attorney-client visiting area because of "the circumstances of [my] previous employment" there and because my name had appeared in the newspaper "in connection with certain allegations."[5] Weiss also invoked the law: she told one of the HRC's attorneys, Esther Olavarría, that I did not qualify as a legal representative under the relevant statute. Olavarría explained that the statute applied only to persons representing aliens in court. But no matter.

We tried again. This time it was my immigration status that was the problem. An INS officer asked me for a driver's license and for proof of my legal status in the United States (I was born in Houston). HRC's supervising attorney, Cheryl Little, who had been visiting Krome for many years, explained to the officer that this requirement had never existed before, only to be told that it was "routinely done." Weiss's assistant administrator, Michael Rozos, emerged to concede that the new requirement was in fact new and that it had been put in place because of heightened security concerns since the start of the Gulf War. When the law provides insufficient cover, "security" becomes the inevitable pretext. After a few months of this sort of thing, Miami attorney Ira Kurzban, counsel to the HRC, had a tête-à-tête with Richard Smith, INS district director. An antagonistic but working relationship, plus the threat of an unwinnable lawsuit, seemed to make the difference. A few days later I was allowed into Krome to interview HRC clients.

"We're in a fight with the advocates for the Haitians," District Director

Smith had told me when we were discussing my student's belongings. "I'll be vindicated," he said and added, "The Haitian community in this town will pull any trick in the book." Two months later my student was deported to Haiti at two o'clock in the morning.

———

For almost a century, immigration to the new United States of America was regulated by local jurisdictions. Most immigrants arrived at major ports, and decisions about how to handle them were made by the port commissioners. Ship captains and shipping companies were usually responsible for holding and returning would-be immigrants rejected by the commissioners. Shawn P. Aubitz, a government historian, notes that "in most cases where aliens were detained it was due to their failure to pass the medical examination." Through most of the nineteenth century deportation was rare. And according to historian William S. Bernard, the California gold rush of 1849 and the subsequent arrival of Chinese who were "largely brought in as contract labor to build the railroads" spurred "the drive for federal regulation of immigration." In the mid- and late 1800s localities began turning to the federal government for funding and assistance. Bernard continues: "In the late 19th century, the federal government built the administrative and bureaucratic machinery that would operate this new federal immigration policy."[6]

Ellis Island, the major port of entry, opened its immigrant-processing operations in 1891. For a great many immigrants, of course, Ellis Island was a symbol of welcome. But, according to a description in the INS's own history of the legendary gateway, in the early 1900s it "was a grueling detention-like penitentiary. It was to many, a nightmare." The INS's *Isle of Hope, Isle of Tears* reports that conditions on Ellis Island were unsanitary and overcrowded: "The food was unsavory and lacking in nutrition—stewed prunes over stale black bread, with little variation. . . . As a consequence of the mental anguish . . . many immigrants committed suicide," three thousand in the first forty years of operation. In the last twenty-five years of its operation, from 1930 to 1954, according to *Isle of Hope*, "the island became a grim detention center." In 1953 a U.S. Supreme Court justice called it an "island prison."[7] A year later Ellis Island closed altogether, later to reopen as a museum.

The Immigration and Naturalization Service announced in 1954 that it was "abandoning the policy of detention," according to refugee expert Arthur Helton, except in rare cases when an alien was considered likely to "abscond" or to pose a danger to the nation or community. This policy continued for the next twenty-six years. The general practice was to release undocumented immigrants pending their administrative proceedings, "avoiding 'needless confinement.'" According to the INS, "The average detained alien of the 1970s was a young male or female noncriminal who either overstayed his/her visa or entered illegally to secure employment." Apprehensions were concentrated on the Mexico-U.S. border, and, again according to the INS, "the Service's concentrated effort [is] to seek out and deport a selected group of illegal aliens—those holding lucrative jobs at the expense of citizens and lawful aliens." However, the INS reported that the decision to detain would continue to depend "upon economic conditions on both sides of the border and particularly upon the labor situation."[8]

Immigration "enforcement procedures" that had long "tended to be casual," in the words of one historian, would become increasingly "brutal," in the characterization of an INS official who resigned because of what she saw. International and domestic factors contributed to the stricter policies. In 1980, over the course of about six months, 125,000 Cubans left the port city of Mariel for the United States. President Jimmy Carter initially welcomed the refugees of what became known as the Mariel boatlift, and they were "processed" at Miami's Krome Processing Center and a half dozen other centers around the country. In 1981 a less dramatic but large influx of Haitian "boat people" (known as *botpipel* even in Haitian Creole) left their country for the United States. Krome was expanded as President Ronald Reagan ordered the mass detention of the Haitians, who were described as "economic" rather than "political" refugees in order to justify denying them political asylum. Attorney General William French Smith said, "Detention of aliens seeking asylum was necessary to discourage people like the Haitians from setting sail in the first place." The use of detention as a deterrent to potential refugees "violates obligations assumed by the executive" under international law, according to Helton, but this policy for Haitians remains explicit today. Meanwhile, although thousands of Cubans would end up in long-term detention, most Cubans who made it to U.S. shores were welcomed as political refugees since they were fleeing a regime opposed by the federal government.[9]

The Reagan years brought what Timothy Dunn calls the "militarization" of the southern border and of immigration enforcement in general. Under Reagan, the federal government also worked out a "contingency plan" for the "detention of hundreds of thousands of undocumented aliens in the case of an unspecified national emergency" and of "alien activists who are not in conformity with their immigration status."[10] In making this plan, the INS noted its shortage of detention space. As the 1980s progressed and Reagan administration policies in Central America helped to fuel the flight of thousands of Salvadorans and Guatemalans, the INS notified Congress of its need for more detention space. Refugees from these countries, too, were detained as part of the administration's strategy to deny them political asylum. From 1973 to 1980 the average daily number of people in INS detention almost doubled, from 2,370 to 4,062.[11]

At home the INS's enforcement strategies were increasingly influenced by the rhetorical and political focus on crime and drugs. A concern with "criminal aliens" was not new. In 1909 the immigration commissioner had reported that the "subject" of "alien criminality" was "of the utmost importance."[12] In the last third of the twentieth century, however, this subject came to occupy a new role in INS policies. Through the 1980s and into the 1990s, prison and jail populations skyrocketed as a result of the "war on drugs." The "Service," as it was often called, was devoting more of its growing resources to locating noncitizen inmates in local jails and state prisons in order to take them into INS custody and remove them more efficiently.[13] The bureaucratic imperative of higher numbers—in this case, the number of "criminal aliens" apprehended and expelled—became a political priority.

In the 1990s it became more difficult to distinguish between domestic and international factors governing detention policies. In 1993 the *Golden Venture,* a cargo ship, landed off the coast of New York with 286 smuggled Chinese on board. This "brought the issue of unauthorized immigration to the forefront of national attention," writes Joseph Nevins. The Chinese were detained, and the Clinton administration continued to detain even those who were granted political asylum by immigration judges "while it pursue[d] a reversal" of those asylum decisions.[14] In the same year the World Trade Center was attacked for the first time by immigrants, and in 1995 an American citizen, Timothy McVeigh, bombed the Murrah Federal Building in Oklahoma City. Once again, the INS had a key role to play in the political movements galvanized by Congress. In 1996 President Bill Clinton signed into law the Antiterrorism and Effective Death Penalty Act (AEDPA) and the Illegal Immigration Reform and Immigrant Responsibility Act (IIRIRA), the latter rushed through Congress to commemorate the anniversary of the Oklahoma City bombing.

Together these laws drastically expanded the categories of crimes for which immigrants who had become legal residents were "deportable" and subject to "mandatory detention." In other words, the new laws "eliminated the INS's discretion to release certain aliens" and required that it detain large numbers of legal resident aliens without setting a bond. The laws also mandated increased detention of asylum seekers and, through a process known as expedited removal, gave low-level immigration inspectors wide authority to return asylum seekers encountered at airports. The number of detainees increased dramatically; a few thousand of the detained were asylum seekers. From 1994 to 2001 "the average daily detention population has more than tripled," an INS official informed Congress, "from 5,532 to 19,533." Striking an appropriate bureaucratic key, one commentator observed that the INS was "the world's largest agency that apprehends individuals." As former INS official George Taylor put it, the INS was becoming a "mini-BOP [Bureau of Prisons]." The agency was unprepared for such a mission, Taylor told me, in terms of infrastructure and "expertise in corrections."[15]

Today the immigration agency holds some 23,000 people in detention on a given day and detains about 200,000 annually. The prisoners are held in the INS's service processing centers; in local jails; in facilities owned and operated by private prison companies such as the Corrections Corporation of America (CCA), the Wackenhut Corporation, and the Correctional Services Corporation (CSC); and in Bureau of Prisons facilities, including federal penitentiaries. Wherever they are held, INS prisoners are "administrative detainees"; they are not serving a sentence. As early as 1935 a Texas judge said it was "most regrettable" that Mexican women arrested for working illegally in El Paso were confined in the local jails "along with women of loose morals and general unsavory reputation." In 2003 approximately 60 percent of INS detainees were in local prisons and jails and in private contract facilities.[16]

Local politicians and business entrepreneurs have taken full advantage of the revenue possibilities in immigration detention. Many asylum seekers aboard the *Golden Venture,* for example, were detained in a York County, Pennsylvania, jail. In a neighboring county, a *Harrisburg Patriot* headline read, "Prison Board Shopping for Immigrants to Prevent Layoffs." A Perry County commissioner told the *Patriot,* "We tried like the dickens to get some of the Chinese . . . but it didn't pan out. . . . If no immigrants are secured, some layoffs may be inevitable." The federal government paid York County $45.00 per detainee per day, although it only cost the prison $24.37 to maintain each prisoner. As the Chinese asylum seekers approached the two-year mark of their detention, the county's general fund boasted a profit of about $1.5 million.[17] A Mississippi sheriff said, " 'We don't always agree with the INS holding them. . . . But we like the money,' " and a Miami INS official confirmed that a jail in northern Florida was "calling us all the time to bring back some business for them." A Nigerian detainee being transferred from Krome to the Monroe County Jail in Key West overheard a jail official and an INS officer discussing vacancies and wondered, "Is this slave trade or what?"[18]

When detentions increased following the September 11, 2001, attacks on New York City and the Pentagon, private prison profiteers saw another opportunity. The chairman of the Houston-based Cornell Companies spoke candidly in a conference call with other investors: "It can only be good . . . with the focus on people that are illegal and also from Middle Eastern descent. . . . In the United States there are over 900,000 undocumented individuals from Middle Eastern descent. . . . That's *half* of our entire prison population. . . . The federal business is the *best* business for us . . . and the events of September 11 [are] increasing that level of business." The head of the Wackenhut Corporation was also optimistic: "As a result of the terrorist attacks in the United States in September we can expect federal agencies to have urgent needs to increase current offender capacity if certain anti-terrorism and homeland security legislation is passed." A colleague asked about the possibility of "internment camps," and the company head reflected, "It's almost an oddity that . . . given the size of our country and the number of illegal immigrants entering our country that we have such a small number of beds for detention purposes, and I think this has become an issue under the 'homeland security' theme, and I think it's likely we're going to see an increase in that area." A White House Office of Federal Procurement Policy official confirmed the trend:

"'If there has ever been a time when the government needs to expand and fortify its base of suppliers for both goods and services, this is the time.'" "Nowhere is this more evident than in the procurement of detention space," adds a former Justice Department attorney.[19]

The INS was transferred to the Department of Justice from the Department of Labor in 1940 by President Franklin Roosevelt. "Transfer to an enforcement agency was a logical step" in wartime, says an INS-produced history of immigration laws. The INS remained part of the Justice Department for sixty-three years. On March 1, 2003, it was "transitioned" into separate bureaus within the Border and Transportation Security Directorate of the new Department of Homeland Security (DHS). For weeks afterward, some agency officials became tongue-tied as they answered their phones with the new nomenclature. Within the DHS, detention became the responsibility of the Bureau of Immigration and Customs Enforcement (BICE).[20] This bureaucratic reshuffling is months old at this writing, but one potential danger is already apparent. The secretive immigration prison world is likely to be pulled even further from public scrutiny.

———

During the two years I worked at Miami's Haitian Refugee Center, talking to advocates and attorneys who were trying to help INS detainees around the country, I began to understand that the Krome detention center had many counterparts. In this book I examine the reasons that people are in detention, but I am not concerned primarily with immigration policy. Rather, this book is about prisons—about a particular American prison system operated by the INS or, since early 2003, by the BICE—with an astonishing lack of accountability, not only to outside criticism, but to the rest of the government as well. It is a prison system that, with a few exceptions, has managed to remain invisible. Once you know about these "facilities," as the sanitized corrections terminology has it, once you have visited a number of them, the map of the United States starts to look different.

Communicating from Miami with advocates in New York and California, I learned about New York City's Varick Street detention center, where detainees have been held for months without seeing daylight or fresh air.[21] From advocates in southern California, I heard about repressive crackdowns on Central Americans' hunger strikes in Los Angeles and along the California-Mexico border. Over the next decade, after more than a dozen prison visits and innumerable phone calls and letters from detainees, I watched the rest of the country fall into relief: Seattle, Washington; Bakersfield, Lompoc, and Berlin, California; Florence and Aurora, Colorado; El Paso, Dallas, Houston, and Laredo, Texas; Oklahoma City and Waurika, Oklahoma; Terre Haute, Indiana; Rush City, Minnesota; Atlanta, Georgia; Gadsden, Alabama; Columbia, South Carolina; New Orleans, Oakdale, Cottonport, Avoyelles, Pine Prairie, Amité, and Lake Charles, Louisiana; Bay St. Louis, Mississippi; Piedmont, Virginia; Ashland, Kentucky; Columbus, Ohio; Salisbury, Maryland; York and Lehigh, Pennsylvania; North Dartmouth and Plymouth, Massachusetts; Hartford, Connecticut; Cranston, Rhode Island; Manchester, New Hampshire; Batavia, New York; Brooklyn, Queens, and Manhattan; Elizabeth, Paterson, and Kearny, New Jersey; Palmetto, Jacksonville, Ft. Lauderdale, and Key West, Florida. Dots began to connect along the 1,800-mile INS bus routes and the air routes of the federal interagency Justice Prisoner and Alien Transportation System (JPATS).[22]

Aleksandr Solzhenitsyn describes the nation within a nation constituting the gulag archipelago. His translator, Thomas P. Whitney, writes, "The *image* evoked by [Solzhenitsyn's] title is that of one far-flung 'country' with millions of 'natives,' consisting of an *archipelago* of islands, some as tiny as a detention cell in a railway station and others as vast as a large Western European country, contained within another country." My own title intends no analogy to the purpose, scale, or often fatal brutality of the Soviet gulag. I use the word *gulag* in its more general sense of prison rather than labor camp. Yet Solzhenitsyn's description of the invisible country all around us could not be more appropriate: "there is where the *Gulag* country begins, right next to us, two yards away from us."[23] The INS prison system is distinct from but often grafted onto the larger American gulag. At this writing, there are more than two million people, citizens and noncitizens, doing time in U.S. prisons and jails. But the INS prison system is in a sense the *American* gulag; its raison d'être is the control of certain non-Americans among "us."

This book is an attempt to leave a record—usually narrative and descriptive, sometimes archival, occasionally polemical—of something the U.S. government has long preferred to keep far from view: the system of immigration detention itself, including the widespread mistreatment of the prisoners inside that system. This book tells just some of the countless stories connected to the U.S. immigration gulag. The consistent purpose of this effort is simple—to make public what the INS and now the BICE try to hide.

On paper, for example, there are agency "standards" regarding immigration detention conditions. These cover attorney visitation, media interviews, law libraries, detainee grievance procedures, and other crucial aspects of prison life.[24] "But by refusing to promulgate these standards as regulations," notes Judy Rabinovitz of the American Civil Liberties Union (ACLU) Immigrants' Rights Project, "the INS insured that they would be difficult, if not impossible, to enforce." This effort to operate outside the bounds of enforceable law is no accident; on the contrary, it is characteristic of INS/BICE tactics, as I repeatedly show.

Many readers will be most familiar with immigration detention in the context of the terrorist attacks in the United States in 2001. It is to that context I turn in the next chapter. "September 11: Secrecy, Disruption, and Continuity" attempts to show that these detentions are best understood not as a meaningful or even well-intentioned response to terrorism but rather as part of the larger context of INS secrecy and excessive authority. The administration of George W. Bush exploited our national trauma to extend federal law enforcement authority, as the long-standing biases within the Justice Department against Muslims and Arabs became politically correct. In crucial respects the September 11 detentions were new; Georgetown University law professor David Cole observes, "Never in our history has the government engaged in such a blanket practice of secret incarceration."[25]

A year and a half after the attacks on New York City and Washington, D.C., a scathing critique of the Bush administration's post–September 11 detention policies was issued, paradoxically, by an arm of the Justice Department itself.[26] Although shocking to some, the details in this report were more than familiar to immigrant advocates. The report documents widespread mistreatment of detainees as well as the Bush-Ashcroft policy of failing to distinguish between "illegal immigrants" and "terrorists." As I argue, this "failure" was the result of calculated political rhetoric, and the verbal and physical abuse of detainees must be viewed as the predictable enactment of such rhetoric by those charged with the day-to-day custody of the prisoners. A typical liberal response to the report on the September

11 detentions is instructive. While apparently sympathetic to the victims of the roundups, many of them isolated from lawyers and family, a *Washington Post* columnist could still write, "After all, [the Justice Department] was establishing a detention system virtually from scratch—and in something of a panic, at that."[27] Even though media coverage of detention had increased significantly since passage of the 1996 laws, the *Post* writer failed to realize that the post–September 11 detentions, isolation, and mistreatment of detainees did not come out of nowhere.

In chapter 3 I return to Miami's Krome prison, where the contemporary era of immigration detention began with Cubans and Haitians and where secrecy already shielded the INS from scrutiny. We see how, from the start, detention guards were conditioned to view all administrative detainees as dangerous prisoners. A former Krome guard describes his isolated journey through this world, giving us the first of many glimpses into the system's ability to corrupt well-meaning employees, in addition to repressing the more obvious victims. In the following chapter, another INS official describes the INS culture that forced her to leave her job when she became too sympathetic to the "undocumented." A Nigerian INS prisoner, too, becomes a dissident (a transformation we will see more than once) as he works to expose the INS's practices.

The immigration agency is further shielded from accountability by its expedient relationship with private prison companies. In chapter 5 nurses working at a Houston detention center operated for the INS by the Corrections Corporation of America refuse to play by the government's dehumanizing rules. In the next chapter INS detainees from around the world organize against bureaucratic injustice in another privately operated, converted warehouse (one INS official has appropriately referred to some detainees as "warehouse case[s]").[28] Here I offer a glimpse into the bureaucratic proceedings of an immigration courtroom, in the same building that houses the jail. One quotidian surprise we find there is a Dominican American INS lawyer comparing plantain recipes with a Berlitz interpreter from Uganda as she tries to convince an immigration judge not to grant political asylum to one of the hunger strikers. The detention world remains isolated, but many paths unexpectedly cross inside it.

I began this book with the hope of publicizing the voices and writings of INS prisoners. Soon enough it became clear that despite the adversarial nature of legal battles and of the "pro-immigrant" versus "anti-immigrant" debate, there are no good guys and bad guys—and yet there are unmistakable victims. Several chapters explore this complexity, which, it should be said, is regularly "discovered" by those writing about prison life. In "The Art of Jailing," a New Jersey correctional officer (CO), once a substitute teacher, talks irrepressibly about "the toughest guys in America" and explains how to use force to control a jail. It becomes more clear that inside a prison, a prisoner is a prisoner, U.S. citizen or not.

The 1996 immigration laws targeting noncitizens expanded the INS detention net so drastically that the lines between "us" and "them" began to blur. People who did not think of themselves as immigrants found they were subject to detention. Difficult as this may be to believe even now, almost ten years after they were passed, the 1996 laws might require the INS to detain, for example, someone convicted of misdemeanor drug possession or of jumping a subway turnstile without paying a fare or even of hair pulling.[29] These laws, like the INS detention system itself, should be examined in a wider context. In chapter 8, " 'Criminal Aliens' and Criminal Agents," we hear from inside the Oakdale, Louisiana, immigration prison, a centerpiece of 1980s rhetoric about "criminal aliens," a term as technically meaningful yet deceptively wielded as "terrorist" now is. Once again, a low-key dissident emerges to shed light on reality: a former Oakdale correctional officer recalls the ruthlessness practiced by INS agents against the agency's nonviolent prisoners.

Chapter 9 continues the exploration of the 1996 laws, focusing on some of the people whose lives were affected by them. Here I also consider what the metaphorical "wide net" has to do with actual steel restraints and the jailer's emphasis on "control." A prisoner from Guyana explains how the laws themselves and the brutality to which they give license are part of the same design; but as the net widened, grassroots resistance found its footing. More victims (an overused but unavoidable term) surface from around the world in small-town Alabama and New Hampshire jails. In the following two chapters, we meet prisoners who may not be "innocent," yet demand our attention as they are transferred from jail to jail, repeatedly humiliated, and confronted with outright violence when they attempt to protest or simply to hold onto their legal paperwork. Again, we meet local jail workers who, like other people, are sometimes compassionate and sometimes manipulative. Either way, the system rolls on; a local INS official concerned about jail conditions is too intimidated to speak up, and INS litigators in Washington consider new ways to isolate detainees from legal relief.

Immigration detainees can be held for days, months, or years. Serving time that cannot be counted, to paraphrase a Somali prisoner, can make INS detention intolerable. In chapter 12 an unusually talkative and thoughtful Denver INS official reflects on his authority under the 1996 laws to keep legal immigrants in detention until he wants to let them out. In the next chapter I follow a paper trail used by the INS to justify detaining people indefinitely when "their" countries would not take them back. INS prisoners from Southeast Asia and Somalia speak about the daily frustrations of prison food, of not having enough blankets in a cold dormitory, and of going mad because they do not know how long the INS will hold them. In 2001 the Supreme Court decided in these detainees' favor, ruling that there is a limit on how long they can be detained.

There remains no limit, however, on how long the INS/BICE can detain certain Cubans in this country. In the last chapter I return to the origins of the current era of detention and look toward an uncertain future. Detainees who came here during the 1980 Mariel boatlift are probably the most lasting victims of U.S. immigration detention. Despite the Supreme Court decision against indefinite detention, the U.S. government continues to assert its authority to detain these "Mariel Cuban" men and women indefinitely, since Cuba will not take them back. Some have been imprisoned for years, even decades, although they have completed their criminal sentences. Of all those whose stories are told here, the Mariel Cubans remain farthest from any hope of justice.

A few more words about the title are in order. Most INS detention facilities are not technically prisons, according to American usage.[30] In addition, it must be repeated, a person in the custody of the INS or the BICE is an administrative detainee—even when she or he is in your nearby county jail, sharing a cell with a sentenced inmate. During a media pool tour of the Hudson County Jail in New Jersey after post–September 11 interest in INS detention increased, the jail warden kept referring to his INS prisoners as "inmates" and then quickly corrected himself by saying "detainees." The distinction may seem trivial, but it resurfaces now and again, especially when the INS attempts to defend preferential mistreatment of those in its custody by denying them participation in educational or work release programs, for example, even when non-INS inmates in the same facility do participate—all on the grounds that they are not "inmates" or "prisoners" but "detainees."[31]

Legalistic distinctions aside, someone who is detained or imprisoned is a prisoner. This may seem obvious enough, but part of understanding the INS is understanding that what is obvious often does not matter. What must it mean to be held in a prison for weeks or months, even for a decade or more, and to be told by the administrative agency renting bed space for you that you are not a prisoner? What does it mean for these men and women that the INS argues that immigration detention is not "punishment"? "I feel like I don't even exist anymore," said one detainee. "And I try to convince my brothers and sisters to tell that to my mom so it'll be easier for her."[32] In the Calcasieu Parish Jail in Lake Charles, there is a large group of Cuban INS detainees. Jail administrators there are concerned with the well-being of these men. One small gesture they have made is to eliminate the typical prison jumpsuit in favor of khaki pants and purple T-shirts. The warden feels that purple might lift the prisoners' spirits. For management reasons, the back of each T-shirt has the words "INS INMATE" stenciled in a contemporary graphic; at least it acknowledges reality.

This book, then, is also about language. In this still-too-invisible system, the lives of bureaucrats, correctional officers, attorneys, clinic workers, and detained immigrants intersect. Some use language to hide the truth, others to tell the truth; some to argue, others to seduce. Who does which is not always predictable, and the truth itself is often elusive. The vast archives littering the immigration prison world range from Supreme Court briefs to graffiti on cell walls to eloquent pleas written on scraps of paper with a dull pencil. In many cases, since we are talking here about immigration prisons, prisoners struggle to articulate their pleas in a language that is not fully their own. Just as often, the language used against them is not fully mastered by their undereducated masters. Looking to the future, the great Walt Whitman wrote:

> The Real Grammar will be that which declares itself a nucleus of the spirit
> of the laws, with liberty to all to carry out the spirit of the laws, even by
> violating them, if necessary.—The English Language is grandly lawless like
> the race who use it—or, rather, breaks out of the little laws to enter truly the
> higher ones. It is so instinct with that which underlies laws, and the purports
> of laws, it refuses all petty interruptions in its way.[33]

A final interruption: for prisoners, the difference between inside and outside can be everything. A Haitian refugee at Krome once said, "Only one thing you know is that you are inside." A writer who visits prisons is not inside. But as more and more people listen and see, as our own archipelago becomes more and more difficult to ignore, we will understand that their inside surrounds us all.

*Secrecy, Disruption, and Continuity*

Start with the unusual suspects: eleven young Israelis selling toy helicopters in rural Ohio malls. In the United States on valid tourist visas, they thought that their employer, Florida-based Quality Sales, had arranged for their work permits, but they were wrong. Early one October morning FBI and INS agents arrived at the apartment building in Findley, Ohio, where the Israelis were living. Oren Behr and Leran Diamant laugh when they mention Findley to me as we sit in Diamant's Tel Aviv apartment five months after their arrests. "It's a hole," says Behr. "It's fucking nowhere." The local residents were friendly, though, Diamant wants me to know.

Diamant was arrested along with nine other Israelis at the apartment complex. Agents tore the place apart and gathered potential evidence, including a Burger King receipt, which still makes Diamant laugh. Behr was picked up at one of the malls. Handcuffed and sitting in a government car, he counted twelve other vehicles in the convoy, some fifteen agents accompanying him alone. In court one day Behr had to be handcuffed and shackled to use the bathroom a few steps outside the courtroom. He could have understood cuffing either his hands or his legs, he tells me, but considering the gauntlet of heavily armed agents, this seemed excessive. He is still somewhat indignant about that detail. He has excellent posture and a short, neat haircut; his friend Diamant has long unkempt hair and slouches comfortably. They both agree that Americans are obsessed with "regulations." Diamant says, "This is the way Americans are." He gets more specific about his cross-cultural observations: "It's not only square. It's sharp, square, and unchangeable."

Behr's mother came to the United States from Israel after he was arrested, but the INS attorney did not want her in the courtroom. The judge allowed her in. Then, Behr recalls, the INS attorney kept saying that they were "bad kids." His own attorney, David Leopold, argued that they were "good kids"; they had entered legally and had not been accused of a crime. During a court recess, Behr's mother approached the INS lawyer to explain who these young people were. They had done their military service in Israel, were in the United States, and wanted to earn some money before returning home. "The [INS] lawyer started to shout, 'They are bad kids! *My* kids are good kids,'" Behr tells me.

In retrospect it may be comical; at the time, according to Leopold, everyone was scared. No wonder that after September 11, 2001, Attorney General John Ashcroft ordered that "special interest" immigration hearings be closed. In the Israelis' case, the Justice Department first claimed they were "special interest nonterrorist cases," then that they were "special interest terrorist cases." Either way, the Israelis were to be kept in jail. According to Leopold, the government said it did not have enough guards to bring the Israelis to court one day, although he notes there were enough to move his clients from the nearby Broadview Heights Municipal Jail in a Cleveland suburb to the Medina County Jail forty miles away.

Elizabeth Hacker, the immigration judge who presided over the case, wrote: "Although the Service alleges that these cases are 'special' it has failed to present any credible evidence of the basis for this finding. Indeed the Service has failed to submit any evidence of terrorist activity or of a threat to the national security. There is no evidence of the risk of harm to the community."[1] The story received media attention because, Leopold says, "there was no evidence of anything." The INS dropped its appeal of the judge's decision to release the prisoners. Nine of them, including Diamant, were released from jail after three weeks, under orders to leave the country, and they returned to Israel. Oren Behr and Yaniv Hani were also freed, but they were ordered to remain in the United States until the government gave them permission to leave. The INS based this restriction on what it called a "safeguard order." Leopold filed a habeas corpus petition demanding an explanation of this order, and two days later the government simply dropped it, allowing Behr and Hani to go home. Leopold has commented, "You hear there's more than 1,000 detainees, and if these cases are any example, you have to wonder if they're just locking people up to make it look like they are getting somewhere on their investigation."[2] He would not be the only observer to draw that conclusion.

"We told them we can't be Muslim if we are Jewish," Rachel Sabah, one of the Ohio detainees, informed me. She was held for two and a half weeks in the North Royalton Jail near Cleveland. She and the others were not mistreated, she said, other than being handcuffed a lot. Her interrogators wanted to know if she frequented any mosques near Toledo. At the time we talked Rachel remained puzzled: "I don't know if it was for the interrogation or if they really didn't understand what is the difference between Jew and Muslim. I thought it was very strange."

When I repeat Sabah's comments to Behr and Diamant, the latter observes, "Americans sometimes don't know what it means to be an Israeli."

"To be Jewish," Behr corrects him.

"I mean, an Israeli, Jewish Israeli," explains Diamant. "Terror is our enemy. This is what we fight all the time." All the detained Israelis had done their required service in the Israeli army. Correctional officers at the Medina County Jail treated the men well out of a sense of camaraderie, as many of them had also served in the military. A few of the local inmates bothered the Israelis at first, because, Diamant says, "they thought we were Muslims." They shouted "bin Laden" and "anthrax" at them. After a while they understood, and then they approached out of curiosity. "Why are you here?" they wanted to know, but the Israeli prisoners themselves did not know why.

After he was arrested, Behr was interviewed by the INS for ten minutes and by the FBI for about two hours. He was detained for a month. At first, according to Behr, the FBI agents told him they found explosives in his car. They were bluffing. Then they said they had photos of Behr meeting "somebody" in a New York airport where he had spent about thirty minutes on arrival. "Bring the pictures," Behr said to them. Because he had worked as a military policeman in an Israeli prison, his mother tells me, he knew some of the tricks. But they were bluffing again. The agents even told Behr they had discovered photos of mosques in the car. Finally, the agents announced they had found maps—Ohio road maps. A quiet man who administered a polygraph test said to Behr, "You know you'll be in jail for a long time." Then he asked Behr what his "suffer limit" was. Meanwhile, agents warned Behr and the others that hiring an attorney would only prolong their detention.

"These guys were pathetic," says Diamant.

"They were shooting to all the directions," adds Behr. "They were dying to hit something."

The Justice Department exploited the national trauma of September 11 to extend its reach in many directions. Immigration courts were among the first targets. Immigration hearings, traditionally open to the press and to the public, were closed in the so-called special interest cases. In response to lawsuits from the press demanding access, the government argued that its investigation was like a "mosaic": seemingly meaningless bits of information could be important to the bigger picture.[3] Meanwhile, family members as well as the media were barred from special interest cases, even as the term went undefined. Attorneys Bennet D. Zurofsky and Regis Fernandez represented Malek Zeidan, a Syrian who spent forty days in the Hudson County Jail in Kearny, New Jersey. The Justice Department designated Zeidan "special interest" and on that basis closed his hearing too. Zurofsky told me that the Justice Department "never put any justification of 'special interest' in writing or otherwise explained it" with respect to his client. When Zurofsky sued in federal court demanding a justification of the "special interest" designation, the Justice Department simply "dropped [it] rather than answer the claims that they had closed [the hearing] in an unconstitutional manner."

Zeidan's individual hearing was opened, and he was released from detention while the case proceeded.[4] But his case had helped to form the basis for *North Jersey Media v. Ashcroft,* a lawsuit brought by media groups to force the government to open immigration hearings, except when it can show that a particular case requires secrecy for specific national security reasons. Fernandez, who represented Zeidan in his immigration case, recalled that throughout this period in Newark immigration court, "people were being chased out of the hallways." Attorneys couldn't get information from clerks about their own clients' hearings. The chief immigration judge, a subordinate of Ashcroft, issued a memo spelling out a few practical guidelines for maintaining secrecy: references to cases should be removed from printed court calendars; the automated system should be set to prevent case information from being available through an 800 number; court administrators should buy large stamps that say "Do not disclose contents of this record," and this message should be stamped on the front and back of the regular blue file jacket covers.[5]

But secrecy was not enough. The Bush administration needed to limit the power of immigration judges who might rule against its wishes. So the Justice Department announced that it could now invoke an "automatic stay" to keep certain people detained even if an immigration judge ordered them released. Immigration judges do not hold their positions by constitutional mandate but are Justice Department employees—"bureaucrats in judges' robes," in Robert Kahn's words.[6] A year after the attacks California federal judge Stephen Reinhardt, who is not an immigration judge and not in the attorney general's chain of command, reflected on the political pressures under which immigration judges must work. The "unprecedented nature of the September 11th attacks" brought these pressures to the surface, but they had been beneath it for a long time: "In immigration cases, the enforcement wing of the government can dictate the policies that bind the immigration judges. It goes without saying that an independent judiciary does not function in this manner."[7]

The Executive made other unilateral changes. Eight days after the attacks Ashcroft announced a new rule authorizing the INS to detain aliens for forty-eight hours without charging them; previously, it could have legally done so for only twenty-four hours. The new rule also allowed the INS to detain an alien indefinitely—that is, for an undefined "reasonable period of time"—in the event of an "emergency or other extraordinary circumstance." Nancy Chang, an attorney with the Center for Constitutional Rights, called the new forty-eight-hour rule "astounding." But a former Clinton Justice Department official said, "It's inevitable that at times like this that the pent-up agenda of law-enforcement gets put forward." He added that "there is nothing wrong" with Congress "acting quickly," and it did.[8]

On Capitol Hill legislators bypassed normal committee meetings to draft language that would become the Uniting and Strengthening America by Providing Appropriate Tools Required to Intercept and Obstruct Terrorism Act of 2001, commonly known by the propagandists' acronym USA PATRIOT Act. Democratic staffers invited David Cole, a Georgetown law professor and one of the most visible and unyielding defenders of civil liberties to emerge in the national debate, to participate with them as an expert because the Justice Department was using experts who had litigated cases against him. But Justice Department lawyers would not agree to Cole's presence, so he sat in the room next to the Judiciary Committee offices in the Dirksen Building. Republican Representative Ron Paul complained that the final language of the bill was "not available" before the vote and anyway could not be read in the time allotted. Among many other changes, the new law extended the INS's authority to detain people indefinitely. Six weeks after the attacks the undemocratic "antiterrorism" law had taken its place alongside the "antidrug" laws of the 1980s and the anti-immigrant laws of the 1990s.[9]

The attacks of September 11 and their aftermath led to a revitalized examination of democracy, but it was not a true dialogue about the often-cited balance between security and civil liberties. First, as Cole puts it, because "what we have done is to sacrifice the liberties of some—immigrants, and especially Arab and Muslim immigrants—for the purported security of the rest of us."[10] Second, because, despite the very real law enforcement imperatives, the national debate had little to do with the realities of law enforcement practice, regardless of whether one is troubled by these. As we cruised along the steel border wall in the San Diego Sector, a Border Patrol supervisor I had interviewed several years earlier candidly stated, "We're not a police state." Then he smiled and said he wouldn't mind if we became one, "since I'm the police." On the other hand, a fifteen-year federal law enforcement officer who lost friends in the September 11 attacks told me: "If you're going to give me too much power, believe me, I'm going to do the wrong thing."

Whatever might have had to do with security was subordinated to "a deeper and more troubling agenda," wrote two former INS general counsels. The nation's top law enforcement officer more or less admitted this himself. He told the International Association of Chiefs of Police, "The critics . . . would have us return to a reticent law enforcement culture of inhibition which existed prior to September 11, 2001."[11]

Oren Behr's mother told me, "We didn't think that in America people can be arrested without giving a reason." The American wife of an Egyptian charged with immigration violations said, "They don't know how painful this is. They're destroying families."[12] But they did know, and there was a reason. One priority, as Ashcroft stated repeatedly, was to prevent future attacks. Another, about which he was less explicit, was to make it look as if the law enforcement agencies that had made serious errors were now on top of things. What thousands of detainees and their families experienced as "destruction" was the strategy of "disruption" articulated by the attorney general. "Aggressive detention of lawbreakers and material witnesses is vital to preventing, disrupting, or delaying new attacks," he insisted in one of many such statements.[13]

Confronted with the critical law enforcement objective of preventing attacks, the Justice Department reverted to the long-established rhetorical tactic of blurring the distinction between alien, criminal, and terrorist. In his "explanations" of who was being detained and why, Ashcroft repeatedly implied that all post–September 11 detainees were terrorist suspects. Rather than "live in a dream world," he told a Senate committee, we must "fight back." How? We must "identify, disrupt and dismantle terrorist networks." Three months after the attacks Ashcroft testified that through "a preventative campaign of arrest and detention of lawbreakers, America has grown stronger—and safer—in the face of terror." Again he described the administration's tactics as a "deliberate campaign of arrest and detention to remove suspected terrorists who violate the law from our streets." Among these were several hundred detained on "immigration violations." Were these "suspected terrorists"? Getting answers was nearly impossible. It is in this duplicitous context that Ashcroft's infamous and calculated words of contempt will survive:

> We need honest, reasoned debate and not fear-mongering. To those who pit Americans against immigrants, and citizens against non-citizens; to those who scare peace-loving people with phantoms of lost liberty, my message is this: your tactics only aid terrorists, for they erode our national unity and diminish our resolve.[14]

"No raids, no roundups, none of that," INS Assistant Commissioner for Investigations Joseph Greene told the press. It is true that there were no World War II–style roundups and relocations of American citizens whose ancestry was suspect. But the extensive infrastructure for detention was in place. In addition to the often-cited 1,200 post–September 11 detainees, a year and a half after the attacks the INS had detained some 1,100 persons in connection with its Absconder Apprehension Initiative and more than 2,700 through its special registration program.[15] Both programs targeted Arab, Muslim, and South Asian foreign nationals.

Fox News commentator Michelle Malkin complained, "Even after September 11, the mainstream media . . . run scores of cookie-cutter sob stories about illegal aliens 'unjustly' detained instead of focusing on the still rising costs to society of an immigration system run amuck." She added that "the speedy detention and deportation of some twelve hundred aliens suspected of terrorist ties gave the illusion of competence in . . . immigration enforcement." Malkin is in agreement with many critics of the INS when she charges that the response to September 11 is at least in part a cover for incompetence. But her own critique of the "sob stories" depends on the attorney general's calculated disinformation. Versions of the administration's smoke screen bear repeating: "Each action taken by the Department of Justice . . . is carefully drawn to target a narrow class of individuals—terrorists. Our legal powers are targeted at terrorists. Our investigation is focused on terrorists. Our prevention strategy targets the terrorist threat." Even those more sympathetic to "illegals" than the Fox commentator might reasonably assume that the twelve hundred detainees were "suspected of terrorist ties." FBI agent Coleen Rowley appeared in the spotlight after September 11 for her public criticism of the FBI's intelligence methods. Less attention was paid to this paragraph in Rowley's letter to the FBI director:

> The vast majority of the one thousand plus persons "detained" in the wake of 9-11 did not turn out to be terrorists. They were mostly illegal aliens. We have every right, of course, to deport those identified as illegal aliens during the course of any investigation. But after 9-11, Headquarters encouraged more and more detentions for what seemed to be essentially PR purposes. Field offices were required to report daily the number of detentions in order to supply grist for statements on our progress in fighting terrorism. The balance between individuals' civil liberties and the need for effective investigation is hard to maintain even during so-called normal times, let alone times of increased terrorist threat or war. It is, admittedly, a difficult balancing act. But from what I have observed, particular vigilance may be required to head off undue pressure (including subtle encouragement) to detain or "round up" suspects, particularly those of Arabic origin.[16]

Since the Bush administration's "new culture of prevention" was intended to prevent the flow of information as much as the commission of crime, we will probably never know how many people were picked up and held and perhaps deported after September 11, or even if any are still being held incommunicado. The Justice Department explicitly stopped releasing numbers in November 2001, less than two months after the attacks. Not one of the "special interest" detainees was indicted here in connection with the September 11 attacks.[17]

———

One friend brought Majid Al Shihri and Lisa Schroeder together, and another tore them apart. After meeting the Fort Worth schoolteacher through a neighbor, "I gave her my phone number," the thirty-seven-year-old Majid tells me by phone. He had come to New York on a visa, which he would overstay, and had driven down to Texas because "it's hot—like Saudi Arabia." He and Lisa were married in a Muslim ceremony. They delayed the civil ceremony because Lisa's father had misgivings about the "mixed" marriage, and after September 11 the topic became especially "touchy," Lisa explains. Meanwhile, according to Dallas attorney Karen Pennington, the Saudi consulate threatened Majid, suggesting that for his own safety he disavow his blasphemous marriage to a Christian before returning to Saudi Arabia.

Shortly after September 11 a friend of Majid called the FBI to suggest they check him out. Majid was not at home when agents came looking for him, so he called the Dallas FBI office himself and invited them over. Lisa remarks that the agent who came to their house "asked the most ludicrous questions," such as "'Do you hold ill will towards the United States?'" She asks me, "Would you say if you did?" Still, she says that the agent was "a very nice man." Four days later he called to say that Majid was "cleared" of possible terrorist connections but that the family should contact the INS. This time agents from both the FBI and the INS came to their home. They arrested Majid, even though the friendly agent suggested to the INS that they leave him alone. "It was like a bad movie," Lisa tells me. The INS agents instructed Lisa that she would have to post bond and that her husband would be home in three or four days. The immigration judge, however, refused to set a bond.

When I first spoke to Majid Al Shihri in May 2002, he had been detained for seven months. He suggested we set up a three-way call with his wife from the Denton County Jail in Texas so she could "translate" his heavily accented English; I asked him to speak slowly instead. "I need help me," he says. "I'm tired, man. Please. I'm tired here." He was having trouble sleeping, and the 4:30 A.M. breakfasts in jail made it worse. He felt harassed because INS agents kept giving him papers to sign, which they said they needed right away, but he didn't understand what these papers were. "I need somebody speak my language. I need lawyer. They say no." With the help of his wife on the outside, Majid had been able to get an attorney.

At one point Majid gave the phone to a U.S. citizen inmate, to help with the "translation." Jimmy had done time in jails and prisons in California, Texas, and Arizona over eleven years, and he said the Denton County Jail was the worst he had experienced. He had just seen an inmate get beaten for asking to see a sergeant after a correctional officer refused to let him use the bathroom. "If they feel like they want to run some kind of punishment on you, they can," Jimmy told me, attributing such actions to their "God complex." He said that county inmates had to pay for medical care, which INS inmates were often refused because the federal agency did not want to foot the bill. His wife was a correctional officer elsewhere in the Texas Department of Criminal Justice, and she was scared about what might happen to him in this jail. A few weeks later Majid told me that the American had been released. *"Insha' allah,"* he said. "God's with him." Months later an INS detainee from Sierra Leone allegedly hanged himself in the Denton jail using "a piece from a mattress pad as a rope," even though he was on twenty-four-hour suicide watch at the time.[18]

Lisa Al Shihri was worried that her husband was going crazy. She had been allowed to visit him through Plexiglas for twenty minutes the day before, after driving forty-five minutes and then waiting two hours. And Majid was worried about his wife. She was having heart problems. "If she die, nobody care. . . . Please, I tired. I need understand why. . . . I scared for my name. I scared for my family." He said I could use his name, though, and he also spoke to the *Washington Post*'s Steve Fainaru and to the BBC. "Maybe I can help some people, some other people."

Majid and Lisa were married in a civil ceremony after he was detained, but the Dallas INS office refused to expedite Lisa's petition for Majid's immigration status adjustment based on their marriage. After almost a year in detention, Majid agreed to return to Saudi Arabia. He was never charged with a crime in the United States. Lisa Schroeder Al Shihri wrote: "The wide net that the INS has cast out to cover up their inadequacies prior to 9/11 has stripped this country of the very basic principles on which it was founded. And it has taken my husband."[19]

———

The "cookie-cutter sob stories" of September 11 detainees did generally neglect the bigger picture: INS secrecy did not begin on September 12. "The official with a secret *feels* powerful," wrote Daniel Patrick Moynihan. "And is." Sometimes keeping the secret is an assertion of petty authority, sometimes it is an instrument of policy, and often it is impossible to tell the difference between the two.[20]

Karen Pennington, Majid Al Shihri's lawyer, worked in California in the 1980s, when Salvadoran asylum seekers were regularly moved from one jail to another to "hide them from their attorneys"—or "to hide [them] from hope," as a Cuban man put it. The practice has varied but has not stopped. "Post–September 11," observes Pennington, "was the first time that they kept them in the same area and just refused to tell you even who they had." Before September 11 Tara Urs, a paralegal with the ACLU Immigrants' Rights Project in New York, could call the area jails for detainee names, but that also stopped. As legal representatives discovered that their clients' names were removed from court dockets, detainees were denied access to phones.[21]

And as the attorney general's subordinate interrogators were telling detainees that they would get out faster without attorneys, Ashcroft himself was assuring Congress that all detainees had the right to counsel. As detainees were denied access to telephones, Assistant Attorney General Michael Chertoff was assuring Congress that they could call lawyers as well as their families. As allegations about the denial of meaningful access to counsel came to light, INS public affairs spokesperson Russell Bergeron, in line with the common pattern, said, "If such an allegation exists, we would like to hear about it." In the same pattern, Ashcroft claimed, "I would be happy to hear from individuals if there are any alleged abuses of individuals, because that is not the way we do business"—this in response to a *Los Angeles Times* report of precisely such allegations.[22]

But something positive was happening too. More than a year after the attacks, reporters were regularly following INS detainees from jail to jail, sometimes even tracking them down after deportation. If the government had to pull out all the stops in its newly uninhibited assault, this was in part because the INS's traditional secrecy was no longer the secret it had been for so long.

Dan Malone says he was naive when, as a staff writer for the *Dallas Morning News,* he started looking into the circumstances of long-term INS prisoners in 1997. During a telephone conversation Malone had with Russell Bergeron, the INS's chief press officer and media relations director, Bergeron referred to a document summarizing the agency's detained population by categories such as nationality and length of detention. Bergeron told Malone that according to the document, fifty-three detainees had been in custody for more than three years because their countries would not accept them. Intrigued, Malone decided to "find out who they were."

Malone filed a Freedom of Information Act (FOIA) request to obtain the names and alien numbers of the fifty-three detainees. A specialist with the Department of Justice/INS FOIA Unit informed Malone that "no records" on this subject had been found "in a search of our Headquarters including our Public Affairs office." The FOIA specialist also said that Chief Press Officer Bergeron denied the existence of the document he had mentioned to Malone. When Malone tried to help out with the search by letting the FOIA specialist know that Bergeron had identified one Kristine Marcy as an INS field officer knowledgeable on the subject, the FOIA specialist responded that she was unable to locate any such INS employee. Malone then called the INS switchboard, which gave him Marcy's number.

The INS continued its refusal to provide the requested information on the grounds that it was protecting the detainees' privacy. Malone observed that the INS cited irrelevant laws to justify the practice of withholding names. One should add that the agency drops the pretense of privacy concerns when it suits the government's interest to discuss a particular detainee.[23] Privacy concerns also become secondary when a larger political agenda is at stake. In the 1980s, for example, the U.S. government violated Salvadoran asylum seekers' privacy—with potentially fatal consequences—by sharing information about them with the government they were fleeing, and to which the United States itself acknowledged most of them would be returned. We know this because of materials provided a decade after the fact to Robert Kahn in response to his FOIA requests. In 2003 a Silicon Valley newspaper reported that Iranians, including asylum seekers, taken into custody as a result of their compliance with "special registration" programs here, were threatened with criminal charges by U.S. immigration officials if they did not consent to interviews, while detained, with Iranian government officials.[24]

INS officials told Malone that their privacy policy was consistent with Federal Bureau of Prisons guidelines. But, in a letter to the FOIA office, Malone pointed out that his own "request to the Bureau of Prisons for the names of all persons incarcerated under a federal death sentence was promptly answered by fax with the information requested." After further denials, Malone and the *Morning News* sued the INS to compel release of the requested information. In a settlement the agency ultimately provided a list of detainees, "criminal aliens" as well as asylum seekers, held for over three years. In accordance with the terms of the settlement, the INS withheld the detainees' last names and identifying alien numbers. But it agreed to deliver letters to all of them from the *Morning News*.

There were not, it turns out, 53 detainees who had been held for at least three years, as the INS had first indicated to Malone. There were not even 294, a number subsequently released to him. There were 851, according to records eventually released because of the lawsuit.

Malone told me that his story originally described these long-term INS detainees as secret prisoners. So that his contacts at the INS would not be caught off guard, he told the INS press office about this in advance. An INS official complained to the newspaper, and Malone's characterization was removed from the story. In the morning, however, the reporter awoke to find his published story with the front page banner "INS Faulted for Secret Detentions." A headline writer at the *Morning News* had seen for himself what the story was about and titled it accordingly.[25]

If the powder blue lintels and molding inside the courtroom of the Bergen County Justice Center did not convey the appropriate gravity, at least the name of the presiding judge in the three-panel hearing of the Superior Court of New Jersey did. With the hum of unidentified machinery coming through the windows, Judge Sybil Moses noted the "inherent logic" that detainees' "access rights" to attorneys could not be assured if the identities of the detainees were unknown. The New Jersey ACLU had sued for the release of September 11 detainees' names and won in the lower court;[26] this was an appeals hearing. Judge Moses asked the government attorney if there was any system in place to monitor the "treatment and detention of foreign nationals" in U.S. jails. Justice Department attorney Thomas Bondy said, "Uh, well."

Bondy recovered quickly. He told the judges that no "record evidence" of mistreatment existed, and, more important, this suit was not about that; it was about releasing the names. Another lawsuit, in a Washington, D.C., federal court, had unsuccessfully attempted to force the federal government to release the detainees' names. Citing a New Jersey statute according to which such records "shall be open to public inspection,"[27] the New Jersey ACLU had filed suit against the state of New Jersey to demand that the Hudson County and Passaic County Jails release the names of INS detainees they were holding. County officials sat at the defense table in the Hackensack courtroom, but Justice Department attorney Bondy and Assistant Attorney General Robert McCallum argued the case. During the recess and after the hearing, McCallum took questions from the press. He wore rimless glasses over his red-rimmed eyes and spoke with a slight drawl. Associated Press reporter Amy Westphal asked McCallum, if the refusal to release names was because of heightened security concerns resulting from the September 11 attacks, why did the agency refuse to release detainee names before? McCallum responded that he was unaware of anyone being interested in these names before the attacks. He added that he could not answer in any case, because he had come out of private practice to work for the attorney general just six days after the attacks.

In both the federal and the state suits, the government defended its refusal to release names on the basis of privacy and national security concerns. The government did not dispute the long-standing and widespread practice of making jail inmates' names a matter of public record, but it contended that this was different. For one thing, Bondy said, when one judge asked about such laws, "that word [inmate] has to be understood in context." These were federal detainees, he explained, not inmates. The local jails hold them under contract with the federal government. Thus any federal policy prohibiting the release of their names must supersede any local rule allowing the release of that information. (Two months later the government argued that a United Nations plan to monitor prisons worldwide "would be unconstitutional in the United States because it does not recognize states' rights.")[28]

Just to be safe, however, the government had "promulgated" a new regulation after the lower court's decision striking down the secrecy policy. The rule stated that "non-Federal providers shall not release information relating to those detainees" held in contract facilities. The rule "covers all pending and future requests for detainee information," according to an INS press release. "The need for the rule was highlighted by a New Jersey court order requiring county officials to release information regarding federal detainees pursuant to state law."[29]

"There's something I have trouble swallowing," Judge Moses said about the Justice Department's having created a new rule to evade a judicial decision during ongoing litigation. She paraphrased the government's rationale: "'We lost in this case and we're going to cure it.'" The government attorney argued that such a move was perfectly legitimate.[30]

The government had another argument to justify its policy: "Although [the INS detainees] may eventually be found to have no connection to terrorist activity, release of their names and personal information at this time would forever connect them to the September 11 attacks." This is from the Declaration of James Reynolds, chief of the Terrorism and Violent Crime Section in the Criminal Division of the Justice Department, submitted to the courts. Reynolds continues: "Given the nature of these investigations, the mere mention of their name in connection with these investigations would cause the detainees embarrassment, humiliation, risk of retaliation, harassment and possibly even physical harm in the United States and in their home countries, if they are eventually deported."[31] Never mind that in a lower court Judge Gladys Kessler had acknowledged the legitimacy of privacy concerns and so, when ordering release of the names, noted that the government could simply allow any detainee who preferred privacy to "'opt out'" of disclosure.[32]

The crowd filed out of the courtroom while Assistant Attorney General McCallum, carrying a leatherette portfolio with a Drug Enforcement Administration (DEA) logo on it, answered more questions from the press. Outside it was a cool May afternoon. Men on scaffolding sanded masonry on the courtroom building. A garden of memorials commemorating Vietnam, Desert Storm, and Beirut included a quotation from the Saudi ambassador thanking the United States for contributing to the "reversal of a brutal aggression and occupation of sisterly Kuwait." Across the street from a bench with "City of Hackensack" stenciled on one of its slats stood the ordinary men who had come to town to argue for unlimited government power. A woman in a blue suit stood with them. A car arrived, they picked up their bags, and they drove away.

The new rule prohibiting jails from releasing information about their federal prisoners took effect on April 18, 2003, when I happened to be at the Passaic County Jail to interview a "special interest" Pakistani detainee. The day after the interview I received a call from the Newark INS public affairs officer, Kerry Gill. He asked whether it was true that I had asked the on-site INS official at the jail "questions about statistics," specifically, about "special interest cases" there. When I said yes (I hadn't gotten any answers, of course), Gill said, "I don't understand why." He told me that my question was "inappropriate" as the attorney general had ordered the district director "not to disclose these numbers" and that I knew this, having been on a media pool tour of the Hudson County Jail when the district director herself said so. Gill said that "the only place to properly pose" questions was to the district director or to INS Headquarters. "You can't go to another INS source," he said.

Moving on from the new "appropriateness" standard, Gill then alleged that I had violated INS detention standards concerning media visitation by trying "to solicit information" contrary to a "directive from the attorney general." When I asked which standard he was referring to, Gill decided that our conversation was over. From now on, he said, my requests for visits with detainees in the Newark District, by order of the district director, would be permitted only when an INS public affairs official was available to accompany me to the jail (though the official would not be present during the actual interviews). I wrote to Newark District Director Andrea Quarantillo, asking her to remove this restriction. She refused and directed me, as Gill had, to the INS Web site, where I could find INS detention standards. Like Gill, she failed to cite any specific standard that had been violated. In refusing to lift the restrictions, Quarantillo wrote: "You sought to obtain information from an INS employee (whom you clearly knew was not the Public Affairs Officer) that the Attorney General has determined is relevant to the investigation of the events of September 11 and not appropriate for release at this time. . . . I have found no evidence or indication on your part that you plan to observe the agency's procedures for the release of official information."[33]

Several weeks earlier Quarantillo had decided not to attend a public meeting set up by immigrant advocacy groups to discuss September 11 detentions with the disrupted communities because the organizers refused to comply with the INS condition that journalists be forbidden from participating. Gill told reporter Elizabeth Llorente, "What we're saying is not that the press cannot be there, covering it, and observing it. . . . What we're saying is that there be no members of the press participating in the discussion, asking questions or making statements." The INS cited the ACLU lawsuit concerning the detainees to explain its position, but the larger reason was the agency's ongoing practice of keeping the detention system secretive and the detainees themselves isolated. Quarantillo's spurious invocation of the detention standards to justify a new and arbitrary media restriction put her squarely in the INS tradition. Three decades earlier a law student who was investigating INS compliance with FOIA regulations had produced a copy of the published Code of Federal Regulations (CFR), which prompted an INS employee to ask, "'Where did you get that? [It] is confidential, isn't it?'"[34]

The 1970s brought some openings in what that student's article in the *Iowa Law Review* referred to as the INS's "insistence on maintaining a system of secret law" and the agency's "pervasive attitude of non-disclosure." These openings continued into the Clinton era, when Attorney General Janet Reno urged a "presumption of disclosure" in responses to FOIA requests. One month after the terrorist attacks on the United States, in the words of the Lawyers Committee for Human Rights, Ashcroft "effectively reversed" these openings. He advised FOIA office employees that, with few exceptions, when making decisions "to withhold records, in whole or in part, you can be assured that the Department of Justice will defend your decisions." The administration went even further when the Justice Department staff "secretly drafted" the Domestic Security Enhancement Act of 2003 in the hope of "making it easier for the government to hide whom it is holding and why, and preventing the public from ever obtaining embarrassing information about government overreaching."[35] The Iowa law student's observations from 1970 could not be more timely: "Whether secrecy is preferred solely to protect the agency's activities from public scrutiny or because it allows a governmental policy of bias against aliens to be implemented behind the public's back is unclear. What is clear is that the attitude exists in the INS and breeds unchecked, low visibility discretion."[36]

—

Between the first and second Gulf Wars, I received a carefully folded paper towel in the mail. It was stapled at two corners to form a palm-sized pouch. Inside were seven small black rubber balls and a broken piece of black plastic. There was no letter with the package.

I met Zakia Hakki, a Kurdish Iraqi woman who had received political asylum in the United States, at a conference of Iraqi opposition groups in New York in 1999. The apparent purpose of the conference was to consider a post–Saddam Hussein Iraq, but Hakki had a distinct if related agenda. She was trying to free two of her sons from INS detention. In 1996, after civil war in Kurdish northern Iraq, the United States had evacuated "some 6,500 Iraqis and Kurds" to the island of Guam, where it has also quietly detained and processed Chinese refugees intercepted at sea.[37] (The United States has used its naval base at Guantánamo Bay, Cuba, to detain Haitians, Cubans, and Chinese, as well as persons captured in Afghanistan, in an effort to keep them outside the realm of any enforceable law.) The Iraqis, write Andrew Cockburn and Patrick Cockburn, "were sequestered until the presidential election was safely over before being admitted to the United States." Two of Hakki's sons were among them: thirty-seven-year-old Dr. Ali Yassim Mohammed Karim, a physician, who had worked with the U.S.-backed Iraqi National Congress, and his brother, who had deserted Saddam Hussein's army after witnessing the destruction of a Kurdish village.[38] Ali's wife and two young children left with him.

In Guam the evacuees were interviewed by the FBI. When they were permitted to enter the United States, Ali and his brother, along with about twenty others, were detained because of allegations that they were security threats. Their attorneys were not able to respond to these allegations because neither the government nor the judge would allow them to see the "evidence." Between 1996 and 2000 the INS used secret evidence against some two dozen people, most of them Muslim. Every federal court that addressed this issue in the past decade found the practice unconstitutional.[39]

Ali had sent the small rubber balls to his mother, and she sent some of them to me. He picked them up from the ground of the Mira Loma Detention Center, a Los Angeles County lock-up in Lancaster filled with INS detainees. Ali described a protest in which three hundred detainees, most of them Spanish-speaking, complained about their lengthy incarceration; many of them simply wanted to be deported. "At 4 P.M., these detainees were attacked by armed officers with machine guns and wooden sticks. Despite the fact that the detainees showed no resistance to the guards, the guards beat these detainees very badly." The *Los Angeles Times* reported that the Sheriff's Department had used "sting ball grenades"—"low explosives packed with rubber pellets"—to control the detainees, some of whom "stripped to their boxer shorts and t-shirts, flinging county issued bright orange shirts and pants onto razor wire atop fences."[40] It was some of these sting balls that Ali's mother sent me. Ali wrote many letters seeking attention for his fellow inmates, but he was careful: "Because of the use of secret evidence, secret charges, and secret witnesses against me, I am in a more vulnerable position than other detainees and, as a consequence, believe that I dare not say or do anything which the INS or any person may use against me. I have made no complaints and I have not participated in any protests. . . . Despite my behavior, which I believe has been exemplary, I was always punished along with the other detainees." Even his silence seemed to provoke his keepers. A deputy "came with a wooden stick in his hand behaving just like a gangster [and] said: 'Today, I'm going to fuck around with you guys.' Then a few more deputies came and threw food on us in a completely uncivilized way while at the same time using foul language." Ali and eighty others were put into segregation. Several deputies came in "and told us that they can torture anybody here, nobody would give a shit."

Niels Frenzen represented Ali and his brother. Frustrated by rulings allowing the government to withhold the so-called evidence against his client, Frenzen enlisted the help of James Woolsey, former director of the CIA, hoping that Woolsey's security clearance would make it possible for the defense team to see what the government was hiding. Woolsey agreed to help. He later explained his concerns about the U.S. government's arbitrary treatment of people it had brought here, as well as the practical implications for future alliances. Quoting the New Testament to illustrate the long-standing expectation of the accused to come "face to face" with their accusers, Woolsey told Congress, "The Iraqis would have been better off in the Roman Empire of the First Century."[41] The publicity associated with Woolsey's involvement helped to pressure the INS into concessions.

In releasing hundreds of previously classified pages used against Ali and the others, the INS explained that these documents had been "erroneously classified."[42] The documents illustrated what Woolsey called "bureaucratic incompetence or impropriety." Among them were depositions taken by INS officials of FBI interviewers from Guam that provide some insight into the U.S. law enforcement community's perceptions of the Middle East. Government witnesses confused Iraq with Iran, according to Woolsey. Journalist Martin Lasden reported the material showed that "while one FBI agent thought that [Ali] might be a spy for Iran, another suspected him of being a mole for Iraq." In the meantime, Ali's wife and the wives of other Iraqis labeled security risks were granted asylum even though their cases were based on their detained husbands' applications. In another case involving the same group of evacuees, Hashim Quadir Hawley, a Kurdish activist, spent eighteen months in detention; declassified INS information showed that an FBI agent doubted Hawley's credibility because "he had provided more information about himself than most of the others being interrogated."[43]

At the heart of all these illustrations is the institutionalized racism that kept Ali and his brother in detention for four years. In one deposition, an INS official elicited testimony from FBI agent Mark Merfalen about one of the Iraqis.

Q. Based on the hours that you spent interviewing him, as well as the sort of answers that he gave you or didn't give you, did you reach any conclusions about him in terms of whether he answered questions . . . truthfully, or were there problems? Did you characterize his answers in a certain way?

A. Hmm. I—it's been my experience working with these people that they, they lie an awful lot. They're very—they don't tell truths too many often, too very many times. . . . They lie a lot. If they can get away with it, to them it doesn't make any difference. If they can get away with it, they think it's fine.

In another deposition—and these are friendly question-and-answer sessions between two government officials—FBI agent John Cosensa explained what he had learned about "the Arab culture" in two classes given by the CIA and "an intensive seminar" at the State Department: "There is no guilt in the Arab world. It's only shame. . . . It's not okay to lie, but it's okay to say something that you don't mean, as long as you don't get caught. . . . In other words, if I lied to you, I'd feel bad that I didn't do what I knew I should do. But there is no—that's part of doing business. In other words, it's not a bad thing. Sometimes it's hard for us to understand."[44]

In summer 1999 five of the Iraqi detainees held with Ali were released under strict conditions of house arrest in Lincoln, Nebraska. Among other things, they had to agree to allow the government to monitor their phone calls and mail. They were also forbidden to speak to the media about possible government efforts to resettle them outside the United States.[45] Ali wrote to President Clinton that he refused to sign an agreement "in which I have to give up all my human rights which have been protected by the Universal Declaration of Human Rights. Moreover, they are violating the constitution of the United States by putting in dilemma an oppressed, helpless, innocent victim to choose either to remain in prison or to surrender to their abusive power and give up all his honor and dignity." Ali's brother, who during one period of his imprisonment was held in segregation for six months, also refused to sign. Both men would be detained for another year and then granted political asylum.

The Secret Evidence Repeal Act that President Bush himself had endorsed during his campaign quickly disappeared after September 11, along with legislative efforts to reform the 1996 laws. Summarizing the factors that contributed to the mistreatment of his Iraqi clients, Frenzen told me, "It's a combination of things . . . stupidity, mismanagement, incompetence, and racism . . . that all just came together in a terrible nightmare." One week into the second Gulf War in 2003, the Department of Homeland Security, into which the INS had been absorbed, issued a statement that Iraqi nationals in the United States would be interviewed and in some cases detained. Public affairs officials refused to say how many Iraqis were being held.[46]

Half a century earlier, a Hungarian man who had lived in the United States for twenty-five years left the country for nineteen months to be with his dying mother. He was detained on his return, charged with being a national security threat on the basis of secret evidence. Justice Robert Jackson wrote: "Quite unconsciously, I am sure, the Government's theory of custody for 'safekeeping' without disclosure to the victim of charges, evidence, informers or reasons, even in an administrative proceeding, has unmistakable overtones of the 'protective custody' of the Nazis, more than of any detaining procedure known to the common law. Such a practice, once established with the best of intentions, will drift into oppression of the disadvantaged in this country as surely as it has elsewhere."[47] Justice Jackson would have understood the seriousness of his analogy, having served as U.S. chief prosecutor at the Nuremberg trials just a few years before. Unfortunately, his was a minority opinion, and these words are from his dissent.

———

On a rainy February day in 2002, Uzma Naheed, a Pakistani, stood at a microphone in New York's Union Square. A rally organized by the Prison Moratorium Project, the Coalition for the Human Rights of Immigrants, and Desis Rising Up and Moving (DRUM) had attracted an impressive number of media representatives. Naheed publicly acknowledged that her husband and her brother-in-law had overstayed their visas, but she did not understand why they were still being held after four months. "Let me know what [they] did," she pleaded in struggling English as a young activist held a microphone to her mouth. "Nobody's telling us what's going on." *New York Daily News* reporter Robin Haas braved the civil rights activists to articulate the prevailing wisdom: How would Mrs. Naheed respond to most Americans' view, she asked the traditionally clad mother of four, that "if it walks like a duck and talks like a duck," it must be a duck?

"I don't think people really worry about Muslims," Naheed's husband, Anser Mehmood, told me—at least not the "real, proper Americans" whom he met in jail, he added with a laugh. Mehmood was already in the visiting area of the Passaic County Jail when Pete Del Rosso walked in and identified himself as the on-site INS official. Several minutes earlier, as we waited in the jail lobby in downtown Paterson, a short ride from Main Street with its Ramallah Halal Meat Market and Al Aqsa Deli, I had casually asked Del Rosso how many "special interest" detainees were at this jail, but he wouldn't say. When Del Rosso handed Mehmood a media interview consent form to sign, Mehmood politely asked for a moment to read it. Then he smiled and said to the INS official, "I was waiting for you guys a long time to fly me back." This was the first time in two weeks Mehmood had seen an INS official here at the Passaic County Jail. Del Rosso did not reply.

Mehmood had been traveling legally between Pakistan and the United States since the mid-1980s. He was in the export-import business. In the 1990s he overstayed his five-year renewable visa. Driving a cab and later his own eighteen-wheeler, he had seen much of this country and its people. Sometimes he would go on the road by himself so that he could work more efficiently; sometimes he would take his wife and children along so that they could spend more time together and so that his children could see the country too. "I met good people at the truck stops," he told me as we sat at a metal table, windows on four sides of us, in a long double row of mostly empty visitation rooms. Mehmood had not been particularly surprised or concerned when, three weeks after the attacks, some twenty-five federal agents came knocking on the door of his Bayonne, New Jersey, home while he slept. He knew that authorities were "coming to Muslim houses. They just want to search us." Initially there were compelling and suspicious details: agents found a flight simulator, a flying lesson logbook, box cutters, and a hazardous materials driving permit. With minimal investigation, the case "evaporated," writes law reporter Jim Edwards.[48] The hazardous materials license and the box cutters were both standard equipment for the truck driver's job. The flight simulator had been a gift from Mehmood to his son Uzair after the boy recovered from a trip to the emergency room for lead poisoning; the four-year-old souvenir logbook was part of the gift. Mehmood's attorney, Martin Stolar, noted that his client was charged only with removing a no-work advisory from his social security card. So why was he held in the Special Housing Unit (SHU) at Brooklyn's Metropolitan Detention Center (MDC), a federal prison, for four months and two days? Why was he denied access to legal help and to his family for weeks? Even after Mehmood was back in Pakistan, "immigration officials said they could not comment on specific cases."[49]

Community organizers held regular weekend rallies outside the Brooklyn prison, located under a noisy expressway and down the road from Halal Brothers Live Poultry, Inc., and a scattering of strip clubs and adult video shops. One organizer said that a prison official told him protesters were making it difficult for prisoners' families to visit. Two of Anser Mehmood's teenage boys, twelve and fourteen, became regulars at the demonstrations. When he was inside MDC, Mehmood told me, he knew nothing about the protests outside. While human rights groups were denied access to the prison,[50] Mehmood was confined with another man inside a cell measuring approximately six feet by twelve feet. He jotted down the measurements on a diagram he drew for me as we sat in the Passaic jail visiting room. "When I lie down, my foot [reached] to the wall," he explained. He is five feet nine. He is wearing a white T-shirt under his green prison uniform. In the MDC cell, if a guard came to tell him something, he would have to stand on his tiptoes and press his ear to a small circle of holes in the steel; to speak, he had to press his mouth to the holes and shout. The lights in the cell were on at all times. At mealtimes guards would order him to the rear of the cell along with his cellmate, and they had to show their hands. Then the guards would open the food slot, put the trays in, and close it. "This is the procedure," Mehmood explained.

For the first two months (October and November), Mehmood was moved each week to a new cell in the SHU. He was handcuffed and shackled to be moved those few feet, and he says matter-of-factly now that this was "very humiliating." Aside from that movement, he was kept inside his cell for twenty-four hours a day. After three weeks he was allowed to make his first legal phone call. When he was first arrested, Mehmood said, the FBI interviewed him at his home for about an hour and was satisfied. "We have no problem with you," Mehmood said he was told. "Now it's up to INS if they want to take you or not." The INS took Mehmood, but even as they left, agents told his wife that she could expect a call from him in four to six hours. They told her he would see an immigration judge the next day and get out on bail. They said he might even get a green card before it was over, since he had been working and paying taxes here for so long.

Bail was never set. "That four to six hours turned into two months" before he was able to see his wife again, Mehmood calmly noted. He had been taken from Bayonne to New York's Varick Street detention center for a day. He still assumed everything would be fine. Only when the Border Patrol came in and chained his ankles, waist, and legs did he become frightened. "Then I start wondering. These guys are shouting like army people. 'Don't move! Don't move!'" He thought they were the military until they took him downstairs amd he saw the Border Patrol vehicle. With sirens blaring, accompanied by New York Police Department motorcycles and what he assumed were FBI agents in sedans, Mehmood and others were moved across the river to Brooklyn's MDC.

When Mehmood arrived at MDC, he alleges, seven or eight correctional officers threw him out of the van, dragged him across the floor, and then threw him against a wall. "They pressed me with their full power," he said. A bone in his left hand was displaced and remains partially numb. His wrists and ankles bled. He recalled that one of the guards pressed his head against the wall and told him, "Just follow what we say or else you are dead." Mehmoud was amazed at what was happening.

MDC-Brooklyn's ninth-floor Special Housing Unit, known by staff as "the shu" and by inmates as "the hole," has about seventy-five cells, each with a bunkbed. It held about sixty "special interest" detainees around this time. (The prison's total capacity is about 2,500.) An Egyptian man was confined to the SHU for two months before being permitted to call an attorney; he was given no soap or towels for a week and meanwhile was interrogated. Correctional officers allegedly stomped on his bare feet. A Buddhist Nepalese man suspected of nothing was held in the SHU for four months.[51] Quite aside from any alleged mistreatment by officers, "just being there" is "detrimental to any person's mental health," an MDC employee told me.

The Nepalese man, who was in his mid-forties, had been selling flowers and working odd jobs in the United States illegally for about five years and was preparing to return to his country. Before going home, he bought a videocamera to film unusual things in America to show his wife back in Nepal: women smoking in public, and tall buildings. From Kew Gardens in Queens he videotaped a building that happened to house an FBI office, and he was arrested on the street. Agents realized their honest mistake right away. Legal Aid Society attorney Olivia Cassin said "a really nice" FBI agent called her to get help for the "suspect." He was being held alone in the SHU, and the agent told a colleague of Cassin that he "cries all the time." After about two weeks, the Nepalese man was allowed to meet with Cassin. At first Cassin just tried to have her new client moved into the general population to break his terrible isolation. He didn't understand what was happening to him, and he spoke practically no English. "But, of course, prisons are prisons, and immigration proceedings are immigration pro-ceedings," Cassin told me. An INS deportation officer told Cassin that precisely because the man cried so often, he could not be moved into the general population or he might "start a riot." "I begged them," Cassin recalled, and finally "their compromise was to put someone in [the SHU cell] with him"—an Indian prisoner who spoke a different language. But at least he had company.

After about a month Cassin's client was moved into MDC's general population, where he was held for another three months. He was never charged with a crime. On Christmas Eve, just before the prisoner's scheduled return to Nepal, the friendly FBI agent brought the videocamera to the prison for him to take home, and Cassin brought a black suit for him to wear on the flight. She left it with the executive associate assistant warden. But the man was sent home without his camera and wearing his orange prison uniform. Cassin said she doesn't know if authorities were just "inefficient" or wanted to "punish him even more." On the flight home, she later found out, the man covered himself with airplane blankets out of embarrassment.

The MDC employee I spoke with noted that immediately following the terrorist attacks there was plenty of "chaos and anger" among staff at the prison. From the roof of the prison, one high-ranking MDC officer had watched the hijacked plane hit the second tower. Two weeks after September 11 the attorney general sent a memo to MDC staff members "to address the emotions of [officers]." He advised MDC staff to act "professionally," warning that to do otherwise might provide the basis for complaints, which could, in turn, jeopardize the terrorist investigation. The employee witnessed one incident in which correctional officers pressed a "special interest" detainee "firmly" against the wall while moving him out for an FBI interview. The witness believed the officers were within the legal limit of force but admitted, "My reaction was confusion. I thought, if this guy is involved, I want him punished. A part of me even thought he deserved to be roughed up." At the same time, he reflected, "Most of these guys are probably innocent [and] they're probably fearing for their lives. I felt really bad for them and even wanted to protect them."

He also wanted me to know that prison staff members often felt they were not recognized for their efforts while the media made heroes of New York police officers, firefighters, even Port Authority workers and emergency medical personnel. After several weeks, the employee said, the sense of chaos inside the prison diminished, and the presence of the "special interest" detainees in the SHU became routine. He added that many blacks and Latinos are regularly locked up for long periods on the pretext of "investigations." INS detainees, in particular, he observed, "literally fall through the cracks [and] . . . sit in these places anonymously for years," but the September 11 detentions were simply more widely acknowledged.

Attorney General Ashcroft likened his new policy of preventive detention to Robert Kennedy's crackdown on the Mafia, when arrests were made for "spitting on the sidewalk" in order to prevent more serious crimes. On the same day that an INS detainee filed suit for alleging that corrections officers had kicked him and pulled his hair to make him face an American flag, a Brooklyn judge ordered the MDC warden to appear in court to justify his use of solitary confinement. But the latter case had nothing to do with September 11 detainees. Peter Gotti, brother of "the late mob boss," had complained that he was kept in solitary "for almost a full day" after being ordered into the general population. Officials reportedly believed he was involved in a plot to kill a Missouri warden in the prison where his brother had died.[52]

Sitting in the SHU twenty-four hours a day for about four months, Mehmood began to realize, "Everything is gone because I am a Muslim." He lost his house and his $42,000 truck, for which he had paid all but $9,000. "The dream of every American, suddenly"—he clapped his hands—"gone." He had not been to a mosque more than a couple of times in many years. In the hole, however, he turned for comfort to prayer and to the Koran. He considered killing himself the first few days, and then he began to pray five times a day in the traditional manner.

"It will take time for me to come back," he said. He was not talking about coming back to the United States, though he would have to wait ten years to do that legally. "To be as a human being. The strong ego inside me [is lost]." Yet he seemed calm and self-possessed as we sat there. He smiled. "MDC convert me to a good religious person," he said. Islam teaches "whatever you lost, you're going to get back."

When Mehmood was moved from the SHU into the general population after four months, it was like moving "from hell to heaven." After two more months, he was moved to the Passaic County Jail, where the mattresses were filthy and prisoners had to send only one sheet at a time to laundry or else they would have none. Mehmood told me without a trace of melodrama, "If you have any pet, like dog or cat, you're not going to keep it in that cell." When Human Rights Watch representatives were finally allowed to tour the Passaic jail after repeated requests, they were prohibited from going into occupied housing areas.[53] MDC, on the other hand, was clean. And not only that. "Criminals [are] so nice—I was very surprised," said Mehmood. He described the other inmates in the general population there as "very loving." "They couldn't believe I spent four months, two days [in the hole] for overstaying my visa." That's when Mehmood told me with a smile that the "real, proper Americans," such as those he met in the general population, are not anti-Muslim. Before he left, all those in his unit came to say good-bye to him individually.

Just after Mehmood was moved to Passaic, his wife and children returned to Pakistan. The United States filed criminal charges against him for altering his social security card. He had paid $100 to a Polish car service driver to help him do it. He was sentenced to time served when he pled guilty. Mehmood was "removed" from the United States aboard a passenger plane two days after we spoke in mid-April 2002. He had worried about his children, who were being taunted as "terrorists" by their classmates in New Jersey. Back in Pakistan now, they were having trouble in school because they did not speak or write Urdu and because "people are hating them because they think they are American." As a father, Mehmood wonders what he should tell them. He had always advised them "to be a law-abiding citizen [and] respect the cops." Now they want to know why their father was taken from them for seven months. "They can't understand," Mehmood said. "It's a big question on their mind." "This is not Lincoln's America," he added.

In 2002 and early 2003 at least four charter flights took large groups of Pakistanis who had no proper documentation—or ties to terrorists—back to Pakistan. The INS called the charters "routine." Such large-scale deportations occur regularly, but this time the media were paying attention, and the *Washington Post* referred to one flight as a "secret airlift." Secretive, routine, or both, the crackdown made news from the *Sacramento Bee* to the BBC and from Quebec to Karachi. The Canadian government issued a rare travel advisory to Canadian citizens born in Pakistan, Syria, Iran, Iraq, Libya, the Sudan, Yemen, and Saudi Arabia about the dangers of travel to the United States. Meanwhile, many Pakistanis in the United States were heading for Canada, and the United States increased the detentions of Pakistanis on the northern border.[54]

From Brooklyn's federal prison in late 2001 came a report that as protestors outside demanded to know the identities of detainees inside, the windows were painted over. At a California prison correctional officers had followed the initiative of the nation's chief law enforcement officer and papered over the windows of cells holding "special interest" detainees. They did it with American flags.[55] Before I left the Passaic County Jail, Anser Mehmood asked me to ask the INS official when he would be able to return to Pakistan. He told me again, "There are people who know this is wrong. That's encouraging."

# 3 | ANOTHER WORLD, ANOTHER NATION

*Miami's Krome Detention Center*

Edward Calejo is the first prison guard I saw cry. Actually, he was no longer a guard. He was standing in the air-conditioned courtroom of Judge Federico (Fred) Moreno, Southern District of Florida, downtown Miami. Judge Moreno had simply asked him, before imposing sentence, why he had done it. Calejo, a light-skinned Cuban American, age twenty-nine, was wearing a blue blazer and wire-rimmed glasses. In the courthouse coffee shop, Calejo's mother told me her son should have made a speech, should have defended himself, should have told the judge about his patience coaching Little League baseball. Instead Calejo choked and could barely speak. "It was a situation I had never been in. . . . I reacted. . . . I don't know what happened."

Krome North Service Processing Center detention enforcement officer (DEO) Edward Calejo was being prosecuted for the beating of a Haitian detainee, David Bernard. According to a statement released by the U.S. Attorney's Office,

> Calejo became angry with Bernard, a non criminal detainee, after a verbal incident in the cafeteria. He then escorted the detainee to the dormitory building and placed him in a small cell. Inside the cell Calejo, without warning or lawful justification, punched Bernard in the head. Calejo then kicked Bernard and punched him multiple times about the head and body. Bernard posed no threat to his safety, Calejo admitted in court today. . . .

"This successful prosecution and the defendant's guilty plea demonstrate our commitment to protecting the rights of all inhabitants of our country," said Assistant U.S. Attorney Mary K. Butler. "It also shows the ability of the federal government to police itself when confronted with criminal misconduct."[1]

The press release seems straightforward enough—to the uninitiated, even reassuring—but to Krome watchers it was an anomaly. For years, Cheryl Little, a relentless Miami immigration attorney, had been asking the Justice Department for the results of its investigations into allegations of mistreatment at Krome without getting any answers. The press release about Calejo was faxed to a reporter who also had asked for those results; she had not asked about Calejo. Apparently the Justice Department had something to prove.

There was another odd thing about the sentencing hearing. The courtroom was packed with character witnesses for Calejo, many of them uniformed law enforcement people (the judge allowed Calejo's attorney to introduce them but declined to let them testify). There was a pronounced absence of olive green INS uniforms, of Calejo's most recent colleagues. After the hearing, I asked the government attorneys whether the evidence against Calejo had come from other Krome officers; I knew that a detainee complaint alone was unlikely to have gotten this far. They would not answer my question because, they explained, grand jury proceedings (at which indictments are handed down) are secret and because prosecutors depend on law enforcement cooperation when they prosecute law enforcement personnel.

Calejo was sentenced to a year and a day in prison on the felony charge of violating Bernard's civil rights. Judge Moreno said that even though the crime was "apparently out of character for this defendant," an example had to be made. He paraphrased Swift: Laws are like cobwebs, sometimes catching flies and letting the wasps go. Calejo had about two months until his "voluntary surrender date." I wrote him a letter inviting him to talk, but he did not respond.

Scott Partridge, a retired Miami Metro-Dade police officer, was one of the character witnesses who did not get to testify. During the recess, he asked me who I was. He gave me his card—"Carib American Systems, Inc. Security and Investigative Services/Executive Protection"—and suggested I give him a call in a few weeks because he might have a good story for me. Two and a half years later I called. I was heading down to Miami from New York and wondered if Partridge could put me in touch with Calejo, whose phone number was now unlisted. We chatted, and Partridge told me that he had written a story about why he liked being a cop. It was a true story. Two kids were playing with a gun when one accidentally shot the other. Partridge got the call. He remembered how he controlled the bleeding until paramedics arrived, at the same time comforting the boy who had shot his friend. "Had I not been up to that moment," Partridge told me, the boy would not have survived. Then he said that the wounded boy was thirteen-year-old Eddie Calejo and that he eventually became Calejo's godfather. Partridge said he would find out if Eddie would talk to me.

"I want to tell you everything. I really want to tell you everything," Calejo says soon after we sit down in the living room of the southwest Miami house he shares with his mother and grandmother. He had done his ten months and decided to explain a few things. He had even asked a friend who worked at the post office to check on my forwarding address, but it had expired. Calejo says he doesn't want to make excuses; he wants me to understand why he did what he did. "I just thought I got a bad rap. That it really wasn't me. The person that went into jail wasn't me. Yes, I did something wrong, but no, I didn't do it for the reasons everybody thought I had done it." In other words, he isn't a racist. He wants me to understand that he did things at Krome he didn't think he was capable of doing.

The counts had made an immediate and lasting impression on him. Counting inmates is a mainstay of prison routine. At Krome the detainees lived in large, collective rooms rather than individual cells. Bathrooms were locked during the counts. "One of these guys got locked up inside the shower," Calejo recalls. "It was a long count. He was in there for an hour, and when we opened the door, the Haitian was on the floor in convulsions." This wasn't Bernard but another Haitian. Krome held about 285 Haitians at the time, out of a total of 412 detainees.[2] "A lot of times, the Haitians would just jump to the floor and do little shows. Sometimes you didn't know if they were acting, sometimes you didn't know if it was real. It's kind of funny because each nationality had their own different way of doing things. Jamaicans kind of kept to themselves, didn't say much. The Chinese would just do little sit-ins. The Haitians would throw fits. The

Latins would speak a lot, would get in your face. You learned all that as you went. You saw all the different reactions of different nationalities, which was interesting."

When he realized that the Haitian was locked in the bathroom, Calejo notified a more experienced officer. "Leave him in there," he was told. So he did, and he soon realized that this wasn't just about the counts. Sometimes officers would "lock them in the toilet and leave them there all night or day. In the toilet. That was some sort of punishment," he explains. "I was new. There wasn't really much I could do about it."

In the stacks of affidavits that the Haitian Refugee Center had submitted to the Justice Department are these lines from a Haitian detainee:

> They say Krome isn't really a jail, we're not really prisoners and this really isn't punishment. Let me tell you how we live. We live behind a fence, of course, and we are supposed to live by a routine, a schedule, rules. In fact, we live however the guards decide we should live that day. On a good day, when we get a good guard, we can stand life. On a bad day, anything can happen.

Eddie Calejo's parents came to Miami from Cuba in the early 1960s, and he was born here. He wanted to be a professional baseball player. He attended St. Thomas University and Florida International University on scholarships while his mother worked two jobs. A serious shoulder injury changed his plans, and he found himself working as a financial counselor at a bank. A friend working for the INS mentioned a job opening at Krome. It wasn't what Calejo had in mind, but the law enforcement culture was not foreign to him. His sister worked as a warrants detective for the Miami-Dade Police Department, and his godfather was a cop. "I didn't want to work at Krome," Calejo says, "because I thought it was a jail." But he thought it might provide other opportunities. Once he had a government position, he could "lateral over" to a job with the FBI or the Bureau of Alcohol, Tobacco and Firearms (ATF). In fact, Calejo tells me, he was on the verge of being hired by the ATF when he was indicted. Five years had passed since the fight with the detainee. In the meantime, he had been promoted twice and sent to the Federal Law Enforcement Training Center at Glynco, Georgia, where he worked briefly as an instructor of other detention officers.

The timing of it all was confusing. Why would he be allowed to remain on the job for five years and receive promotions if the beating had been reported right away? A case had to be prepared against him, but that was only part of the answer. As Calejo told me many times, "I'm not going to deny anything. I never denied hitting [Bernard]." But, he says, "it was really weird [because] in all that time I had been there, I had never seen anything" result from investigations of officer misconduct. "There's a lot of [officers] out there that have been taking women back into the dormitory and raping them. Some weren't raped, some were consensual. [But] that was happening all the time. All the time. And investigators were going out there all the time. Nobody ever came up with anything."[3] Sexual abuse of prisoners is a common practice,[4] and INS detainees are especially vulnerable for the simple reason that they can be deported. As a 1993 Justice Department investigation "concluded" in another Krome case, "[Detainee's] version of rape and forced oral sex is corroborated only by her subsequent statements to public health service personnel. There are no witnesses nor any physical evidence. . . . Moreover, [the woman] has been deported to Haiti. Under these circumstances, this matter lacks prosecutive merit."[5]

The investigations to which Calejo was referring were the result of ongoing and increasingly organized complaints to INS Headquarters and the OIG. Local groups, including the Haitian Refugee Center, the Florida Immigrant Advocacy Center, the Catholic Legal Immigration Network, and the American Friends Service Committee, had forced the government to create at least the appearance of concern about allegations of abuse at Krome. Even when INS Headquarters officials wanted to clean up Krome—and even their staunchest detractors recognize that some have—they were unable to do so. Between a well-intentioned political appointee in Washington and an isolation cell in the Everglades, there are layers of recalcitrant career bureaucrats. At times the middle-management recalcitrance is strong enough to prevent alliances from forming between its own superiors in Washington and its subordinates in the detention camp. A group of anonymous Krome officers sent a memo to their supervisor complaining that thirty-nine women and children were being held in a single room at the detention center, where they had to "eat their meals on the floor" and share six beds. The officers wrote:

It has been known, that when officers address issues of concern to all that are involved, and past practice, is to label or cast the officers as trouble makers or whiners. We hope that by reporting some of these violations we can instill a new attitude of caring, professionalism and concern. We feel that this [is] not only a human rights issue but also a safety and legal issue that I.N.S. can not afford to ignore. We further hope that by speaking the truth, none of the officers will receive criticism or retribution by management for trying to do the right thing.[6]

In 1998 attorneys Little and Joan Friedland wrote to INS Commissioner Doris Meissner to ask about the status of one investigation. An Angolan woman seeking political asylum was being detained in a Miami hotel with her small children. She had complained to Friedland and Little that a detention officer posted outside her room pressured her throughout the night to have sex with him. The OIG determined that this was not a criminal matter and referred the allegation to the INS's Office of Internal Audit (OIA), analogous to a police department's internal affairs department. Commissioner Meissner responded: "The OIA has completed the investigations. . . . The allegation that [the detained woman] may have been the recipient of improper advances . . . [is] unsubstantiated. The investigation did disclose several systemic issues. These findings regarding policy and procedures concerning women and children detained as a result of a petition for asylum have been forwarded to senior agency management for review and action." While she was commissioner, Meissner herself told Congress that the INS needed better oversight.[7] A veteran staffer of a nongovernmental organization told me that Meissner was "too nice" for the job. Under her signature on the letter to Little and Friedland, Meissner added a handwritten note: "I hope you are seeing progress under the new leadership at Krome."

Krome leadership had been juggled before. At the time Calejo was being investigated, a new Miami District director, Walter "Dan" Cadman, had recently moved into the district office on NE 79th Street in Miami. Calejo speculates on the connection: "I think that he wanted to make an example of somebody at Krome because he was trying to straighten Krome out." A year after Calejo's guilty plea, Cadman took a "voluntary change" in job assignment from Miami after the OIG examined his role in a "deception of Congress"—a cosmetic cleanup of the Krome detention center before Commissioner Meissner and a congressional delegation arrived for an inspection. According to the OIG, Cadman "was a willing participant in efforts to mislead INS headquarters and then to mislead and delay the OIG investigation." In 1986 Senior Special Agent Cadman had been designated staff coordinator for the Alien Border Control Committee, which developed mass detention contingency plans. After the Miami deception, he became "chief of counterterrorism" at INS Headquarters, a position he held on September 11, 2001. Congressional pressure forced him out of that job, but Cadman still had the support of INS management, one Headquarters official told me. Because he was considered loyal, this official said, he was transferred to "a plum job" in Madrid.[8]

———

The wilderness west of Miami is one of America's heartlands. North toward Lake Okeechobee, Jamaicans cut cane. South toward Homestead, Mexicans and Guatemalans pick tomatoes and strawberries. Anti-Castro Cubans practice paramilitary exercises in the nearby swamps. The "river of grass," as the Everglades is known, drains slowly south and southwest, still recovering from the damage of sugar industry pollutants. In the 1960s the Krome Avenue site outside the backwater town of Miami was cleared for a Nike missile base, one of many built on the perimeters of potential target cities during the cold war.[9] In 1980 and 1981 large groups of Haitians and Cubans made their way to South Florida. The Army Corps of Engineers, which had built the canals crisscrossing the Everglades, now converted the missile base into "a turn-around facility" for "aliens" who would either be returned to their countries or moved to facilities designed for long-term housing. At least that was the designers' plan. But almost immediately Haitians were being detained at Krome "for an indefinite period."[10]

Although U.S. immigration law mandates a case-by-case determination of applications for political asylum, policies coordinated by several federal agencies have always treated different groups in different ways. There are exceptions, but in general, and not surprisingly, detention and asylum policies serve foreign policy goals. Like the Salvadoran and Guatemalan asylum seekers during the 1980s, Haitians have been forced to seek protection from the same country that has helped to sponsor the repression from which they are fleeing.[11] In 1992 a group of Haitian asylum seekers detained by the INS in a CCA jail in Laredo, Texas, sat down in a recreation room to protest arbitrary release policies. Officers in masks and riot gear broke up the peaceful sit-in. A detained Haitian woman told the *Laredo Morning Times*, "Oh God, [the guard] beat the Haitian. He put him on the ground and put his foot on his neck. He did it just like a Haitian."[12]

Krome soon became overcrowded as Haitians were detained en masse under what a federal judge would decry as "a program at work within INS" to single them out for discriminatory treatment. Twenty years later Miami INS was still excusing its problems by saying, accurately, that "the Krome facility was never designed for detention."[13] Today, Krome is overflowing with Haitians again as the United States detains them in order to deter their countrymen from fleeing too.

Overcrowding at Krome provides a useful lens onto national detention policies. INS officials have attributed problems in the detention system to the fact that the agency was never prepared to handle the large-scale incarcerations mandated by the 1996 immigration laws. The reasoning is sound, but it only tells part of the story. From the early 1980s, the beginning of what might be called the contemporary era of INS detention, crucial inadequacies have been in place. But these were not accidents. The infrastructure of detention centers and the mentality of the bureaucrats and guards operating them have perpetuated the problem they sometimes tried to solve and sometimes tried to hide: "processing centers" were prisons, and everyone knew it, even if they had to deny it in public. Pacification and repression were, therefore, in order and inevitable.

As early as 1981 the INS Southern Regional Office sent a "survey team" to Krome. The team made a variety of suggestions, from treating the water to eliminate fecal bacteria from the system serving detainees to piping in music and clearing ball fields. The report even suggested the possibility of team uniforms for soccer—"the Haitians' favorite team sport"—while cautioning that "the nature of the game which frequently excites the spectators may present some problems."[14] To be fair, the report was written by middlemen. These INS officials do not write the laws governing the detention or release of those in custody, nor will they oversee the soccer games or interrupt the proposed piped-in music to announce a count. (Neither the music nor the soccer uniforms materialized.) Whatever the efforts to make detained time more bearable, viewing every aspect of daily life through the clouded lens of "security" makes prisoners out of human beings. The builders used prisons as their guiding image, so control superseded humane treatment. Fifteen years later the Krome clinic director said there were almost daily complaints that the water caused stomach problems and skin irritation; to avoid the latter, the clinic suggested that detainees wash less often.[15] The most detailed recommendation in the early Krome survey concerns the fencing.

> All of the perimeter fences present a top horizontal plane with the bottom level of the fences being parallel to the highest contour of the ground, the outermost fence has six (6) strands of barbed wire affixed to the top of the fence in a "Y" angled configuration of three (3) strands each. The middle fence has a single roll of 36" diameter concertina wire affixed to the top of the fence. The innermost fence has three strands of barbed wire affixed to the top of the fence and angled away from the compound area.[16]

All of this predates the fear of the "criminal alien" that would become a touchstone of late 1980s political rhetoric; in fact, the word *criminal* does not appear in the fifty-page survey.

Fenced into their own contradictions, the middlemen try to hide the problem they are creating. Krome "presents a harsh, uninviting appearance to all who enter whether they be staff, visitors, or alien detainees. *This harsh perception could easily lead to the belief of mistreatment however untrue it may be.*"[17] Maybe the Southern Regional survey team was already aware of mistreatment. Perhaps they were only foreseeing the inevitable. Several years later a detained Haitian woman described her experience of the harsh Krome landscape:

> [The female officer] called us out early and made us all take plastic bags. There weren't any gloves the way there was supposed to be for any kind of dirty work. Then she told us to pick up the trash in the yard. There wasn't enough to go around because we pick that up regularly anyhow, so she ordered us to start picking up rocks. The rocks here are sharp, white coral, and you can hurt yourself easily on them, especially without gloves. But there weren't even enough of them to go around, and [the officer] sent us squatting and crawling to look for small stones and even pebbles. This all began to hurt, and some of the women began to cry.[18]

The 1981 Krome survey noted that INS detention officer training at Glynco, Georgia, where Calejo would serve as an instructor after administering a beating, was geared to short-term detention. Krome, however, had to be ready for "indefinite detention." So the report recommended consultations with federal corrections professionals to increase training in "long-term detention techniques." On-the-job training taught officers how to view the aliens in their custody. Calejo tells me: "They instill in you that everybody's bad." He would sometimes argue with other officers, reminding them that the detainees were only locked up for immigration violations. "But you know how they justified things?" he says, still amazed. "They [said], 'Oh no, don't look at it that way. They could be criminals in their country.'" He adds: "You're brainwashed over there. 'These are all scumbag inmates. For all we know'—this is what they'd tell us—'for all we know, they're murderers in their own country and coming over here.' That's the frame of mind that we had."

A young man and a young woman are speaking to each other through not one but two layers of internal camp fencing. In all likelihood, they were deported to Haiti long ago, because their picture appears in a collection of early Krome photographs.[19] All of the prisoners in Gary Monroe's book are wearing street clothes, and why not? The Krome survey notes, without much ado, "The BOP in Miami has the capability to manufacture clothing to our specifications. This source will be fully utilized for all detainee clothing needs." Ten years later a detained Haitian activist and refugee had gone for more than a week without eating, leading a hunger strike that united detainees of different nationalities. Dehydrated but extremely patient, he explained that the issue at Krome was not individual officers. Yes, one of the hunger strikers' demands was that abusive officers be disciplined. "My problem," he told me, "is the structure, the way this place is run." He was wearing a standard orange prison uniform. In a French-language poem that he signed, though he asked me not to use his name, he too noted the landscape, the "incurable grayness" of it, and the way "the olive green dominates the orange."

———

"You know what it is?" Calejo asks. "All those guys are cop wanna-bes. That's what it is. All those guys out there want to be cops, and there's no way they can be cops. They got a badge, you know? They got a badge. People that can't get into real law enforcement—because that's not law enforcement—but they go around saying, 'Oh, we're officers,' and 'We're this and that.' They're nothing. But they have that complex, you know?

And I tell you this because when I first got there and got my badge, I felt the same thing. I tell you from experience. I was going, 'Wow, I got a badge and a gun now.' They gave me a gun, and I hadn't had any training. I had never shot a gun, and they gave me a gun." (In one recent year, five INS officers committed suicide with their weapons.)[20]

Discipline in the Krome cafeteria "was just another ridiculous thing," Calejo continues. When he was doing time himself, prisoners in the dining hall sat wherever they wanted to and got up as they pleased. "We were supposed to sit them down, each in their own spot. We were baby-sitters. Sit there, sit there, sit there." One day David Bernard was the last in line; Calejo recalls closing the gate behind him. Bernard skipped ahead in the food line, and Calejo called him on it. "He got in my face and said, 'You don't tell me what to do. I do what I want.' So we had it out right there, and he took his tray and walked." It might have ended there, but one of Calejo's supervisors, a lieutenant who had come to the INS from the Bureau of Prisons and who would help to convict his subordinate, had seen the whole thing. The lieutenant told Calejo to "take him to isolation and take care of him." Calejo understood. The "Stipulated Facts" signed by all parties in the plea agreement say that the supervisor advised Calejo and another officer "to escort Bernard to a small cell . . . for counseling." "Isolation" did not necessarily mean the so-called disciplinary segregation units described in the INS's *Service Processing Center Design Guide,* although those could be bad enough. "They'd lock you up with no bathroom, no water," Calejo recalls. "It was like a storage space, but it was used as isolation. Anything that we could use—and I say 'we' because I did it also, okay? I'm not proud of it—anything that we could use to isolate them, to make them suffer."

*Abuse* is a word that can be abused, and sometimes over the years I have wondered how often detainee stories are exaggerated to make a point. A beating might make the newspaper; despair probably won't.[21] But not only have the stories recurred with consistency over decades and from around the country, every once in a while someone like Eddie Calejo steps forward with nothing to gain. When I spoke to him, I realized that the situation at Krome was worse than its harshest critics had probably imagined.

I had a totally different frame of mind. I hated going to work there. I really did. Because I was locked up—they made us work twelve-, thirteen-hour shifts. It wasn't eight-hour shifts. You worked twelve-, thirteen-hour shifts locked up in that environment with a bunch of people wanting to get out. . . . A lot of things we did out there weren't right. I mean, we make guys stand in line—they just stand there, just to stand there. "Don't move," you know. And we'd make them stand there all day long. Or we told them, "Go get a piece of paper. Go clean that. Go stand over there. Don't move. If you move, you're going to isolation."

For everything, the threat was isolation. I [did] things that at the time I thought weren't too bad, like I'd lock somebody up in the bathroom, and I really wouldn't think about it. I was saying, "Well that's for not being where you're supposed to be." I never went out of my way to beat anybody up. There were guards that, if you didn't do something, would slap you. Guards did that. At the time I was out there, there were about one hundred guards. I'd say 60 percent of them slap you right across the head, kick you in the ass. They would humiliate people. . . .

If you had inmates fighting, you think they broke it up? It turned into a boxing match. It turned into a ring. All the guards [would say], "Now you guys got to fight," and make the inmates fight. It was a show. I hated it.

Accompanied by another officer and by his supervisor, Calejo took Bernard to an isolation area, "a cage." On the way back there, he called Bernard a faggot in Creole; he had picked up a bit of the Haitian language on the job.

We gave him a little push to go in, and he didn't want to go in. And we pushed him again, and he fought back. And when he fought back is when I went at it with him. And that's when I hit him, and that's when the fight went to a whole different level. I look back at it, and I was wrong. I was. I admit it. . . . We got in a fight, and I took advantage of the fact that I was wearing a badge. But I never intended for it to go where it went. I had a lot of training in college, I took martial arts and I knew how to defend myself. He thought he was going to kick my ass, and that pissed me off. So, you know, one thing led to another.

The word *torture* can be abused too. While explaining that in the United States it occurs only "in aberrational situations and never as a matter of policy," a United Nations report gives examples of "torture and other cruel, inhuman or degrading treatment or punishment" in this country. These include the 1997 sodomizing of Abner Louima by New York City police, the 1991 beating of Rodney King, and, in the Justice Department's official version, the 1995 Calejo-Bernard incident.[22]

Off a stretch of Miami highway called the Tamiami Trail, not far from a Miccosukee gaming complex and a billboard advertising airboat rides through the Everglades, a Confederate flag was often planted in the mud where big-wheeled pickup trucks splashed around for recreation. A short service road runs from SW 177th Avenue, also known as Krome Avenue, to a small guardhouse, and behind that, a parking lot. One enters the lobby and from there, through a locked door, a hallway of offices. There is another layer of security and locked doors to get to the yard and the dorms—a fairly standard jail setup. "When you pass that administration building," Calejo tells me, "that's where the world begins. Another world begins."

The Calejo-Bernard incident was not an aberration in the Krome world, and Haitians were not the only victims. Even when guards were not watering down the food simply out of malice, the cafeteria was the site of confrontation and humiliation. The very fact that it was a place where prisoners might be able to relax for a few moments seems to have invited the worst of officers' inclinations. Krome detainees have regularly complained of being rushed through their meals in a scenario conjuring a mix of impatient security guards and fraternity hazing; a BOP food service administrator once recommended "expedited feeding" at Krome to handle all the prisoners.[23] In 1991 a group of about seventy Chinese asylum seekers wrote "No discrimination, no insult, for freedom—an open letter to American people":

> This incident happened on May 1, 1991 when we were waiting in the line for lunch. That day, on the counter of the cafeteria, there was a plate of unclean dish; and none of the Haitian detainees before us picked up that dish. The officer on duty did not say nor do anything about it. When it was the turn for a Chinese detainee to pick up his dish, this officer told him to take that dish, which was unwanted by anybody else. As soon as this Chinese detainee slightly showed that he did not want it either, he was very rudely dragged out of the line by the officer and was not allowed to have lunch. After this incident, all the Chinese detainees had a sit-down protest. Seeing this scene, another officer threatened us by saying: "I hate you fucking Chinamen the most, tomorrow all of you will be sent back to China," then he pointed at one detainee's forehead and made a gesture of shooting with his hands and said: "Bang" "Bang". . . .

Because of the incident of racial discrimination against Chinese in the cafeteria, Chinese detainees organized a sit-down protest. We quietly sat down in order, and waited for our attorneys to negotiate with Krome Detention Center authorities. To this quiet, peaceful protest, the Detention Center dispatched dozens of officers and dragged some Chinese detainees out. We then stood up and tried to protect our country fellowmen. At this point, the officers attacked us brutally; three of us were beaten down to the ground and seven or eight of us were injured. After this incident, flying in the face of the facts, Krome authorities accused the Chinese detainees of attacking the officers first, and later on, they used the same story to cheat the press.[24]

A guard makes a prisoner use a dirty tray: that hardly seems worth our time. Armed officers attack detainees who are sitting on the ground: that's hard to believe. And the trajectory from one to the other is played out again and again in the prison world. The "structure" of the system—"the way this place is run"—ensures it, whether inside immigration detention or the larger gulag to which the immigration system has attached itself.

The way Krome is run means arbitrary power on the inside and disinformation on the outside. In 1996 a Nigerian detainee told me that an officer had walked into the men's dormitory "shouting [and] boasting." The officer, whom he named, took down his own pants. The detainee told me, "[The officer] asked if we're man enough to fuck his ass . . . [if not] he'll fuck our ass." A second officer challenged detainees by asking "anyone who calls himself a man" to come forward. "There were reportedly some seventy witnesses to this incident." Miami INS spokesperson Lamar Wooley refused me a tour of Krome, in violation of the INS's own media visitation guidelines, saying it would be disruptive. He said a group media tour was more likely to be permitted. A group of journalists and photographers, including representatives of the *New Times,* the *Washington Post,* the *Los Angeles Times, Newsweek,* and the *Miami Herald,* and me, then requested a tour. Speaking for District Director Cadman, Wooley denied access again. He told me, "Nothing unusual has happened or is happening to warrant this type of coverage." After letters were sent by local advocates to the INS commissioner and by Amnesty International to the district office, a media tour was finally allowed. None of the original requestors was included. An Associated Press reporter was asked to direct the pool tour. When I told him how the tour had come about, he said he knew that the INS must have been up to something to offer a tour when he had not requested one. Then he asked me not to use his name. He said he still needed the INS to return his calls.

Meanwhile, I had sent a letter about the sexual assault allegation to District Director Cadman, who forwarded it to the Office of the Inspector General. The Ft. Lauderdale OIG later told me that it could not comment on whether my complaint had led to an investigation or, if it had, what the results might have been. The Freedom of Information Act has provided valuable openings into the government tendency to secrecy; my request for information was at first denied, but on appeal, I was provided with multiple copies of my own letter—and also, to my surprise, with the news that the officer who had threatened the Nigerian was "reprimanded" and sent back to work.

Internally, investigators were well aware of the Miami nightmare. Documents released to me included a short memo to an assistant director of internal investigations from a special agent:

> In the last two weeks this office has received a number of allegations regarding the Krome Detention Facility. The offenses range from, assault by DEO, to intimidation by DEOs, a DEO who dropped his trousers soliciting aliens to penetrate his sphincter and forcible rapes by other aliens. In 1995 we have logged in 12 cases and as [of] today March 26, 1996 we have four. I suggest we meet with Detention and Deportation and consider some strategy or possibly consider addressing some of these issues in a joint program review.

The assistant director replied with a handwritten note: "I agree we have a problem."

Critics have charged that the Office of Internal Audit, where this memo circulated, simply does damage control and that it also retaliates against whistleblowers. One Washington INS official told me that the chief of the OIA is only there because "his high-level colleagues have nothing to fear from him." It's not the kind of thing most employees waiting to qualify for a government pension are going to say publicly, so the insulation from accountability remains intact. Whistleblower cases that make the news tend to concern allegations of agency corruption or lax law enforcement. The abuse of detainees remains off this particular map.[25]

When I visited Lulseged Dhine at Krome, the thirty-six-year-old detainee and self-appointed ombudsman was in a wheelchair talking heatedly to fellow detainees and officers alike. Dhine had produced detailed accounts of individual cases as well as conditions at the detention center. He had been awarded a commendation for saving a detention enforcement officer's life in a laundry room chemical accident at the Florence, Arizona, Service Processing Center. At New York's Varick Street Service Processing Center, he wore a wire to help bust a drug-dealing officer. Dhine had been detained for almost nine years; it would be nine years and forty-five days before he got out. Then he would be deported to Ethiopia. In 1978, after his family was murdered by the regime in Ethiopia, fifteen-year-old Dhine had walked to the Sudan. A Christian relief agency helped the Ethiopian Jew to enter the United States legally. In Washington, D.C., Alisa Solomon writes, Dhine's "trauma caught up with him: he found escape in drugs. After several convictions—all misdemeanors carrying sentences of less than a year, which he served in full—the INS picked him up and began deportation proceedings in 1990. It was then that Dhine began fighting."[26]

While detained in New York, Dhine had helped the People for the Golden Vision, a church-based grassroots organization founded to assist the detained Chinese asylum seekers who had landed in New York on the *Golden Venture,* to organize a demonstration outside the federal building that houses the Manhattan detention center. He was transferred to Florence. INS officials said the move was to "'accommodate his request for fresh air and outdoor recreation.'"[27] The laundry incident in Arizona had landed Dhine in a wheelchair, and he was then transferred to Krome. Now he was providing regular information to the Florida Immigrant Advocacy Center and maintaining contacts with reporters around the country.

Deputy Assistant Regional Director Rita Nixon's contribution to a Krome inspection report is divided into sections. *Issue:* Bonds tracking. *Issue:* Docket control. *Issue:* Pod visitation. Her last entry is a unique category. *Issue:* Detainee Dhine.

Mr. Dhine regularly grants interviews to the press. He loves the attention. Needless to say his accounts of his case and his treatment while in Service custody are greatly exaggerated and extremely biased. . . . Due to the sensitive nature of this case, Headquarters is directly involved. . . . Mr. Dhine remains a major disruptive force at Krome. Due to a prior problematic incarceration history he is given preferential treatment and basically catered to by the medical staff. He continues to contact the media with inflammatory reports.[28]

Nixon recommended that "a public relations specialist on site be pursued to deal with all media involvement." She certainly had a point about the disruptive effect of long-term incarceration in a processing center never intended for such a thing. But there was no sign of an on-site media specialist the day a more accommodating Krome leadership allowed me to sit with Dhine in a high-traffic area of the camp.

The government's "Krome SPC Back-Up Material" confirms practically all of Dhine's complaints, from the inadequate laundry service to a vermin-infested health clinic, and even his allegation that detainees working in the clinic were forced to collect laundry stained with blood and "other body fluids" without the use of cleansers.[29] Dhine and the inspection team also agreed on something else. Nixon wrote: "Morale is extremely low. There exists an overall attitude of one 'team' vs. the other. . . . In a recent 'town hall meeting' conducted on site the issue of morale was brought up by an officer and he was told by a member of upper management that his morale was his problem. This was done in the presence of a large number of employees." Dhine wrote in an open letter:

> The INS officers work 12 hour shifts, and they get only 3 fifteen minute breaks, if they are lucky. They do not get any time to eat lunch or dinner or to get any time to relax mentally. . . . Mentally this is not good for the officers so they do not handle the detainees well. They are abused and then they abuse us. If they can not even take a break to use the bathroom, they are not going to be willing to listen to our needs or handle situations in a manner that will decrease tensions. They also need to be treated humanely.

———

Calejo and I speak again in 2002 in his Miami home. The large-screen television is on again, and Calejo asks if I remember his grandmother, who had been sitting there watching it the first time we met. I do. She and Calejo's mother have since died. He is living here now with his wife, about thirty minutes and a world away from Krome. The camp is larger now and more modern, but guards still bark, "You have no rights. . . . The only right you have is to be deported"; "This is my camp and you do what I say"—all this to visitors who have come to see detained family or friends. From inside, allegations continue that guards sexually abused detained women.[30] Calejo is a regional sales and service manager now, busy helping to open up new Home Depots around Miami. "Seems like another lifetime," he says, though certain things stick with him. One is: "The guards are worse than the inmates." Another is: "I felt like I was a prisoner also."

Even when he did some tough-guy work, playing the "good soldier" as he puts it, Calejo felt that he never really fit in. He thinks the trouble started when he was assigned to organize a relief effort for South Florida after Hurricane Andrew devastated the area in 1991. Krome was used as a distribution center. Assistant Camp Administrator Rozos put Calejo in charge, and he told higher-ranking officers to follow Calejo's instructions on the distribution of relief supplies. Calejo's superiors were not pleased. To make matters worse, Calejo recalls, he saw officers stealing food that had been donated for hurricane victims. He reported this to Officer-in-Charge Constance Weiss. "And that's where all my problems began. . . . I was seen as a rat, and I wasn't a rat. These people were taking food from other people that needed it." After that rough start, Calejo tells me, he "was always kept out of the loop." When he tried to convert an unused grassy area into a soccer field for inmates, just as the higher-ups had recommended ten years before, his colleagues ridiculed him.

Calejo does not claim to be an angel. After a fire in the men's dorm he helped to throw a few detainees around, and he slapped a Jamaican prisoner once for getting in his face, though he says the two apologized to each other later. A Salvadoran refugee once told the American Friends Service Committee, "We call them soft blows, blows with charm, blows with affection, when they don't break a bone with one blow. Maybe they slap you, even in the face, but if they don't fracture your bones or poke out your eyes we say, no, they hit me with charm."[31] Calejo often just walked away when he knew that other officers were "taking care" of situations the way he would later take care of Bernard.

His biggest mistake with the fight was the cover-up afterward. He and his colleagues knew it had gone too far. They said, "Let's mark you"—punch him in the chest hard enough to leave marks, then take some photos and claim that he had acted in self-defense. Calejo was scared, and he went along with the idea. Five years later, after the promotions and the teaching job at Glynco, federal investigators came through Krome again. Calejo talked to his colleagues, the ones who had helped him out, and they all got their stories straight. But this time one of them was wearing a wire, and another led him into FBI video surveillance. Calejo served ten months in the Federal Correctional Institute (FCI), south of the Krome detention center. At the sentencing hearing Calejo's lawyer had tried to convince the judge that prison would be too dangerous for him since he was a law enforcement officer, but the judge was unmoved. When he got there, Calejo hoped to keep a low profile, but other inmates knew right away who he was.

"I slept for two months with one eye open," he says. Sometimes before going to sleep he would find newspaper clippings about his case resting on his pillow. Meanwhile he was being pulled into the racial politics of the prison. Blacks saw him as a law enforcement official who beat up a black prisoner. "Latins," as they say in Miami, although not necessarily befriending him, warned the African American prisoners that they would back Calejo up if he were attacked. He soon discovered why he was getting so much attention. Inmates from the minimum security camp where he was incarcerated sometimes went to Krome on work detail. As Calejo explains it, "[Officers at Krome were] feeding them stories before I even got [to FCI]. . . . They were saying I beat him up handcuffed. You're not allowed to have handcuffs inside the [Krome] jail. But they spread many stories about me. Basically they were trying to turn all the black guys in the jail where I was against me, and at first it kind of worked." Even after all this time Calejo wants to stress that the Bernard incident was not a matter of race. "What happened between Bernard and me was personal," he insists.

What happened at FCI, however, was racial and personal. Eventually Calejo had to fight an African American inmate who confronted him. "I gained respect with that fight. After that, everything worked out okay, and then people got to know me and talk to me." When it was over, the inmate pulled Calejo aside and apologized. He explained that he was a South Florida correctional officer himself, though "nobody knew," doing time on a drug conviction. "Isn't that a bitch?" Calejo asks. "He says he had no choice."

Relations with the other inmates became bearable. Calejo was asked to join in a baseball game one day. "They have a lot more liberties there than they do at Krome. . . . They put me on third base. Nobody knew if I could play or not. They were trying to hit all the balls as hard as they could at me, and I was catching everything. . . . I'd seen a lot harder." He was in the best physical condition of his life when he got out, but that doesn't mean it was easy being in. With a few exceptions, the guards were "assholes." Although this was a minimum security, dormitory-style setup, officers would try to make inmate life miserable however they could. "Small things, like having a comb or a toothbrush or a piece of food. . . . We had our little lockers, and the officers would come around and take your stuff away. It really had no meaning to them. It was no harm. But they would take it away from you. And then that's when I understood. God, I did some stupid things too, because I used to do the exact same things, and I used to treat these people in the exact same way that these people treat us."

Calejo told the correctional officers what he thought: " 'You're doing the exact same shit I used to do. And you know what? Until that day when you're put in my position . . . you're not going to know what it's like.' They didn't like that. But hopefully, they heed my warning."

The harassment in the federal prison was petty, though. Calejo didn't see any real guard-on-inmate violence there.

"Not like at Krome," he says. "Krome's just a different world. It really is. It's another nation. If they really wanted to punish me, they would have stuck me in Krome for six months."

# 4 | "ENFORCEMENT MEANS YOU'RE BRUTAL"

The "nigger roast" took place in the office parking lot. An INS supervisor was frustrated by the number of Somalis applying for political asylum in his district. These were "affirmative" applicants, meaning that they were not being detained but were presenting themselves voluntarily at the INS office to apply for asylum. The supervisor decided "to make an example" of one Somali to discourage others from applying. He handcuffed the applicant and forced him to sit for about half an hour in a locked car, with the windows shut, in the midday heat. The car was parked in front of the main entrance to the building. Judith Marty, another supervisory asylum officer, complained to the director of her office. She found out that he knew what was going on, and he justified the supervisor's action by saying, "'I'm not trying to prosecute them. I just want them to quit coming here.'" Marty, who is forty-seven, told me the incident made her think of Alabama in the 1950s, but this was Los Angeles in the 1990s.

Prejudice inside the INS against Africans is a nationwide phenomenon, tending to focus on Nigerians in some parts of the country and Somalis in others, depending on which communities predominate in a particular area. "It is not a highly sophisticated manner of thinking that you're dealing with," Marty says of the attitude that permeates the agency. "All they can see is, I got aliens in front of me flooding my door. How can I get rid of them?" Over the years Marty voiced discomfort about this incident as well as subtler forms of cruelty—what she calls "the intentional abuse of applicants." The result: "I'd be treated as a nigger-lover or alien-lover. . . . They'd turn on *me*." She experienced the bureaucratic retribution of being denied interesting international assignments, having her office moved, having her computer access restricted, and receiving negative job-performance ratings. Marty had already resigned from the INS when she spoke to me but was still hesitant at first about speaking out. "Unless you can beat them, they can do scary things to you," she says of her former employers. She filed complaints through official channels with the Office of the Inspector General. These went unanswered. She expresses astonishment that attorneys representing immigrants do not complain more about the mistreatment of their clients, but she concludes that they too are afraid "to make waves" that might affect the outcome of their clients' cases. Now she is an immigration attorney representing asylum seekers in southern California.

Marty relates a story she heard about the Border Patrol picking up an undocumented Mexican in Arizona and driving him around for six hours, even though the detention center that they were supposed to go to was nearby. They kept driving in the desert heat until the already dehydrated prisoner vomited. "They love to do that," she adds, almost in passing. She also recalls asylum applicants who claimed fear of persecution based on their sexual orientation. INS officers would force those applicants to show their "walk" in order to "prove" they were gay. Marty specializes in handling these cases now.

"Does it sound like a place out of control?" she asks. "The mentality is that they're, quote, *aliens*. Which means they're subhuman. Then you can do anything to them."

—

One day the prisoners lined up to show their blue plastic identification cards to an officer who was checking eligibility for release from the place Tony Ekpen Ebibillo dubbed the Krome North Persecution Center and English detainee Peter Medcraft, a bit more dryly, called Krome Sweet Krome. When Ebibillo reached the front of the line, he said, the officer told him, "'Get the fuck out of my face. You Nigerians, I can only help you to stay *in* Krome and not to get out.'" Five years later, in 1996, another Nigerian at Krome accused the same officer of singling out Africans in general and Nigerians in particular for abuse: "[The officer] asked me if I was ready to be deported and I told him that I'm still waiting for my court date. He then told me that there is no way that he is going to . . . let me get a court date. He then told his co-officer at the front desk to put me on the list of those being transferred out to [the jointly run Bureau of Prisons/INS facility in] Oakdale, Louisiana, the next day. He told me that all he wants to hear is my accepting to be deported back to Nigeria."

At first Tony Ebibillo went through a typical immigrant experience in America: plucked from his apartment for overstaying his visa, he was roughed up by the U.S. Border Patrol in South Florida, then locked up at Krome, where his personal belongings were taken away and never returned; he was verbally abused, held in isolation cells, and denied access to telephones and writing materials. Eventually he would spend much of his time documenting his experiences in detention, as well as collecting affidavits from fellow prisoners about their suffering. Ebibillo became another example of someone leading a normal life, albeit on an expired visa, who was transformed by circumstances into a dissident inside the American gulag. A 1991 Krome hunger strike demanding fair release policies and humane treatment attracted attention from the media and from Washington immigration officials. Ebibillo's participation, and perhaps leadership in the strike, would contribute to making him even more a target of INS threats and abuse.

"The officers were laughing when someone passed out from hunger," Ebibillo reported, "saying, 'You see, that one has been carried away, that's how you will be.' The officers were annoyed, as if the strike was against them. We were just doing something for our benefit, we just wanted some fairness, some justice in Krome. We weren't doing it to hurt anybody."

Ebibillo was ordered deported, but he resisted each time INS officers tried to put him on a plane. "Sending me back to Nigeria is like sentencing me to death," he told me. His father, his uncle, and he had openly criticized Nigeria's military rulers. His application for political asylum was denied. But this is not the story of his alleged political problems in Nigeria; it is the story of his treatment by immigration and public health officials in America.

On December 6, 1991—when Ebibillo had been in the United States for eleven years and at Krome for one year—INS officials took him from an isolation cell to the clinic, telling him he that looked sick. He later wrote, "INS agents and medical staff . . . tied my hands, legs, waist, and arms to the bed face down. They then admitted to me that they were trying to make me sleep, boasting that I will wake up to find myself in Nigeria. . . . [The medical staff] started to give me two injections and four capsules after every four hours. I lost complete consciousness the following day after I recorded eleven injections and about twenty capsules."

Attorney Cheryl Little obtained Ebibillo's detention medical records, though only after initial refusals by Krome's clinic to provide them, despite Ebibillo's permission to do so. These records provide a rare glimpse not only into the treatment detainees can suffer when far from the spotlight but also into the fabric of lies and half-truths that the INS manufactures when put on the defensive.

Deportation officer Kimberly Boulia was "the officer in charge of the letter *E*," as the INS employee answering the telephone at Krome put it. That meant Ebibillo was one of her cases. Boulia swore that Ebibillo "was given medication, 30 minutes prior to his flight, to calm his violence."[1] Clinic medical records show that he received his first doses of Thorazine and Benadryl from Dr. Aida Rivera at 9:00 A.M. on December 6, the day before his scheduled deportation. Doses were repeated every few hours for twelve and a half hours and resumed at 6:30 the next morning. At 2:55 P.M. on December 7, just after more Benadryl and more Thorazine and a few hours before Ativan was added to the menu, the record states: "P[atien]t requesting to know how many more injections he'll receive. . . . P[atien]t in 4-point restraint to avoid causing harm to himself and others." Ebibillo asked them to stop, saying, "It's getting to be too much." Then, he wrote, "they turned me over so I was facing up and then strapped me back to the bed."

According to a note at 7:45 P.M., the four-point restraints were removed just over an hour earlier. Then, at 8:25 P.M., thirty-five and a half hours after the medicating had begun, Ebibillo was "escorted" by deportation officers and a registered nurse to the "processing" area of Krome. When he briefly regained consciousness in the INS van, he found himself handcuffed, shackled, and straitjacketed. His mouth was taped shut.

Supervisory detention enforcement officer (SDEO) Billy Blakely picks up the narrative for us in a memo he wrote to Joseph Kennedy, chief of detention (also known as "captain"). Accompanied by DEO Lashley and a nurse, Blakely arrived at the Miami international airport and made arrangements to board Ebibillo on an American Airlines flight ahead of the other passengers.

> I opened the door of the van and instructed Mr. Ebibillo to exit the van. Immediately he went into a kicking and screaming rage. Mr. Ebibillo started to kick and yell that he didn't want to go, and that he was not going to get out of the van. We finally managed to remove Mr. Ebibillo from the van and got him upstairs to the departure area taking him directly to the aircraft. While attempting to place him on the aircraft he became very violent; he threw himself on the floor, started kicking strongly and yelling; it took four (4) Officers to carry him aboard the aircraft.
>
> During this time the ticket agent began to board the passengers, and Mr. Ebibillo by this time was really causing a commotion which was getting the attention of the passengers and the flight attendants. We proceeded to place him in his seat and that's when Debby Garner, Supervisory Boarding Attendant along with Rossi James, Captain of aircraft approached myself and the aforementioned persons with me and stated to us that because of the commotion Mr. Ebibillo was causing they had no other choice but to instruct us to remove him from the aircraft because he was beginning to frighten the other passengers.
>
> I (SDEO Blakely) then tried to explain the situation with the detainee and that he was being deported, along with the fact that the PHS [Public Health Service] Nurse which also was there to escort the detainee during this flight had administered a sedative to the alien earlier (but had not effected him in any way noticeable). This did not assure Ms. Garner nor Mr. James considering that Mr. Ebibillo continued kicking and moving around in the seat.
>
> Mr. James, Captain of the aircraft at that point again stated to me for the safety of the other passengers he could not allow the [Immigration] Service to transport Mr. Ebibillo on that flight and that he wanted us off his flight immediately.

Blakely's account would seem complete if not for a few salient details provided by American Airlines employees. They remembered seeing Ebibillo on the plane surrounded by four men, one of whom was holding a syringe. Ebibillo had "tape strapped over his mouth and nose extending around his head and [was] making a loud groaning noise." He was wearing only one shoe. An airline employee who had been called to the scene said that one "[immigration] official continuously elbowed Tony in the rib cage area every time he would move, knocking the wind out of him. . . . [He] would hit him so hard, Tony's eyes would roll upward." In an attempt to explain the beating, an immigration officer told airline employees, "Tony's sedative was wearing off and we could not give him another sedative for another hour."[2]

Again the INS was unable to deport Ebibillo, this time because American Airlines officials refused to transport him in his condition. A flight supervisor said that "since the authorities refused to ungag or unstrap Tony, she and [the plane's captain] were worried that during the course of the [nine-hour] trip Tony would not be able to go to the bathroom or to even drink water." Another airline employee said "that customer service was also an issue." When airline officials told immigration officials that Ebibillo could not fly that way, one of the INS officers called an American Airlines employee a "bitch" and went into a rage himself, telling them, "You can't mess with the federal authorities, we have an exclusive agreement." He also "threatened her with a $5,000 fine."

According to a former Miami INS trial attorney (that is, an attorney who represents the government in proceedings before an immigration judge), a PHS official would typically accompany a tranquilized deportee en route to monitor his or her health. She added that the PHS worker usually "makes a vacation out of it"; for example, the nurse accompanying a Lebanese victim spent a weekend in Paris. In fact, it was because Krome employees were talking about a colleague's "vacation" that word generally got around when a prisoner was being drugged. Ebibillo recalled that when he resisted the second deportation attempt, a Krome officer was especially angry at him for having spoiled a trip to Rio de Janeiro, where they were to have spent a night on the way to Lagos.

This was the third time INS had tried to deport Ebibillo, and it might have been doing so illegally. Sitting in the Ft. Lauderdale jail, Ebibillo wrote another of his protest letters, certain that if he continued to document the details of what he had been through, eventually someone would help him. This time, his five-page handwritten statement was submitted to a congressional committee that was urging the creation of an Immigration Law Enforcement Review Commission. In his "Testimony of I.N.S. Brutality at Krome Detention Center, Miam[i], Florida, U.S.A.," Ebibillo explained his resistance to the previous attempts to deport him:

I refused to board the aircraft for th[ese] reasons: First, my application for political asylum was still pending at the Board of Immigration Appeal[s]; Secondly, I.N.S. agents lost my property in their storage without just compensation; and, thirdly, I.N.S. agents were trying to deport me to Nigeria even though an immigration judge stated that I should only be deported to Nigeria if Holland—the country that I had designated in the event of deportation—refuse[d] to accept me. I.N.S. agent[s] failed to find out if Holland will accept me as required by the Law.

At eleven o'clock on the night of the third deportation attempt Ebibillo was back at Krome, being medicated again. Clinic records note that from midnight until eight o'clock in the morning he "slept normally . . . in 4 p[oin]t restraints." Ebibillo later wrote a letter to Florida newspapers to try to interest them in his situation: "When I regained full consciousness . . . I discovered to my great astonishment that this kind of brutality can even take place in the United States, the champion of human rights in other parts of the world."

During his detention at Krome, Ebibillo was threatened repeatedly by deputy camp administrator Michael Rozos, as well as by Captain Joseph Kennedy and other Krome officials. "As a matter of fact," he said, "when I told Mr. Rozos that I couldn't go home, he told me that he has many ways of sending me back home. He told me that he can send me home by straitjacket, handcuffed, shackled, and drugged."

Rozos, whom Ebibillo once described as "power-drunk," was fond of wearing a gun on his hip even though he was guarding administrative detainees. Rozos once told *USA Today* that the detainees in his custody were "scumbuckets"; his boss later explained that the remark was taken out of context and that the detained population included aliens "of uncertain background" and others "with criminal charges pending but who have not been convicted."[3] What he didn't say is that Rozos's authority allowed him to create "criminals" when it suited him. He had threatened to use criminal charges to send Ebibillo to a federal prison if he did not willingly return to Nigeria. When officers returned from the airport with Ebibillo, Rozos was immediately informed, and Ebibillo was moved to the Ft. Lauderdale jail for about ten days. Then Rozos made good on his threat: Ebibillo was charged with a federal offense. "I told him that I am prepared for anything,"

Ebibillo said later. According to the indictment, Ebibillo "did knowingly and intentionally, forcibly assault, resist, oppose, impede, intimidate and interfered [sic] with officers of the United States Immigration Service."

The affidavit from officer Boulia attached to the indictment in *United States of America v. Tony Ebibillo* states: "The defendant throughout this process [of attempted deportation] was restrained in a straight jacket, had ten pound weights on each leg and was injected with medication. The defendant was still able to forcibly assault U.S. Immigration and Naturalization Detention and Enforcement Officer, Officer Lashley, by kicking him in the arm and chest." Boulia herself had not witnessed the episode; her statement says that she was only "advised" of the "facts" that she relates.[4] Nevertheless, on the strength of these charges, Ebibillo was locked up in the Metro Correctional Center in Miami. He was lucky enough to draw a dedicated public defender, Lori Barrist, whose office gathered the accounts of the airline employees. Otherwise, in all too typical fashion, we would be left with only the "official" version of events, the version in which Ebibillo would be the assailant.

After a month in the federal prison, Ebibillo wrote to Little at the Haitian Refugee Center: "I was devastated and shocked to know that officials who enforce the U.S. immigration laws will have to lie, fabricate stories, and cover up the truth in an apparent effort to get me convicted of a crime and subsequently deported." Ebibillo saw the INS's game for what it was. A few months later he wrote to Little again: "Since Krome realized that they can't convict me if the case goes to trial, they decided to employ the tactic of delaying my trial, hoping that the effect of incarceration will eventually force me to surrender and accept their offer that I should plead guilty in exchange for time served. However, this strategy will fail, since I am prepared to fight on as long as it will take to reach the ends of justice." In a report on the U.S.-Mexico border, Human Rights Watch noted that such "counter-charges" are an effective method used by the INS to prevent abuses from being reported. "Beatings or other abuses" by immigration officials often occur after a person is "arrested, handcuffed, and subdued. By charging beating victims with assault on a federal officer and other felony charges, the agents [seek] to conceal their own misdeeds."[5] Nine months after putting Ebibillo in federal prison, the government dropped the charges against him. He remained at MCC, however, now back in the custody of the INS rather than U.S. Marshals.

In August 1992 Hurricane Andrew devastated South Florida, and many prisoners were transferred out of MCC. Over the next year Ebibillo was moved to the Federal Correctional Institute in Mariana, the Lake County Jail in Tavares, the Wakulla County Jail in Crawfordville, the Federal Detention Center in Tallahassee, and back to MCC. In the year he was held at Krome, he was also sent temporarily to the Port Manatee Stockade and the Ft. Lauderdale jail. At times, neither reporters nor attorneys could locate him. The INS typically moves its prisoners in the middle of the night without first allowing them to contact family members or attorneys. Ebibillo was not given reasons for these transfers, and he assumes, as INS prisoners around the nation have, that they are a method of punishment and intimidation. The INS publicly denies such a policy while internally acknowledging transfers as "discipline."[6]

Consider the words of another Nigerian:

> The officers here talk to and threaten all detainees. They say that they are God over us, and show no sign of respect. They put us through all sorts of emotional distress. If you as a detainee try to point this out to them, you get transported out of Krome to any county jail of their choice. . . . The lack of communications on each detainee's case, as well as the long periods for which they are being held is a serious issue. . . . The long periods we have to wait for our case[s] gives us a lot more stress.

The writer, Ope-Agbe A. Bariu, had been at Krome for fourteen months and in that time was transferred back and forth to about six county jails in Florida. His name appeared in the *Miami Herald*,[7] and the next day he was approached by a Krome lieutenant. "You put a good show . . . I saw your handiwork," Bariu told me the officer told him. Bariu was in the clinic at the time for chest pains, and several immigration officials came to see him, to put a face with the name; PHS employees pointed him out to INS officials. Days later, Bariu was transferred to the Monroe County Jail in Key West.

But "before they did take me, they beat the shit out of me," he said by phone from the jail. A group of eight officers led by the lieutenant "rushed" Bariu when he said he was not a criminal and should not be handcuffed and asked for time to collect his files from a Krome administrator. He reported injuries to his head, ribs, shoulder, and face. "I didn't provoke it," he said. Then, with his hands cuffed behind his back and legs shackled, he was taken to the clinic, where, Bariu said, an INS officer told a clinic employee "to get the doctors to write . . . [that] he got into a fight here, that's why we're shipping him out." He remained cuffed and shackled while he was given an EKG. In the clinic the lieutenant allegedly told him, "The only way you're going to stay here in Krome is over my dead body."

"They intimidate people here at Krome," Bariu said. "That's why none of those guys want to say anything. . . . They're scared." The next month Bariu was transferred to the Avoyelles jail in Marksville, Louisiana, his arms and legs shackled for the bus ride. "Well, they have just showed me a new form of their extreme and limitless power," he wrote from Marksville. Soon after, Bariu was deported to Nigeria.

As Tony Ebibillo became an activist and was punished for it, he grew increasingly determined "to give a more comprehensive account of [his] experience to any news media . . . willing to let the American people see the abusive, destructive, and hidden part of their government." Without the use of copying machines, he would write multiple copies of the same detailed letters to send to various journalists. In 1991 a story about him appeared in the African American community paper, the *Miami Times.* Two years later—and two months after his final asylum appeal had been exhausted—the *Washington Post* ran a front page story on him, focusing on forced tranquilization. Five days after the *Post* story appeared, the INS had prepared its own summary of Ebibillo's case. My requests to the agency for a copy of the report went unanswered, but Representative Carrie Meek's office obtained one for me. The summary asserts that an investigation by the INS and the Public Health Service "discovered no wrong doing *[sic]*." It also accuses William Booth, the *Washington Post* reporter, of "manufactur[ing] a quote which he attributed to a PHS physician in Krome" and of reading incorrectly the relevant medical reports. "Whether or not the *Post* reporter willfully misinterpreted the medical information is unclear and open to speculation," the summary stated.[8] Booth denies that he manufactured the quotation.

In its "findings," the INS highlights "the most important portion" of the INS/PHS policy on matters relevant to this case: "'Under NO circumstances will the alien be medicated solely for purposes of restraint.' It has been found that medication has been administered only for the treatment of diagnosed illnesses." This is obviously the crux of the matter, since the agency's internal report, its director of public affairs, and the PHS doctor at Krome all insist on this version of events. But they are using the stated policy to mask what really takes place. In other words, although there was apparently a psychiatric diagnosis of Ebibillo, the INS report's own chronology strongly suggests that the diagnosis was manufactured to justify sedating him for deportation. One day, Ebibillo resisted deportation; the next day, the PHS physician "determine[d] him to have 'passive/aggressive personality disorder . . . and [to be] potentially aggressive and capable of hurting others or himself.'" On the basis of that "diagnosis" he was tranquilized.

Several years later I asked Russell Bergeron, INS chief press officer, about the circumstances under which INS might sedate a detainee. His answer was unequivocal:

> INS does not sedate detainees. . . . We have no jurisdiction and no authority to sedate anyone, and we do not. We cannot administer sedation to people, and we simply don't do it. If an individual is sedated, it's because a medical decision has been made by competent and qualified medical doctors that an individual needs to be sedated because of a psychological or physical medical problem.

Is it possible, though, that a joint decision would be made between INS and another agency, such as the Public Health Service, for the purposes of what in law enforcement is called "chemical restraint"? Again Bergeron was unequivocal: "No. It's not our decision. No. We don't chemically restrain people. It's not our decision. So any time, if you have an INS detainee, and that individual has been sedated, it's because a medical authority has determined that that individual needs to be sedated for medical reasons. Period."

Bergeron and I moved on to other questions, then he returned to the earlier topic. "The question about the sedation disturbs me," he said. "Where are you going with this thing? What's the point of all this?"

I told Bergeron that over the years I had heard several accounts of the forced medication of detainees.[9] The issue had resurfaced in a story I was writing about Nigerians. Bergeron elaborated on why he found the question disturbing:

> The fact of the matter is that, you know, it's real easy to make this sound as if that is some kind of horrendous practice, okay? when in fact, number one, the detention authorities within the federal system, be it BOP or INS or whatever, you know, we do not make those decisions in terms of whether or not an individual needs to be sedated. Those are medical decisions made by medical authorities. Number two, when an individual has to be transported, we have to concern ourselves with the safety and security of all the people on board, and if you have someone who has psychological problems, okay, and psychiatric problems, that make them a threat if they're not kept under sedation, you know, then it would be negligent of the government *not* to issue the medication, in the same way that if you had an individual who had been diagnosed in that way and they were not in detention, and they were in a medical facility, it would be negligent of that medical facility not to issue that medication to the people, because they have a responsibility to protect their employees and the other patients at the hospital.

I quote Bergeron at length because if we follow the train of thought instead of excerpting a soundbite, then we can see how the concept of medical diagnosis begins to merge with the concept of physical threat. I tried to ask about "use of force" guidelines for medication, presumably analogous to law enforcement agency guidelines for using stun guns or even shackles. Bergeron cut me off:

> Let me make it very, very clear and very easy for you, okay? We do not have nor can we administer sedation simply for restraint purposes. Okay? That's all there is to it. *And there is no provision for us to go to the medical authorities and say, well, we think that this guy might give us problems; would you go ahead and sedate him? We can't even do that, okay?* The only thing that can happen is that the medical authorities can say, this individual has psychological or physical problems which justify sedation.[10]

In the case of Ebibillo, the internal memos from Krome make it "very, very clear" that officials did precisely what Bergeron says they may not do. INS officers asked medical authorities for help deporting Ebibillo. And unlike the agency's chronology, composed after the *Post* story appeared, the memos were written as the situation unfolded. Krome Lieutenant Nestor Meiggs wrote to one of his superiors:

> Subject: Disturbance in the Processing Area
>
> . . .
>
> On wed20 Nov 91, on or about 06:30hrs, detainee ELIBILLO, Expen [sic] Tony A#28392576 while at the processing area, he was asked to change his clothing in order to get ready for his departure.
>
> Detainee Elibillo was asked numerous times by this Supervisor to get ready with negative results.
>
> While I was handling to him part of his civilian clothing, Elibillo assumed a position that clearly showed he was getting ready to fight, and in a very hostile manner stated that he was not going to leave this Country.
>
> Necessary force was used to subdue this detainee in order to change his clothing and get him ready for his departure.
>
> It is my opinion that this detaine[e] is a very dangerous person with no respect to a uniformed Officer, very hostile that will require the assistance from medical Staff in order to control his violent mood preventing him from hurting anyone.[11]

Officer Meiggs's memo format complies with INS guidelines on "preparing memorandums";[12] and his words about Ebibillo's "violent mood" and "preventing him from hurting anyone" seem to indicate that the officer has also been trained to use the cover of psychiatric diagnosis for the medically assisted use of force. If there were any lingering doubt, it is dispelled by a handwritten sentence followed by Captain Kennedy's signature at the end of the typewritten memo: "I concur with SDEO Meiggs request for medical assistance in order to remove this detainee." Medical records indicate that the doctors complied with the request.

Bergeron suggested that I contact the PHS. The INS Miami District director had similarly written to Human Rights Watch that deportees are only medicated by the PHS, and "information concerning their procedures can be obtained directly from that agency." It's difficult to imagine what these men thought the PHS would say. When I reached Damon Thompson, press officer for the assistant secretary of health, Bergeron's double-talk was fully exposed. I asked Thompson what the PHS guidelines were for tranquilizing INS detainees. He replied that the PHS does not have its own guidelines on this and that its employees who are detailed to the INS "simply follow the INS policy." He explained that PHS employees detailed to the immigration agency are "responsible to the INS and work as INS employees. . . . [They] answer to the INS and go by INS policies." While their salary is paid by the Public Health Service, he continued, "they become de facto employees of that agency and follow the guidelines of that agency. . . . You really should be asking the INS."

If I had met Lupe Rivera and Milissa Grace sooner, I would not have had to work so hard to separate public relations from reality. Rivera and Grace are nurses who used to work in the INS's Houston detention center clinic. Rivera sent me an e-mail after seeing my article about her old employers, the Corrections Corporation of America, in the *Texas Observer*.[13] A few months later, over plates of Mexican food in downtown Houston, I ask the nurses about the INS spokesperson's contention that only medical personnel can make the decision to tranquilize troublesome detainees.

"How easy is *that* to manipulate?" Grace asks rhetorically. "Tell your nurse to do it, you've got a cheesy-ass nurse—"

"You've got a psychiatrist that's going to give you a diagnosis," adds Rivera.

"'Cause you're paying him money on the side," says Grace.

They both say they're fairly certain that in two and a half years they never actually saw the psychiatrist who "diagnosed" detainees at the Houston Processing Center—in other words, he didn't actually see the prisoners.

Needless to say, Rivera and Grace no longer work for CCA, which is why they are willing to talk freely. Grace laughs about how the guards used to ask the nurses, "Can't you give 'em some Thorazine?" referring to detainees they wanted to control. But did they really expect nurses to do it? "Yes, they used to do it," she tells me—meaning before she and Rivera supported each other in resisting the pressure to mistreat detainees.

Rivera recalls a detainee scheduled for deportation who "was totally combative and just refusing to cooperate." He was Nigerian too. "How are you going to load somebody on a commercial flight that's combative and raising all kinds of hell? So they wanted me to go over and inject him with something." She says she refused. To do otherwise would have been medically inappropriate because the clinic didn't have a file on this detainee, she says. He wasn't "our inmate."

"[This was] the first time I locked horns with Pam Fugazzi [then the CCA warden]," Rivera notes, "and she just realized that maybe she hired the wrong person, that couldn't be manipulated." Rivera, a registered nurse, was the clinic manager. "So then they got the psychiatrist to call me up." Without seeing the detainee, the INS contract psychiatrist urged Rivera to tranquilize the man. He would order the medication, and a guard would pick it up from a local pharmacy. "And once again I said, 'Is this my inmate? Does he have a chart?' No. Then I'm not going to do it."

I ask Rivera what she means by "our inmate." After all, she was working for CCA, and CCA was under contract to the INS. She answers, "Yes, but [the INS] had these secret inmates. He was an Immigration 'hold.' I don't know who he belonged to." In other words, he had not been processed into the CCA facility as an INS detainee. If he had been, the clinic would have had a chart on him. Warden Fugazzi called Rivera in to ask why she was not cooperating. Rivera relates the conversation to me: "I said, 'cooperating with what?' . . . I said, 'Why would I want to do that to somebody that hasn't been processed, and is not our actual inmate with a patient chart?' She said, 'You can do it as a favor.' And I said, 'You know what? I can lend you five dollars as a favor, but I cannot inject somebody against their will'—I mean, you know, you just can't."

Fugazzi, now retired, acknowledges that she might have asked Rivera to sedate the Nigerian man "in the spirit of working with the INS," but notes that Rivera "was correct in refusing to do that." The INS then hired a local nurse to do the job in the middle of the night, and the man was successfully deported, Fugazzi recalls. "Ultimately I was very comfortable with that decision."

In December 1993 the INS successfully deported Tony Ebibillo in restraints but without medication. "In the first INS operation of its kind," according to the *Los Angeles Times,* "the agency chartered a plane . . . to return 74 male and nine female prisoners to Nigeria, a cheaper alternative than flying them commercially. The detainees were held at Oakdale, in jails throughout Louisiana and in Miami. The Nigerian government finally issued travel documents for them. The operation took months to plan."[14] Contrary to the INS line implied in the *Los Angeles Times* article, not all the prisoners were criminals. Ebibillo was never charged with a crime, aside from the trumped-up charges that were later dropped. Moreover, Ebibillo and detainee Olu Balogun both believe that a number of the deportees had been petitioning for asylum and, in Balogun's words, "had not exhausted [their] avenues in the U.S." I first heard from Balogun in 1999 after he had managed to return to the United States and was again detained. Independently and years apart, Ebibillo and Balogun gave me similar accounts of their treatment at the hands of U.S. authorities, on one end, and Nigerian security forces, to which they were handed over by the Americans, on the other.

Four or five buses, Balogun recalls, pulled onto an airstrip near Oakdale, where hundreds of officers from a variety of federal agencies were waiting. It looked like a "war was going on." When I asked former Oakdale correctional officer Richard Franklin about Balogun's description, he said: "That's how they do it. He wasn't lying. They surround the plane with shotguns aimed. You make a wrong move, they've already been given the order to shoot you. And the guns are aimed until they get on that plane and the officer on the plane gives them the wave that we got everybody secured. And then you still stand there until that plane hit the runway and take off." Balogun also says that some detainees tried to resist and were beaten and forcibly injected. All were shackled hand and foot, and, once inside the plane, they were shackled to their seats. He witnessed another detainee being "choked" and "injected" on the plane. The INS never answered my FOIA request about this flight.[15]

Both Balogun and Ebibillo report that all the deportees were handed over to Nigerian security forces and put into detention facilities at the Lagos airport. "We were marched out of the plane," Balogun recalls, "to be handed over to the military." While he was being questioned, Nigerian officials slapped him repeatedly in the face. "That's just the normal process," he calmly informs me. Then he describes the three phases of interrogation. In the first, officials wanted to confirm that he was a Nigerian. Then they beat him for "destroy[ing] the image of Nigeria" in the United States and "grilled" him about the crimes he had committed here. Finally, he was questioned to ascertain whether he was a CIA agent. Balogun was left in his cell without food for eight days and was unable to contact a lawyer or family members.[16] The local media in Lagos covered the return of these U.S. prisoners, and Balogun's family tracked him down to pay the equivalent of $400 for his release. The *Los Angeles Times*'s Dianne Klein, again apparently taking cues from INS spokespersons, as too many reporters regularly do, made no mention of the deportees' being handed over to the same Nigerian forces that were being condemned by the State Department for human rights violations. Three months before the flight General Sani Abacha had annulled Nigeria's democratic election and imprisoned president-elect Moshood Abiola. The aviation reporter for a Nigerian paper, however, confirms this part of Balogun's and Ebibillo's stories: "The 46 deportees with drug related offences were handed over to the National Drug Law Enforcement Agency (NDLEA), and the 32 others . . . were taken for interrogation by State Security Service (SSS) officials."[17]

———

In Houston Olu Balogun said he felt offended by the portrayal of all Nigerians as "fraudsters," though he freely admits that he himself committed fraud. But his attorney also represented Nigerians without criminal convictions of any kind and observes, "You have a lack of credibility as a Nigerian which you have to overcome. . . . [It's] almost like the [immigration] case is secondary." He adds that the immigration judge's distrust is so strong that the case is never heard.

"You're Nigerian, you're lying," is how another Texas lawyer sums up the agency's attitude as conveyed to him by clients. The Immigration Service's response only strengthens the anecdotal case against it. "The Nigerians in the system have credibility problems because they lie," not because of any "predisposition" against them, according to a Washington INS official who prefers not to be identified. He mentions a couple of examples of fraudulent Nigerian immigration cases and says, "Don't misunderstand me—I'm not saying that Nigerians are more prone [than other nationals] to false claims." Then he gives me another example of a Nigerian who allegedly lied.[18]

"Nigerians are"—brief pause—"problematic." That is Houston District Director Richard Cravener's first reaction when I ask him whether "Nigerians present a unique challenge in terms of credibility." He had misread "Nigerian" as "Nicaraguan" in my written questions and thought it would be an easy one, he tells me. Then he explains that "there is an increasing amount of [financial] crime attributed to Nigerians" and that they present "a law-enforcement challenge."[19] Cravener stresses that his view does not influence decisions on particular cases; in fact, the criminal aspects of a case typically have been adjudicated before it reaches him. In accordance with INS guidelines, his decisions on parole are based on an assessment of the detainee's likelihood to flee and on the danger he might pose to the community. When I ask if he feels that stereotypes about Nigerians and fraud might influence how Nigerians are treated in the INS system, he replies, "I honestly don't think so."

Richard Cravener was born in Mercedes, Texas, near the Mexican border. His father was in the Border Patrol. "My job as a kid was to keep his law-books up to date." The constant changes in immigration law made this an ongoing task. He remembers the five-inch-thick stacks of inserts for the black three-ring binders containing updates of statutes, operating instructions, and "regs." By the time he went to college, Cravener was "pretty much an expert in immigration law." He and his brother both joined the Border Patrol, and for a while father and both sons served at the same time, in New York, Arizona, and California. Today Cravener says with matter-of-fact pride that he has held "almost every officer position in the Service" and volunteers that he is one of 7,744 federal employees who make up the Senior Executive Service, a body created by Congress, in Cravener's words, "to ensure that there would exist in the government a cadre of senior executives who would be able to keep the government running consistently and uniformly regardless of what political circumstance might occur." As district director in Houston, he made the news for his involvement with some of the INS's biggest alien-smuggling busts. His "biggest challenge is providing the proper amount of service to the community."

Cravener's reflections on his career embody an institutional tension inside the former INS that for years led would-be reformers of various political stripes to call for a split in the agency. The INS had two mandates, which some critics inside and outside the agency considered at odds: service and enforcement. In short, the service side is intended to help deserving immigrants stay here; the enforcement side tries to keep out the illegals and to find and expel them when they get in. Whatever dedication an individual agent might feel to the "service" function of "the Service," the "agency culture" of the INS was one of law enforcement, according to Chris Sale, former INS deputy commissioner.[20] After the attacks of September 11, the idea of reorganizing the INS was revived, and in

December 2001 Cravener was appointed director of the Office of INS Restructuring. In early 2003 the INS ceased to exist; the service and enforcement branches were finally separated into the Bureau of Citizenship and Immigration Services and the Bureau of Customs and Immigration Enforcement, both within the Department of Homeland Security. At the old INS Headquarters on Eye Street in Washington, an official there told me, the new agencies were known as the Bureau of Keep 'Em In and the Bureau of Kick 'Em Out.

The enforcement culture remains stronger than ever. But long before September 11, 2001, it encouraged extremism in the way the designated defenders of our borders see the outsider. Whoever the current targets might be, there is a continuum from the policy-level discrimination in offices down to the treatment of prisoners by guards. The Immigration Service reflects and implements prejudices that exist in society; it probably helps to create them as well. Chinese, Haitians, Indian Sikhs, Africans, Arabs of any nationality—the list goes on, and changes with circumstances. The rhetoric of border protection conditions one to view all "illegals" as inherently, or at least potentially, dangerous invaders. District Director Cravener believes in administering the Immigration Act for many reasons, he says, among them protecting "the integrity of the border, prohibiting entry of terrorists, drug lords, those kinds of things." The overwhelming majority of people violating the "integrity" of U.S. borders are Mexicans looking for work. Still, a supervisory Border Patrol agent once told me in the same breath how Mexican border-crossers crawl through sewage *and* break the law. His men in the San Diego Sector keep alcohol with them to wash their hands after contact with aliens. To describe countries whose economic woes force people to come to the United States (Mexico, Pakistan, the Philippines, for example), the Border Patrol supervisor used the term "high-risk," as if the nations themselves were prone to infection. And he made the surprising observation that before a steel wall was erected between San Diego and Tijuana, "human waves" of Mexicans were crossing over in such numbers that "you'd think it was Chinese coming at you." In fact, before the Border Patrol was created in 1924, one of the principal missions of the "immigration inspectors on horseback" was to apprehend Chinese crossing the U.S.-Mexico border.[21]

It's easy to criticize the armed Arizona vigilantes who went after Mexican border-crossers in early 2000, but perhaps more dangerous in the long run is the fact that a *New York Times* reporter sympathetic to undocumented Mexican farmworkers can nevertheless refer to them as "a formidable army" within the United States. The Chinese invaders had become Mexican invaders: one hundred years ago, some of those California Chinese were going to be detained in empty grain warehouses on the pretext that they were carrying the plague, but a federal court intervened. A contemporary labor journal fumed, "The almond-eyed Mongolian is . . . waiting to assassinate you and your children with one of his many maladies." More recently, in a special survey of Nigeria, the *Economist* reported: "Abroad, the country has become a byword for advance-fee scams and drug-peddling"—the "law-enforcement challenge" to which Cravener had referred. Judith Marty told me that from the asylum units to the detention centers "the whole system was tainted [by] that prejudice about Africans," which has nothing to do with any "real evidence" of crime or fraud. But once prejudice becomes policy, it can be difficult to separate fantasy from reality. Whatever the basis for the accusations about lying and crime, there is something besides objectivity at work here; the *Economist* report also informs readers that money in Nigeria is literally "dirty and smelly" and "infested with the sorts of microbes that cause diarrhea."[22]

I asked Marty what she imagined the official who locked the Somali asylum applicant in a hot car was thinking. "He thought he was doing the right thing," she said. "He was a traditional INS person. They don't do things by the law, they do things by force. Enforcement means you're brutal."

Tony Ebibillo was always optimistic. He wrote from one Florida jail: "I am quite sure that everybody will agree with me that despite the fact that I was residing here illegally, I still have the right to be treated humanely." Later he wrote from Nigeria: "[The INS] picked me up from Ft. Lauderdale County Jail on the pretense that I was schedule[d] for a court hearing on the status of my case. [Instead] I was taken to Ft. Lauderdale International Airport for deportation." Former correctional officer Franklin confirms that INS practice too, and the next one Ebibillo describes: "INS agents deported me penniless in spite of the fact that I had $860 in my commissary account at Metropolitan Correctional Center, Miami; they refuse[d] to even allow me to take a sheet of paper with me; and I was severely brutalized and deported wearing prison uniform." The jail kept his sweater, jeans, and bloodstained underwear in storage. "I pleaded for a delay of my deportation so that I can collect my money . . . but they refuse[d] and forced me into a chartered aircraft after receiving merciless punches, strangulation of the body and banging of the head. When I got to Nigeria, the military detained me for . . . bringing Nigeria['s] name into disrepute while I was in the USA. I'm out on bail pending the final dispensation of the case in the tribunal."[23]

Six months later, Ebibillo's sister told me by phone from Europe that her brother was out of immediate danger and trying to leave Nigeria again.

# 5 | THE WORLD'S FIRST PRIVATE PRISON

Warden Charles Martin invited me to join his staff for a lunch of fried
fish and cole slaw prepared by inmates in the kitchen of the INS's Houston
Processing Center, owned and operated by the Nashville-based Corrections
Corporation of America. We ate in the conference room, where the walls
were decorated with faded photos of other CCA facilities. Directly across
from me sat a man named Jimmy Cook. When we introduced ourselves,
I asked if he worked for the INS or CCA. He said he couldn't tell me that.

He was kidding. Cook was a CCA employee and the assistant warden
at the Houston Processing Center. He hardly said a word as we ate, but
when he finished he sat back, folded his arms across his chest, and softly
volunteered that he enjoys the challenge of corrections. I asked what the
biggest challenge was. He replied matter-of-factly that it has always been
to break a man who thinks he can't be broken. Cook had been at the
Houston Processing Center for just a few weeks, having come from a CCA
facility in Louisiana. He was a retired major from the Texas Department
of Criminal Justice and a rancher from Madisonville, Texas. When he
talked about breaking a man, he made it sound like a seduction. You bring
him to you, he said. You go down to his level so you can talk to him. And
you do what you say you're going to do, whether that's locking him up
or letting him send out extra letters. Cook could still remember his first
time. A prisoner from North Carolina had come in thinking he was

tougher than everyone. By the time he left, he was a model inmate. Cook felt good that he helped the man, and occasionally he still received letters from him.

Cook's deadpan joke didn't come out of nowhere. The INS's culture of secrecy works on many levels, and there is even an aesthetic of secrecy. The Houston Processing Center is a faceless "contemporary" building near Houston's international airport, nestled among the shipping companies at the intersection of Export Plaza and Consulate Plaza, a short drive from airport hotels, long-term parking, and rental car lots. At the lobby entrance is a welcome mat with the CCA emblem in red, white, blue, and black, and there are rosebushes too. Some people don't know even that this place is a "processing center," the chief of security told me approvingly.

I submitted my requests for a tour of the Houston Processing Center to CCA headquarters in Nashville, to CCA's Warden Martin in Houston, and to the Houston INS district director's office. At first, all approved. Then Martin told me the tour was off because the INS district director had changed his mind. "I didn't have a problem" with it, Martin told me, and if the INS would agree, "I'll ease you around." After a second request, the INS gave its approval. If all of this seems trivial, it is. But where there is no accountability, the arbitrary use of authority governs the trivial as well as the substantial. One insidious aspect of the private contractor's relationship with the INS is that it pairs bureaucracies that are hostile to public scrutiny. The buck stops nowhere. While the INS pretends to be open to scrutiny, the corporate offices of CCA make no secret of their antipathy to oversight, at least not in materials directed to shareholders. In a recent annual report, CCA warns that one of the "risks inherent" in this business is that "the private corrections industry is subject to public scrutiny."[1]

My tour of the Houston Processing Center is conducted by Assistant Warden Cook and INS spokesperson Luisa Aquino. They guide me down the wide main hallway, a CCA logo beckoning at the end of it and a sign on the wall in English and Spanish:

PROFESSIONALISM

POSITIVE ATTITUDE

PRODUCTION.

Groups of men, most of them brown- or black-skinned, dressed in bright yellow jumpsuits are knocking on the window from inside the library. They are locked in. The library is being used as a temporary holding area. The men are gesturing for the attention of their keepers, who studiously ignore them. Cook refuses to let me go in and speak to them, reasoning that they might say something "confidential" about their own cases. To explain away their clamor, he tells me that "they get all excited" in this male facility whenever a woman comes through. A second group of men comes to the open doorway of a room filled with exercise equipment. One asks Aquino in Spanish who she is; he thinks he has seen her before. Aquino, a native of Mexico City, doesn't answer him, but she tells me the man has probably seen her on television. She used to be a reporter for Telemundo, the Spanish-language network, covering immigration and "blood and guts" crime stories in Houston. She left to take a job with INS Public Affairs because it paid better.

I ask to see the segregation cells, since in many other INS facilities detainees have complained that these rooms are used arbitrarily for punishment. Sometimes, it seems, they are punishment cells and sometimes medical segregation units. Lupe Rivera, the former CCA nurse who won awards from the city of Houston for her control of tuberculosis in this detention center, told me that she "was always fighting with the chief of security" about the use of the rooms. There is a pause after my request; the assistant warden, the INS spokesperson, and the chief of security exchange looks. Then they take me to see two adjacent rooms, each with a shower, a toilet-sink unit, and a bed. A sign on the door to one of the rooms designates it "S7." Inside, the words FUCK AMERICA are neatly stenciled on the wall in large block letters. Aquino explains that the rooms are indeed used "if anyone gets rowdy for some reason" but that "most often . . . it's because of a medical reason." The longest someone would stay in one of these rooms for disciplinary reasons is two or three hours of "cool-down" time, Cook says, until "they realize they made a mistake." What about the disciplinary procedure, a hearing in which, according to INS regulations, inmates are allowed to call witnesses and to contest the charges against them? Cook assures me that these hearings take place. "You don't just go back there and get them," he says.

"They still have rights," Aquino adds. Even though they are "illegal aliens," and contrary to what many people might imagine, she assures me, "they're all entitled to due process. They still have civil rights, they're all humans, we're all human beings."

Assistant Warden Cook nods in agreement.

Nigerian detainee Kenneth Efe wishes that he *had* been put into a segregation cell, which he alternately calls "lockdown" and "lockup." Instead, he alleges, he was locked into some sort of small shower room when he was judged disruptive. The first time, he had complained to the on-site nurse because he thought he had an ulcer. It was "paining me seriously inside," he says. "The lady said I'm disturbing her. . . . They didn't even put me in the lockup. I would prefer that. But they lock me in the shower [where there is] water on the floor. . . . I have no place to sit down."

Efe says that he was held in the shower room for three hours without medical attention. He complained to the night shift captain, he told me, and was instructed to submit a request for medical assistance. A doctor told him that his stomach was fine. Two days later he was given some Maalox. The pain persisted. It might seem surprising or unlikely that the professional medical staff inside a prison would react the way Efe claims it did. I have no confirmation that the incident in Houston happened as Efe described it, but his story is a familiar one. Nominally independent medical staff in jails and detention centers have used their position to punish prisoners. One nurse at Wackenhut's Jena Juvenile Justice Center in Louisiana reported that another nurse " 'jacks offenders up against the wall and throws water on them' and refuses to give the boys their medications if they don't act right."[2] The two nurses who worked in the CCA clinic at the Houston Processing Center under a previous administration told me that one of their former colleagues would withhold Motrin pain relievers from inmates to punish them.

Efe had been detained for two years when we spoke in December 1999. He stowed away on a ship to escape his native Nigeria after stabbing a policeman in self-defense when he was being beaten for his participation in a political rally.[3] The vessel took him to Galveston, Texas, and the INS held him at the Wharton County Jail and the Houston Processing Center. The CCA officers "just want to piss you off," he says, so that you'll react "and they get a chance to lock you up." Just after our visit, he wrote in a letter: "The world need to know how we're treated here. This is hell on earth." But Olu Balogun, who has been detained in several facilities around the country, has a different perspective on Houston's CCA personnel. "The guards are pretty much okay, you know, fair," he tells me. "There's no kind of abuse. They're just doing their job: to detain us."

This is no small compliment. The industry leader in private corrections had compiled such a notorious record that even its promotional material was defensive: "While its detractors are crying more loudly than ever and are given free voice by an attentive media, CCA's customer base continues to grow."[4] But conditions and treatment vary widely from place to place, and the personalities of those in charge may be the most significant variable. Houston Warden Martin seemed committed to running a decent operation at "Export Plaza," as some locals call the Houston Processing Center, using the name of the street it's on; Export Plaza stands apart from the patterns of mistreatment extensively documented at other INS detention centers and county jails and at other CCA facilities.[5] When local immigrant advocacy groups complained several years ago about heat and overcrowding in the dorms, for example, Martin met with them personally after the INS leadership refused to do so, said Blanca Alvarez of Madres y Familias Unidas, and he promised to address the problem "as if it were his own house."

As for Ken Efe's complaint, Martin acknowledges that small temporary rooms, including a "holding room" with a shower, are sometimes used to confine a detainee when it is inconvenient to take him to a segregation cell, but he insists that no one would be left in such a room for more than a couple of hours. Later he says it would be for an hour or less, "until they have time to move them or whatever." Martin continues: "Inmates have a way of manipulating the way things happen and how long they happen . . . [they] have a tendency to exaggerate . . . they got a good exaggerate mind." By way of example, he says an inmate might report that he was beaten thirteen times and that the beating lasted from five to ten minutes. "Can you imagine someone getting beaten for five to ten minutes? . . . Inmates seem to think that whatever they say will help them out in the long run," he cautions me. "You have to be real careful with what inmates say sometimes." And that little shower room? Martin reminds me, in our phone conversation a few weeks later, that he had shown it to me during the tour. But no one had shown me that room, and Martin himself had not even come along on the tour.

The warden and the detained young man agree on one thing. "This place is just like prison," Efe says. "It's not like detention." INS officials have argued that detainees and prisoners/inmates are not the same thing. Technically, they are correct, though CCA itself refers to the Houston Processing Center as "the world's first privately designed and built prison."[6] The distinction is understandably lost on many of the men and women who are locked up, and it means even less to the many thousands who are "detained" in prisons and jails alongside non-INS inmates. Given his career, Warden Martin knows the distinctions, but he's not interested in splitting hairs. "We call it a detention center," he admits, but as far as the "structure," the "escape risks," and the "quality of life"—"they're basically the same."

"The warden is good to us," Efe tells me. "He treat us like we are all the same." Martin visits the dorm, Efe says, "to tell us by the grace of God we're going to go out of here."

After his dorm visits, Martin can leave the mind-numbing concrete and Plexiglas of the inmate areas and go back to the administrative offices that he has enlivened with Ansel Adams posters, potted plants, and fish tanks. "I like to see things living around me, because everything is dying," Martin explains. "The older you get, the more appetite you have for life." He was only in his early forties when we met, but he is a twenty-one-year veteran of the Texas Department of Criminal Justice, an African American Texan who did not foresee a lifetime in corrections when he was working for $1.90 an hour as a dishwasher. Then he was offered $5.95 an hour plus room and board as a corrections officer at the Ramsey Unit in Rosharon, south of Houston. Eventually he would spend eight years as warden of Eastham Prison Unit, a maximum security facility in Lovelady, near Huntsville, where he grew up.

Martin's parents were farmers and ranchers, not corrections officers. "I was very intimidated by prisoners," he says. "I thought they all killed people." A friend helped to convince him to make the career change. As for those dorm visits, "I'm sort of a hands-on type warden. The way to get to the root of the problem is to face the problem head-on. . . . I like to be available to the inmates. . . . Some things that don't mean a lot to you mean a lot to them . . . [so] at least you listen." He sees what former Krome detention officer Eddie Calejo learned the hard way. Martin tells me about a letter he received from a prisoner doing criminal time in Texas who will soon be transferred into INS custody at the Houston Processing Center.

The prisoner wanted to know what items would be available at the CCA commissary. It might seem like a small thing, Martin tells me, but to the prisoner it's important. (Presumably the prisoner was not told that CCA commissaries have been reported to sell merchandise at dramatic mark-ups—a $9.90 pair of sneakers for $30; a $5 portable radio for $26.77—while prohibiting inmates' families from bringing them items purchased on the outside.)[7]

Martin seemed candid, but he was also somewhat reserved. He wouldn't allow me to take his picture or to use a tape recorder when we talked. Maybe his caution was due in part to the fact that INS spokesperson Aquino was monitoring our interview. When I told her that it was awkward for her to sit in, she responded, "I'm just here to facilitate the interviews that took place with the detainees." Those interviews had just ended, but she stayed. The warden readily admitted that he would avoid the media if there were a problem at his facility. Then he offered me the name of a karate school run by a friend of his. He wanted me to write an article about that and suggested that the favor would be returned. Journalists are only interested in what they want to be interested in, he told me. "I don't want to talk to them then."[8]

My tour included a look inside one of the dorms, a large room dominated by about twenty rows of steel-framed bunkbeds. There was not much movement in the room. A prisoner wearing headphones sat at a table filling out immigration forms. Others washed or shaved in the collective bathroom. There is a kitchen area with a microwave oven and an ice chest. There are television sets. There is a row of lockers in which the detainees are permitted to keep what the chief of security calls "comfort property." He has also "provided a multiple of games" to help the men pass the time. It is a well-intentioned and utterly perverse notion that a few board games will help these men to tolerate months and even years of sensory deprivation and administrative detention. After a few minutes, my eyes adjusted to the cavernous room. Here and there a gray blanket stirred. Men shifted around in their bunks. I realized that a great many of them were sleeping through the day.

Less than two months later, in the aftermath of a hostage-taking by Cuban INS prisoners in a Louisiana jail,[9] holes were drilled in the dorm doors at the Houston Processing Center, Balogun would tell me. That way tear gas canisters could be fired into the rooms in case of trouble, a guard reportedly told him. During the tour, I saw Balogun through a Plexiglas window, holding a manila file folder of documents. A few days later he called to tell me that the Houston Processing Center is regularly overcrowded and that between fifty and eighty men sleeping on mattresses on the floor had been moved out before the tour and returned to the facility after it ended. Warden Martin called this "hearsay," but Aquino acknowledged that at the time of my tour two groups of detainees were being organized for deportation by the Justice Prisoner and Alien Transportation System. To my surprise, she also acknowledged that it is not uncommon for the center to be temporarily overcrowded as prisoners are being moved through it from around the state, because of its proximity to Houston's George Bush Intercontinental Airport. The INS in Houston is less defensive than its counterparts in New York or Miami, to take two examples. Aquino spoke frankly: "If people are sleeping on the floor, we try to accommodate them and make them more comfortable while they're there." She added that they are only in that situation for "four hours or so, and then they're out. We certainly don't like to overpopulate, simply because that creates a little bit of tension."

The Houston Processing Center has a capacity of about five hundred beds. "Normally the higher concentration of aliens is Mexican," Aquino told me. Everyone else is OTM, agency shorthand for "Other Than Mexican." Among non-Mexicans, Central Americans and South Americans make up the largest groups. There were also approximately forty-five Cubans who had already spent about two years detained in Houston. But the numbers are always shifting. Aquino explained: "We move people around constantly. There's always a flow." She was acknowledging one of the greatest sources of frustration for INS detainees, even in the best of circumstances. The "flow" is often used as a control measure. Officials take advantage of the network of beds to keep the detained immigrant population shifting. The warden's secretary at the Avoyelles Parish Jail in Marksville, Louisiana, told me, referring to INS prisoners, "It's not good to let them stay in the same place together for long . . . they tend to want to get their heads together."

The flow is also a matter of business. A group of detainees who *wanted* to be deported wrote that the financial arrangement between CCA and the INS gave them "a very strong feeling of detention fraud."[10] For a four-hour stay, CCA charges taxpayers the full $52 "manday" fee. In the prison hallway, Aquino, Cook, and I walk past postings for "Accident-Free Days" and "Yesterday's Closing Stock Price" for Prison Realty (neither was updated). A company promotional packet depicts a gavel slamming down beneath the encouraging words: "ONE OUT OF EVERY TWENTY PEOPLE IN THE UNITED STATES IS EXPECTED TO SERVE TIME IN PRISON." When projections showed no need for new prison beds in Florida, a CCA lobbyist told a reporter, "That leaves us trying to find a way to provide some services for the department [of corrections] that they don't want." The president of TransCor America, Inc., a CCA subsidiary that transports prisoners, told *Mother Jones* magazine, "When we have an escape, it hurts our stock price." A former CCA corrections officer told a reporter: "They gave us a rundown saying two slices of bread per inmate costs this much. . . . If you cut corners here, it would mean a possible raise for us."[11]

The first two privatized prisons in the country were immigration detention centers: Wackenhut's in Aurora (near Denver) and CCA's in Houston both opened in 1984. When CCA was first awarded its Houston INS contract, it had not built a facility. So it locked up its first immigration prisoners in rented motel rooms and soon had its first escapes when the inmates pushed the air-conditioning units through the walls. "Since then," testified Ohio Congressman Ted Strickland, a former correctional officer, "for-profit prisons have created a multi-billion dollar industry and are as likely to be traded on Wall Street as be listed as defendants in litigation." In 1996 two inmates escaped from the Houston Processing Center and were recaptured. These turned out not to be INS prisoners at all: "Faced with empty beds, CCA had imported 240 sex offenders from Oregon." The company had managed to do this behind the backs of local officials. Prison commentator Alex Friedmann writes: "Private prisons would be great if the primary purpose of the criminal justice was to warehouse inmates without providing them with meaningful opportunities for rehabilitation."[12]

I spoke with two warehoused men that day in Houston, and as our separate interviews ended, Olu Balogun and Ken Efe each had the same impulse—to share the stories of detainees whose patience had run out. Balogun offered a scrap of paper with a note written on it: "2 persons (Spanish) attempted suicide because of prolonged detention." In Dorm 4, just days before, a man had tried to slit his throat with a razor. In Dorm 7, a month earlier, a man had cut his wrists and was found "lying quietly, bleeding." Efe told of another who "tied a rope around his neck" and tried to hang himself after being held for so long after he had agreed to his deportation.

"A lot of it is just attention-getters," opined Assistant Warden Cook. As for the suicide attempts, he has seen a lot of them over the years, but he doesn't take them too seriously. They just want "to see the warden or the INS quicker . . . a lot of that is just a ploy and a game." If a ploy, it's a desperate one. "It's very frustrating," explained Balogun, who had been detained for almost two years when I met him and would be detained for two more. "People are even willing to risk their lives to go back to their country of persecution just to avoid detention. They are tired of prolonged detention."

"The problem is the INS," Balogun continued. "They don't really care about our welfare. They don't come to talk to us." Then he offered the kind of insight that comes from being on the inside. "That's the strategy the INS are using right now—to frustrate asylum seekers so they can give up and sign their deportation [papers] to go back home." Many are signing, he said, because "there's no hope of being released."

If the keepers and their contractors are occasionally difficult to predict, it is safe to assume they will resist any challenge to their arbitrary authority. In 1992, when a group of Romanian asylum seekers at the Houston Processing Center went on a hunger strike, CCA headquarters in Nashville declared that they "had 'lost their right to talk to the media.'"[13] That time, the local INS overruled and allowed the interviews. For my visit, CCA headquarters permitted interviews but required that my questions for the detainees and for its employees be submitted in advance to corporate headquarters; CCA has also required this of researchers looking into some of its other facilities. The INS itself has never asked me for my questions before I have interviewed detainees in the agency-run facilities, though an INS representative in Houston wanted to know "the nature of the interview" I was planning. And a New York attorney reports that the INS has strongly discouraged detainees at the Wackenhut detention center in Queens from giving media interviews. At first glance these restrictions might seem reasonable. But, like much of what is justified by the INS and its surrogates in the name of security, this monitoring of detainees' contact with the media is simply unnecessary, except as a matter of intimidation and control; in Texas a journalist can visit an inmate on death row without having her questions prescreened by the authorities.[14] Just as it had at first declined to give me a tour, the Houston INS initially denied my request to interview the two detained Nigerians. Why? Because, according to INS Community Relations officer John Ramirez, "on both, litigation is pending." This was ridiculous. It simply meant that the men had filed habeas corpus petitions seeking release from detention and applications for protection against being returned to possible torture in Nigeria. The INS's Aquino later added that her agency felt interviews "were not in [the detainees'] best interest." The detainees themselves disagreed. After a second request, the agency relented. Balogun later said that when he was given the form authorizing our interview, Aquino tried to discourage him from signing it, saying that "it might or it might not affect [his] situation with the INS." He was not swayed. "I have been here two years, so there is nothing else I have to be afraid of. They couldn't do more than what they have done already."

Olugbemiga Olayinka Balogun is not the sort of prisoner you will read about in an Amnesty International fund-raising appeal. Balogun first came to the United States on a student visa in 1984. Three years later he completed a B.A. in accounting, with a D in financial management. Three years after that he was convicted of credit card fraud and sentenced to five years in the federal penitentiary at Talladega, Alabama. Like many Nigerians detained in the United States, he knows his rights, he fights for them, and he does so in English—a combination that does not endear him to the INS.

As a "criminal alien," Balogun would be moved from Bureau of Prisons custody into INS custody so that deportation proceedings could begin. He was transferred to the INS Service Processing Center at El Paso, where he joined fellow detainees in filing a lawsuit against the INS, an action organized by another Nigerian who was eventually deported. The suit alleged abusive treatment by guards and inadequate health care. Years later, El Paso Service Processing Center prisoners still had serious complaints. They were spending twenty-three hours a day locked down in the packed dormitories, their heads "only inches apart," many resting on books wrapped in shirts since they were not given pillows. They had to request toilet paper from a "cage officer" each time they went to the bathroom. They only received two regular meals on weekend days, and they were not allowed to talk in the mess hall. They had minimal access to the under-stocked law library. They were not allowed to have radios to listen to music. When they arrived, detainees were told they would see a judge within four-teen days; one of them had gone twenty-one months without seeing a judge and "consider[ed] himself kidnapped."[15] Conditions like these do not result from mere "poor management," as the title of one government report crit-ical of the INS puts it. They are a program for making the detained men's and women's lives miserable. When Balogun was detained in El Paso, he managed to obtain a phone card from MCI by using a false social secu-rity number. "I was desperate to make phone calls to my people in Africa," he explained seven years later. He was indicted, pled guilty, and paid MCI a restitution, and he was transferred again to serve more time before being deported. "It's just a change of location," he would muse. The change took him through several correctional facilities in Texas and Oklahoma, until, in 1992, he was moved to the INS/BOP-operated Oakdale, Lousiana, detention center. Despite Oakdale's notorious history,[16] for Balogun "the treatment was very nice."

After being deported in 1993, Balogun had come back. In 1996 he was picked up at Houston's Intercontinental Airport, en route from Cancún to the Bahamas, for using a French passport and a false name. According to INS documents, he said he was "drifting about in the hope that [he] could return back home if things change."[17] At the airport, he requested political asylum. "Do I have the right to remain silent?" he asked the officers screening his asylum claim. Then he said: "I will answer to the best of my ability." He was detained at the Houston Processing Center.

Even as he fought, Balogun accommodated himself to his situation, and he was cooperative enough with his keepers that he was able to mail me thick packages containing newspaper clippings, court filings, copies of INS memos on parole guidelines, and relevant congressional testimony. One assistant warden wrote a letter of support for Balogun, calling him a "model inmate," but INS decision makers were less sympathetic.

"What he did was badger them a lot," said Thomas Brannen, referring to his client's *pro se* lawsuits and FOIA requests. Unsympathetic as Balogun may seem, he and attorney Brannen were in a position to be more than frustrated with the black hole of INS procedures. When we met, Balogun's claim for protection in the United States existed in the form of an appeal under the international Convention Against Torture (CAT). But even winning his appeal would not necessarily mean release from detention. Under regulations guiding CAT claims, "The Service can maintain him in custody even if he prevails," in the words of one immigration judge. Brannen is the first to concede that his client "did some things wrong." But, he said, Balogun "doesn't deserve to spend the rest of his life in a U.S. jail if he wins his case."

Two weeks after the tour, Balogun called. About ten detainees, all of whom had been held for a year or more, staged a hunger strike for five days to protest the uncertainty of their situation and their lengthy detentions. The local INS took it in stride. "It wasn't a threatening situation," said spokesperson Aquino, "it was just all talk and no bark." Local consulate officials, on whom the INS depends to arrange travel documents for deportees, worked with the agency to keep detainees calm. "They're not INS," Aquino explained. "They can go in and just say, 'Look, it's not INS, it's us. . . . If you'll just be patient you'll be out of here shortly.'"

Warden Martin, however, said that there was no hunger strike at all. "All our hunger strikes are usually prematurely thought of. . . . I call them 'incidents' until we see that it's a hunger strike," he noted. Either way, the purpose of the action "is to be able to manipulate the system." He said this as an observation rather than as criticism. But he also said that he does not remember any consulate officials coming in to calm the inmates. CCA promotional literature makes the enigmatic claim that "sometimes responding to public and media inquiries on government's behalf is beneficial to them."[18] Perhaps the warden was just trying to help. Yet somehow only the detainees have credibility problems.

In November 2001 Balogun lost his last appeal; two months later he was returned to Nigeria with other deportees on another charter flight. U.S. government procurement arrangements for a comparable deportation charter stipulated: "No crew rest in Nigeria. INS does not want to stay in Nigeria more than 2 hours."[19]

———

Exploiting the hopelessness of detainees is a strategy that the INS and its contractors have been using for a long time. Yet sometimes the institutional cruelty is so stark that the system falters by turning its own enforcers against it. "You start having so much sympathy that you feel like you're being held captive yourself. That's exactly what happened to us." Milissa

Grace is talking about herself and her friend Lupe Rivera. "We met in prison," Rivera says with a smile. Grace and Rivera, who talked to me about forced sedation, had both answered ads and been hired at the Houston Processing Center's medical clinic in the mid-1990s as employees of CCA. Grace is what they call an "Anglo" in Texas, from the Dallas area, who has rarely left the state. When I ask Rivera where she is from, she gently but pointedly informs me that she is from Pasadena, just outside Houston, and that two generations ago her grandfather helped to build the San Jacinto monument in the center of town. On the wall of the Good Neighbor Clinic where Rivera now works as the nurse manager of pediatrics, there is a poster of Mexican revolutionary hero Emiliano Zapata with the caption, "I would rather die fighting on my feet than live the rest of my life on my knees." Rivera tells me that she was active for many years in the Chicano movement; the poster was a gift from a Chinese medical resident at the clinic.

Grace and Rivera both like to laugh, and they're both willing to fight. Grace tells me: "They hired the wrong nurses when they hired me and Lupe. . . . We cared, and we weren't supposed to care." Together, the nurses tell me about their first impressions of the CCA clinic where they met. Each had been instructed to wear whatever she felt comfortable in, and, being nurses headed for work in a clinic, they both chose to wear scrubs. It turned out that they were the only nurses wearing scrubs. Over our lunch at El Paraíso, a few blocks from Rivera's clinic, the women finish each other's sentences. Grace begins:

"I walked in the clinic and all of the nurses—"

"Street clothes, cleavage, Lee's Press-On Nails—"

"Little short skirts and high heels—"

"I was shocked. And smoking during pill call—"

"Besides that," adds Grace, "who wants to go into a dorm full of sixty horny men with cleavage? And the nurses are giving me hell over wearing scrubs!"

The warden suggested to Grace that she wear something more "office-like." Grace was already thinking of quitting but decided to wait until she met the new clinic manager; "If she looks like Tammy Baker, I'm out of here." Guadalupe Rivera, the new manager, looked nothing like Tammy Faye. Equally appalled at what they saw around them, the two nurses bonded quickly.

Grace and Rivera seem to have nothing to prove and nothing to hide. So I start by asking if they think critics of prison privatization are overstating the case when they claim that, to save money, companies cut corners at the expense of prisoners' physical well-being. Rivera doesn't even hesitate. She tells me that when she arrived as clinic director, the first thing she did was to go through medical records, and she immediately noticed that adult detainees with hepatitis B were being given pediatric doses of medication because it was cheaper. Clinic workers, who were CCA employees, were expected to go along with the program, though Rivera received permission from the warden to fire a nurse for withholding insulin from a prisoner-patient (it was the same nurse who as punishment had withheld Motrin). Rivera knew how to gain some leverage by putting everything in writing, with copies to CCA's local and corporate offices.

"Remember when [the warden] said, 'Once again, you've been reduced to writing?'" Rivera asks Grace nostalgically.

Grace turns to me. "And Lupe was burning that paperwork up," she says admiringly. Later she adds: "Lupe single-handedly turned this place upside down. I just followed along."

Rivera counters: "I won them awards, Milissa," referring to the recognition she had received from TB Control of Houston.

Rivera recalls a patient with a seizure disorder. The medical staff claimed he was faking because they needed to justify denying him the necessary treatment. Grace explains: "We did things the right way. That was the problem. It was all about money." The nurses laugh about arrangements they made with a local Wal-Mart to get eyeglasses for detainees who needed them. The money for glasses was already in the budget, Rivera insists. All she did was go home and read the INS policy manual.

"How hard was that?" she says, amused but still incredulous. "I took the stupid manual home with me when I started working there, and finding out, well, you know, they have a right to this, and they have a right to that." Even though INS regulations stated that detainees were entitled to these medical services, Rivera found she was fighting company policy.

"What did [the warden] always say? If it's costing you money, put 'em on a list." Meaning what? I ask.

Deport them, she explains; get rid of them. CCA's warden "was in it for profit, you know. That's why you only got teeth *pulled*. You didn't *fix* nothin'. She was being their puppet," Rivera explains, focusing on the warden again. "Her job was to keep those costs down."

On the subject of cost-cutting, the nurses segue easily from CCA's treatment of detainees to the company's treatment of its own employees. Grace explains that the warden, assistant warden, program director, and chief of security all received year-end bonuses if overtime pay to wage-earning staff had been kept to a minimum. To make that happen, management used salaried staff to cover extra duty, such as escorting detainees to outside hospitals. More insidiously, salaried staff were sometimes punished for mistakes with "in-house suspension," referred to as "days off without pay." In other words, Grace explains, you worked on your days off without any additional compensation.

The officers or guards are all "trapped," says Grace. "We say, they sold their souls to CCA."

The nurses are sympathetic to guards who have little college education and wouldn't be able easily to find a job with comparable pay. "What was that guy's name that could barely read and write?" Rivera asks Grace. "That country guy . . ." The obvious alternative would be the Texas Department of Criminal Justice (what is elsewhere called the Department of Corrections), but working in "*that* kind of prison" is a different thing.

When I ask about guard-on-inmate violence in the detention center, Rivera tells me that she approached the program director about certain guards "being confrontational, and making these situations get out of control." "[The director] says, 'Well, you know, we hire them for that reason.' And I said, 'What, the ad says "Cro Magnon" or something like that?'" South Carolina civil rights attorney W. Gaston Fairey has alleged that CCA "us[es] terror rather than sufficient numbers of adequately trained staff" to control its prisons. Fairey has represented INS and non-INS inmate plaintiffs suing CCA for alleged mistreatment. He says that while prison violence is typically committed by low-level staff, in CCA facilities "we're talking [about] senior officials—chiefs of security, shift supervisors. That's the difference." Fairey also remarks that "the INS-CCA association goes way back"—that is, to Houston—and that "the government knows" about the allegations that have been made against this company.[20]

The nurses start recalling "incidents," as the officers and bureaucrats like to refer to them. Once, a guard sprayed a fire extinguisher under the door to one of the dorms, just to scare the detainees. The prisoners thought they were being teargassed and started breaking windows. Then the "riot team"—guards who receive special training every few months—went in with their shields, batons, and "little helmets," what Grace calls "their nasty little SWAT-team-type equipment" to "scare 'em with all their big stuff." This time the CCA guards did teargas the men and then threw them into segregation.

On other occasions it seems to be the INS that was responsible for violence against detainees. "Immigration would . . . call an inmate out to go to the Immigration side [of the facility] for their 'interview,' they would call it," Grace recounts. "It was not unusual for inmates to be taken over there and get the shit beat out of them, and they bring 'em to us [in the clinic] and say they got in a fight." Sometimes the INS would hold detainees in what Grace calls its "secret cells" next to the agency's offices (physically inside the CCA structure but bureaucratically distinct). This was apparently to avoid processing these prisoners through the clinic, as in the case of the detainee whom the INS wanted to have sedated even though the clinic had no chart on him. Later Grace explains that the cells were not really "secret"; they were just called that informally. She adds that beatings were not common. "It happened enough. It wasn't a tremendous amount, or we probably both would have quit sooner than we did."

Rivera says, "We never really had any problems with inmates, Milissa and I, but a couple of the nurses in the clinic did have enemies—"

"We treated them medically . . ."

"Nobody ever cussed me, nobody ever acted menacingly toward me . . ."

"They were human beings."

"They were our patients."

"And we weren't guards."

The defining event at the Houston Processing Center for both Grace and Rivera was a forty-eight-day hunger strike by five Indian Sikhs. By the time it was over, Rivera had quit and Grace had been fired. Rivera quit because she couldn't take it anymore. Grace was fired because she married one of the hunger strikers.

Sikhs are a religious minority in India. They consider the state of Punjab, which was divided between India and Pakistan in the 1947 partition, their homeland. Amnesty International has documented the often-fatal persecution of Sikhs by the Indian police.[21] The Sikhs detained in Houston had applied for political asylum and been denied. Their cases were on appeal. Local Sikh community organizations had written to the INS offering to take the men in while their cases were pending, since a standard rationale for detention in such cases is that the applicant might disappear. INS refused the offer.

When the Sikhs began the hunger strike, one of them had been detained for over three years. Manjit Singh, the man Milissa Grace would marry, had been detained for two years and two months. Now they were asking to be either released or deported. The lengthy incarceration was pushing them to abandon their asylum claims, just as Olu Balogun would observe. But as the strike wore on, local activists were holding demonstrations outside the detention center, and the local press was paying attention. The keepers tend to downplay hunger strikes as long as they can, because to acknowledge them at all is the first concession, but this one was hard to deny.

Rivera recalls the warden's reaction: " 'Don't let 'em die on us.' " Eventually, the hunger strikers were moved into the clinic for full-time observation. The nurses were able to convince them to drink Ensure, a liquid nutritional supplement. "Till [the physician in charge of all the CCA clinics in the area] came in and said, 'Well, why don't you just give it to them on the rocks, Lupe?' " Grace remembers buying butterscotch-flavored Ensure. "Lupe and I were doing whatever we could to keep them alive. . . . And they didn't feel like they were eating when they were drinking Ensure."

According to the nurses, the warden was waging her own psychological warfare. "Pam Fugazzi sent out to one of the finest Indian restaurants there was and got all this Indian food and put it in that room with them for like twelve hours," Grace recalls, becoming angry again. But Fugazzi later tells me she brought in the Indian food at the suggestion of the local Sikh community, and she adds that this episode was "one of the worst moments of [her] career with CCA." Fugazzi respected the hunger strikers—"I felt they were inappropriately detained and they were protesting in a way that was appropriate to their religion"—and she felt caught in the middle.

Whatever the motivation for bringing in the Indian food, "[the Sikhs] didn't touch it," says Grace, her tone shifting to one of respect. "They did not *touch* it." Rivera adds that guards would sometimes bring in food too, or come by the clinic specifically to "provoke" and "agitate" the Sikh hunger strikers. "They did everything they could to break their spirit," Grace tells me, and later: "That was our heartfelt problem—that CCA was cruel."

But there were also officers who liked the striking detainees. Grace shows me a photograph of someone wearing a pink, plastic Barbie mask, his body wrapped in one of those gray prison blankets, sitting on a bed next to Manjit Singh, who is dressed in white, and smiling. The man in disguise is a CCA officer trying to cheer up the hunger striker. Grace mailed the photo to Fugazzi because she wanted to drive her boss crazy. By this time, Rivera had left CCA. "I really ran amok after Lupe was gone," Grace admits.

Grace also readily admits that her decision to marry Manjit Singh was "one of the stranger things" she has done in her life. She tells me for the second time, "I'm a self-diagnosed obsessive-compulsive caregiver. If I didn't do what I'm doing, I'd probably be out under the bridges, asking those guys when their last chest x-ray was." But with Manjit, there was also love. She'd later swear to it in an affidavit:

[The Sikh hunger strikers] had very good reasons for what they were doing, and before long I found myself doing anything I could to help them get through this difficult time. I was given unlimited access to them because I was the only one who could keep them drinking liquids. I spent a lot of time in Manjit's cell because he was one of only two that could speak good English. We shared pictures of our families and we became very close. He was funny and bright and the bravest man I ever knew. . . . Through our continuous association I fell deeply in love with Manjit during that time, and before long I realized that he was in love with me too.

One day Grace walked into the Houston Processing Center with a pastor whose name she had found in the Yellow Pages after her own pastor refused the invitation. "I just walked him in the front door is all I did," she explains, contesting CCA's accusation that she had sneaked him in. "Walked him in the front door and signed him in myself. . . . He had a suit, with a carnation on, carrying a Bible. But nobody questioned me, because I had just been promoted. I'd just been given Lupe's job." Indeed, the CCA memo from Warden Fugazzi announcing Grace's promotion praises her "increasingly responsible role in the clinic."[22]

The day after the memo was issued, Grace married Manjit Singh in the clinic. She was about thirty-five years old, and he was twenty-five. She showed me photos of the ceremony. Lupe Rivera's husband had notarized the marriage license; Grace's daughter was the witness. Three days after the wedding, Grace was fired. In CCA's confidential Employee Problem Solving Notice, Fugazzi wrote: "By becoming involved in this type of employee/inmate relationship, you knowingly and willfully endangered the security of this facility; therefore, your employment is terminated. Action: Termination."[23]

Manjit Singh was finally deported. Grace understood that the INS was not going to release the five Sikhs. She spent her new free time pressuring the dilatory Indian Consulate to issue the travel documents required for the United States to carry out a deportation, so that the other men could go home. Once Manjit was gone, Grace petitioned the INS for his return; she was a U.S. citizen, after all, and he was her husband. Not surprisingly, INS challenged the validity of their marriage. So Grace left Texas for the second time in her life. In the village of Honshon Pur, she married Manjit Singh again, this time in a Sikh ceremony. I saw a snapshot in Rivera's clinic of the couple in traditional Sikh wedding dress. The wedding made the local television news back home—"A Houston nurse followed her heart halfway around the world"—in a follow-up story to Grace's termination two years earlier. The INS dropped its challenge after the second wedding, but three years later the American Consulate in New Delhi had not issued Singh a visa to come to the United States.

"I knew for sure that I was going to be fired," Grace reflects. "And I knew that [the hunger strikers] would die in there if there wasn't someone making sure they didn't." That's why she had convinced them to start eating after her marriage while she pursued their travel documents. As we sit in her living room in a subdivision north of Houston, Grace says, "I saw something I really, really hated I had never seen before. . . . It was tearing us all up. . . . The whole idea that they were locking up these people and holding them for years and years just because they wanted to come to this country." We watch some home-video footage of her trip to India, but she quickly becomes self-conscious. Like any stranger's honeymoon photos, these images manage to put intimacy on public display even while conveying that the real story is a private one. "All they really wanted was to either be set free or go home, that's all. Three and a half years is a long time. And that didn't seem unreasonable to me."

She adds: "Why I took it up as my personal crusade, I'm not so sure, to tell you the truth. But I did. And overall, it was a good experience for me."

# 6 | "KEEPING QUIET MEANS DENY"

*A Hunger Strike in Queens*

Like plenty of other people at their jobs first thing in the morning, the Wackenhut employees were griping about bad coffee. They were also commiserating about their prisoners. A maintenance man had just come from a bathroom: "[They're] fuckin' pigs. . . . I don't do sanitation. I tighten toilet seats. But if it's dirty, I don't tighten *shit*." An officer added, "They don't know how to sit properly. . . . They make a fuckin' mess."

I was sitting on a plastic chair in the lobby of the INS "contract facility" in Queens, New York, waiting for a Ugandan man's political asylum hearing to begin. On the lobby wall is a framed blue and white banner with a company logo: a map of the world and the words WACKENHUT COR-RECTIONS above it. But there is no INS or Wackenhut sign on the outside of the building; in fact, there is no sign at all, other than the street number (182–22 150th Avenue). The building itself is hidden in plain sight among the loading docks of Active Container Station, Amerijet International cargo service, and the like, off South Conduit near John F. Kennedy Airport. The location makes good business sense. The prisoners are commodities while they await transport—or, in some cases, release—earning the company about $50 per "manday" in federal taxpayers' money.[1] That one warehouse looks like the next is an additional convenience. Outside of Denver, at another Wackenhut/INS detention center, also a renovated warehouse, I commented to the administrator that I had driven right past the place. Like the security chief at the Houston Processing Center, he was pleased and said they like to keep a low profile.

In 1954 a former FBI agent named George Wackenhut began a private investigative business. A decade later the company won its first federal contract, providing security for the Department of Energy's Nevada Test Site. Wackenhut would go on to provide protection to, among many others, Cape Canaveral Air Station and the Kennedy Space Center (a joint venture with Northrop Grumman and ICF Kaiser), some twenty U.S. embassies around the world, Ryder Argentina cargo trucks, and various "gated communities." The company reportedly has also helped to break a coal miner strike in Kentucky and carried out a campaign of harassment on behalf of British Petroleum against an independent oil shipper who revealed its role in negligence leading to the *Exxon Valdez* disaster. The Wackenhut Corporation earned nearly $2 billion in 1998, with its subsidiary Wackenhut Corrections Corporation (WCC) operating about fifty prisons and detention centers, including a few in Australia and England.[2]

The Ugandan asylum seeker waiting for his hearing in Queens was Emmy Kutesa. He was among a group of Wackenhut detainees who had gone on a hunger strike in summer 1999 to protest their long imprisonment. Immigration detainees can be "paroled" or released at the discretion of the INS district director while their cases are decided. The terminology can be confusing: in the criminal justice system "paroled" means getting released before a sentence has been completed, but INS prisoners are not serving sentences. They are "administrative detainees," being held in custody while their cases are processed or to await deportation. As advocates like to point out, it simply makes sense, and it is humane, to let people out if they have shown that they can make a good case for staying in the United States. But reasonableness and humanity vary, and in the immigration system they vary by district. The New York District has an especially restrictive parole or release policy.[3] Emmy Kutesa had been detained for seventeen months when he joined the hunger strike with other detainees frustrated by a seemingly interminable legal process and by a limbo status made worse by the expedient relationship between the INS and its private contractor. Here is Kutesa trying to explain why a hunger strike is the only meaningful weapon for someone faced with this arrangement:

Immigration, they're federal. Wackenhut, they don't know why you are here. They're here to keep you here. . . . When you don't eat, they feel worried. You may get sick. . . . If you die in their detention . . . they will get it hard to explain why. . . . [They will have to decide] where to take your dead body. . . . [They will have to say] a detainee died because he was demanding parole.

Kutesa's seeming languor makes it hard to say whether he was determined or simply resigned to his struggle. Either way, his name had been circulating among journalists and activists in New York because he was the last holdout among the Wackenhut hunger strikers. In late August activists staged a demonstration outside INS offices in Manhattan to support Kutesa as his protest entered its fourth week. The Immigration Service issued a press release that began with this surprising heading: "THE NEW YORK INS WANTS TO CLARIFY THAT THERE IS NO HUNGER STRIKE AT ITS CONTRACT FACILITY IN QUEENS." This was damage control intended for media accustomed to taking government spokespersons at their word. But those with some experience of the INS detention system would recognize the transparent tactic of denial. When demonstration leaders walked into 26 Federal Plaza and forced an impromptu hallway meeting, INS Community Relations representatives began by "denying that the INS had ever denied there was a hunger strike," according to an activist with the Center for Immigrant Families. After a few minutes, the INS conceded its earlier denial and admitted that there was in fact a hunger strike going on.

There had been others. In late 1998, for example, the *New York Times* reported that frustrated asylum seekers at the Queens Wackenhut refused to eat and that there were several suicide attempts: a nineteen-year-old Iraqi Kurd in solitary confinement slashed his arm with a razor and tried to hang himself; a thirty-four-year-old engineer from Congo drank a mixture of painkillers and Ben Gay ointment in water; and an Albanian man took an overdose of antibiotics.[4]

This time the frustration boiled over differently. At the end of July detainees smashed chairs, broke a Ping-Pong table, and one threw a carton of milk at a guard. Referring to these incidents, New York INS Public Affairs officer Mark Thorn emphasized that "there is no place for violence" in the Wackenhut facility. He intended no irony. Detainees did not deny these incidents, but they tended to put them in a broader context, one in which violence *against* detainees is not unusual. On July 27, the first day of the hunger strike that began in the wake of these outbursts, a Nigerian asylum seeker wrote a letter to his pen pal in Florida through an arrangement sponsored by a religious advocacy group to help break INS prisoners' isolation.

> There is something I'll like you to be aware of, there is a big riot going on in this detention center and it's really serious, some detainees have been injured serious in the process of restraint, the officers here used excessive force on them, people (detainees) are also on hunger strike. The objective of the strike is that the INS should do something about the local parole program which is not all that effective. . . . Things are going from bad to worse here. . . .
>
> We all heard the story about [John F. Kennedy Jr.'s plane] crash, it was really a tragedy. . . . At times God does things that are beyond human understanding but there is a purpose for everything he does.

An attorney representing another asylum seeker who had been detained for six months said his client told him that Wackenhut officers had been "roughing them up"—pushing people, for example, instead of giving them time to get in line—and that this kind of mistreatment helped to precipitate the strike. His client, also Nigerian, had urged his fellow prisoners to protest.

According to detainees, more than one hundred of them, or more than half the total, refused to eat. Here is a general picture of who was detained in Queens two months before the strike. Of 194 detainees, 160 were men. They ranged in age from eighteen to fifty-nine. The countries with the largest representation were Sri Lanka (30 detainees), China (29), Nigeria (23), Sierra Leone (16), and Ghana (15). The other countries of origin were Afghanistan, Albania, Algeria, Bangladesh, Brazil, Burkina Faso, Cameroon, Chad, Congo, Czech Republic, Dominican Republic, Ecuador, Egypt, El Salvador, England, Ethiopia, Guinea, Haiti, India, Iraq, Ivory Coast, Jamaica, Kosovo, Lebanon, Liberia, Macao, Mali, Mauritania, Pakistan, Poland, Russia, Rwanda, Somalia, Sudan, Syria, Togo, Uganda, Ukraine, Uzbekistan, Vietnam, Yemen, Yugoslavia, and Zaire. At least 13 of the 194 had been detained for a year or more.[5]

Officials of both the INS and Wackenhut cracked down on the multi-national hunger strikers by confiscating juice and water, putting participants in solitary confinement, transferring protest leaders to other facilities, and threatening to force detainees to sign deportation agreements. All of these are practices regularly reported from around the country, and over many years, by INS detainees who have attempted hunger strikes and other peaceful protests. Meanwhile, the INS district office in New York plugged into the usual pattern by vigorously disputing this account even while conceding ignorance of day-to-day operations inside the facility. The INS minimized the number of detainees refusing to eat and denied the use of retaliatory tactics, claiming that water remained available in the dorms and acknowledging that juice may have been confiscated so that it would not be thrown at guards.

An INS spokesperson did confirm that several detainees were transferred but explained that this "was a precautionary action" taken against the "instigators." In a letter to the Committee Against Anti-Asian Violence (CAAAV), one of the groups spearheading support for the strikers, New York District Director Edward J. McElroy acknowledged ordering that certain detainees "be removed to a more secure environment" but only as a result of their "physically menacing the guards, throwing heavy objects, and destroying the dorms." He also accused CAAAV itself of "an act bordering on irresponsibility" for protesting the situation "before gathering all relevant information." An INS spokesperson declined to reveal the names of the five detainees who were transferred, or the locations of the facilities to which they were moved, citing the confidentiality of asylum seekers. This is a legitimate justification when actually used to protect the detainees, except that the INS violates confidentiality to suit its own purposes.[6] As for the transfer of protest leaders, that too fits a long-standing pattern of INS repression in which detainees who forcefully speak up for their rights are sent to facilities far from their attorneys and support networks.

Another of those transferred from Wackenhut gave an account of "physical menacing" at the Queens facility. After complaining about a five-month wait for a response to his political asylum appeal, this Nigerian wrote:

I was treated very badly. [The officers] kicked and beat me for reasons I did not understand. When I asked why I am being frustrated this way, they just ignored me and kept pushing me around. After some time had passed, I began to be very ill, both mentally and physically; I was emotionally stressed out and depressed, and not me alone, but my fellow inmates. When we would not take the punishment any longer, about 150 detainees (out of 198 people who were detained there) decided to go on a hunger strike.

When they heard about the hunger strike, they armed themselves with riot gear to disperse us, but that amount of force was not necessary. They came in to our dorm and began by beating us. They took four other inmates and me to solitary confinement (or the *hole*). It was very violent; I was crying and thinking about back in my village, saying to myself, I should stay there and die, rather than going through this torment here in the United States of America.

On the 28th of July 1999 they transferred the other four inmates and me to a new prison here in York, Pennsylvania. The name of this prison is the York County Prison. To this day I have not heard anything from the INS about my appeal case.

Four months later the man who wrote that statement was allegedly kicked and beaten by a correctional officer at York County Prison in an argument over the television. When the detainee was put into disciplinary segregation and charged with attacking the officer, two other correctional officers put their objections to that lie in writing, according to a source at the jail. Back in New York, the man's attorney wondered where he should go to complain about his client's mistreatment.

It was a good question. Accusations of abuse against the INS and its surrogates, whether county jail or private sector employees, generally disappear into a whirlpool of circular logic and self-protecting bureaucracy. Asked about accusations that guards had threatened the Wackenhut hunger strikers with having to sign some kind of document agreeing to deportation, the INS spokesperson told me that such claims were "absolutely untrue," adding, "If there was any kind of abuse or threat to any of them, we would want to know." Yet as we spoke, the grassroots organizers who had spoken to the detainees and who would walk into the INS office were in the plaza in front of the spokesperson's office, trying to make those allegations known. When *Village Voice* reporter Alisa Solomon asked Wackenhut officials about the allegations of beatings, she was referred to an INS Community Relations official, who told her, "If it occurred and were an issue, I would have heard about it, and I haven't heard about it."[7] It was the same official who, in the hallway with activists, had denied the agency's previous denial.

———

Most INS detainees never get an attorney;[8] Emmy Kutesa is represented by a former president of Uganda. When G. Lukongwa Binaisa walks into the Wackenhut lobby, the desk guard greets him with amiable, sarcastic pomp, putting on a generic foreign accent to welcome "Mr. President." Soon the Luganda-language Berlitz-contracted interpreter[9] arrives wearing a long, white gown. She takes the seventy-nine-year-old former president's hand and kneels to greet him. He smiles broadly, his battered, maroon briefcase and white Stetson pith helmet on the plastic chair beside him.

In 1979 former Attorney General Binaisa became the second man appointed to serve as president and head of a provisional government after the overthrow of Idi Amin Dada. Less than a year later he was placed under house arrest when he tried to dismiss the military chief of staff, to ban political parties in an effort to "achieve the politics of consensus,"[10] and, by his own account, to make inroads against government corruption. Some twenty years earlier, when he was a young man, he had been imprisoned for resisting British rule. Now, as an immigration attorney, he has agreed to take on Kutesa's case free of charge because they are both from Uganda and because Kutesa managed to get in touch with him from detention.

The courtroom, with its grim, TV-courtroom-set ambience, is part of the detention center building, though the court has its own authority that governs access and visitation. The players are Kutesa, attorney Binaisa, the INS attorney, the judge, and the interpreter. Kutesa is wearing the standard-issue bright orange detention uniform, or "pyjam," as he calls it, with the block letters WCC/NYC stenciled down the leg. Looking on and occasionally falling asleep are the khaki-clad court officers who can be fired anytime, one later explains, no matter how many years they've worked here.

The judge, who sits before a large plastic emblem with the words "Department of Justice/Executive Office for Immigration Review," and the INS prosecutor working to deny the Ugandan man protection are both employees of the Justice Department, although they work for different agencies within that department. Moreover, the immigration judge, as we have seen, is not a judge in the usual sense of the word. "They're really just employees of the Attorney General," says one expert on international refugee issues.[11] Yet as the hearing begins, it is the INS attorney who seems suspicious. She wants to know if there is a business relationship between the Berlitz interpreter and the former president that might bias the proceeding. She asks because they seem to know one another.

"No, I just know him because we speak the same language," the interpreter explains.

"We're both from Uganda," adds the former president.

"He was the *president* of Uganda," the judge cheerfully informs the INS attorney. "It's like having Jimmy Carter come!"

Well, not exactly Jimmy Carter. In a series of subway and "dollar-van" rides Binaisa—who likes to save money by taking these independently operated vans, which cost fifty cents less per ride than the city bus—shares some undiplomatic thoughts about whatever crosses his mind. He searches his memory for the exact insult that once landed him in jail back home, something about British rule smelling worse than a backed-up sewer, and he beams with pride. Today, he continues, it is the International Monetary Fund and the World Bank that continue the colonial enterprise. British intelligence still runs much more of the world than the naive Americans realize. The British are happy, for example, to have a couple hundred thousand Nigerian professionals living in exile in the United States. Keep the educated people out, give a petty dictator a fleet of Mercedes, plenty of whiskey and women, and you can control nations, Binaisa explains. Americans understand little of this, he goes on, because their country is so large. Moreover, who remembers what the American War for Independence was really about? Americans should be fighting for their government to pursue those ideals for everyone, not just for themselves. Instead, we have presidential candidate George W. Bush. "Compassionate conservative," Binaisa scoffs. What is that supposed to mean? Verdict: "absurd." Then there is this Khalid Muhammed organizing a "Million Youth March" in New York City. Verdict: "ridiculous." And Kweisi Mfume, chairman of the National Association for the Advancement of Colored People (NAACP) and former head of the Congressional Black Caucus, changes his name from Frizzell Gray, yet he makes recommendations to President Clinton about sanctions against the Sudan, recommendations that are patronizing to that country, so he is using a name from his homeland while insulting his true ancestors. American blacks could pressure their government to have more humane policies in Africa, the way American Jews do for Israel, but—Binaisa lowers his voice and leans a bit closer as we ride the subway through Queens—American blacks have no real connection to Africa. In fact, they don't really know the first thing about it. He tells me that he once told a reporter his "candid" opinion that then-mayor David Dinkins wasn't fit to run an African village and was then shocked to find his comment in print.

In the dollar-van, which Binaisa notes is called a "matatu" in Uganda, Kenya, and Tanzania, after the driver has closed the door with a home-made rope-and-pulley contraption and we are well on our way, we discover that we have gotten on the wrong van. An ugly stretch of highway runs by a desolate field behind the airport. "Like Uganda," says the former president. Beside him is a man who says that he lives here and that it is beautiful. The man is bouncing up and down in his seat and sitting sideways so he can look steadily out the window, and he keeps referring under his breath to "Papa Doc," presumably because Binaisa, with his chubby, round face and pith helmet, reminds him of Haiti's *Baby* Doc, Jean-Claude Duvalier. When another passenger explains that we are headed toward Far Rockaway instead of the subway station at Jamaica, Queens, Binaisa, who still has to make a two-hour trip from the detention center to his home in New Jersey, becomes incredulous about the very name of the place.

"Far Rockaway?! What do they do there?!"

No one bothers to respond, except the bouncing man, who does not even turn around. "They eat, drink, shit, sleep, breathe," he says.

The former president does not seem to hear him.

During a break, the INS attorney makes small talk with the interpreter of whom she had seemed so suspicious, in her bureaucratic role, an hour before. The attorney is from the Dominican Republic, her husband is from Kenya, and they want their children to learn Swahili. They already speak English and Spanish. But she observes that there is a shortage of good Swahili teachers in New York. She wonders if Swahili is similar to Luganda, the language of the asylum applicant. She laughs to discover that their native countries share a national dish, mashed green plantains, known as "mangu" in the Dominican Republic and "makote" in Uganda.

"You cook it the way we cook it?" the INS attorney asks, smiling with surprise.

"Yeah," says the Berlitz interpreter.

"No way."

Meanwhile, the twenty-eight-year-old Kutesa sits quietly at the table with them. He looks weak and exhausted, not having eaten now for a month. For the last three of those four weeks he has been held in a segregation cell, released back into the dorm only a day before this hearing. Privately, Binaisa indicates his disgust for such mistreatment, but it is not an issue in the courtroom. The focus is on a procedural or clerical mishap. An appeal that Binaisa thought he had filed with the appropriate office in Virginia turns up in the INS attorney's files, and no one can say why. In an unusual move, the judge generously offers to grant Kutesa a new hearing because of the confusion. But his offer is conditional on Kutesa's agreeing to end the hunger strike.

"You should start eating," Judge Donn Livingston tells him. "Everyone's worried about you." The applicant agrees to eat. A new hearing date is set, three weeks away. Outside the courtroom, in a corridor between sets of locked doors, a guard smiles and tells Kutesa he looks better. They shake hands, and Kutesa is returned to his dormitory. Outside at a bus stop, Binaisa tells the *Village Voice* reporter and me that his client has agreed only "reluctantly" to end his strike. Kutesa himself will explain that he has only modified and not ended it, to comply with the judge's request.

At the new hearing three weeks later, Binaisa uses his diplomatic skills to give a primer on African history and current events to the judge and the INS attorney, both of whom admit to being confused. Officials cannot reasonably be expected to have expertise on every country from which a potential refugee arrives, but one must question the system in which no independent expert need be present when someone's life may be at stake. In this case, it is just happenstance that the applicant's attorney is more than expert.

In 1990, four years before the genocide in Rwanda, a civil war began there "when armed Rwandan exiles, primarily Tutsi, launched an invasion from neighboring Uganda to assert their right to resettle in their homeland and share political power with the country's Hutu leaders."[12] Emmy Kutesa was a lieutenant in Uganda's Museveni-led National Resistance Army, out of which some of those armed Tutsi factions were organizing themselves to invade Rwanda, and he faced a dilemma. His mother was a Hutu living in Uganda, and she was married to a man from the Muganda tribe. Uganda recognizes patriarchal lineage, so Kutesa himself is ethnically Mugandan. His father had been kidnapped in 1982 by Milton Obote's government soldiers because of his ethnicity and his support for pro-Museveni rebels. The father never returned, and eleven-year-old Emmy joined the rebels. In 1986 Museveni took power. Seven years later, out of loyalty to his Hutu mother, or fear for her safety, as well as his belief that it was wrong for ethnic factions to arm themselves and violate national sovereignty, Kutesa passed military information to the Rwandan army via an uncle who was a Hutu. He was discovered and arrested by Museveni's government troops.

At military police headquarters in Kampala, "they tied my hands behind my back," Kutesa explains. "They dipped my head under water and I couldn't breathe—I was sucking in water. I still denied everything, and they kept putting my head in the water. . . . I was beaten with wooden batons on my head and on my face—that's why you are seeing the wounds and [scars] on my face." The torture continued. Police placed a bag over his head, suspended him by his arms from the ceiling, then suspended a weight from his testicles. Unable to "reach down to relieve the pain," Kutesa says, he finally lost consciousness.[13]

After this testimony the judge suggests a recess. During the break, the attorneys discuss the recent heavy rainfall that left many New Jersey homes without electricity. "I could get used to it in another country," says the Dominican American INS lawyer, "but not here."

Kutesa, according to his testimony, was taken from police headquarters to a military hospital. "A trained soldier," as his lawyer puts it, he managed to escape from the hospital one night after hitting a guard on the head from behind with a bucket of water. He followed railroad tracks into the sugarcane fields, sleeping by day and walking at night. He hid briefly near his mother's house so they could see one another. In February 1994 he crossed into Rwanda. In April war broke out when a plane carrying the presidents of Rwanda and Burundi went down. Kutesa fled again, this time with his uncle. They lived in Burundi until 1998, when the killing intensified there. They fled to Kenya but still felt unsafe, since refugees were being sent back to Rwanda from that country. "My uncle told me that America is a country that respects human freedom, and they are going to give you help," Kutesa tells the immigration court. His uncle got him on a plane from Nairobi to Amsterdam. The plane went on to Sweden, where some people who "were blacks," not Swedes, met Kutesa with a false pass-port and put him on a flight to the United States.

Which city? he is asked now in court.

"New York," he replies in English.

"New York," repeats the interpreter.

Which airport? he is asked.

"JFK," he replies.

"JFK," repeats the interpreter.

The worst day of his life was when his father disappeared. The second worst was the day he himself was arrested at JFK. When he began to tell the INS airport officer his problem, the officer complained that too many people come here asking for political asylum. "I was wondering if it was a crime, you know," Kutesa said later. He tried asking about the United Nations headquarters, which he knew was in New York. He tried to explain his situation to an official, but the official kept interrupting him and threatening to send him back. Meanwhile, his leg was chained to a chair for some twelve hours (he was accompanied to the bathroom when necessary). "You know, in my country we didn't even have that kind of chain . . . when they see you in that kind of chain, even your mother she won't come near you." A sympathetic INS official, a woman, became angry about this treatment, but it continued. When he was moved, he was secured with "another belt which I have never seen in this world," one with wrist shackles attached. He was put into a van and driven to a dark warehouse area. "I thought I was going to be killed." He is not the only INS prisoner whose treatment has led him to imagine such a fate. Inside the warehouse he was strip-searched, then given the orange uniform. When he saw the beds—a dorm of 40, among Wackenhut's 26,500 beds worldwide—he understood that this was a prison and that he was not going to be killed. A detainee from Ghana showed him how he was expected to make his bed there. The next morning breakfast was served at 6:15. Kutesa could not eat.

Kutesa's day in court was not the first time the INS had heard an account of his torture. In March 1998, after about four weeks in detention, he was given a "credible fear interview" by an asylum pre-screening officer. The officer had found his account "specific, detailed and credible." In the boilerplate language of the procedure, "Applicant has demonstrated that there is a significant possibility he could establish eligibility for asylum." In certain jurisdictions, at certain times, that would have been enough for Kutesa to be released while his case made its way through the system. Kutesa could be awarded asylum by an immigration judge, or by the Board of Immigration Appeals, but it is the district director who has the authority to grant parole, and each of the country's thirty-three district directors has wide discretion in parole decisions. There is "no enforceable national policy," explains Miami attorney Joan Friedland, who wonders aloud why INS Headquarters does not order "less punitive alternatives" to detention when appropriate.

During the Wackenhut hunger strike, coincidentally, the Lawyers Committee for Human Rights released a report criticizing the New York District's overly restrictive parole policy. The group noted the case of a Somali woman who had been raped in front of her children because of her membership in a minority clan and who was detained at Wackenhut when she arrived in the United States. Attorneys requested that she be released to stay with family members legally residing in this country. An INS officer responded "that the only individuals who would be released from Wackenhut were those who were 'near death' or [were] government witnesses."[14]

Toward the end of a credible fear interview, the officer typically asks about an applicant's criminal background. Kutesa saw the question in another light and responded, "I was arrested only once in Uganda and once here in the U.S."

"What do you mean by arrested in the U.S.?"

"I was detained here at this place," he said.

In spite of the "credible and consistent" account he had given, Kutesa would remain detained at this place for well over a year, waiting to tell his story to the judge.

Although no one challenged Kutesa's account of his ordeal at Kampala police headquarters, the judge and the INS attorney explored other avenues of testing his credibility and the degree to which he merited the official protection of the United States. Judge Livingston, for example, wondered whether Kutesa had violated his military obligations by passing along confidential information.

"Did you promise to defend Uganda?"

"I agreed to defend the people of Uganda but not to attack their neighbors and not to fight tribal wars," Kutesa responded.

The judge persisted, asking whether the applicant had not violated some oath by giving away military codes. Kutesa was becoming frustrated, leaning forward in his chair, trying hard to explain: "The war was not between countries, the war was between two tribes. . . ."

Rather than get bogged down in African politics again, the judge took a new tack. If Kutesa remained in the United States and were required to join the military here, would he do so?

"I don't want to join the army ever again. . . . Politics can force people to go to other countries and fight. . . ."

"So you wouldn't fight for this country?"

Kutesa's head was in his hands now. It would depend on whether it was for a "good cause," he ventured, "but fight for the interests of one cause, no."

But would he obey a law that might require him to join the army?

"From what I have heard about America, that it is a democratic country, I think they cannot force you to do something you don't want."

The Q-and-A was in danger of unraveling. The judge returned to his concern. "If you were required to serve in the military, would you serve faithfully even if you didn't agree with your mission?"

"To be in the army you have to be a citizen."

". . . My question is, are you going to sell secrets if you're allowed to remain here?" At this point Binaisa objected. No one had ever accused Kutesa of "selling secrets." The judge repeated the question, then asked: "If you're allowed to remain here, you may be allowed to serve in the military. [If so] will you serve faithfully or only obey the orders you agree with?"

Kutesa was visibly upset. The next day he would tell me, "I was very, very tired. They were asking stupid questions sometimes." He told the judge: "As a well-trained soldier, you are taught to defend the country and its citizens and its property, but if it comes to fighting certain tribes . . . I wouldn't fight."

The judge then asked Binaisa, "Why is he not the Benedict Arnold of Uganda?" Binaisa patiently explained the political context of Kutesa's actions, emphasizing that the concept of treason did not apply since this was not a war between countries. Eventually the judge revealed that he may have been playing a convincing devil's advocate, though continuing to miss Binaisa and Kutesa's point. "I think there is an exception [to following orders] when your government is involved in inhuman conduct," he said.

"Good afternoon, sir. I'm here on behalf of the government. . . . Are you aware that there is a reporter in court?" The INS attorney, with an over-size plastic green-and-white Krispy Kreme mug on the table beside her files, began her questioning with this indirect shot at Kutesa's credibility. She was referring to me.

"Yes," Kutesa answered. He and I had spoken privately several times already.

"And you're not afraid that your asylum claim will be exposed internationally?"

"As long as I'm not in Uganda," Kutesa said, that's not a problem.

The trial attorney went on to ask a few questions, following the judge's lead, and doing her job of trying to poke holes in Kutesa's story where she could, though she presented no concrete evidence or theory contradicting his story. At one point she even tried to implicate Kutesa in the Hutu massacre of Tutsis in Rwanda. Wasn't he aware of all that killing when he passed the military information? she demanded. Binaisa objected again, explaining that the genocide had not taken place until four years later.

As the INS officer had done eighteen months earlier, Judge Livingston ruled that Kutesa's testimony was credible and consistent. But a grant of political asylum depends on one's ability to prove the likelihood, if returned home, of persecution based on membership in a particular social, religious, or political group. Livingston decided that although Kutesa had a legitimate fear of return, it was not a fear that put him into any of the protected categories. Instead of political asylum, he granted Kutesa the form of relief known as "withholding of deportation" in accordance with the international Convention Against Torture, which prohibits signatory countries, of which the United States is one, from sending people back to countries where they are "more likely than not" to be tortured. CAT protection, as it is sometimes called, is certainly better than nothing, but it does not carry all the benefits of political asylum, such as the possibility of a green card and eventual citizenship. Nor does it provide the opportunity for family reunification, and Kutesa's two children were still in Uganda.

"The respondent is ordered removed," announced the judge into a tape recorder. ". . . It is further ordered that the respondent's removal to Uganda is withheld." He asked the trial attorney about the status of an FBI fingerprint clearance on the applicant. Then he explained that the Service could not send Kutesa back to Uganda now but that it still had the option of sending him to a third country, if one would accept him. Binaisa asked the judge to postpone his ruling until a new report about Uganda was published. Due out from Human Rights Watch in a month, it would include a section on the danger to soldiers in detention.[15] He hoped it would sway the judge to grant his client asylum, but the judge held firm and granted only the lesser CAT relief.

"The question," the judge said, "is whether they'll let him out of custody," and he laughed. In other words, the decision to parole him was still in the district director's hands. "He's a spy," said the judge, summing up. "When he goes back . . . he's going to be hung up by his private parts." Then he made sure Kutesa understood the decision and told him, "You're going to have to be patient. . . . I'm sure you're going to be released pretty soon . . . [but not] right away. . . . Are you eating?"

When Kutesa called from Wackenhut the next day, he told me he was relieved to have been awarded relief under the Torture Convention, though disappointed that it would not be as easy to see his children as it would have if he had been granted asylum. He was plainly exhausted, physically and emotionally. "I feel scared," he said, "because the INS is very tricky and I don't know how long I'm going to stay here." A deportation officer had come to ask him about contact information for a non-profit organization that had promised to provide him with a place to live. Even a skeptic would take that to mean that the INS was moving toward releasing him. "This may be to calm me down, to give me patience," Kutesa said.

He would continue his two-day-a-week strike as a way of insisting on parole. "I feel like I don't know. I don't know what I can tell you. I feel hopeless. I don't see my future. . . . As I'm still inside, I feel desperate. I'm confused." A week later he informed me that he was preparing to refuse all meals again if he did not get released within a month. "I wouldn't like to hurt myself. . . . I'm just forced to do that."

When Emmy Kutesa describes his newly modified hunger strike, the version he began after the judge urged him to eat in exchange for a new hearing, it becomes clear that he is involved in a negotiation with his keepers, a negotiation of language as well as action. I ask Kutesa why he had agreed to end his hunger strike, and he responds: "In fact, I didn't stop the hunger strike. I started eating yesterday and haven't stopped the hunger strike. But it is because of the pressure they put me. For example, the judge told me I have to start eating so I can be strong. He doesn't want me to be sick, so that I can come for my hearing. And my attorney advised me the same."

In addition, he says, the INS officer-in-charge at Wackenhut, Teresa Regis, and INS deportation officer Evaristo Robinson had spoken to him privately and asked him to eat "at least something." His first reaction was to decline. "I was not feeling very bad because I'm taking water, I'm taking juice, I'm drinking tea with milk. So I wouldn't like to start to eat, but the pressure they put me, I felt it was impolite to refuse all the time. . . . I told them I will start to eat, but I will eat once a week. One meal. And they tried to insist that I have to eat at least something every day. I don't have to eat much, but a little every day. And I told them, OK, I will eat twice a week, on Monday and Friday. So yesterday I ate my dinner." He had turkey and rice. "They are pushing me to eat. [Officer Regis] told me she has to push me to eat because she's worried about me. Her aim is me to eat, to end the hunger strike, but I didn't cooperate with them."

Kutesa talks about time, about the months of waiting. But why a hunger strike to make the demand? "I have no other way of showing them that I'm asking for parole. . . . Because where we are, it's very tight, you know. You cannot do anything. You cannot do anything."

Then he continues with no apparent transition: "You know, last year, I was upset, and I was very depressed, so I tried to kill myself." Technically we are discussing parole; in reality we are talking about hopelessness. The act of protest sometimes seems to be a negotiation not just between the keeper and the kept but between demand and despair. "You know, when I was upset, I made some problems in the dorm, so they took me into segregation." He had stopped taking medication for depression (Paxil) and stopped eating too, though he did these things "with no aim." He was thinking, "Why do I have to be here? . . . Maybe I will die, that will be better." Another detainee had tried to wake him up. Because Kutesa is easily upset when he's depressed, he pushed the other man. That's why he was taken to segregation. "And I came to segregation, I took one of my bedsheets, I tied it up, and hanged myself. You know, this bedsheets is old bedsheet, and they wash them every week in the machine. They are old." He rubs his fingers together as you would to check the quality of a fabric, indicating how thin it had become. The sheet tore, and he fell. An officer discovered him, and he was taken to Jamaica Hospital in Queens for three and a half weeks. That was a full year before the hunger strike we are talking about now.

When the protest of August 1999 began, Kutesa was in the hospital again. He was returned to the detention center one day into the new strike. "I ate my breakfast because I was not sure they were serious," he says with a smile. Another detainee asked, " 'What are you doing?' . . . [and] I joined my fellow detainees." After eight days of drinking water but refusing food, some of the strikers were separated from the others. This is another standard tactic to break up protests. Kutesa was put into segregation by OIC Regis. "The water was cut off. I couldn't wash my hands after urinating. I was complaining all the time," he says. The toilet would not flush. He was moved to another cell where there was water. While he was in segregation, officials checked him every four hours. Kutesa admits to being uncooperative about being awakened for blood pressure checks. He was already have trouble sleeping, and the doctor had discontinued his medication for insomnia. "So I was feeling like the medical staff are disturbing me, they are just checking me, they don't give me medicine for sleeping. And if I don't sleep, I feel disturbed. I feel disturbed in my mind. . . . The help I need, they don't do that. They don't help me in the way I want. But they used to tell me that they want to know how I'm doing."

Kutesa believes he was put in segregation to pressure him into ending the hunger strike. "That's what they always do, and that's the purpose of closing the water. Because when they cut off the water, they put water outside in the jugs, so that if you want water you tell the officer . . . so that they know you are drinking water, and how much you are drinking." The INS acknowledges that hunger strikers are segregated and monitored for medical reasons, which includes regulating what they eat and drink. This is standard prison procedure, adapted by the INS from the Bureau of Prisons. The prison or detention center, after all, is responsible for the safety of those in its custody. What officials omit in their explanation is the role that segregation and medical monitoring play in the power struggle of the protest.

Kutesa explains that food is also left outside the segregation cells of hunger strikers. "But for me," he says, "they used to put the tray inside my room." The smell made him sick, but officers refused to remove it. He was being singled out. "[Officers] said that they are doing me an offer. I said I don't need any offer." He became angry and threw the tray against the door. The following day an officer came to his cell with a written explanation of the charges against him. The officer said, "'Last night you disturbed the security and you threw the food. Do you accept the charge?'" Kutesa tells me, "I didn't answer him, I just kept quiet. And he told me that keeping quiet means denying. Then he asked me if I am going to sign the forms. I kept quiet. Again he said, 'Keeping quiet means you refuse.'" INS procedure requires that a detainee in disciplinary segregation be given a written explanation of the charges against him, as well as a hearing and the opportunity to dispute the charges. Compliance with this requirement is spotty. The next day officials again brought food into Kutesa's cell, and again he threw it at the wall. Another officer brought another charge sheet. "He ask me if I accept the charge. I kept quiet. I never answered him. He said, 'Keeping quiet means deny.' He asked me if I would sign the forms. I kept quiet. I didn't answer him. He said that means I refuse. And he went." Officers returned regularly to speak with Kutesa, using a videocamera to record their meetings.

Though Kutesa would be the last of the hunger strikers, he had begun as one of a large group, and theirs is a story of political organizing under pressure. Via fleeting signals in hallways and through windows, participants kept track of who was *not* participating in the strike in each dorm. "From beginning, it was A-dorm whereby some people ate. . . . In my dorm [i.e., A-dorm], there was a young guy from Haiti who ate, and one guy who had kidney problems [he ate also, though for a different reason], and two Chinese guys; there were five out of twenty-four. In C-dorm, it was just one guy [who] ate; that dorm is taking forty people. In B-dorm, they told me—I asked one guy when we met in the clinic—he told me it was about six people, I can't remember, six eating. . . . D-dorm, all of them they participate . . . because we had good communication." He didn't think any of the women participated; the men had no communication with them. After the strike the building's internal windows were tinted.

When I relay INS's contention that only one dorm had refused to eat, a rare laugh breaks through Kutesa's fatigue: "Yeah, they always lie, they always lie."

In surprising ways, a bit of humanity can show through the faceless bureaucracy. When New York INS District Director Edward J. McElroy responded to the letter from the CAAAV about the hunger strike, he wrote: "The tone of your letter and emergency vigil notice suggests that I am on some personal crusade to make intending immigrants miserable." The letter continues: "I understand that my position makes me an easy target for those who wish to advance or protest certain immigration policies. But to attribute my actions to personal agendas is wrong and hurtful." At a rally outside INS offices a few weeks later, a young activist from CAAAV urged spectators not only to send a "fax barrage" to the district director and to "make his life miserable" but even to "get his home number if you can. . . . Harass him!"

McElroy once wrote to Amnesty International, responding to the group's concerns about detention policies in New York, "In my District, *I have a facility.*"[16] The facility, of course, is a federal one operated by a private company, but McElroy's proprietary sense is common among wardens talking about "their" jails. McElroy's personal connection to the detention center is apparent again in the letter to CAAAV when he defends conditions and employee practices during the hunger strike by recalling a bit of local history: "In order to meet my legal obligations as established under the [Immigration and Nationality] Act, I fought for and established a detention facility near JFK Airport that could be used strictly for the lawful detention of individuals attempting illegal entry to the United States. The Wackenhut center is the result of that effort." In spite of the personal imprint on these policy statements, INS spokesperson Mark Thorn admits that interviews with this district director are extremely rare.

At Wackenhut's INS facility in Denver—or is it INS's Wackenhut facility?—I was a given a tour so thorough that I had to cut it short myself. But Patrick Cannan, Wackenhut's director of corporate relations in Palm Beach Gardens, Florida, warned me that the New York INS would be much more reluctant because of the city's diversity and the array of advocacy groups there, and, he explained, corporate headquarters would need the New York INS's approval before it could grant a media tour. Cannan had been in town for the opening ceremony in 1997. A smaller Wackenhut detention center in Rosedale, Queens, had been shut down; two years and $13 million later, the 65,000-square-foot warehouse had been converted, and Wackenhut signed a five-year, $49 million contract with the feds. There would be about one INS or Wackenhut employee for every two detainees at the new facility.[17] At the time, Cannan recalls, INS spokesperson Thorn told the local media, "'Enjoy it today, because after we're in operation, this will be a rare occurrence when we can have people walk through here.'" Then Cannan adds: "Maybe he's backed off on that since, I don't know. But I don't think he wants media going through there, for example, during a hunger strike, or just an opportunity for some of the detainees to get a point across to the media inside the facility. They can write letters, they can make telephone calls, things like that. But [Thorn] doesn't think he wants the media going through there to give them an opportunity to get their—actually to cause, from our standpoint, anyway, a disruption."

Before shifting gears there at the end, Cannan had been surprisingly frank about the policy to minimize the detainees' opportunities to speak out. He was right about Thorn's response, which came wrapped in the more predictable bureaucratic packaging. Media tours were allowed only before the center was "populated," because their "concern is the individuals" and, of course, because of "security." The New York District's restrictive policies apply to the press as well as to parole. In-person interviews with detainees are allowed, but, although some detention centers permit reporters to visit with prisoners for hours at a time, day after day, New York has its own idiosyncratic rules: a maximum of one in-person media interview of one detainee per week, and that interview lasts a maximum of thirty minutes. Why? "On the record," says Thorn to preface an amalgam of meaningless catchphrases, "we do it for the operational security and for the safety." The public affairs role of hiding INS operations from the public without being challenged is so ingrained that Thorn hardly bothers to make coherent sentences out of the denial. Since he doesn't have to explain his rationale to anyone, even the clichés are half-baked.

———

Because I had used up the available slot speaking with Emmy Kutesa, I had to wait until the next week to speak in person with Armando de la Vega, another hunger striker. I arrived to discover the detention center staff had not received the paperwork from INS authorizing my interview. A gruff Wackenhut officer pointed me to the pay phones I should use to call an INS official who was just upstairs. I walked across the small lobby, past the stacks of New York *Newsday* and an Arabic-language paper. (Detainees would report that newspaper distribution, one of their few links to the outside world, was halted during the hunger strike. That's another INS tactic, common across the country. Kutesa later said that in *Newsday* he had read an expression of support from the Latino Workers Center, letting him know that he was not alone: "That made me strong in my hunger strike." So apparently the newspaper ban was not total, but one can see why the INS would want it to be.) The pay phones didn't work, and the gruff but friendly officer invited me to use the lobby desk phone. He looked up the detained man's "alien number," handed me the phone, and gave me the INS official's direct line, none of which is a trivial favor in the obstacle-riddled INS world. I was put on hold, then disconnected. The officer was sympathetic. Later he would give me about ten extra minutes for my interview with de la Vega.

Armando de la Vega had operated a fast food business— *"comidas rapidas, como McDonald's"*—in Ecuador. He too was in the United States seeking protection from state-sponsored torture back home. Trying to do something about getting ripped off by auto-body repairmen in a major city, he found himself in a fight against corruption organized by a municipal mafia of judges, police officers, and car thieves, according to his application for political asylum. He began receiving threatening calls, then one day was kidnapped from his place of work. He was taken blindfolded to an unknown location, held in a small room, and tortured. His eyes fill with tears when I ask him about it. "It's like going back there," he says weakly; ". . . it was a day more or less like today . . . I'm remembering it now, and it's too powerful for me, it's too strong, it's very hard to answer you." And so we move on, since I am really here to document the protest, and our time is short.

"I found myself on a hunger strike," de la Vega explains somewhat formally in Spanish, "waiting for my situation to be clarified." We are seated across from each other at a small table in the visitation booth. Guards occasionally glance at us through a window, until someone shuts the blinds, controlled from outside the little room. On de la Vega's wrist is a yellow plastic ID bracelet with his name, country of origin, and alien number handwritten on a slip of paper laminated into the plastic, a perfect emblem of the odd combination of amateurishness and institutionalization that characterizes these detention centers. Around his neck he wears black beads and a medallion with a figure of Christ. He is thirty-four. His breath smells strongly of mints. He is talking more about the experience of being on hunger strike than about his motivation for the protest.

"I was really coming apart. I couldn't even get up out of bed. . . . I asked for a doctor. . . . The officers said no. They thought I just didn't want to get out of bed, so they took me by force and tied me to a wheelchair. I was so weak, I didn't feel anything anymore. My life seemed like it was about to end. I wasn't exactly sure what was going on. I thought they were taking me to a hospital, but they took me to a punishment cell. When they left me in that cell, in segregation [he says this word in English], I thought I was in the hospital. . . . And then I realized I was in a solitary room. It was my worst nightmare. My brain started trying to remember the time when I was locked in a room in Ecuador again. I asked, 'My God, where am I?' I knocked on the door and started to scream, 'What's happening?' Then I realized I was in a punishment cell. I realized that instead of taking me to get medical attention, they had taken me to a punishment cell."

He would be kept there for two days. On the first day medical personnel came to visit, telling him that he would die if he did not eat. On the second day, de la Vega recalls, "an immigration official came to manipulate me, telling me that I should eat, because if my attorney hasn't done anything, it's because he didn't want to—that my fight should be with my attorney." It comes as no surprise to those familiar with hunger strikes in INS detention centers over the past decade that an officer would be standing at de la Vega's isolation cell at the Wackenhut facility in Queens, telling him, with no justification, that he should blame his attorney and not the INS for his bad luck.

"I said that my attorney had done everything he could," de la Vega continues, "including to ask for parole, but they had denied me everything, including parole. I don't understand why they denied me parole precisely *during* this demonstration, when my attorney had requested parole well before." Robert Cisneros of Brooklyn's Central American Legal Assistance confirmed that he sent four parole requests to the INS district director over several months and that he literally received no answer until the denial arrived at his office by fax the day after the hunger strike began.

"Considering all of this," de la Vega concludes, "I *believe* that the INS took revenge against me for what the press was digging up about the problems here at Wackenhut. So when the press, the television, and all the media were coming directly to me, and my name was appearing in all the papers— I believe, and I'm convinced now more than ever, that the Immigration Service took revenge." De la Vega's name appeared day after day in New York's *Daily News, Newsday,* and *Diario/La Prensa.* In addition to letting his attorney know what was happening, de la Vega spoke with the Latino Workers Center, which put the press in touch with him. That's the way communication with prisoners often works. The network of local activists and media put this hunger strike in the public eye. Stories also appeared in the *New York Times,* in the Chinese-language *World Press,* in the French-Creole-English *Haïti Progrès* (my own), and, a few months after the fact, by a CAAAV activist, in the now-defunct, hip-hop magazine *Stress.* But in the often-surprising dialectic of power, it seems to be the INS's reaction to de la Vega's name in the papers that led him to think of himself as spokesperson: "The press used my name because, as the Immigration Service told me, I was the spokesperson for what was happening in this place."

The power struggle in Queens unfolded. After two days in seg, de la Vega was returned to his dormitory. Although he was still feeling weak, he says, doctors never came to treat him. Five days into the hunger strike, he had received no treatment beyond medication for nausea. He also complained that he was not receiving the psychiatric medication prescribed for him since his incarceration. He had been seeing a psychiatrist at a local hospital once a month, and a therapist once a week, to help him with "the nightmare that refuses to be erased from [his] mind." Finally the Wackenhut nurse gave him a pill. He didn't know what it was, but it helped to calm him. He was returned to the segregation cell for another day. An INS deportation officer came to ask him why he was on a hunger strike. De la Vega explained again that he was demanding a response from the INS. The officer told him that he should eat, then left and returned with something like milk that he said contained vitamins. De la Vega agreed to drink it for the sake of his health. "He tried to manipulate me using that, to say that I was eating, because the press was still saying that I was not eating. He was trying to manipulate me, and he's someone who can be very persuasive." The official offered to move de la Vega out of the segregation cell, because, in de la Vega's opinion, it looked bad in the press. But he wanted to move him to a new dorm where de la Vega didn't know anybody, so, as much as he hated that cell, de la Vega refused. This was not just a question of company but one of organization, and both men knew it. That's why group prayer services were prohibited and internal windows were darkened. The officer said that de la Vega's dorm was too crowded now because of new arrivals. In fact, he was finally taken back to that dorm by a Wackenhut officer, and there was plenty of room.

De la Vega pauses a long time when I ask how many days his hunger strike lasted: twelve. The gruff but friendly guard arrives to say that our time is up. I ask de la Vega if he wants to add anything, and he drops the details to make a broader statement: "The problem in this place is that the immigrants are suffering with fright, they are suffering with the fear that the Immigration Service or the judge will deny them political asylum, and that's why everyone detained here is so afraid. They don't dare denounce anything that goes on here. So some of them support each other, and some don't, because they think that by not supporting others, they are going to save themselves." He concludes by asking that "the entire community . . . be concerned about these people." On my way out, I thank the guard for going out of his way to help and for giving me a few extra minutes with de la Vega. He responds, "Don't tell anybody." An immigration judge granted de la Vega relief under the Convention Against Torture, and he was freed after a year and a half of detention in Queens.

In the Wackenhut lobby there are blank complaint forms preaddressed to the INS's Office of Internal Audit in Washington. There is a sign posted near the flyers:

> YOU DESERVE TO BE TREATED WITH
> PROFESSIONALISM AND RESPECT.
> DO YOU HAVE A COMPLAINT OF MISTREATMENT?
> WE WANT TO KNOW.

A week before the hearing that Judge Livingston set up in exchange for the pledge to eat, Emmy Kutesa was dragged from his bed and beaten, he alleged. About ten men in his dorm had written a letter to the INS complaining about the officer assigned to their area. The dispute was about control of the television as well as the officer's refusal to take a sick detainee to the clinic. Having received no response for about two weeks, the detainees refused to line up for the count. "I was one of them," Kutesa said. He remained in bed, was pulled out of it by two officers, and was dragged down a corridor where he finally "insisted to stand up" on his own. Instead, he explained, "one [officer] was stepping on me, another was kneeling on my back." While the one on his back held his arms, the other "kicked [his] shoulders first, and second under [his] eye." This time he was relieved when told that he would be put into segregation for six days. Kutesa reported the incident to the Wackenhut supervisor and to an INS deportation officer. A local attorney contacted Kutesa to interest him in a lawsuit, but Kutesa feared, quite reasonably, for the effect on his case and on the possibility of parole.

Kutesa was lucky. His detention lasted less than two years, and he was eventually released rather than deported. Friends and advocates with the Lawyers Committee for Human Rights threw a party for him. After a big meal, Kutesa said, "I slept like I was dead."

There were other protests by INS detainees that summer. As the New York hunger strikers dwindled to one man, between fifteen and fifty INS detainees jailed in Manchester, New Hampshire, were refusing to eat, and an immigration official promised to meet with them to discuss their demands. Outside Los Angeles, in Mira Loma, INS prisoners removed their orange jumpsuits and threw them onto the barbed wire, demanding to be deported rather than held indefinitely. Detainees at the Piedmont County Jail in Virginia began a hunger strike, and the leaders were quickly transferred to other jails. A group of Cubans at the Mansfield County Jail in Texas began a hunger strike and all were moved to the INS Service Processing Center in El Paso. These are the protests that we know about. At Wackenhut's INS detention center near Denver, prisoners decided against beginning a hunger strike, fearing that even a peaceful action could jeopardize their chances of being released.

In November 1999, exactly one month after his release, Emmy Kutesa spoke at a forum in lower Manhattan titled "Justice for INS Prisoners," sponsored by some of the groups that had supported him and his "fellow detainees" during the hunger strike. Other panelists (an attorney, an expert on prison privatization, local activists) remained seated during their presentations, but Kutesa stood up when he spoke, because, he politely explained, that's the custom in his culture. He was dressed in a coat and tie, and it was the first time that many of us had seen him in anything but the bright orange "pyjam." He spoke softly but audibly and clearly. Kutesa, who had dropped out of school when he was eleven, began by reminding the small audience that Uganda "is a country in Africa. . . . Everyone has heard of the continent Africa." Then he told us about being tortured in his country and about escaping into the hands of U.S. authorities. He spoke in some detail about his detention but eventually decided to take questions rather than try to tell everything.

"It's very hard to explain what happens in nineteen months and nine days," he said. "It's a long book."

In late spring 1995 immigration detainees in Elizabeth, New Jersey, engaged in a situation, an uprising, a melee, a riot, or a disturbance, depending on your terminology. They broke a lot of glass and destroyed furniture. The contract guards, none of them harmed, fled to the parking lot and called for local law enforcement backup. The most surprising part of this milestone in INS detention history is the Service's own postmortem of it.

The three-hundred-bed facility housing primarily asylum seekers was owned and operated for the INS by the Esmor Corporation. INS Commissioner Doris Meissner directed the Headquarters Detention and Deportation Division to review and investigate the June incident. The result was a seventy-two-page report[1] that reads very much like a report from Amnesty International or Human Rights Watch. It details complaints that immigrants' advocates could recite in their sleep: meaningless prisoner grievance procedures, arbitrary use of disciplinary segregation, verbal harassment, physical abuse. The report also notes the theft of detainee property (a category often overlooked by advocacy groups), the practice of waking detainees in the middle of the night "on the pretext" of security checks, and complaints by female detainees "that they had been issued male underwear on which large question marks had been made in the area of the crotch."

One distinguishing feature of the INS report is the concern with public relations: "Some of the decisions made by Esmor had a serious nega-tive impact upon relations between the INS and the general public since, in the public perception, INS is inextricably linked to the operations of the Elizabeth facility." In fact, the INS's Michael Rozos, formally assistant administrator of Miami's Krome detention center, was the officer-in-charge at the Esmor facility when it erupted. What happened at Esmor could hardly have come as a surprise. Elizabeth Llorente's excellent reporting on the detention center for the Bergen *Record* had practically predicted it. But in a bureaucracy, especially one in which the potential victims have no political or economic leverage, prediction is less important than dam-age control after the fact. According to George Taylor, Atlanta INS chief of detention, Headquarters officials exploited the buffer of private prison companies to shield themselves from accountability. He added: "There's no real governing body to drop the hammer when the hammer needs to be dropped."

Private company and government agency used one another. In 1988 Esmor had submitted a proposal to the Justice Department for an INS detention center to be built in the San Diego area. Confronted with the red tape of "state and local government agencies, local zoning regulations, environmental requirements and community organizations," Esmor sug-gested a "bold and innovative" solution. It would contract with the Viejas Indian tribe to lease acreage. "Because the Viejas reservation is considered a sovereign nation by the Federal Government, it therefore is not bound by the same state and local governmental and environmental regulations as are other locations in the San Diego area." Barbara Muller, a member of the Viejas tribe and an activist with one of the community organiza-tions with which Esmor seemed concerned, said, "It's kind of ironic to put a prison facility on an Indian reservation in America to house people from Mexico and Central America who are also Indian." Muller's sister Elida said, "We're already a prison, we don't need another jail."[2] The deal never went through; tribal chairman Anthony Pico later told me the coun-sel had turned instead to gaming "to establish an economic base for the tribe."

After the Elizabeth debacle, the Long Island–based Esmor Corporation became the Sarasota-based Correctional Services Corporation. CSC oper-ated a non-INS juvenile detention center in Tallulah, Louisiana, that was taken over by the state after repeated allegations of prisoner abuse. CSC was also forced to give up operation of its Youth Development Center in Pahokee, Florida, after a judge compared it to a "'Third World country that is controlled by . . . some type of evil power.'"[3] In the Pacific Northwest, CSC was having more success, and in 2002 the company received a new contract with the INS for a detention center in Tacoma to relieve overcrowding in the CSC/INS facility in Seattle. The new prison would be converted from an old meatpacking plant.[4]

It is worth pausing over the career of one member of CSC's board of directors, William Slattery. Slattery had been New York INS district director and was then promoted to the Headquarters position of executive associate commissioner for field operations. In 1996 some of Slattery's colleagues demanded that Commissioner Meissner remove him. According to the *New York Daily News,* Slattery's colleagues said that he "sat on allegations of brutality on the Mexican border that exposed poor training and supervision of border agents. Slattery was [also] accused of threatening disciplinary action against managers who reported problems." The *Washington Post* reported allegations that Slattery called off raids on Korean garment factories "after he was invited to social events with factory owners." The *Daily News* reported that "a former INS agent has alleged that Slattery obstructed a 1994 conflict-of-interest probe of Slattery's romance with agent Rosemary LaGuardia." The couple was later married. LaGuardia taught an ethics course at the INS officer training center in Glynco, Georgia, and she was later convicted of stealing from a department store.[5] Slattery left the INS and joined the CSC board.

Back in New Jersey, INS officials had decided for the sake of efficiency that Esmor itself should sell the rights to and equipment in the detention center, which it did, to the Corrections Corporation of America. The reaction of a *New York Times* columnist, John Tierney, can help us to understand how little the media seems to understand about the way the U.S. government operates. It is certainly a positive sign that the details of INS contracts made it into a column at all. But Tierney misses the point by accepting the INS's pallid mea culpa in the Esmor report, because he seems to have no knowledge of the agency's long-standing evasion of accountability. Tierney writes that CCA, which took over the Elizabeth contract, is "still running it to the satisfaction of the INS"—hardly reassuring to anyone who knows a little about INS or CCA operations.[6] CCA itself warned investors about the "risk" of "public scrutiny." In one suit against

CCA, Gaston Fairey represented Salah Dafali, a Palestinian, and Oluwole Aboyade, a Nigerian, both of whom were allegedly assaulted and then transferred after contacting the media about conditions at the newly satisfactory CCA/INS Elizabeth prison. The suit alleges that "CCA operated the Elizabeth facility under a policy or practice that authorized CCA staff to use abusive practices to control and discipline the refugees detained at the Elizabeth facility."[7]

About a year later the New Jersey INS district director banned the Jesuit Refugee Service from giving Bible classes at the CCA-run facility because it had discussed a taboo subject with the detainees: detention. The class had been reading Matthew 25: "I was a stranger and you took me in. . . . I was in prison, and ye came unto me." District Director Andrea Quarantillo said, "It was understood by all parties that detention issues would not be topics for discussion." Quarantillo also explained, "INS has no objection to Matthew 25 or any other Bible passage and does not seek to censor them. We only request that detention issues not be included in the lesson plans." Almost comical—but for the fact that the rate of suicide attempts in INS detention in Elizabeth is higher than in the New Jersey Department of Corrections, Llorente discovered.[8]

A young Swiss detainee—noting that not all of the guards are "compliant" and that many of them "suffer as well"—told me, "It's very clear that whole system is designed for intimidation." He had been detained in Elizabeth for just five days.

—

"Discipline, or rather 'dis'plin,' was their slogan," writes Nobel Laureate Wole Soyinka of what he calls the "poli-thug state" of Nigeria under military dictatorship in the 1980s.[9] The military and police "notion of 'dis'plin' was not to take offenders to the local magistrate court . . . but to make them do the frog-jump. For the uninitiated, this exercise requires that you attach your hands to both ears while you jump up and down in a squatting position."

Felix Oviawe, a state assemblyman from Benin State in Nigeria, gets down on the floor of his friend's house in Canarsie, Queens, to show me a variation on this ritual of humiliation. Because he was a democratically elected local politician who had opposed the military regime, Oviawe felt his life was in danger after the 1993 coup d'état in Nigeria, and he fled the country in search of political asylum. But he was not harmed in Nigeria. Arriving at New York's Kennedy airport, he acknowledged having a false passport and told U.S. immigration officials that he wished to apply for asylum. He was sent to the INS Esmor detention center in Elizabeth. After the 1995 disturbance, Oviawe—who had not been among the protesters—was transferred with about two dozen other immigration detainees to the nearby Union County Jail in Elizabeth. It was there that corrections officers forced him to kneel naked on the floor.

Oviawe loves politics. At his friend's house in Canarsie, on a short visit to New York, he spends his days watching C-SPAN on a giant-screen television. On the day that we speak, in May 1998, Congress is debating tobacco legislation. I convince Oviawe to turn off the volume so that I can record our interview. The only furniture is the tall director's chairs we're sitting in. On the walls are a couple of African masks and a poster of Malcolm X. "Right from time, when I was young, I picked interest in politics," he tells me. He is forty-three. "I read about people . . . who fought for the independence of Nigeria from Britain."

His father was a miller who sold wood to carpenters. Felix earned a bachelor's degree in mining engineering and was elected student association president at Federal Polytechnic in Akure. After graduating, he became the production manager in a cement company. He also taught physics and engineering at a technical college. In 1991 he was elected to the House of Assembly, the equivalent of a state legislature in the United States. He campaigned to improve the standard of living for the people in his district, the majority of whom were subsistence farmers—better roads would make it easier for them to bring their produce to market—while others worked in the oil industry. "There will be grading of roads and tarring of roads, and provision of water for my people," he says, as a congressman filled the screen; he had muted the volume but left the set on. As chairman of the Lands and Mineral Committee of the House of Assembly, he resolved a dispute with a neighboring state over oil deposits discovered by Shell. Twenty-two months after he was elected, on November 17, 1993, General Sani Abacha overthrew the democratically elected government of Moshood Abiola. The Houses of Assembly across the country were dissolved. "The crisis was on," says Oviawe. "I had no alternative. . . . I came seeking political asylum."

His brothers were already living legally in this country. One was an engineer in Los Angeles, the other a pharmacist in Miami. They bought a plane ticket for Felix, and he arranged a false passport because his diplomatic one had been seized. "I came in a different name," he explains to me. "When I got to the international airport, JFK, I went straight to Immigration, asking for political asylum. Then the Immigration took all my documents. I now presented myself as Honorable Felix Oviawe, because I came in a different name, you understand, and I told them the reason."

Oviawe stands up to tell me what happened after the transfer to the Union County Jail. "We are coming out from the van, about thirteen of us. As we are coming out, your hands are tied. A guard would grab you, throw you on the floor. You understand me? And someone else grab you, throw you back to the van. Somebody push you out again, then they throw you on the floor, another one would pick you, just continuous like that. They started beating us. Started beating us. Even while they were taking us to the cell, [a guard] said he feel like killing somebody. One of the guards, he said he feel like killing somebody. So he grabbed me by my shirt." Oviawe grabs my shirt from behind to demonstrate. "Beated my head on the wall. You understand me?"

"So we were now taken to the cell. 'Get into the cell.' We were asked to strip ourself naked. Three of us: myself, a Ghanian, and another Indian boy. We were three. We were asked to strip ourself naked, right in the cell there. Then we were asked to kneel down. We were asked to be on our knee. You are naked. Then, the next person to you, you grab his ear, you draw him by the ear, as you are on your knee, then the other one would drag the other person. We were there for more than three hours."

In the Canarsie living room, Oviawe explains that he and his two cellmates formed a small circle, each holding the ears of the person in front of him. "The guards, they started coming around. When they come around, one of them, very huge guy, he spat mucus. In short, it was so horrible. You understand? Some other [officers] started coming, to come and see if we had ever stood up from that kneel. We were there for more than three hours."

Oviawe pauses a long time. He has told this story many times by now. I ask him what he had been thinking as he kneeled naked on the jail floor. "My thinking was that maybe they were going to kill us. That was where my mind was going. It was the Ghanian boy who told me that they won't kill us, that I should have hope." It didn't seem like such a stretch for Oviawe to think he might be killed. "I just couldn't believe that things like that could happen here when they started doing that to us. For a good two days, it was continuous. In the night, at about nine, they would come around. You would remove even your underwear . . . we didn't have blanket, no nothing. They would increase the AC." He tells me that when the guards left, but left them naked, he wrapped himself in toilet paper to try to keep warm.

"In short, I just don't want to remember. I started having different kind of dream. There is a brother of mine who died here in 1988. I dreamt of him. He came and he said, 'What are you doing here?' In a dream. I told him: 'Here am I.' He said I shouldn't worry, that he was coming to get me out of there."

Oviawe tried to speak with the correctional officers. "I told them, you know I am a majority leader. Please. Don't do this to me. And they started teasing me and said, 'Majority leader! Majority leader!' And they grabbed me"—Oviawe himself is laughing now—"and they hit my head on the wall. You understand me? They started teasing." His laughter trails off, and he says, "Oh no." He pauses again and takes a breath. "I think I lived to respect this country because of what's happened in the long run. You don't just do things like that and go free." His very next sentence returns him to the van: "I thought they were now going to kill us. That was my thought." But this drive was to the next jail. It was a long drive, and the guards were armed. At some point Oviawe realized they were in Pennsylvania.

"Since I was already out of Union County, I knew I was going to make it."

Felix Oviawe had arrived at the Union County Jail along with about two dozen other detainees. These included a number of Indian Sikhs, as well as men from Finland, Albania, Nigeria, and Mauritania. The detainees were met by a gauntlet of correctional officers, some working their normal shifts, others called in especially for the "Esmor detail." The "beat and greet" reception included kicking, punching, and, according to the indictment brought by the New Jersey prosecutor's office, "plucking detainees' body hairs with pliers, forcing detainees to place their heads in toilet bowls, encouraging and ordering detainees to perform sexual acts upon one another, forcing detainees to assume unusual and degrading positions while naked, and cursing at and verbally insulting the detainees."[10] The pliers, it would turn out, were pincers used to cut plastic flex cuffs. Officers were also alleged to have forced their prisoners to chant "America is number one!"

Three Union County Jail officers were convicted on multiple criminal charges, including official misconduct and witness tampering. (One of the three primary defendants was not accused of abusing the detainees but of orchestrating officers' perjured testimonies to the grand jury.) The three men received prison sentences of seven years, with parole eligibility after a year or a year and a half. Jimmy Rice, Charles Popovic, and Michael Sica all, if I am not mistaken, shed tears at their sentencing. About eleven other officers subsequently pled guilty, and most received sentences of community service.

Defense attorney Anthony Pope's strategy was to depict the correctional officers alternately as heroes and victims. In his opening statement he criticized the "gross overreaction" of the prosecutor's office, calling it "the most unjust thing . . . you've ever seen in your life." As Americans, he instructed the jury, it is not just an opportunity but "by God, your obligation . . . to question your government." Bob Valaducci, another defense attorney, added depth to the anti-authoritarian argument. Our forefathers understood, he said, that when the enormous resources of the state are used "against one individual . . . it's not a very fair fight." Pope took every opportunity to remind jurors that the detainees were "illegals." "You know you had no right to come into this country, correct?" he asked an Indian man. In his closing statement, Pope repeated that what happened at the Union County Jail really began at Esmor, "which is housing people who came here illegally"—a fact that tells us "what kind of people they are."

The prosecutor's office went so far as to locate victims who had been deported and bring them back to Elizabeth for their testimony. Although Pope was right that much of the detainee testimony seemed rehearsed, possibly for the purposes of a civil suit that was being filed and would depend on evidence of lasting injuries, the overwhelming and consistent testimony of what happened that day was simply too much for the defense team. Witness Harpal Singh described the way that he was moved from the van into the jail: "Like you have a bundle of wood—he just picked me up and threw me outside." And if the testimony of a succession of detainees was not enough, the testimony of other correctional officers (COs) who had been promised immunity sealed the outcome. CO Juan Espinosa said of the detainees, "They were just mild people who just took it, actually."

Pope also did his best to challenge the repeated usage by witnesses of words like *abuse, beating,* and *torture,* and he tried to take advantage of the linguistic babble to imply that the detainees' testimony was coached. In his cross-examination of Balvir Shah, Pope first got the witness to answer yes to the question, "Do you feel that someone using a curse word at you is a form of abuse?" Shah had said that guards forced him to kneel and then told him to fuck himself.

"So they used the word *fuck?*" asked Pope. "You realize that the word F-U-C-K is used in a lot of different ways?"

Shah said, through the interpreter, "All I know is that this means you have sex."

"So you heard the word, and you assumed that someone wanted you to have sex, correct?"

"This is what he meant, the two of you [prisoners] have sex together."

"Sir, how do you know what he meant?"

"It could only mean that. It mean nothing else."

"Excuse me," Pope said to the court, and then, to the witness: "If someone said *go fuck yourself,* you would think that meant go have sex?"

"You can't do it on yourself," Shah responded.

There was laughter throughout the courtroom, which made the witness smile, and Pope himself smiled.

The judge said: "He told you."

Pope wrapped it up: "You heard the word F-U-C-K and you believed in your mind that's what he wanted you to do?"

"Yes."

Margarita Smishkewych, the supervisor of court interpreting services, who loved talking about the Spanish landscape and passionately quoted lines from García Lorca as we stood outside the courtroom, told me this trial was the most challenging of her career.[11]

Balvir Shah testified that "it was paining a lot" when he was thrown around by officers, so he "made a big sigh."

Prosecutor: "What do you mean you made a big sigh?"

"I said *hi,*" Shah seemed to say.

"You said *hi?*"

"Yes. In Punjabi, when you get injured, this sound comes out of your mouth automatically."

———

Pope's cross-examination on cursing was a fascinating if flailing excursion into linguistics, but it did not seem to help his clients much. On the other hand, when he broke down witnesses' accounts of heads being pushed into toilets, he seemed to break down their credibility as well. Pope managed to take the mind's moving picture of a CO forcing a prisoner's head into the toilet and edit it down to a single frame. What came before or after became indiscernible. Pope asked a detainee who claimed to have pushed back against a CO's hand, "If someone was constantly trying to put your head down, that would mean, wouldn't it, that your head was up?" Detainees who testified to having seen this act now admitted seeing a prisoner's head poised above a toilet but not in it, not touching the water. Pope returned to another of his themes by reminding jurors that not only is prison a different world from the one we are used to, but these detainees were from the Third World, and they had been in transit all day in the June heat, and the toilets had been cleaned the night before, and the prisoners might have just been drinking—the civilized COs might have been pulling their heads *out* of the toilets. Far-fetched as this may seem, Pope had made an impression by showing that so much of the testimony seemed overly practiced. There was no doubt that terrible things had happened that day at the jail, but I wondered if this dramatic detail had really been one of them.

From the windows of the courtroom one could see down to the adjacent Revolutionary-era cemetery in bleak, downtown Elizabeth. The trial was an important show for local law enforcement, and on the street county correctional officers gathered to protest the prosecution of their fellow officers. In the hallway outside the courtoom, one court officer, who was listening in whenever his other duties permitted, recognized me as a regular and asked one afternoon what had happened that day. I told him about the cross-examination on the toilet allegation.

"We had done that," the man said. "That's no big deal. It was a tool to fuckin' influence people." We had not yet introduced ourselves. Once we had, Frank told me that he used to work in the Union County Jail alongside some of the defendants and that forcing prisoners' heads into toilets and stripping them naked were common practice. I asked if I might jot down what he was saying.

A couple of weeks later Frank and I speak at length over several pints of Killian draught in a Hoboken restaurant-bar. Using a tape recorder seems touchy since the convictions in *New Jersey v. Rice* relied on clandestinely recorded conversations, but Frank doesn't mind. "You're not going to put me in jail," he says.

He orders a glass of ice for his beer. The confused waiter brings him ice water. "Nothin' for nothin'," Frank says to me in one his favorite punctuating phrases after sternly instructing the waiter simply to bring ice, "it's cold beer."

Frank had been a correctional officer in the Union County Jail for about ten years, although he no longer worked there at the time of the incident. His grandparents were born in Russia and Poland. His father was born in Newark and worked for General Motors. After a brief stint as a substitute teacher (low pay) and garbage company dispatcher (boring), he found a secure job in the corrections business. His first guard job was at the state prison in Rahway, a "dungeon" where inmates served lengthy sentences and where most of them were—he lowers his voice a moment—black. Then a former Union County inmate suggested that Frank get himself transferred there.

Frank is nostalgic about the jail. "It was pretty peaceful. There was plenty of cells, there was plenty of food. The guys who were going to jail at that time kind of knew each other"—neighborhood winos who needed to dry out, for example. "It wasn't that hard tough crowd, whereas ten years later it certainly was a hard tough crowd." That was 1979, and ten years later, with mandatory drug sentencing guidelines helping to overpopulate the jails, Frank's "nice little spot on the beach" looked a lot different to him.

"We're stickin' six pounds of shit in a five-pound bag at this point," he says. "You try to be fair, but how fair can I be? Call the county manager and tell him you're sleeping on the floor at night. It wasn't fair to put that burden on me. . . . It's pressure for everybody. The place was a powder keg. It finally blew up." Frank was talking about a riot at the Union County Jail. I hadn't asked about it, but it was clearly a formative experience.

"I never seen so many beatings in my life. Nothin' for nothin', [the inmates] were going to beat *you*"—he names four officers who were jumped and beaten by the rioters—"I don't think [the prisoners] fucked anybody, but they spit on 'em and [said] 'fuck you guys' and shit. And they always told you, if you ever get caught, you don't want to challenge the guy, you don't want to show your authority. Take your shirt off if you can. Just sit there and do what you gotta do. You realize that help will be there, and when the help gets there, then you can play the game, kick their ass. I think that's exactly what happened. It took about forty-five minutes. But when the jail was retaken, you know, when the men were back in position, they literally beat the shit out of them. I seen 'em put a mop bucket on a guy's head and hit him in the head with a fuckin' nightstick. This guy's ears still gotta be ringing. . . .

"Thank God they didn't get me. . . . That was by far the scariest day I ever had in my life." Perversely, I cannot hear his next words without Martin Luther King Jr.'s echoing behind them. "I think after that everything is inconsequential. Know what I mean? I'm really not too concerned about anything after that."

Although Frank feels that those post-riot beatings were justified, he does not think they are the most effective method of controlling a jail. "I think it's so much more effective to embarrass and humiliate a prisoner than it is to kick his ass," he explains. "You're kickin' his ass, that gives him the red badge of courage."

Frank takes pride in the fact that he was respected by prisoners as well as fellow officers. "I would make it my business to walk through every tier every day. That was my business, because I wanted to talk to these guys. I wanted them to have a little trust, a little confidence in me. I wasn't there just to be there when there was problems. I wanted them to kind of know me, and that I'm not here to take advantage of you. But when you took advantage of a prisoner—there's guys fuckin' prisoners—it's not appropriate. Unacceptable. You have to do something to this guy, 'cause if you don't do something to *him*, you're going to get no respect from the other fourteen guys."

He gives me another example. It's the "very sad story" of a young black inmate who wore thick glasses. A stronger prisoner used to force him to wash his jail uniform. The young prisoner complained to Frank but was terrified that he would be discovered complaining. So Frank told him not to worry and approached the stronger prisoner.

"'What'd I do?'" Willie demanded. (Frank does a convincing Northeast urban black American accent, not a caricature.) "I ask *you* the questions," Frank said to Willie. "How you get pressed uniforms in the fuckin' county jail? You got more creases than I got." He made Willie get a dirty uniform. "Put that piece of shit uniform on, then go back in that tier and sit in your bunk and shut your mouth. And if I hear another word out of you, I'll be back tomorrow. Today we started with uniforms. Tomorrow I'm going to put your fuckin' head in the toilet. Okay?

"You wanna call your lawyer, go ahead and call your lawyer. Tell him that you don't have a fresh uniform today. You're in the county jail, and you don't have a fresh uniform. You go tell your lawyer that." Frank enjoys telling the story, but he hasn't forgotten its pedagogical purpose. "He doesn't get hit. There's no reports written. And now when I go back on that tier the next day, I seen him in his bunk. 'How you doin', Willie? You all right? Everything OK? Good man, Willie, good man.' And you walk through. It's just business, you know what I mean? But I gained more respect that day for doing next to nothin'. . . .

"That whole toilet bowl thing: that's like an insult in jail. I'm not saying that that's common practice, but it beats the hell out of beating a guy. You going to give me a hard time? Listen, you jerkoff—boom! That's what I can do to you. You bring them down to a fuckin' ant in a moment, you know what I'm saying? It's better than beating them up. Jimmy Rice can beat them guys up, there's no doubt about it, right?" The principal defendant in the detainee beatings case, Rice is a tank of a man whom prosecutors charged with "pumping up" the other guards. Frank is solid, but he's short and a little plump.

"What's better? Stick their head in the fuckin' toilet bowl. It don't hurt you. It's humiliating. It don't really hurt you. And if Jimmy wanted that guy's head *in* the bowl, *in* the water, it would be *in the water,* there's no doubt about that. He got arms like you got legs. Fuckin' guy's gigantic guy, he's gi*gan*tic.

"Two more my friend, all right?" Our waiter brings the beers and a fresh glass of ice.

"Kickin' the shit out of a guy isn't going to do anything," Frank continues. "But that has to happen too. There has to a be a duke, man. I'm not a big tough guy. But I worked in jail where there's big tough guys. Nobody, but nobody, was tougher than Stanley B.—toughest guy in

America. Ronnie K., Louis P., Arnie O.—these guys are *men,* man. We're kind of like businessmen. They wear a uniform, and if you get out of line, you're going to have to talk to these guys. . . . I was in there for ten years. I seen twenty, thirty ass whippin's. Big beatings, man. But I never saw a [prisoner] complain about it. Guys came out of the hole two or three days later, shook your hand. . . . 'Sorry for all the trouble I caused, it'll never happen again.' And the jail, it ran like a clock."

He takes another sip of beer. "P. J. was another great jailer, another guy who could run a jail. He was an Hispanic." One night, Frank recalls, he and P. J. were working the midnight shift. P. J. had just finished watching Johnny Carson, and one of the inmates was "howling like a fuckin' wolf."

P. J. says, " 'Fella, let me tell you right now, you better shut your mouth or you're going to regret it.'

" 'Fuck you.'

"I'm standing there, and P. J. says, 'Get me a pail of water.' I go in the back, I get a pail of water. . . . P. J. takes the whole fuckin' pail of water, wings it at the guy. Cold water. Guy's sitting there in his fuckin' jail uniform, right?

" 'Get me another pail of water.' Gets another fuckin' pail of water.

" 'Open the window.' It's fuckin' November. It's about fuckin' thirty-five degrees outside. This guy gets a chill in him. P. J. says, 'Now listen, you son-of-a-bitch, you'll be quiet real soon.' Sure enough, two, three minutes later, man, quiet like a baby.

"I says, 'We going to go give the guy a warm uniform or what?'

" 'Fuck that guy, give him a warm uniform in the morning.' "

"So what are you thinking?" I ask.

"That's the way to run a jail. No reports. There's eight other [inmates] seeing it happen, you know what I mean? We didn't hurt this guy. We didn't do a thing to this guy. You know what I'm saying? You hit him with cold water in thirty degrees, thirty-five degrees. It's very painful, you know, but it's not kicking his ass. . . . Go tell your lawyer that I hit you with a pail of cold water and opened a window. See if she's going to believe that. See if she can *prove* that. What's wrong with that? I'm not saying that it's *right.* But what's *wrong* with it? . . .

"Guys knew how to jail then. They were real good jailers. I'm telling you, man, there's a real art in jailing. It's a real art. Some guys can do it and some can't. I think for prisoners too. I think some prisoners really know how to do it, and other prisoners have a real tough time doing it. You can spot the guys who are having a tough time. You try to help those guys a little bit, some guys who have psychological problems. . . . We're white guys—you get tossed into an institution that's all black, you're in a lot of trouble." Especially, he adds, if you're a "regular" guy, as opposed to somebody like, say, Jimmy Rice.

Frank found out about the officers' indictments by reading *USA Today* on a flight home from Las Vegas, and he was immediately afraid for them. "Nothin' for nothin'," he says, "Jimmy Rice is a very aggressive kid." Prosecutors emphasized that the detainees called to testify in *New Jersey v. Rice* had not been involved in the Esmor riot. But Frank notes, as the defense lawyers had, that the Union County guards were told the detainees were coming from the scene of a riot. Frank makes clear that he doesn't know what happened at the jail that day, but he's comfortable speculating.

"He's a very aggressive guy, and I would imagine when he tells you, whether you're in the bar or in the jail, 'Go this way,' I think it's in your best interest to go that way. He's a fuckin' Popeye, man. He's a big, tough guy. I've seen him wipe guys in the bar just like I've seen him wipe guys in the jail. Jimmy's not out of character. That's the guy he is. He's not [just] a big guy, he's a *tough* guy. And I think he felt somewhat slighted: he told all the [detainees] to move. They didn't move." Defense witnesses testified that the detainees remained in the vans when ordered by Rice to get out; one CO testified for the state that the prisoners huddled in fear. "I think [the officers] took advantage of them. They didn't speak English, they probably figured they couldn't really recognize them . . . it's like kickin' a fuckin' scared dog. *I* could never do that. *You* couldn't do that. But these guys kind of thrived on it. . . . I understand these [detainees] were causing some shit in the van on the way over, [saying] 'Fuck you guys,' [and] 'Hey man, fuck this.' I understand one guy pissed in the van or something. So now they're going to kick the shit out of 'em when they get inside? Fuck it, who cares, get a hose, wipe the fuckin' thing out."

"Jimmy's not a bad kid," he continues. "Jimmy's a good soul, man. He'd help you much more before he'd hurt you. But I think they got caught up in a frenzy. I think there was no leadership. . . . I think that frantic mentality took place. That fuckin' mob mentality, that pushin' and shovin' and smackin'. And I think once Jimmy did it, sure Popovic [a codefendant] did it . . . and I'm sure all the way down the line. I'm sure that Dougie Wynn did it." Officer Douglas Wynn had been granted immunity from prosecution in exchange for his testimony. Here Frank's anger surfaces. He feels sure that the COs who testified against Popovic, Seca, and Rice were equally culpable but, in standard criminal justice procedure, had traded testimony for immunity. A prosecutor's assistant admitted as much when she told me her office could have indicted every CO at the jail that day, but they wanted convictions, not just indictments.

Wynn, an African American and a former football player—a big man— seemed more frightened than any of the detainees while testifying to the roomful of COs and their families. He was shaking when we spoke for a moment in the hallway afterward. Weeks later the judge would have to clear the courtroom when CO supporters jeered and spat as the guilty verdicts were announced.[12]

——

"There's a lot of dark side to this country. . . . The word *foreign* makes them despise you. People have a lot of hatred."

Even three years later, Ghanian immigrant Eric Mensah—his birth name was Kwadjo, which means "Monday-born son"—could not understand how he got caught in the Union County incident. After experiencing racism in Chicago, Miami, and New Jersey, Mensah had to endure the racism of Union County correctional officers, and he was one of them.

Mensah picked me up from the train station in South Amboy, and we drove to his home in the Township of Old Bridge. On the way he gave me a racial-geographic tour of the place, telling me he was forced to sell his property in nearby South Amboy because of his color. He seemed to want to tell me everything about his life, though he asked me not to use a tape recorder because he didn't want to lose the movie rights to his story. Mensah's mother, in traditional African dress, sat watching television as her son and I ate pizza.

Then thirty-six, Mensah had left Ghana at the age of seventeen and gone to Romania. A friend of his father was close to the dictator Nicolae Ceausescu, so his family was able to have a successful tractor equipment business. But Mensah's goal was the United States; he was living in inner-city East New York, a section of Brooklyn, when his three-month visitor visa expired. One day INS agents showed up, but he refused to open the door, and they left. Soon after, agents walked into his psychology class at Manhattan's City College. "They handcuffed me right there," Mensah said. He was briefly detained at the Varick Street detention center. He still remembers the strip searches, and "the noise [was] overwhelming."

After he was released and collected his belongings from the courtyard where his girlfriend had scattered them, Mensah got his life back together and moved up to Harlem. With legal assistance, he obtained a green card, and he worked various jobs, including one with American Express and another as the food services manager at the United Nations. In 1992 he became a U.S. citizen and took advantage of the opportunity to change his name for no fee. He took the civil service exam and by 1994 was working as a correctional officer at the Union County Jail, a job he hoped would lead to the police academy. "My main profession was supposed to be an architect. I missed that opportunity."

Mensah never really enjoyed being at the jail: "I'm just there to do an eight-hour job." It didn't help that his tires were slashed and fellow officers told him, "Go back to Africa, you fucking monkey," or that one of the defendants in the case kept a Ku Klux Klan hood in his locker. The place was run by "jaundiced white boys," he said, and then apologized to me for his language. Mensah's theory of the prosecutors' strategy in *New Jersey v. Rice* is compatible with Frank's: use the black COs and their harbored resentments to bring down the guilty white ones. On the day of the incident Mensah was called in to help with the Esmor detail because he speaks several West African dialects. Sure enough, in the jail sallyport he met a Nigerian detainee sent over from Esmor—here's where the movie rights could come in—and the prisoner's only relative in the United States turns out to have been working in a hair salon with one of Mensah's close relatives down South. In any case, Mensah did little but watch the events that unfolded—or perhaps he didn't watch. Either way, he admits that he did nothing, and that's what he was prosecuted for.

"When you abuse people, that's when the adrenaline gets high. To be part of the clique, you have to abuse inmates. . . . The institution is built up paramilitary style. Your first 101 is that you don't report anything to the director." Mensah pled guilty to obstruction of justice. He was sentenced to do community service work at a soup kitchen. He almost lost his wife because of the stress of the trial.

Now Mensah was selling real estate in New Jersey. He was staring down at the table and fiddling with a pen he had used to doodle flowery shapes on a paper plate when he told me that sometimes he thought about moving back home. "I know life is not fair," he said. "But come on."

———

"It's a prison mentality," says Frank. "When you're sitting around, when you're hanging around with a lot of tough guys and there's a lot of tough things going on, you certainly do become a tough guy. I mean that's part of the business. There's no doubt about that." He adds that the jail hiring practice is getting less and less selective, even as the inmate population continues to swell. "You're getting the bottom of the barrel. You're getting guys who can't fuckin' spell their name. You're getting guys who are cheating on the test. These guys are not me and you taking the test. These are guys who should be janitors—not even janitors. These guys should be fuckin' criminals, but they're not inside the jail, they're outside the jail. You know what I'm saying?"

Here is what he's saying: "I don't want shoe salesmen, I want corrections officers. There's a big difference. If they want to sell shoes, or you want to sell carpet, go right ahead and go there. . . . But the jail job is a very personal job. . . . [There's] a lot of pressure in there. . . . [The inmates'] lives are being destroyed, their wives are getting divorced, or their wives are fucking their cousins. A guy's sitting in jail, he can't do nothing about it—you have to know when you can lend a hand to a guy, when to kick a guy in the ass. It's a very delicate situation, you know. And I think a lot of guys don't know how to juggle that act. That's what makes a good guard from a bad guard. Anybody can sit there and be a robot. Anybody can sit there and be a fuckin' Gestapo—Jimmy Rice, that was his job. He was a big, tough guy, so we used him: Jimmy, you sit in the office, drink coffee, and when we need you, we'll call you. And when we call you, we expect you to act in a certain way."

Frank cannot quite believe that his old friend and the others were going to jail themselves. "I don't think there were any people there rooting for the Indians," he says, referring to the Indian and Pakistani witnesses. "It was like 180 people in the courtroom, 150 were rooting for Jimmy, and the fucking Indians won." As we leave the restaurant parking lot in Frank's car, the olive-skinned attendant gives him change, pronouncing *three* as *tree.* Frank laughs, and says the guy sounds like an Indian. "That's funny, isn't it?"

Felix Oviawe had told me he believes in America because the defendants in *New Jersey v. Rice* were tried and convicted. And he said so before giving up his asylum petition, which became unnecessary after he won a green card in the State Department lottery.

Frank believes in the Constitution too. That's why he remains bothered about what happened at the Union County Jail that June day. It was bad enough that the correctional officers overreacted, bad enough that the state went after them, but then his old colleagues surrendered their rights to the overzealous government agents.

"These guys didn't have enough sense to just turn around and say, 'Fuck you, I'm an American. I don't have to talk to you.'"

Trucks loaded with fresh-cut timber still roll through southwestern Louisiana, though much less frequently than they used to. Today they pass fewer pulp mills and plywood plants and more prisons and jails, as well as a sprawling casino complex that lights up one rural stretch just south of Oakdale. The Santa Fe railroad terminated here and connected to the Missouri Pacific, and nearby river mills built in the nineteenth century made the lucrative timber industry possible. "Oakdale's frontier character has served it well," wrote a local historian.[1]

In the 1980s the region's largest employer was a paper mill; it has since closed. Unemployment in Oakdale reached 31 percent, and the average annual salary was $7,000. But the frontier spirit was still alive, and an enterprising Lebanese immigrant whose family had settled in the area saw a way to save the town. George Mowad was a general practitioner who used to treat local athletes free of charge and was an announcer at high school football games. He was also Oakdale's mayor. Mowad led a successful lobbying campaign to bring a new federal detention center to his town. The prison had actually been planned since the Reagan Justice Department "began incarcerating refugees as a matter of policy in 1981," writes Robert Kahn. Mowad would later tell Kahn that immigration prisons are "'a recession proof industry,' because if the U.S. economy suffers, the world economy will follow, which will lead to more undocumented aliens coming to the United States, and thus more employment for Oakdale."[2]

The new contract did bring new jobs, although Barbara Doyle, sole reporter for the *Oakdale Journal,* told me there has also been a downside. Locals left other jobs to work at the new prison. Police departments were especially hard-hit, Doyle said. Sometimes people would apply to a local police department to receive the training, only to leave for a job with the Bureau of Prisons. Doyle also noted, "We do not have the housing or the shopping malls to keep the money here." Still, the town celebrated its victory, and the edition of the *Oakdale Journal* proclaiming "We Got It!" now hangs in the Mowad room of Beth's Catfish Kitchen. At the local library, for some reason, the folder on the Oakdale prison is empty.

At a courthouse in Shreveport a clerk could still locate a copy of *McFarlane v. INS*.[3] On January 6, 1992, one Albert A. R. McFarlane, "on behalf of all Aliens/Detainees"—the names of twenty-two others were carefully listed in a clerk's small hand to show they had been sent copies of the judge's order—wrote a letter asking the American Civil Liberties Union to investigate "the constant deprivations of 'Human Rights' as well as 'Civil Rights' at Oakdale." This postscript is included: "When the Federal Bureau of Prisons knows about my initiative, please be advise[d] that I might be placed in 'Lock Down Segregation.'" Attached to the letter is a class-action lawsuit brought by the aliens/detainees against the INS and the Federal Detention Center (FDC) at Oakdale. The requisite self-taught jailhouse legalese alternates with grim lucidity:

> This Action arises under the laws of the United States, and the United States Constitutional Amendments . . . [and] under the Federal Rules of Civil Procedure (FRCP) that are hereby invoked. . . . The Immigration and Naturalization Service along with the Federal Bureau of Prisons, knows exactly what's taking place in this facility, but plays blind to the facts.

What are those alleged facts? Inmates who refuse to work are locked in segregation; the INS pressures detainees to agree to "accelerated procedures" in their cases; prisoners in the "Oberlin 2" segregation unit have no access to immigration law materials. There is more:

> All Aliens in this said unit are given a shower every two days, and must be handcuffed to and from the showers. Harassment by officers is a joke for

them, and racial slurs are echoed quite so often; it has become a routine for all officers to them it's a joke! It can take an alien/detainee up to two weeks or more to get a simple telephone call to his lawyers and loved ones. Alien has virtually no rights whatsoever to write the media, because on most occasions the letter will not ever leave the facility.

The complaint asks for no financial damages award. Instead, it "prays" for the "relief" of investigations into Oakdale, a proper law library, lawyers, and an end to "involuntary servitude." Added to this general list is the prayer that one particular detainee held for almost two years receive a decision on his case.

Attached to the lawsuit is a page-and-a-half typed document, "Policies of the I.N.S.":

> The intricate and inhumane treatment of Aliens/Detainees are so over-whelmingly high, that the I.N.S. is scared of being exposed.
>
> The purposes of holding aliens/detainees here are for deportation proceedings; but most detainees will let you know that they are going through another period of incarceration which is worse than that which they went through in a criminal penal institution. . . .
>
> The recreational facilities, which it is called; is similar to pig's sty! Wherein one must sit in the hot sun because one is locked in there for over two hours without being able to move or take part in any form of sporting activities whatsoever. . . .
>
> Only animals are treated this way! and someone in their right state of mind who believes in "God" would never in their right mind do such thing. . . .
>
> Immigration Judge's gives "Bonds" which most of times are virtually impossible for Aliens/Detainees to post, and which can range from $5000.00 up to $150,000.00. . . .
>
> The I.N.S. and its system of hypocrisy has virtually left Aliens/Detainees rejected, deprived, discarded and demoralized of their "Constitutional Rights" to life, liberty and freedom. . . .
>
> I, myself and my co-author are constantly considering and thinking if this is the So-Called-American-Dream; wherein one has virtually no "Rights"; and wherein one must suffer the consequences of a crime and its convictions two different times for the same offenses.
>
> Prepared, authored and edited by Mr. Albert A. R. McFarlane and Mr Derrick Whonder; Advocates of Human Rights

The case was transferred from the Eastern District to the Western District of Louisiana, where Judge James Trimble dismissed it.

Just a few months before the aliens/detainees had filed their dead-end class-action suit, the August 30, 1991, issue of *Southern Pride,* the newsletter (or, as the masthead puts it, "communication publication") of FDC Oakdale employees, included this item from the inmate systems supervisor: "All areas of ISM [Inmate Systems Management] are operating smoothly. There now seems to be a consistent flow of incoming and releasing detainees. If that is a sign for the future, the future definitely looks bright." In the same issue the warden gave a "hearty FDC welcome" to fourteen new correctional officers. One of them was an African American named Richard Franklin, whom I would meet about ten years later. I hadn't finished setting up the tape recorder at our first meeting when Franklin started telling me that when he worked in Inmate Systems, where aliens/detainees were processed into the facility, he used to see INS agents "jump on inmates"—that is, attack them—and then cover up their actions "by writing memos."

A New York woman whose husband was being detained in Louisiana by the INS had been given Franklin's name when she was looking for someone who might know a local immigration attorney. The New York woman, in turn, gave his name to me, and when I called Franklin immediately agreed to come to my motel room in Alexandria, not far from where he lives. He showed up with a friend, a former cop with a pending antidiscrimination suit against a local police force, who never introduced himself, amiably declined a drink of water, and eventually resorted to eating chunks of ice from a paper cup. It was summer in Louisiana. Franklin was dressed neatly in black slacks and a tight black shirt, with a gold chain around his neck. He's not a tall man but he's solid, a former high school football player. Like the nurse in Houston who married the Sikh detainee, Franklin gave no sign of having something to prove. She had been hoping to tell her story to Sally Jesse Rafael, and Franklin had been trying to get *Dateline* interested in his.

Richard Franklin was born and raised in Alexandria. His father, who died less than a year before we spoke, had been a bus driver for Rapides Parish. His mother had been working for the U.S. Postal Service for eighteen years. In 1998 Franklin graduated from Grambling State University with a bachelor's degree in criminal justice. He liked the idea of law enforcement administration, maybe with the INS, maybe with the BOP. Maybe he could be a probation officer. He was still young; there were possibilities. On the BOP application for the position of correctional officer was a short essay question: "Correctional officers must be able to remain calm and make sound decisions quickly in emergency situations. Describe what you have done which demonstrates your ability to respond quickly and calmly in emergency situations. Relate examples of critical, hazardous or life-threatening situations which required you to make decisions under pressure." Franklin printed his answer:

> It was a rainy night and I was driving my car with my wife and daughter, riding alone with me. As I attempted to avoid another car I went into a ditch full of water, and my car went under. I was able to stay cool and calm as I assisted my wife and daughter out of this sinking car. I feel I respon[d]ed quickly in this life-threatening situation and demonstrated the ability to think under pressure.

Franklin was hired. After a week of classroom training and three weeks at the Glynco academy, his starting salary was $18,900.

What he recalls about his first day on the job is the noise, but it wasn't a threatening noise: "[The inmates] wasn't hollering profanities or anything, they was just hollering, 'Hey, how you doing? What's your name?' and different things like that. I kind of felt comfortable. I got comfortable in the job. I really quickly came to see that it wasn't the inmates, it was the people you were working with—that was the problem." I remind Franklin that we're talking about inmates with criminal convictions.

"I looked at it like this. You had to spend eight hours there. We worked eight-hour shifts. If you were respectful and honest with them, they were going to be respectful and honest with you. And any shift I ran, it ran smooth. Never had to write an inmate up, never had to send an inmate to lockdown. The shift ran smooth. And it was basically watching your back, on who was the next officer coming in, who might say this about you, or might say that about you. That basically was it, though. I just never had a bad problem with an inmate." Within six months Franklin was promoted to R&D, or Receiving and Discharge—not packages, prisoners— officially called Inmate Systems Management. FDC Oakdale Warden L. R.

Turner, who had welcomed Franklin and the others in *Southern Pride,* decided to retire. Turner was "a very good man," Franklin says. "Everything really started to trickle downhill once he retired."

We were sitting at the little table in the motel room. We would talk there for a couple of hours, pausing now and then while he flipped through one of the large ring binders of memos, documents, and letters he had brought along. Our conversation continued the next day at his apartment, where he lives with his wife and three daughters, and where he was dressed in old work clothes and surrounded by even more binders and file boxes. Most of these were for telling his own story of racial discrimination, harassment, and retaliation in the Bureau of Prisons. But we talked mostly about the INS prisoners. Franklin acknowledged that they sometimes caused problems. For example, a fight between Mexicans and Jamaicans escalated and they threw pool balls at the guards. Such things happened, but Franklin truly considered them responses to mistreatment by INS officers. The INS spokespeople, I noted, would probably insist that any mistreatment by its officers is the exception.[4]

"You know," Franklin explains patiently, "working around these guys"— the aliens/detainees—"and being around them, and having a rapport around them, it's not like that. They are mad for things INS has done to them. And from every inmate or detainee I done met, INS done had some terrible, bad dealing with them—where they done either beat them up, or they done something to their paperwork, or they done done something with their money. [There's] always a problem. I mean, they always have a problem with INS. And, why the [INS officers] are so gung-ho about jumping on these inmates, it's just unreal to me."

Officer Franklin kept track of the details he observed. He tells me he felt like a cog in the machine when watching INS agents beat a man down. But he also refused to go along, and after just six months on the job he was writing memos giving his own version of events.

Oakdale's Federal Detention Center for INS detainees is on the well-manicured campus of the larger Bureau of Prisons Federal Correctional Complex. In addition to the INS detention center, the campus includes a federal prison for inmates doing time, a lower-security work camp for sentenced inmates, a building housing the immigration courts, and a credit union for employees. The INS administrative offices are just down the road, past a ball field, outside of the BOP complex. Behind that INS building, like so many others around the country, are lines of vans and buses. The windows of the green and white bus marked "U.S. Immigration & Naturalization Service" are whited out.

Officially, the INS detention center known as FDC Oakdale is operated *by* the Bureau of Prisons *for* the INS. In practice, Franklin explains, the two agencies "have a unique relationship. They work hand in hand." Equally important, many of the agents of the two agencies know one other, and they drink together and hunt together. The old racial divides are another constant source of tension, on the job and off. A Confederate flag was flying down the road from Oakdale when I visited. The *Oakdale Journal*'s Barbara Doyle, intending no pun, acknowledged that the town is "clannish."

INS generally moves its inmates in and out of the BOP-run FDC between midnight and 6:00 A.M. "It's always done at night," Franklin says. He has worked both shifts. "I done worked them coming in, and I done worked them deporting them, when they're leaving out. . . . So I done seen them [INS agents] come in there one, two in the morning and start a ruckus. For no reason at all." Sometimes, Franklin says, the detainees were in a good mood—"They glad they're being deported"—and the INS agents would simply provoke them: " 'Your ass is getting out of here today, huh? We ain't going to have no trouble from you, huh? 'Cause you know . . . we'll beat your fuckin' ass.' When you talk to somebody like that, that's starting hostility. It makes a person hostile. And they used to do it all the time, just a constant thing." Franklin says he regularly heard Oakdale INS officers talk about stopping the bus just to show a prisoner "who the boss is." "They thought they were what I call the 'top shit' of INS. They were the ass-kickers. . . . They talked about it and bragged about it."

—

The backward logic of corrections was part of contemporary INS detention from the start: if someone is locked up, then by definition he must be a security threat. Even the absence of danger must be viewed as danger in disguise. As Eddie Calejo summed up about the conditioning of INS guards at Krome, "For all we know, they're murderers in their own country." When the inmate simply can't take it anymore, as at the Esmor prison in Elizabeth, then suddenly the violence of the jailer has become justified. And here we are speaking only of asylum seekers; things can only be worse for the inmate who actually has a criminal conviction of any kind on his record.

Between 1980 and 2001 the combined prison and jail populations of the United States rose from about 500,000 to almost 2 million.[5] Mandatory sentences for drug crimes in the 1980s played a key role in the increase. The 1986 Anti–Drug Abuse Act not only increased the prison population, it helped to lead to an increase in the INS detention population. That year, the INS began its Alien Criminal Apprehension Program (ACAP), which entailed devoting more resources to locating aliens doing time in prisons and jails in order to apprehend and deport them more efficiently. Political rhetoric of the 1980s brought together two indefensible enemies of the state: the criminal, especially the drug criminal, and the alien.

Eric Sterling, now president of the Criminal Justice Policy Foundation, was counsel to the chairman of the House Subcommittee on Crime in 1986, and he was actively involved in creating mandatory sentences for drug crimes through laws that took discretion out of the hands of judges. In Ofra Bikel's documentary *Snitch,* Sterling says his role in drafting those laws was "probably the greatest tragedy of my professional life."

These laws came about in an incredible conjunction between politics and hysteria. It was 1986. Tip O'Neill comes back from the July 4th district recess, and everybody's talking about the death of Boston Celtics pick Len Bias. That's all his constituents are talking to him about. And he has the insight: *Drugs, it's drugs. I can take this issue into the election.* He calls the Democratic leadership together in the House of Representatives and says, "I want a drug deal. I want it in four weeks." And he set off kind of a stampede. Everybody is trying to get out front on the drug issue . . . I mean every committee—Merchant Marine & Fisheries, Interior and Insular Affairs—not just the Judiciary Committee—Foreign Affairs, Ways and Means, Agriculture, Armed Services—everybody's got a piece of this out there, sort of fighting to get their face on television talking about the drug problem.

These mandatories came in the last couple days before the congressional recess, before they were all going to race out of town and tell the voters what they're doing to fight the war on drugs. No hearings, no consideration by the federal judges, no input from the Bureau of Prisons. I mean, even the D[rug] E[nforcement] A[dministration] didn't testify. The whole thing is sort of cobbled together with chewing gum and bailing wire. . . . And we see what these consequences are of that kind of legislating.[6]

"That kind of legislating" foreshadowed Congress's anti-immigrant rush to mark the Oklahoma City bombing anniversary in 1996, as well as passage of the USA PATRIOT Act six weeks after the September 11 attacks.

In 1986 the INS and the BOP also began a joint effort to house "criminal aliens" whose sentences were completed, in order to deport them. They would be held in the nation's largest immigration detention center to date, FDC Oakdale. The INS commissioner at the time was Alan C. Nelson, who, after retiring from the Service, would become a consultant to the restrictionist Federation for American Immigration Reform (FAIR) and a supporter of California Governor Pete Wilson's proposal to prevent U.S.-born children of illegal aliens from automatically becoming U.S. citizens.[7]

The year the Oakdale prison opened INS investigators prepared an internal report on "the newest criminals," describing "organized ethnic crime groups" said to include Chinese gangs, Japanese and Vietnamese organized crime groups, Canadian motorcycle gangs, the Sicilian mafia, the Israeli mafia, the Greek mafia, Korean rings, Colombian and Marielito-Cuban cocaine rings, Nigerians, and Haitian-controlled drug rings.[8] The INS report wryly observes, "Rastafarians are not just noted for Reggae," though ten years earlier a detailed special report from the El Paso Intelligence Center on the Rastafarian movement had warned, "It is important to remember that not all Jamaicans are Rastafarians and not all Rastafarians are criminals."[9]

—

The first time Richard Franklin saw the INS "ass-kickers" at work, the inmate was Jamaican. Franklin was working the computer in R&D, logging in the new arrivals. The usual "processing" was in progress: inmates being moved in, fingerprinting, mug shots, property storage. A new detainee wanted his box of property so that he could count the money he had come in with and make a note of it. "The guy just wanted his property. That's all he was asking for," recalls Franklin. The Jamaican had good reason to want to count his money. Franklin flips open one of the binders: "I have some paperwork here where a guy worked hand in hand with me"— he's referring to a fellow officer who will join us but who prefers anonymity.

"He gave me all this paperwork off different inmates. Well, staff members stole these inmates' money, the money that they were being deported with. And I got some of the amounts here." He hands me a single-spaced document, maybe a dozen pages: inmate names and alien registration numbers alongside dollar amounts left behind in their accounts after deportation. "$700 dollars was stole, $524 dollars, $311 dollars, $731 dollars . . ."

The Jamaican didn't get to count his money. "Two of the INS officers picked him up and slammed him to the floor head-first," Franklin continues. "When they did that, the other two officers walked in from INS, and they start kicking him and punching him and telling him he wasn't going to get nothing, and cursing him out. . . . I can remember the inmate. I was sitting in the computer room with the door open. They were about from where I'm sitting now to that wall." He gestures beyond his friend perched on the edge of the motel bed to the wall about fifteen feet away.

"I can remember the inmate telling me, 'Young brother, you going to let them do me like this? Are you going to let them do me like this?' And one of the INS officers . . . punched him in the stomach. They locked him in the cell. They never took the cuffs or the shackles off of him. They left."

That detail about the cuffs and shackles matters to CO Franklin, because it tells him something about the agents: not only will they brutally beat a man without reason, but they will violate procedure to do it. Typically, after dropping off prisoners with the BOP, INS agents would take their chains with them. But in this case the INS agents left the Jamaican man in INS chains in the BOP processing area. "These are *their* shackles and chains. They left." Soon enough, however, they returned, memos in hand. They already had "two other BOP employees to side with the story," Franklin says, "Then they wanted me to go along with it. I was the only left-out one. I told them no. I'm not signing that. I'm not going to go along with that. That didn't happen like that." He wrote up his own version of the incident. "And that's when I started getting, 'You not a team player. Whose side you on?' You know, 'These fucking inmates, who care about them?' You hear that all the time. From INS *and* the BOP. They work hand in hand. If it's to do an inmate in, he going to get done in."

I ask Franklin, somewhat apologetically, what it was like to watch the Jamaican man get beaten down fifteen feet from him. He replies: "I'm a peon in the system. They really didn't care what I thought. And whether I went along with it or not, the inmate still got sent to the hole. Their version of the story compared to my version of the story—[they would say] 'We going to win regardless.' I had to stand fast against that hate. I'm not going to participate in that. That was wrong. Every time I see it, I'm going to report it, whether nothing gets done about it or not. Every time I see you all mistreating an inmate. With memos. Because the BOP has a stickler for [memos], and INS has the same thing. Every time something done, they want it on paper. Write it down. Put it in memo form, and we'll take it from there."

Paper and paperwork: these words appear twenty-five times in my sixty-five pages of interview transcript with Franklin, and twice the transcriber wrote "[shuffles papers]." In my own paperwork now is a blank copy of the Department of Justice Bureau of Prisons Incident Report. On the back of it, I jotted down what Franklin said when he handed it to me: "When you want to get an inmate in trouble, that's all you need." He explained: "You got a lot of officers that know this. 'All I got to do is put the paper on you. When I put the paper on you, you going to the hole.'"

It was dangerous enough for Franklin to challenge a supervisor for calling him "boy" in front of other officers and inmates. But his refusal to go along with the unwritten procedure for writing memos challenged the infrastructure of denial. Just as one of those Houston nurses had so admired the other for using the institutional obsession with paperwork to her own advantage, so Franklin's tone of voice conveys his respect for inmates who knew how to do the same: "These Nigerians . . . put the paperwork on anything. *Anything.* They was watching. They made us so tight." For example, they could make sure their outgoing mail actually went out. "Everything they sent out that prison was documented. It was roped out. They made appointments, you know." Usually an inmate would deposit mail in a mailbox on the yard, and later an officer would collect it, but that doesn't mean it would be sent. "These [Nigerian] guys would get their [BOP] counselors to walk them to the mailroom so they could hand-deliver that mail to the officer, watch him stamp the mail, watch him sign the card, so they'll know, 'I got your signature on my card. This mail going out.'"

INS officials like to remind journalists and lawyers that there is a grievance procedure available to all detainees. Franklin's initial response to that does not show up on paper. He rolled his eyes. Then: "That's baloney. An inmate or detainee can put in for a grievance [and] it's, 'We going to take

it to the proper procedure, it's going in the proper file, 'File 13,' the clos-
est garbage can. . . . I guarantee you, I guarantee, I could walk to the Bureau
of Prisons right now, and if I'm hired, go on back on to the job, inmate
don't say nothing to me, I look at him and say, 'You going into the hole.'
I go to the lieutenant's office and say, 'He looked at me like he was going
to jump me.' . . . [The lieutenant will say,] 'Write me a memo.' Within
an hour he'd be in the hole. My word is law. The inmate could be totally
right. What I say goes." How often does that happen? "That goes on all
the time. That's constant. That's every day."

Then there's the legal paperwork, the inmate's lifeline. Even on the outside, as Franklin knows, it can be an interminable battle against unac-
countable power. When I ask for his take on the recurring allegation that
detainees have been deported while their cases are still pending, Franklin
replies: "They do it all the time. I done seen inmates come in there crying, with the paperwork in hand, saying, 'I go to court tomorrow.' . . .
[But] the young officers that they bringing in, they teaching them to have
this bully-type attitude. . . . These inmates are nothing to them. And that's
just the way that they feel."

The "bully-type attitude," once again, implements national policy. In
the early 1990s, as the so-called war on drugs was widening into the unac-
knowledged war on immigrants, the Immigration and Naturalization
Service reported to Congress that the "due process requirements" for handling "criminal aliens" "contribute to administrative burdens and delays
in the administrative deportation process." A publicity video of the
Oakdale prison's opening ceremony concludes with military band music
as the words "An Opportunity for Due Process" scroll across the screen.[10]

One day in FDC Oakdale's Oberlin A, a lockdown unit, officers were conducting a routine search for contraband. Franklin explains what happened:
"They took some legal paperwork from an inmate, and the inmate wanted
[that] legal paperwork," so he started yelling about it. The officers "geared
up" to "rush" the unarmed but angry Jamaican detainee. "That's going on
all the time. Some inmate got to be rushed." When the inmate set his mattress on fire, the lieutenant on duty held off the "rush" and simply closed
the Jamaican's cell door and locked the food trap on it. The lieutenant let
the room fill with smoke. The inmate, Franklin recalls, was "foaming all
at the nose, beating on the door to let him out, and the lieutenant stand-

ing there laughing at him." Franklin names the lieutenant. "When they finally opened the door, the inmate collapses, they drag him out, but they laugh. They put out the fire, but they're laughing about it." The lieutenant told the unit's head officer to write a memo. "'Just say he set the cell on fire with the mattress.'" Then they cuffed the inmate and dragged him to the hole.

Franklin's mention of the food trap in the cell door seems to remind him of something. "Sometimes, you leave those traps open, them inmates they'll throw piss on you. But they'll do it if you done done something to them. They respect you if—[say] I come down on the SHU [Special Housing Unit] block. This detainee know he hadn't seen my face on that block. 'Hey, sir, how you doing?' He'll talk to me. 'Is officer such-and-such around?' 'Cause we all wore name tags. They knew who they wanted to get. So if you done done them something, you going to get something done to you."

Again, Franklin seems to be overstating his case. But it isn't *his* case. The details of the stories Franklin tells me were only incidental to his own complaints against the BOP, even though these incidents helped to make it impossible for him to work within the federal prison system. In any case, is Franklin really saying that inmates would never go after an officer without a "reason"? He gently interrupts me. "I understand. Let's put it like this. I have never seen, in my eight years of Bureau of Prison experience . . . I just never seen an inmate get totally, completely out of the box with INS or with BOP [so that the inmate] deserved to get something done to them . . . I just ain't seen that." As for what an officer should do if he's just walking by a cell and an inmate throws piss or shit on him, "Write him up. Write him up. What else you going to do?"

Were there any officers who saw things Franklin's way? "It was very few. You know, I was considered radical. When I fought the system, employees that didn't even know me or didn't have nothing to do with it fought against me. And basically, it was to keep their job." Around the time Franklin was fighting the system in Louisiana, an INS investigator working in Philadelphia described the way in which agency discrimination against Africans extends beyond the prisoners to officers who try to help them. INS investigator Archie L. Graham told Deborah Sontag that "he felt particularly uneasy with two agents called 'the African killers' because they singled out black immigrants from Nigeria and Sierra Leone. 'They went out specially for them, and they'd tear up their papers and throw them away,' he said. 'I didn't go along with it. I'd say, "That's not right." They'd say: "You don't like it, go back where you came from. Go back to Africa. We'll deport *you*."'" Graham is African American.[11]

But INS arbitrariness is not always linked to skin color. In the lobby of the immigration court building down the road from FDC, a white INS detention enforcement officer chatted with me for a few minutes: "I'll tell you what's wrong with the system. They make up their own policies around here. . . . We got discrimination. We got retaliation. We got violations. We got favoritism." He was talking about the treatment of detention officers, not detainees, and he asked to remain anonymous for fear of losing his job.

It goes on and on, almost unbelievably. Almost. Franklin describes the calculated cruelty that could be worse than outright physical violence: "The beating, that's bad. [But] I done seen INS come in there on inmates they don't like and spit in their food. . . . When they come in with the bus, they bring the inmates off the bus, line them up, we go outside, pat-search them down. [The INS agents] tell you, 'See that son-of-a-bitch in the back, he mouthed all the way here. We got something for him.' An inmate got a look on his face—'Oh, shit, what's going to happen to me when I get in here?'" Franklin reminds me that many of the INS and BOP officers know each other, so working together against a shackled alien/detainee arriving on the government bus comes easily to them. "Almost every time we had a bus, they had an incident." Franklin snaps his fingers for rare emphasis: "Automatically, they got attitude with that inmate. Don't know him from who-shot-John. Just from what the INS officer done said, your ass is in for it. So they lock them up in the cells back there, they start passing out the trays. They'll put everybody in one cell, and take that one and put him over in another cell by himself. Isolate him from everybody else. They'll spit in that food. Stir it up. Spit inside that food and hand it to him. And then peek in the window while he eating it and laugh. I done actually seen them do this. It's funny to them. That's a night's work."

At the Oakdale prison's ribbon-cutting ceremony in 1986, BOP Director Norman Carlson said: "I'm sure there will be critics who will say it's too plush."[12] Richard Franklin says: "If a detainee, an inmate of INS, comes up and says something happened, it has happened. I'm telling you to believe it, because if I hadn't seen it with the naked eye, I probably would have a different view. But from viewing it and seeing it and being a part of it for eight years, they not lying.

"Look, these inmates are done in. No respect. Your manhood is taken away when you locked behind them doors. And that's just it. You not considered a man to them. If you not wearing the green INS uniform, or the white and gray BOP uniform, you not considered a man. You considered some of the scum of the earth. You're a criminal, and that's just it."

Laurie Kozuba looked at the built-in china cabinet in the dining room of her Mesquite, Texas, home and started to cry. Things whose permanence she had long taken for granted suddenly seemed fragile. It had never occurred to her that her husband of eleven years, a legal permanent resident and U.S. military veteran, could *be* deported. But Laurie Kozuba is a U.S. citizen, and her husband, Danny Kozuba, is not. A reporter had called to ask what Laurie would do if her husband lost his case and was, in fact, deported. She was sitting at her computer and staring at the china cabinet. She cried, she explains, "just because it's always right there." In that moment the Texas girl who had grown up on Civil War reenactments along Interstate 10 with her father—she remembers how he would set his 35 mm camera inside a mockup of a nineteenth-century box camera—understood that if her husband lost, she would have exactly two choices.

"I can choose my husband or my country. And I think that my country can go to hell."

Laurie's father's family immigrated to the United States from Alsace Lorraine and settled in New Orleans, where he was born in 1921. When he was eight, his family moved to Houston. Laurie's mother's family came from Germany, via Tennessee, to the Dallas area, where Laurie was born in 1959. In this quick history, she wants me to know that her father's father was excommunicated from the Catholic Church because he married an

Episcopalian. "One of my father's old mantras was that my rights end where the next guy's house begins. And that I cannot demand rights that I'm not willing to give other people. That is democracy to me." She adds that she does not consider herself idealistic. "[But] I always believed that, beneath it all, Americans were fair-minded."

Danny Kozuba's life is summarized in a flyer produced by his wife. His father had come to the United States legally from Canada via Ellis Island after writing letters to the Dallas Chamber of Commerce and securing a job as a plumber. The family followed in 1958, when Danny was five. At fifteen, Danny began working. Eventually, he would own and operate a commercial kitchen installation business. During the Vietnam War, he served in Germany and was honorably discharged. Laurie adds—this is not in the flyer she hands out—"Danny doesn't even like to be called a veteran because he feels it dishonors the guys who actually went to war, even though he had no control over that whatsoever."

When Laurie and Danny met, she was nineteen and he was twenty-six. Just as vividly as she recalls his custom-restored '68 Chevy Stepside pickup, she still sees his face from that time, a lifetime ago, when he had a drug problem. "He looked horrible. Horrible. And his skin was ashen, his cheeks were sunken, and he looked like a walking dead man. And I knew then that he was in serious trouble. He was either going to die or go to jail." He lived and was convicted of methamphetamine possession. She was relieved that he went to jail because "that meant there was a chance—that he had a chance to get his life back, that he could be okay." In 1992, while Danny was still doing time, they married by proxy; contact visits were prohibited. Laurie visited him once a month, driving 426 miles round-trip to Navasota, Texas.

Danny served three years and upon parole in 1993 was detained by the INS, which began deportation proceedings. According to the law, his convictions made him "deportable," so now an immigration judge would give him a chance to explain why he should not be deported. At these hearings immigration judges are interested in learning about such things as family members who are U.S. citizens, community ties, how long one has lived in the United States, successful work history, military service, and rehabilitation. In Danny's case the judge was satisfied and granted him a waiver of deportation. After six weeks of detention in the Houston Processing Center, Danny was released on bond. But the INS appealed the judge's decision, and the case sat before the Board of Immigration Appeals (BIA) for more than two years.

In the meantime, immigrants bombed the World Trade Center, an American citizen bombed the federal building in Oklahoma City, and one of many successive waves of anti-immigrant hysteria swept through Congress. In 1996 Congress passed and President Bill Clinton signed into law the Antiterrorism and Effective Death Penalty Act (AEDPA) and, six months later, the Illegal Immigration Reform and Immigrant Responsibility Act (IIRIRA). Taken together, these brought unprecedented changes in U.S. immigration laws. They dramatically expanded the categories of crimes for which legal residents could be deported. They eliminated the opportunity for people like Danny Kozuba even to *apply* for waivers of deportation. And the government applied the new laws retroactively. The law had changed after Danny Kozuba's deportation was waived by an immigration judge and after the INS's appeal was first filed, yet now he was no longer considered "statutorily eligible" for "relief." On Good Friday, 1997, the Kozubas received a letter from the BIA. The INS had won its appeal of the judge's decision. The last line of the letter, Laurie says, was like a kick in the chest: "Daniel Kozuba is ordered deported."

Their lawyer's advice was to change the law, so Laurie decided to try. She wrote letters to representatives and senators but found no help. "They don't want to hear it. He is a 'criminal' . . . not to mention that he's an 'alien.' Well, the man's been here all his life, he's contributed to the infrastructure of this country, he served this country in the military, how can he be an alien?" In a rare moment, her sentences start to fracture under the pressure of her indignation. "Granted, he's a legal permanent resident. But you're telling me that this little piece of paper, this sort of official, you know—people can be living together and still be married, you know what I'm saying?" To make matters worse, "there's a lot of great immigrations issue organizations out there, but nobody dealt with criminal aliens." That would change, in large part because of Laurie's efforts.

"I didn't think we had time for somebody else to start a coalition," she continues. "I got a computer, I got the Yellow Pages out, and I got the fax number for every single immigration lawyer in Dallas." She wrote a letter outlining her case—her husband's case—and faxed it to the lawyers, asking them to share it with clients who might be in similar situations. By the end of 1998, just a year later, she had heard from perhaps two hundred families. She wrote summaries of their cases too. "I just started gathering these profiles, I wasn't sure what I was going to do with them yet." Since a coalition needs a name, Laurie and her sister-in-law started playing with acronyms. "I wanted to make sure that the message comes across: these are citizens and immigrants who are bonded together." Her group would be called Citizens and Immigrants for Equal Justice: CIEJ, pronounced *siege*. She liked the ambiguity. Who was besieging whom?

To the extent that they created a siege, CIEJ did it in Washington, D.C. Laurie has been there to lobby officials more times than she can count. New York University law professor Nancy Morawetz and her students helped Laurie with "Immigration Law 101," she says. She was hooking up with immigrants' rights groups, and before long CIEJ would be at the center of FIX 96, a nationwide campaign to reform the 1996 immigration laws.

"That's when I [really] learned about detention. . . . I was still sort of blissfully ignorant. Because if I had realized then what this was really going to do, it would've scared the shit out of me. . . . You have to listen to the pain and anguish of the families every day. You're there when they are deported. You are there when they call and tell you about the horrendous conditions that their loved ones are being forced to live in. Detainees call you, and you get letters from detainees: 'Ms. Honorable Laurie Kozuba'—it's just amazing, amazing, the helplessness that people are feeling, and they are literally begging for their lives."

Danny eventually won his case, but Laurie's work continued. "Where's the redemption?" she asks. "Where do we finally say to a person, I guess you've proven yourself, I guess you've rehabilitated, I guess I'll get off your back?"

In Houston, at one of the early CIEJ vigils, a little girl had held up a sign almost as big as she was. "I guess I just snapped," Laurie recalls, "because the sign said, 'Please Don't Take Our Daddies.'" Laurie put a photo of the little girl and her sign on a CIEJ brochure. An aide to Texas Representative Lamar Smith looked at the photo and said, "'She's going to be better off without him.'"

———

Marlon Rajigah only served four months on Rikers Island, but when we met in summer 2002 he had not seen his eight-year-old daughter, Natalia, in two years. The reason: after his criminal sentence was completed, the

INS not only detained Rajigah unnecessarily while his deportation case was adjudicated but also kept him far away from his wife, his friends, his home, and his young daughter. I met Rajigah's wife, Rita Dave, at a CIEJ rally in New York days before her husband was to be transferred into INS custody after serving four months of a six-month sentence for a statutory rape conviction. He had no previous record. Rajigah and his wife maintain that he was falsely accused. After being convicted by a jury, Rajigah rejected a judge's offer to serve no jail time in exchange for an admission of guilt. After he served the sentence and INS began deportation proceedings, both the judge and the district attorney who had prosecuted him wrote letters to the INS recommending Rajigah's release from custody. The judge and prosecutor also separately noted that they had never contemplated the "immigration consequences" of Rajigah's sentence.

A native of Guyana, he had been in the United States for twenty-two years. Dave, born in India, had been here for thirty years. She was in real estate and became a personal injury lawyer; he was a mortgage broker. Both were "legal," and their daughter was a U.S. citizen by birth.

"We were so American that we never thought this could happen to us," Dave told me at the rally. She didn't want to use her own name back then. She still believed that if she kept a low profile and didn't make trouble, the INS would resolve her husband's case humanely. "Thanks for the peaceful demonstration," a New York City Police Department captain had said to her as he left Manhattan's Federal Plaza.

After Rikers, Rajigah was held briefly at the Varick Street detention center, within walking distance of the downtown rally. Then he was shipped to FDC Oakdale. Every weekend Rita and Natalia would fly down to Alexandria and make the one-hour drive to FDC. The tidy lawns and flowerbeds, deceptively reassuring in the dilapidated town, helped Rita and Marlon to tell a white lie to their five-year-old daughter. "She didn't know it was a jail. She thought it was my workplace. Even though the surroundings were kind of strange, and I was in a uniform, she was little, so we tried to play it off," Rajigah tells me when we meet at Louisiana's Pine Prairie Correctional Center. He had been transferred here, where visitation hours are generous for family members who have to travel considerable distances, but Dave visited without Natalia now because she was old enough to figure things out. Talking to me near the federal courthouse in lower Manhattan where she was doing research for an INS prisoner housed with her husband, Dave had finally choked up as she recalled the low ledge separating her from her husband in the visiting area in Pine Prairie. They are not allowed to touch, she told me. They may hug when she leaves. She said that Assistant District Director Craig Robinson of the INS New Orleans office told her: "'You love your husband so much, and you want him to be free—why don't you just leave the country?'"

Rajigah tells me, "I've seen people down here just totally destroyed [by] everything. Their wife has left them, their kids have grown up. I know this guy left his kid since she was five years old, and now she's a teenager. He doesn't even know what to say to her on the phone anymore. And so it does destroy you. I'm getting to a point where, even though I'm talking to my daughter on the phone—I know she's familiar with me, but . . ." He doesn't finish the thought.

Marlon and Rita have had to borrow money to pay the exorbitant phone bills. Jail phone contracts are structured to raise rates above the norm so that the additional revenue can be divided between the phone company and the county operating the jail. An INS official toured nine county jails holding INS detainees and reported that in eight of them, prisoners could only make collect calls. The official wrote to his colleagues: "The telephone system is a big money item to these County Sheriffs and while they are very willing to work with us to meet our requirements [on other issues] when you start to negotiate about toll free calls and taking money out of their pockets we need to be sensitive to their needs."[1]

A key moment in the history of prison architecture arrived with the radial design exemplified by Jeremy Bentham's panopticon.[2] Lookout areas were placed at the center of living areas that radiated outward like spokes, so that officers could see as much as possible from where they stood. But prisons are also designed so that it is possible to stand at the heart of one and keep everything in view and at a distance at the same time. At the Pine Prairie Correctional Center, the warden and his assistant warden took me inside a control booth. We looked out through Plexiglas windows, across a hallway, through another set of Plexiglas windows, and into a crowded "pod" of uniformed men staring blankly, sleeping the day away, playing cards, or, in one case, trying to mop up water leaking into an open bathroom and shower area.

The dreary windows upon windows that hide as much as they show, even under the fluorescent lights, are almost unimaginable from the open pine prairie outside. This jail, like others, is easy to miss. I had driven north along Highway 13 from Eunice, listening to a Cajun French call-in radio show. The hosts and callers were exchanging information on the French names for local birds: the nighthawk, the cedar waxwing, the armadillo (that last caller apologized for not sticking to the topic). "*Un autre call,* Charlie," says the host. I made a brief stop at a little service station where the marquee, above the gas prices, advertised homemade boudin and cracklin' (Cajun sausage and fried pigskin). I was driving slowly because people in Eunice had warned me that the Highway Patrol looks for speeders along this stretch. Still, I almost missed the correctional center. What caught my eye is what was supposed to catch my eye: orange dots in the green and wired landscape. The inmates in the yard were squatting, or down on their knees, picking up rocks or garbage, I suppose. A uniformed man stood over them. At Krome the young Haitian prisoner had written about the "uniform of contempt." His shame was just what an eighteenth-century prison "reformer" had intended when he advocated prisoner clothing that would be "comfortable, yet humiliating."[3]

About an hour after seeing the jail yard from the outside, I was looking at it from the inside. Rusting weightlifting equipment was scattered across a large, paved "recreational area." A row of pay phones, one next to another to make privacy almost impossible, stood along the edge of the pavement. The staff and I were on a shaded walkway fenced off from the yard. The entire yard, including its lucrative phones, was unprotected from the blazing Louisiana sun. I commented naively on the lack of shade, and the general manager of Louisiana Corrections Services, Inc. (LCS), which owns and operates the facility and other jails in the area, laughingly pointed out that trees are for hiding and escaping.

Jean Genet wrote of his penal colony in the sun: "Everything transpires there in a cruel light which I cannot refrain from choosing as a sign of lucidity."[4]

When we headed back inside, Deputy Warden Drew Bergeron used one of the oversize keys from his heavy key ring. It looked like something from an old prison movie—the *clink* is audible in our recorded interview—and Warden Gary Copes jokingly referred to the key ring as his deputy's purse. All of the gates' locks are controlled remotely, Bergeron explained, and these keys are used in the event of a power outage. He was using them now even though there was no problem with the electricity. The keys have an even more practical function than unlocking gates. Along with the concertina wire, the surveillance screens, the logbook officers use to record the time they look at the surveillance screens, and the uniforms of humiliation, the heavy keys are a symbol of control.

And then there are the chains. In ancient Athens, one term for the local prison literally meant "the place of chains."[5] Every day, back and forth between "facilities" in America's immigration archipelago, the INS's administrative detainees are transferred by bus, van, and plane, usually in "restraints." It's procedure, and it's worth a brief detour here.

On the East Coast, Emmanuel Yvenie found out about shackles and jail regulations. She was at home with her husband and her sister one night after they had all worked their shifts in a chicken processing plant in Salisbury, on the Chesapeake Peninsula. In Haitian they call their work *fè treypak*, making tray packs. They were here legally, having been allowed in to pursue their political asylum claims and to work after being intercepted by the Coast Guard. Yvenie's permission to be in the United States ended when her asylum claim was denied. Her husband's claim was still pending, however, and if he were to be granted asylum, his wife would likely be able to stay with him. Nevertheless, the INS arrested her in the middle of the night. She was driven through an area crisscrossed by the Underground Railroad to the Wicomico, Maryland, jail.

She was distraught, crying, and spoke no English. There was no Haitian interpreter at the jail. The jailers decided that she must be suicidal, so they followed procedure: they stripped her, put a paper gown on her, and locked her in a cold cell. She was pregnant, and after a few days in solitary, she miscarried. Fortunately, her sister had been locked up with her because she refused to stop screaming until the jailers did something. Officers took Yvenie to a hospital, arms cuffed and legs shackled. Her legs remained shackled while she was treated.

INS's Baltimore District Director Benedict Ferro said, "It would be hard for me to imagine [such treatment]. I would presume [jail officials] followed their own guidelines on escorting and restraints." He was right. Wicomico Warden John Welch explained that shackling was indeed jail procedure and that under this procedure they "always treat everyone equally." He also explained that if the doctor is willing to sign a release form to take responsibility, then the escorting officers may remove the restraints. "All my people are looking for is, who's going to take the responsibility if

I take these off and this girl jumps up from the table and runs? . . . Just because she was a woman and she was hemorrhaging makes no difference to me."[6]

In Pine Prairie, when Deputy Warden Bergeron brings Marlon Rajigah into the conference room across from the warden's office to speak with me, it seems obvious from the body language and the lack of any "backup" that no one feels even remotely threatened by Rajigah. Even the warden, who had warned me about Rajigah's complaints, never suggested any such thing. Yet Rajigah's legs are shackled, his hands are cuffed, and the cuffs are attached to a chain encircling his waist. I ask Bergeron if he will remove the handcuffs for our interview. He hesitates and looks over the prisoner's shoulder to the warden standing in the doorway. They agree to remove the waist and wrist restraints only and make a show of telling Rajigah to "behave."

"This doesn't exist," Rajigah tells me after they leave. "This whole situation here. [People are supposed to think] it's only 'aggravated felons,' terrorists, that are being deported, [that] it has nothing to do with writing bad checks or nothing like that. . . . They think it's all dangerous people that are being deported. They don't understand."

He is referring to one of the most insidious aspects of the 1996 immigration laws, the redefining of the term "aggravated felons," crucial to the widening of the net. On one of her visits to New York, Laurie Kozuba had walked me over to the New York University law school to get me a copy of an article by Morawetz that lays out some of these changes.

> The most publicized aspect of the new laws is their Alice-in-Wonderland-like definition of the term "aggravated felony." This term plays a central role because it is one of the triggers for mandatory detention and deportation. As the term is defined, a crime need not be either aggravated or a felony. For example, a conviction for simple battery or for shoplifting with a one-year suspended sentence—either of which would be a misdemeanor or a violation in most states—can be deemed an aggravated felony.[7]

Even this "most publicized aspect of the new laws" was not public enough. Seven years after the laws were enacted, Chief Justice William Rehnquist seemed not to have heard the news. In a case challenging provisions of the

1996 laws that prohibited certain legal residents from having a bail hearing to ask for release from detention during the course of their proceedings, this memorable exchange took place between Rehnquist and ACLU attorney Judy Rabinovitz:

RABINOVITZ: "The question is what—what constitutes an aggravated felony. Misdemeanors constitute an aggravated felony as well. . . ."

REHNQUIST: "What—what do you—what do you mean, misdemeanors constitute an aggravated felony?"

RABINOVITZ: "I know it's somewhat shocking, Mr. Chief Justice, but, in fact, the way that aggravated felony has been defined so broadly . . . the courts have held that even misdemeanors can be aggravated felonies."[8]

In Atlanta the INS circulated a memo to local prosecutors to ensure that petty crimes resulted in the deportation of legal residents. The 1996 immigration laws mandated that many crimes resulting in a sentence of a year or more would trigger the new retroactivity provisions. Nationwide, more than 90 percent of criminal convictions are the result of plea bargains, not trials.[9] The Atlanta memo therefore urged prosecutors to reject guilty pleas that would not conform to the time scheme triggering detention and deportation. "NOTE: THE ALIEN IS NOT REQUIRED TO SERVE THE SENTENCE, AS LONG AS IT IS IMPOSED." In other words, detention, deportation, and destruction of families are triggered even when the defendant was not required by the criminal justice system to do any time. The memo continues: "If possible do not plea bargain an Aggravated Felony down to a non aggravated felony. . . . This is important to assure the aliens' swift removal. . . . You may encounter alien defendants that return to court to have their sentences amended to avoid removal/deportation i.e. reduced from twelve months to eleven months. Try to avoid this, by reducing the sentence the alien may avoid removal. Contact INS if you have questions on these cases."[10]

Marlon Rajigah's large brown eyes look exhausted. His dark black hair is thinning on top but falls frizzy and thick to his shoulders. At our meeting he is very different from the neatly groomed short-haired man in a photo his wife showed me in New York. He sits very still, as if his body knows to conserve its energy.

"They have successfully managed to keep [all of this] away from the American public for so many years because they have certain things in place. It's a design. And when you're in it, you understand why they were able to do that." When I ask him to tell me about the design, what he sees from the inside, Rajigah sketches a nexus of literal chains with the less visible but no less restrictive pettiness and prejudice that govern this system. "First of all, the shackling and the handcuffing. They put you in that psychological state of thinking you are still a criminal, to prevent you from thinking otherwise. That's the first and foremost thing: they get you thinking as a criminal. And secondly, they deprive you of all—almost all—contact, as much as they can, with the outside world. Most of the time your attorney can't get to you."

Rajigah says that INS officials encourage the jailers to lock detainees in segregation on a variety of pretexts, and that this serves two purposes. "First of all, [the disciplinary record] goes against you. And second, when you get locked up in the hole, you can't get phone calls, you can't get access and visits." Rajigah says that often detainees are transferred to different jails when they manage to establish contact with an attorney or to file a complaint in a local court; detainees around the country have reported the same practices.

According to Rajigah, prisoners at Pine Prairie are regularly beaten, though he himself has not been. "It's because of Rita. Because they know. We have complained about them threatening us, and Rita has been writing letters. So they know. We've already put them on notice. That's the only reason. Half the stuff I've done here—if it wasn't for people on the outside, my jaws would have been broken. . . . They beat you for anything here. They'll deny it. But whenever they beat INS [prisoners], if it's really bad, they ship them [to another jail]. . . . And if somebody calls to find out something, they'll ship them right away." Like former corrections officer Richard Franklin, Rajigah emphasizes that beatings are only the most dramatic part of what is unbearable about prison life. "They'll take your holy book and throw it in the toilet because you have no recourse. You can't write a grievance, because you're back on square one. You're just at their whim and their mercy."

Warden Copes had wanted to speak to me about this prisoner before I made the trip down. Although he would call Rajigah "Rashim" throughout our interview, he was well aware of him and his New York wife and of the fact that the two of them were putting their complaints in writing. In person, Copes told me: "You're going to interview one today that complains about everything. I mean everything." I tell Rajigah that Copes said he complains every day.

"I have no reason to lie," Rajigah counters. He had been detained elsewhere, and he knew the differences between jails. "Vermillion Parish wasn't bad, the only thing that was bad there was the food. The COs over there were excellent. They don't bother you. I never had a problem at Vermillion Parish. I can say that. It's not a nice place, but still, it was not as psychologically testing as this place. They're always on you [here]. One guy got put in the hole because his I.D. was like this"—he flips his clipped-on I.D. badge around backward. "The wind blew it. So they called him and said, 'You're I.D.'s supposed to be like this,' and he said, 'Well, the wind blew it.'"

"When you wash your clothes, you can't hang it on the rail. You have to put it in your locker. That's how stupid and ridiculous it is. You can't hang your towel, and you can't hang your clothes. Nobody knows the logic for that. It's little, little stuff—and you can go to the hole for that—little stuff that don't make sense that's very trying. People on the outside are going to think, oh—but when you live this stuff every single day, it gets to a point—it's not the big stuff that kills you, it's the little stuff that gets to be very tedious and annoying and drives you over, you know?"

Shortly before our interview, the staff had walked me through a dorm after we viewed it from inside the control booth. Many inmates lay in their bunks with thin blankets pulled over their heads. One man was stretched out, ignoring the visitors, listening to a small radio he had suspended with a strip of rag from the bunk above him. The LCS general manager noticed it and said something to the deputy warden, who said something to the inmate, who took down the radio.

As we left the dorm a Cuban prisoner approached, asking if I was with Immigration. The deputy warden waved him off. "Life is here bullshit," the Cuban said in heavily accented English and then asked loudly why he couldn't speak to me if this was a free country. Outside, Warden Copes asked his deputy two or three times if he could remember the prisoner's name. Months later the Cuban, an INS detainee, would write from a different Louisiana jail: "If something happens to me for complaining in here please don't forget about me."

Warden Gary Copes and LCS General Manager Richard Harbison have known each other for years. Harbison worked as a local news reporter when Copes was a police chief. Copes jokes that Harbison never stopped following him, and Harbison says that they are on the same team now. We are in the same conference room where Rajigah and I will talk. Harbison goes right into his sales pitch: "They see us trying, they try a little bit harder. We've had almost no problems with INS [detainees]. . . . When you tour the facility you're going to notice the cleanliness of the facility. . . . You're going to see a facility here that's somewhat unique." He will repeat the line about cleanliness when we're inside one of the dorms, at the very moment that the stench of the open bathroom area hits me.

Copes jumps in. "Let's not forget, we're dealing with detainees that don't want to be here. So everything is not going to be peaches and cream with them. You're going to have some of them—and you're going to interview one of them today, I'm sure—that complain about everything. I'm sure you've interviewed those kind before. They complain about everything. You're going to interview one today that complains about everything. I mean everything. [But] you're going to find out that it's a good facility and the vast majority of those inmates here do not want to be here, but they understand that this is a penal institution. . . . We try very hard to do the right thing. But you're not going to please everybody."

Copes acknowledges the problem of the INS's "detaining" people alongside sentenced inmates: "I don't think that some of these detainees should be in a penal institution. I don't know what the answer is. Don't get me wrong. I'm not the person that makes those decisions. . . . I think that we have some problems here, in this country, we have some problems in the way we do it. I don't know what the answer is . . . but I will tell you there is some talent here, state and INS. There are some intelligent INS people that we have here." Copes is one of the few prison personnel I have met who actually refer to the prisoners as "people."

General Manager Harbison agrees: "When a man serves his time, either release him or deport him back to his country. Why hold him indefinitely? That's just not fair. And this company—the directors, the owners—all feel the same way." Then he adds one of the more surprising sentiments of the day: "We're also citizens—we have no control over what the government does."

Harbison's real concern is the business, and he is not worried: "This company will not stand or fall on INS inmates. So we will take them because we are a for-profit organization. If the government finally said [let] them all out, send them all home, do whatever—that's fine. We applaud that. We'll fill up those bunks with other people."

Gary Copes is the fifty-three-year-old son of a Louisiana farmer and the husband of a Syrian woman. This area still produces rice, soybeans, and sugarcane, but farming no longer provides many jobs. There are a few oil rigs nearby, but most of the oil work is south of here, nearer the gulf and offshore. Copes tells me that the sheriff in Allen Parish pushed for the jail, which opened in 1999, "to put some people to work," but he admits that he's not proud of the salaries for his two hundred employees, starting at $6.50 an hour, going up to about $24,000 a year for the captain and lieutenants. Still, around here that's "not a bad-paying job."

Copes has been in corrections for twenty-eight years, and he runs five jails in Texas and Louisiana for LCS. He says that he has never had a complaint lodged against him and that he once arrested a corrections officer for mistreating an inmate, though he declines to go into details. He has also been indicted—and acquitted—for his alleged role in the severe beating of Cuban detainees at a jail in Tensas, Louisiana.[11] His apparent willingness to address questions of prison violence head-on leads me to ask if he thinks brutality is necessary for a prison to function. "I don't think you can answer a question like that by saying yes or no. Because let's face it, there are some situations out here in which an individual has to protect himself. There's no question about that."

The general manager cuts in: "That's not brutality."

"Right," says the warden, then continues his own, more nuanced if ultimately self-protective train of thought. "But when does it *become* brutality? See, from a person whose perspective is on the outside looking in, like yourself, it's probably a totally different ball game than a guy like one of these young, twenty-two-, twenty-three-year-old correctional officers out here who just got out of training for four or five weeks. He goes into this huge dormitory, with seventy inmates in there. All have been convicted of a felony—even the INS inmates have been convicted at some point of a felony." The warden is wrong about that—INS inmates have not necessarily been convicted of felonies—but the fact that he thinks so illustrates the success of propaganda about "criminal aliens."

"He walks in there. It's smoky, it's noisy, and it's just him—or her." He repeats: "Or her. So they're in the middle of this thing, okay? There's a guy smoking a cigarette in the bunk area, which is totally against state of Louisiana fire marshal regulations. It's against the law. You go back there and how do you handle that? You know, 'Please put the cigarette out.' That's the way we teach them to handle it. 'I'm going to have to write you up for that.' So that's just a little piece of paper. You write them up, and here this person goes crazy on you. 'You're not writing me up!' How do you handle that, see? And when does it become brutality? Obviously we know when it becomes brutality. When more force is used than is necessary.

"But what if that individual starts cussing, screaming, hollering, carrying on, and there's no physical stuff going on? This young officer just lets that slide? Because he's afraid? Or because he doesn't know what to do, maybe, Mark. Maybe he's physically afraid, he may be afraid of *you*, in the media, if you understand what I'm trying to say. He may be afraid of the courts.

"So he walks out of there and leaves that alone. 'Okay, I'll just get out of here.' What happens then? Everybody in there walks all over the rules. 'Hey, we can violate these rules any way we want to now. They can't do anything to us.' Or does this young officer make a decision? 'Okay you're comin' out of the dorm with me. You're comin' on, because you're not going to talk to me like that. You're not going to show that disrespect, because you can't do that when you get out into the public, out in the free world, because if you do, you're not going to have a job'—you know what I'm trying to say? So you tried to get this individual out. He refuses to come out. What do you do? See? Do you just let them run rampant in there? Or do you make some decisions as a young officer, 'I'm going to make a decision, you're coming out with me one way or the other. You're going out with me because you can't show this kind of disrespect, and you can't violate our rules like this.' Does that make sense to you, what I'm trying to say, how difficult this is for some of these people?"

It did make sense, and it convinced me more than any antiprison activist or polemic ever did that the only solution for jailer and jailed is the abolition of prisons as we know them. It was in listening to this career corrections man whose perceptions I believed, regardless of the truth of particular, disputed incidents, that I saw most clearly how prisons create the very problems to which they are supposedly society's response. Marlon Rajigah said of his jailers at Pine Prairie: "These people are very impulsive, and that makes them very dangerous."

Harbison announces that it's time for lunch, but Copes wants to finish making a point. "I would be willing to say there's not very many journalists or judges or district attorneys or defense attorneys that, if somebody walked up and spit blood in your face or threw urine in your face, that you wouldn't fight—[that] you wouldn't just do whatever you had to do."

Now Copes remembers a Cuban prisoner from a few years back. He digresses from the point he was making to something he admits he doesn't understand. This Cuban detainee had begun a hunger strike but realized after a few days that he didn't have the willpower to stop eating. So he wired his own mouth shut with jumbo paper clips. Then, the warden says, the prisoner spit blood into a captain's face. Under medical supervision, Copes emphasizes, he had the paper clips removed. "And he hates me because . . . I had them taken out. Now why would he hate me for that?"

Deputy Warden Bergeron, the man with the ring of old-fashioned keys, is soft-spoken, but in the jail cafeteria he starts to chat in the rich accent of Cajun Louisiana. Bergeron's father did some research into family history and found that his people first arrived in New France—later to be the French Canada of Danny Kozuba's father—as stowaways on a ship from old France, then found their way down to what is now Cajun country with thousands of other Acadians exiled by the British.

The day after Bergeron told me about his stowaway ancestry, the Acadiana Edition of the Baton Rouge *State-Times/Morning Advocate* ran a story about three Turkish seamen who jumped from a freighter carrying "wire coil and zinc ingots" on the Mississippi River. After making it to shore at Waggaman, Louisiana, on a "makeshift raft made of scrap wood, empty oil drums and personal flotation devices," they were moved to the notorious Orleans Parish Prison, even though, according to a Border Patrol agent, there was "no reason to believe these individuals are armed and dangerous." The story ran next to a syndicated "Diary of the Planet," which described a volcanic eruption on Japan's Tori-shima Island, uninhabited since all the residents fled previous lava flows some sixty-five years earlier; migrating sand dunes in Nigeria that had forced five thousand farmers off their land; and sandstorms causing respiratory distress in Iran. Below that was a story about the indictment of two inmates in the Calcasieu Parish Jail in Baton Rouge for the second-degree murder of another inmate.[12]

Drew Bergeron tells me that he used to work for Western Union. In the 1970s he went "from climbing telephone poles" to a job at the Louisiana State Prison at Angola, one of the nation's most infamous and violent prisons at the time. He used to see grown men break down and cry when they were booked and finally realized what was happening to them. Warden Copes interrupts his deputy when he notices that one of the blue-uniformed kitchen worker inmates is wearing sunglasses. He asks Bergeron to ask the inmate about it. The deputy warden calls the prisoner over. The prisoner explains that these are prescription glasses. Bergeron asks if he has a copy of the prescription, and the prisoner says yes. Bergeron turns back to his gluey mashed potatoes; the conversation is over. The prisoner goes back to work, and an awkward silence hovers over the table until the general manager breaks it: "All our meals are nutritionally balanced."

The inmates have already eaten, but several are nearby working in the kitchen. One of them brings over some brown paper towels for us. The general manager volunteers that the company saves money by not providing napkins to the inmates. "Most of these folks wouldn't use them, anyway," he says.

—

Not all of the placards at the CIEJ rally where I met Marlon Rajigah's wife were as succinct as the one that had moved Laurie Kozuba. One proclaimed, in alternating red and black letters: "WARNING!! LEGAL PERMANENT RESIDENTS IIRAIRA [sic] CAN DESTROY YOUR LIFE." What would a passerby make of that, or of the "Hispanic" family with its American flags posing with that sign? Exacerbating the usual secrecy of INS operations, the new laws were unusually complex. This would become apparent when the Supreme Court took up *INS v. Enrico St. Cyr* in 2001.

Enrico St. Cyr came from Haiti to the United States as a lawful permanent resident in 1986. A decade later in Connecticut, he pled guilty to selling a "controlled substance" and thus became "deportable." If the INS had taken custody of him at that time, St. Cyr would have been eligible for a waiver of deportation, like the one Danny Kozuba was granted based on his ties in the United States and other individualized factors. Before the 1996 laws took effect, just over 50 percent of such waivers were granted. Because the INS did not begin proceedings against Enrico St. Cyr until 1997, he was subject to the new, retroactive laws. Detained in the Hartford Correctional Center along with about 120 other INS prisoners, St. Cyr filed a writ of habeas corpus, which eventually made it to the Supreme Court. When the Court heard the case in April 2001 St. Cyr had been in INS detention for two years; he had served about three years for his criminal convictions. The outcome of *INS v. St. Cyr* would affect thousands.

Not only did the Justice Department apply the 1996 law retroactively, it also argued that its decision to do so was not reviewable by the courts. The relevant statute reads: "Notwithstanding any other provision of law, no court shall have jurisdiction to review any final order of removal against an alien who is removable by reason of having committed" certain enumerated criminal offenses, namely, the newly broadened range of offenses. Much of the oral argument before the Supreme Court in *St. Cyr* centered on the question of Congress's intent in passing these laws. The Justice Department argued that its intent was to prevent someone such as Enrico St. Cyr from seeking any federal court review of INS actions; even habeas corpus challenges were not to be available. The prisoners argued that habeas review is so fundamental that, to eliminate it, Congress would have had to do so explicitly.

Habeas corpus is sometimes portrayed as a last-ditch loophole through which criminals crawl away from justice. In fact, as Justice John Paul Stevens wrote in his majority opinion, "At its historical core, the writ of habeas corpus has served as a means of reviewing the legality of executive detention, and it is in that context that its protections have been strongest." A group of legal historians filed an amici curiae, or friends of the court, brief on behalf of the prisoners in *St. Cyr*. They wrote:

> The writ of *habeas corpus* was available to persons subject to civil detention in a wide range of contexts in England prior to 1789. The INS may be analogized to 18th century executive agencies such as the British Navy, administrative bodies such as the Sewer Commissioners, our courts of "inferior" (limited) jurisdiction. As both case law and commentaries confirm, unlawful detention by any such bodies could be corrected upon issuance of *habeas corpus*.

The historians list a startling range of premodern prisoners for whom such relief was available both in England and in the United States: sailors impressed into the British navy; a juror who was committed for contempt in London because he had voted to acquit a defendant; an African slave purchased by a Virginia man and confined on a ship ready to depart for Jamaica; a young woman who had been apprenticed as a teenager to a music teacher, then handed over as the man's mistress; a wife who was taken "violently into custody" by her husband; a fourteen-year-old servant who fled his Pennsylvania master; a twenty-seven-year-old man "indentured" by his own mother. Many early habeas petitions were filed on behalf of debtors who were locked up. The historians note that habeas corpus relief "applied to all non-enemy aliens detained within the realm."

The Justice Department argued that its authority to detain Enrico St. Cyr lay outside the traditional scope of habeas protection because he and the other prisoners were attempting to assert their right to a waiver that is available only as a matter of executive discretion. Justice Stevens summarized the government's position:

> Notwithstanding the historical use of habeas corpus to remedy unlawful executive action, the INS argues that this case falls outside the traditional scope of the writ . . . It acknowledges that the writ protected an individual who was held without legal authority, but argues that the writ would not issue where "an official had statutory authorization to detain the individual but . . . the official was not properly exercising his discretionary power to determine whether the individual should be released."

The INS was arguing that the prisoners were not entitled even to a *consideration* of a deportation waiver.

Even the judges acknowledged the complexity of the issue they had to decide. Justice Stephen Breyer said, "It reminds me of these brainteasers in the newspapers."[13] Another commented that he didn't even know how to pronounce the acronym "IIRIRA" (the consensus seems to be *EYE-ruh EYE-ruh*). Nevertheless, a familiar theme quickly emerged for anyone who had read a few government briefs in immigration cases. Deputy Solicitor General Edwin S. Kneedler was arguing that when it comes to immigration, the courts must respect the tradition of granting the Executive practically unlimited power—he calls it giving the attorney general "extraordinary deference"—and in this case, he couched the need for such power in euphemistic terms. Kneedler told the court: "It wouldn't be at all surprising that *in the climate in which Congress acted,* what Congress wanted to do was to vest the final determinations on questions such as" retroactively applying the law to past convictions "in the Attorney General."[14] In other words, considering the climate, it makes sense to assume that Congress intended to limit judicial review of the INS.

The "climate," of course, was the anti-immigrant hysteria that had reached a peak in the mid-1990s. In his decision Justice Stevens stripped away the euphemism: "[Congress's] responsivity to political pressures poses a risk that it may be tempted to use retroactive legislation as a means of retribution against unpopular groups or individuals." In a footnote Stevens added: "The INS appears skeptical of the notion that immigrants might be considered an 'unpopular group.'"

As for the "power of the Attorney General," to which the courts are instructed to give "extraordinary deference," Kneedler explained that "allow[ing] the alien to remain here" after the consequences of a criminal proceeding that has made her or him deportable "is a matter of grace, in no sense is it a matter of right." That is, a deportation waiver is a matter of executive discretion.

Justice Ruth Bader Ginsburg: "There's a lot of discretion in Federal agencies, but there's also a concept of abuse of discretion, and you seem to be saying no, there isn't. . . . The discretion is there but it's kind of a lawless discretion. Is that what you're telling us?"

Kneedler: "The fact that it's not judicially reviewable doesn't make it lawless."

The justices voted 5 to 4 to preserve habeas review and to eliminate the retroactive application of the new laws in cases involving plea bargains made prior to the enactment of those laws. In his dissenting opinion, Justice Antonin Scalia wrote: "The Court has created a version of IIRIRA that is not only unrecognizable to its framers (or to anyone who can read) but gives the statutory scheme precisely the opposite of its intended effect."

Meanwhile something extraordinary was happening in INS offices, as if in a parallel universe. As these complex questions made their way through the courts, as INS received more funding, and as the detention and removal numbers kept rising, elements inside the INS itself were sometimes criticizing the 1996 laws as forcefully as were the members of CIEJ.

> Imagine your neighbor is a legal permanent resident who came to this country when she was four years old. At age 18, she was convicted for a minor, nonviolent offense for which she paid a small fine and served no time in prison. She is now 40 years old, owns her own business, is married to a U.S. citizen, is the mother of three U.S. citizen children, and is active in her church. She travels out of the country and on her way back, at the airport, she answers a questionnaire truthfully by admitting that she has been convicted of a crime. She is detained, put into immigration proceedings, and now faces deportation to a country to which she has no ties, and whose language she does not speak.
>
> As a result of the 1996 law, your neighbor cannot be released while her case is being heard even though she does not pose a threat to society, and she is likely to appear at her immigration hearing. And at her immigration hearing, the judge is not permitted, under the 1996 law, to consider her strong ties to this country . . . The [immigration] judge must order her deported. Her children will lose their mother, a family is irreparably divided.

The INS press release refers to the "wide net cast by the 1996 laws" and the "unjust, harsh results" of detaining people like the hypothetical neighbor and denying them the chance to have their cases heard.

> INS is strongly committed to enforcing the law, and we will continue to do so. And we believe justice is served when we remove the criminal threat from our communities and our country. Justice, however, is more than words in a statute or a deportation order. It is doing what is right and fair for each and every person.[15]

The statement was issued more than a year before the Supreme Court heard the case of Enrico St. Cyr.

How is it possible that the INS could issue such a criticism of the detention policies that its agents were enforcing and that its governing department in the executive branch would defend in front of the Supreme Court? Consider the Antiterrorism and Effective Death Penalty Act, which expanded the categories of crimes that could lead to deportation and also limited the discretionary relief available. Wake Forest law professor Margaret Taylor writes: "Even as the INS began to implement AEDPA, the Clinton Administration was pressing for parts of it to be amended. This perhaps ameliorated the unease of some executive branch officials toward some of AEDPA's harshest provisions, as the administration hoped that a congressional fix was in the pipeline." According to Taylor, the administration's interest in amending the new law "also required the INS to develop political capital with Congress at a time when key members were intensely critical of the agency and most particularly of its record of deporting criminal offenders."[16]

Philip Schrag has described the "secret negotiations" leading up to passage of AEDPA and IIRIRA, and he quotes Senator Patrick Leahy, who attempted to slow things down: "I dare suggest, there are not five Senators in here who have even read the conference report or have the foggiest notion of what it is they are voting on." The details were secondary because members of Congress were in a hurry to pass legislation in time for the one-year anniversary of the Oklahoma City bombing. And so, what Margaret Taylor calls the "stealth amendments"—"expanding the grounds of deportability, severely restricting discretionary relief, and requiring detention of virtually all criminal offenders"—became law.[17] Even if Clinton was credible in saying, as he signed the bill into law, that it made "ill-advised changes" in relief available to long-term legal residents, his wavering was little comfort to the desperate families who had been contacting Laurie Kozuba and CIEJ. The government's lawyer could refer to the "climate" in his plea for a merciless interpretation of the law, but climate is a phenomenon of nature, and laws are made by women and men, even if they choose not to know what they are doing when they make them.

The list of names and of cases becomes an archive, and the archive becomes a memorial, as life stories are pared down to a few sentences. Laurie Kozuba was determined to show members of Congress that real lives were at stake. She spoke to the press from the steps of the Supreme Court while CIEJ held vigils around the country. If the oral arguments were complex even for a Supreme Court justice and the slogans on CIEJ placards a bit much to decipher on the run, the CIEJ profiles that Kozuba had been gathering spelled it out, less hypothetically than the INS's surprising press release had.

"Charlie" Jaramillo, a Colombian, pled guilty to possessing $40 of cocaine. He had been in the U.S. since he was eight. His wife and children are U.S. citizens. When he applied for citizenship himself, seven years after the crime, the INS detained him.

Panamanian-born José Velasquez had been living legally in the U.S. since 1960. In 1980, he pled guilty to conspiracy after telling an undercover agent at a party where he might be able to buy cocaine. His wife and three children are U.S. citizens. Eighteen years later, he was detained by the INS.

Adrian Sanchez moved to the U.S. from Mexico when he was four. His children are U.S. citizens. In 1990, he spent three months in jail for selling marijuana to an undercover agent. Eight years later, the INS detained him for five months.

Zafar Iqbal, forty-five, came to the U.S. from Pakistan in 1982. His wife and children are U.S. citizens. In 1994, he pled guilty to a fraud charge and spent two weeks in jail. Four years later, the INS arrested him at work and detained him for a year and a half.

Ihsan Elias Dawlett came to the U.S. from Iraq in 1973. He was fifty-eight and became a legal permanent resident. His wife and three children are U.S. citizens. In 1994, he received a five-year suspended sentence for writing a bad check to purchase $1500 worth of supplies for his construction business. Four years later, the INS detained him.[18]

In Kozuba's home state of Texas, the INS launched Operation Last Call, targeting resident immigrants who had three convictions for driving while intoxicated. On Labor Day weekend in 1998, reports Jake Bernstein, the agency rounded up "over 500 people, 104 in El Paso alone. The Mexican consulate in El Paso interviewed 91 of the Operation Last Call detainees. It found that the average time spent living in the United States was 21.6 years. Ninety percent of them had children and 81.7 percent of those were U.S. citizens. Ninety-one percent had jobs."[19]

In 1996 the INS deported 4,247 "criminal aliens" who had been legal permanent residents; in 1999 that number had risen to 10,663. This does not include those who were detained and released. Days before the Supreme Court arguments in *St. Cyr*, the *New York Times* quoted Representative Lamar Smith, "a leading architect of the 1996 law" and former chair of the House Judiciary Subcommittee on Immigration and Claims. "These individuals who committed serious drug trafficking crimes are just the kind of individuals who I feel should be deported," Smith said. "Without the 1996 law, these are the kind of individuals who take advantage of loopholes."[20]

Laurie Kozuba said of Smith: "He has got to have a heart in there somewhere. It's just how you get to it . . ."

———

In the central control room at Pine Prairie, a correctional officer follows the warden's instruction to demonstrate the technology for me by zooming in on a prisoner asleep in an isolation cell. When they actually walk me through the special housing wing, I never see the man, only clipboards on the walls outside each cell. Later, in the conference room, Marlon Rajigah groans when I ask him to describe being in the hole. At the Oakdale prison, he had been put in the hole for refusing to work; detainees are paid $1 a day, but Rajigah says he wasn't sentenced to work; he was a detainee, not sentenced at all. At Pine Prairie, he says, he was sent to the hole for filing grievances.

"Being locked up in a regular jail is bad enough. When they put you in the hole, it's just a small cell with two bunks in it. . . . Sometimes, if you're lucky, you get a window, but [there] is always plastic on the window, so you hardly have any light in there. So you're locked up in a room with somebody else for days. Sometimes forty-five days, sometimes ninety days, you live with that person." Why does someone get put in the hole? "They make up whatever they have to make up. So the officer can just put you in the hole if he wants. . . . It's very claustrophobic. And I'm claustrophobic to begin with, so most of the times I would just lie down and keep your eyes closed when you have anxiety attacks."

He is suddenly speaking in the second person as he lets himself remember. "Like you want to get out of there. You have anxiety attacks. You just try to lay down and sleep and pretend that you're somewhere else most of the time. . . . After the first ten days you don't see anybody. Unless you're there with a cellie, you talk with your cellie. But the two of you don't see anybody else. You hear voices on the outside, and you're looking through the glass, and then it dawns on you that there's something else out there, and you want to get out. The world seems so small. And you want to walk. You can't even walk around. You jump down [from your bunk] and you're on top of the toilet."

In the hole at Oakdale, the light is always on. "They dim it, but it's always on. And literally, the top bunk is like six inches from the light, six or seven inches, so it's impossible to sleep when the light is on if you're in the top bunk. . . . You tie your head, but you get a headache with a towel on your head so tight all day. And you don't move. So all day, twenty-four hours a day, you're wrapped up with a towel on your head. And you're lying on the bed, and the only time you get up is when the food comes. You get up, you eat, then you jump back up on the bed. And you tie the towel again, and you stay there until—you just wait for time and wait for time and wait for time."

Like so many other prisoners, Rajigah shifts easily from what he has suffered to what he has seen. He recalls the van ride from New York's Varick Street detention center two years earlier, when he was being moved with two Mexicans and a young African woman. None of them knew where they were going—standard INS procedure. Rajigah says that when officers told the woman she was being deported, "She starts hysterically crying. She says, 'But what about my baby? I have a young baby. It's not even a year old yet. And I don't know where the baby is. Someone has the baby, but I have to come out.' But they didn't care. So the woman said, 'What about my baby?' And I just kept hearing this. . . . And the guy just kept telling her, 'That's not our problem, ma'am. We're just supposed to deport you.' She was deported. But God knows what happened to her baby."

Rajigah's face and his body seem heavy with what he has witnessed. He is a songwriter, and he has written many new lyrics in detention. He's hopeful about Jimmy Cliff's positive response to a few of his songs (back in New York, his wife, Rita, would show me Cliff's autograph on a page of Marlon's lyrics). As Rajigah talks about the songs, despite the fear and isolation and intimidation that went into them, something lighter comes into his voice. I ask how he has held onto this other part of himself.

"You have to. I can't let myself go. But it's like trying to keep a bubble underwater. You know what I'm saying? You can't let up at anytime, or it's going to come up. . . . Especially it's hard after I hang the phone up, and I know I can't call back. I mean, I know I could, but there's also the financial thing. Sometimes phone calls get interrupted because the [automated voice] comes on and says, 'One minute more,' when I'm talking to my daughter. . . . And she can't understand why I'm not coming home for her birthday.

"But because of the profits that my body brings physically, they're telling me that these jails need me more than my family needs me. That's what it comes down to. The important thing is, jails in Louisiana being able to survive. So if they have to sacrifice me and my wife and my daughter and my whole family, it's okay. So long as they create jobs down here and the government looks good. That's the underlying part. There's no humanity at all in INS. They don't care what happens."

# 10 | "SPEAK TO EVERY MEDIA"

*Resistance, Repression, and the Making of a Prisoner*

"All prison reporting is a lie," writes Jennifer Gonnerman in her account of a rare journalistic tour of Rikers Island.[1] Her point is that neither prisoners nor guards can speak freely. But her observation is true in another sense as well. Often when prisoners do talk, they have only one thing to talk about: being imprisoned. This prison within the prison can create distortions of its own.

Rose Livingston of the *Birmingham News* wrote a story about a Cuban detained by the INS in the federal penitentiary in Talladega, after which the Cuban was released. "Mohammad found me [after] he heard about that," Livingston told me. She was referring to Mohammad Bachir, who was being detained by the INS in an Alabama county jail. Livingston spoke to Bachir a number of times by phone. She also spoke to local and national INS officials involved in his case; she had it out with one whom she felt was obstructing her. But when she met Bachir for the first time in person, Livingston too would confront prison reporting's uncertainty principle.

Mohammad Bachir was being detained by the INS for a seemingly good reason. Although present in this country legally, he had been indicted for parental abduction (kidnapping his son) and for stalking his U.S. citizen wife. In Massachusetts Bachir served a total of two years on multiple contempt charges stemming from the parental kidnapping charge. Then the criminal justice system freed him. If he had previously become a U.S. citizen, that would have been the end of that. But he hadn't. So the INS detained the thirty-eight-year-old and began deportation proceedings. Because this was after passage of the 1996 immigration laws, he was not given the opportunity to ask an immigration judge for a waiver of deportation based on his ties to this country and the severity of his crime. Immigration detention is not supposed to be an end in itself the way a prison term is; rather, it is the first step in "Detention and Deportation" or "Detention and Removal" (successive names of the INS division). Bachir was not deported, however, because no country would take him. He is stateless. His parents fled Haifa during the 1948 Arab-Israeli war, and Bachir was born in a United Nations–run refugee camp in southern Lebanon. He has a "green card" in the United States (they're not actually green anymore), but he has citizenship nowhere. Under law that would later come before the Supreme Court, the INS could detain Bachir indefinitely. He was one of several thousand detainees in this situation, and he was one who decided to do something about it.

The INS's "detention standard" specifying that interviews with detainees who are the "center of attention" may be restricted could have been written with Bachir in mind. He is just the sort of detainee INS officials would like to keep out of the spotlight: four years of hunger strikes, one after another, forcing jail officials and INS officials to make special arrangements for him, and irrepressible attempts to organize his fellow detainees and break through the secrecy of the INS detention world. Bachir was constantly stringing and restringing networks of communication between local and national media interested in his case, attorneys, human rights organizations, and other detainees. He would happily give reporters the names and phone numbers of INS officials to contact about his case. He did it all nonviolently and legally. In short, he was what any jailer hoping for a relatively stress-free day would consider a troublemaker. So the authorities kept trying to get rid of him—without setting him free.

On the tape of a radio interview that never aired, Mohammad Bachir explains to a reporter what the Organization of American States (OAS) is.[2] This is August 1998, three months after he was picked up by the INS in Los Angeles. He is in the agency's San Pedro Service Processing Center in the Los Angeles District. The well-intentioned reporter seems unsure what to ask, and Bachir sounds tired. After a week leading a hunger strike in which four hundred detainees participated, he has now been at it for another twenty days on his own. He is trying to tell the reporter too much at once, mixing up the dull, procedural frustrations with allegations of outright brutality. All these meld together for the prisoner who understands them as manifestations of the same system, but it confuses reporters and listeners, making them uncertain of what the real issue is. Bachir tells the radio reporter that the caseworkers at San Pedro have no information on the detainees' cases. Some inmates are sleeping on the floor. The immigration judges are denying bail, and no one can get out. Guards carry guns, which is "not appropriate" because these are civil, not criminal, detainees. There are beatings. And, oddly, perhaps in a kind of public relations mode, Bachir tells the reporter, "People don't believe in the INS anymore," as if they once had. Then he tells her that he has shared his complaints with an OAS delegation that met with groups of detainees and then met alone with Bachir. It was as if the detainees, the detention center administration, and the human rights group all acknowledged his status as spokesperson.

When I first spoke by phone to Bachir, the mixture of intemperance, determination, and desperation was already apparent. Bachir could change his voice like an actor to make you understand how bad things were, but that doesn't mean he was being dishonest. On the contrary, Atlanta INS Chief of Detention George Taylor would tell me that Bachir's problem was that he thought too much about others and not enough about himself. In other words, he wouldn't back off; so his keepers weren't going to back off either. In this unpredictable case, Taylor seemed to have a certain respect for Bachir, while a national refugee advocate told me that Bachir had "a sort of enraging serenity about him" that would drive him crazy "if [he] were a cop." The advocate suggested that Bachir "flips the bird" at INS through his use of nonviolence. "I will never give up," Bachir told me in that first conversation. "When they say I'm stubborn . . . the more they do bad things to me, the more I'm going to go forward. The more they're hurting me, the more I'm going to go against them—in civil way, in nonviolent way."

Bachir wanted the OAS to talk to representatives of various detainee groups. These were not the INS's groupings but Bachir's. "They should talk to one person who represent people who crossed the [Mexican] border," he began. "I want them to talk to someone who represent the ABC," he continued, using the acronym for *American Baptist Churches v. Thornburgh*, a case that had forced the INS to reconsider the claims of Guatemalan and Salvadoran asylum seekers. "I want them to talk to someone who's entitled to a bond and has no criminal record, or a nonviolent criminal record, and he have American wife and children." He had a list of names ready. Then he told me about allegations of guards' using stun guns against prisoners at the camp. He said that he had been placed in segregation for speaking with the local media. He even gave me a fax number where he said I could contact him through a friendly officer.

There was another typical thing about that first conversation. Bachir wouldn't let me off the phone. "They can't keep me forever," he finally said in a relatively calm voice. He was saying good-bye. And then the pitch of his voice rose again, and he started all over: "Mark, they cannot send me to Lebanon, because I'm a stateless refugee . . . They know I have green card, I have family, I have to be released. They just making it hard on me because I making it hard on them. . . . I'm one of no-man-land. One of the newspapers wrote about me, he's one of no-man-land . . . but I'm going to go forward. Whatever I see wrong with them, I'm going to say it's wrong what they are doing. Like one time—sorry, it's the last thing—like last week, they tried to hit somebody here and choke him . . ."

The El Centro SPC, or Service Processing Center, is located about 115 miles east of San Diego in California's Imperial Valley. As the term "processing center" implies, it was built for short-term housing, but like the INS's other SPCs around the country, it has become a de facto prison. It also became overcrowded in the wake of the 1996 mandatory detention laws. More than half of the three hundred to four hundred detainees at the time were Mexican, Central American, and South American. There were a large number of Cubans and Southeast Asians as well, whose native countries would not accept them and who were being detained indefinitely .

Spring and summer 1998 were a tense time in the valley. Frustration had peaked on a March night when INS agents entered the dorms and turned on the lights to search for drugs, according to INS authorities.[3] A Jordanian detainee told the *LA Weekly*'s Ben Ehrenreich: "When they do a search, we lose legal paperwork, pictures of our families, phone books. They throw them in the trash." In Ehrenreich's account, an inmate protested, a guard assaulted, and a twenty-minute riot ensued. The detainees refused to leave their dorms when heavily armed guards massed outside. These were what the INS calls a "tactical intervention team" and what the prisoners call "goon squads"—agents dressed in black with no markings indicating their agency or names, with riot helmets, ski masks, pepper spray, billy clubs, and, this time, guns with wooden bullets. FBI crisis negotiators arrived and stayed through the night; they left with a list of detainee complaints.

A few months later El Centro detainees went on a hunger strike, and one of their complaints was that they had not received a response from the FBI to their March complaints. This time the detainees went public, recognizing their strategic error in assuming the FBI had really been there to help them before. They produced two pages of crowded type with ellipses instead of periods, written in the form of a memo:

FRIDAY, JULY 3, 1998
TO: EL CENTRO INS DETENTION STAFF/AND MEDIA TV
FROM: THE WHOLE DETENTION CAMP

The memo mentions the March incident (though without mentioning that after the initial assault, detainees had taken over the dorms):

THE OFFICERS DRESSED IN ARMY FATIGUES . . . ALONG WITH 3-FEET
WIDE BATONS . . . INDISCRIMINATELY CAME IN NUMBERS OF DOZENS
AND STARTED HITTING INMATES IN THIS FACILITY IN THE FACE, HEAD,
AND BODY . . . WITHOUT ANY TYPE OF JUSTIFICATION. . . .
.IT SEEMS AS IF THE FBI ITSELF ONLY WANTS TO HEAR WHAT THEY WANT
TO HEAR AND NOT ANY OTHER IMPORTANT FACTS ON OUR BEHALF OR
SIDE . . . WE WANT TO KNOW HOW COME THIS ACTION HAS NEVER BEEN
DIGGED UP OR RESEARCHED IN A MORE PROFESSIONAL STATE.

In an article about the July hunger strike, which may have involved as many as three hundred detainees, the Spanish-language *La Opinión* recounted the familiar prisoner complaints of violent reprisals by guards against nonviolent protesters. An INS official from Detention and Deportation in Los Angeles told *La Opinión* that his office takes such allegations very seriously and was still awaiting a "formal complaint."[4] It's the standard method of evasion, variations of which were deployed by Ashcroft and his subordinates after September 11. Los Angeles INS could have gotten a copy of the detainees' memo from Roberto Martinez, a veteran human rights worker with the American Friends Service Committee's (AFSC's) US/Mexico Border Program in San Diego. Martinez had received a call from a detainee who wanted to give him a copy, and he went to the detention center to get it.[5]

There's something else worth noting in the detailed letter. It conveys the frustration of prisoners who thought they were finished being prisoners and on their way back to normal lives, or at least to the outside. But these were men picked up in the widening net of post-1996 mandatory detention laws, under which even someone given a suspended sentence by the courts could be detained by the INS. A former INS general counsel called the laws "draconian" and a Senate staffer predicted the emergence of "tent cities."[6] The distinctions between us and them were getting blurry. "WE HAVE CHILDREN, DAUGHTERS, SONS, WIVES, MOTHERS FATHERS, GRAND-MOTHERS, GRANDFATHERS, AUNTS, COUSINS, UNCLES, AND ALL IMME-DIATE FAMILY MEMBERS LIVING HERE IN THE U.S." The prisoners who wrote that letter have something important in common with the legislators who wrote the repressive immigration laws, or at least they are forced into the same logic: their plea for humanity is made through the colors of nationality. Thus, although these men are subject to detention and deportation precisely because they are *not* U.S. citizens, regardless of their time and connections and family here, it is to that de facto ideology of *belonging* that they appeal. Opposing the widening net, they are implicitly arguing instead for a wider conception of "American," one not based on legal citizenship.[7] "THE MAIN CONCERN IS THAT WE ARE AMERICANIZED . . . WE HAVE BEEN LIVING IN THE U.S. ALL OF OUR LIFES." They go on to acknowledge that they have made mistakes and ask for a second chance, based on their personal histories and connections. They want reasonable bonds set, and they also want some compassion.

ANOTHER TOPIC WOULD BE VISITING. THIS FACILITY AND THE COURT OF LAW . . . ALREADY HAS RIPPED APART DEEP-ROOTED FAMILIES, PARENTS FROM SONS, CHILDREN FROM THEIR FATHERS . . . AND NOW WHEN WE GO TO VISITING . . . WE CAN'T EVEN HUG OR A FAREWELL KISS. THERE IS NO TYPE OF CONTACT WITH YOUR LOVE-ONES . . . WE HAVE BEEN DEPORTED ALREADY.

Some protests are more substantive than others, and some are more organized than others. Authorities were compelled to take the El Centro hunger strike of July 1998 seriously on both counts. The strikers understood what was at stake when it came to contact with the media and not giving the INS justification for harsh response. INS prisoner resistance is rarely violent, but the detailed declaration of nonviolence issued by these strikers is unusual:

> Any officer who tell the barrack that other barracks are eating, don't believe them. . . . Any detainee who is sick, please go and eat. . . . INS officer will try to intimidate you, don't fall into it, walk away and no violence. Let them try to use violence against you, don't reply with any violent act. You are on hunger strike to prove to INS that they can not violate your constitutional rights, and try to take you away from your family. . . . Your children are your life. Don't allow the INS to separate you from them . . . Everybody should call their families and get support. Family ties are very important. We don't want to put our families and our children through emotional situation.

PLEASE NO VIOLENCE

NO VIOLENCE

NO VIOLENCE

In his contacts with the *LA Weekly, La Opinión,* and Telemundo, with Amnesty International, the AFSC, and the Arab-American Anti-Discrimination Committee, Mohammad Bachir did two things that the INS had wanted to prevent. During a hunger strike, the demands that lead to protest share a platform with the inevitable complaints related to the protest action itself; Bachir communicated the range of complaints, and he also connected other prisoners to the outside world. Notes from his conversations with Amnesty International staff members reflect this.[8] Authorities have denied protesters access to water; Bachir hands the phone to a Jamaican detainee who has lived in the United States for twenty-four years. El Centro is overcrowded, and some fifty inmates, including a seventy-year-old man, are sleeping on the floor; Bachir hands the phone to an Iraqi national. Guards are forcing hunger strikers to walk through the cafeteria line; Bachir hands the phone to a young Colombian who was allegedly placed in a segregation cell after complaining that a guard had tried to incite violence.

In another handwritten petition that month, the El Centro detainees asked that media and human rights organizations "enter and investigate INS inhumane treatment." This one is in Bachir's handwriting and is signed "spokesman: Mohammad," followed by signatures representing five lettered barracks. A week later Bachir was transferred to another jail, a move that El Centro's director, Hector Najera, called routine, though Bachir says he had been scheduled for an interview with the Spanish-language network Telemundo the following day. According to a statement from Martinez's AFSC office, Najera finally "seemed to be negotiating in good faith with the detainees, offering bonds to some and prohibiting guards from carrying guns into the barracks and mess hall."[9]

Bachir told me that while being transferred to San Pedro, near Los Angeles, he was thrown down and beaten, still in handcuffs, and that an INS supervisor later apologized to him, saying this mistreatment had nothing to do with the hunger strike. This detention camp, also known as Terminal Island, was built as a naval facility and, as Bachir himself noted, later held Japanese Americans interned during World War II. It was from here that he explained to the radio reporter what the OAS is. Bachir told me that the hunger strike leaders had all been transferred or released from El Centro. "He [Najera] got rid of most of us who know the law and know what we are doing, and he is just controlling the situation. A lot of controlling there right now. I believe people are afraid right now to continue hunger-striking at El Centro because what happened to me." The alleged beating and reprisal had been reported in the newspapers and on television. The AFSC statement paraphrased Nelson Guerrero, the twenty-eight-year-old Colombian to whom Mohammad had handed the phone: "If the leader of the strike can suffer this type of retaliation . . . the rest of the detainees are worried what would happen to them if they were to continue the strike."

Before Bachir hung up the phone that day from Terminal Island, he asked me if I had ever heard of the Iraqis held on secret evidence, and he handed the phone to Mohammad Jwer Al-Ammary, a pilot who had defected from Saddam Hussein's air force and was one of those brought here by the U.S. government and then unexpectedly detained along with Dr. Ali Karim and others. Bachir also reported that a Mexican detainee had hanged himself in a segregation unit that very day; the man was scheduled to be deported the next day. Nine hours later a second detainee had tried to kill himself. Bachir alleged that he himself was surrounded by a contingent of INS officers, private Lyons Security guards, and a male nurse, threatening him with a sedative injection if he did not agree to be moved to a segregation cell without the explanation from the camp director that he was demanding.

Also in September 1998, according to Betty Molchany, an attorney with the Arab-American Anti-Discrimination Committee, charges against Bachir for stalking his estranged wife were dismissed by the criminal court. But that was now irrelevant to Bachir's detention by the INS. That's the law. His life in detention was far from over. The INS considered him dangerous, and every time he protested his detention, quietly or not, he gave them another reason to keep him detained.

I soon lost track of Bachir. But the world of INS detention, even with all its black holes, can be surprisingly small for those who know how to get attention. In summer 1999, a year after the hunger strike at El Centro, I was following a protest at the Hillsborough County Jail in New Hampshire. Erroll Hall, a Jamaican, had been transferred from Hillsborough to the Rockingham County Jail in New Hampshire, and from there he mailed me an Associated Press clipping from the Concord newspaper.[10] According to the story, several of the transferred detainees "still refused food to protest their treatment, according to Mohammad Pachir [sic]": there he was again. Then he turned up in Batavia, New York. The *Buffalo News* reported that after speaking with the press, Bachir was transferred from the Batavia detention center to the DeKalb County Jail in Atlanta. A local INS official "denied that Bachir was transferred because he contacted reporters and said all he could say was that Bachir represented a security risk at Batavia."[11] Bachir himself later told me that as a hundred Chinese detainees began a hunger strike at the DeKalb County Jail in Atlanta, although he had nothing to do with it, INS bused him over to Alabama.

Bachir summarized the transfers with an unselfconscious graphic, written in his extremely legible, grade-school-style handwriting:

INS moved me several times because I speak to the Media, Human Rights Coalition Attorneys, Hunger Strike to protest my long incarceration:

CA→ Oregon→ Washington State→
New Hampshire→ MA.→ New York→
GA.→ South Carolina→ Alabama.

In fact, the graphic is deceptive because it only refers to states and not to individual jails. By the time Bachir got to Alabama, he had been held in about seventeen facilities in those nine states during about three years of detention, so far.

In August 2000 Bachir called from the county jail in Gadsden, Alabama, and left me this message:

> Hello, Mr. Dow. This is Mohammad Bachir. How are you? Today, August twenty-fifth, it's around four o'clock. The INS made a threat to me this afternoon that if I continue my hunger strike and I talk to the media, they will move me to South Carolina, to Columbia Care Center in South Carolina, hospital. They made a threat to me that I cannot talk to any media and I have to stop hunger strike and stop publicity. Otherwise they threaten me to move me. I told them they can move me any place they want—I'm going to continue my hunger strike, and I'm going to speak to every media. It's not fair what they're doing to me. I just want to let you know. Okay. Thank you very much. Bye-bye. I don't know when they're going to do that, it's going to be any time around right now. I just want to let you know, Mr. Dow. Thank you. Bye-bye.

It's a small speech, really, transcribed here in full from the answering machine. And it's all there: the politeness, the clarity and directness, and the persistence that almost imperceptibly becomes desperation. Even when leaving a message, Bachir says good-bye and then continues. What is not on the page was in his voice: the fear that by virtue of his determination becomes a quiet defiance. No wonder so many of his keepers came to respect him—and so many others did whatever they could to shut him up.

Because of the lapse in my contact with Bachir's case, I had to work backward a bit. I spoke to Bruce Chadbourne, the INS's assistant district director for Detention and Deportation in Boston. He knew about Bachir's case because the jurisdiction and the paperwork had been transferred to his district from Los Angeles. For a brief, confusing time, Boston had jurisdiction while Bachir was held in Alabama, which is in the Atlanta District. Needless to say, all this made it more than a little frustrating for Bachir, whose requests even to be considered for release had to be routed to the proper office first.

"Now Atlanta has the case and the body," Chadbourne told me before he shared a few thoughts about Bachir. "We had a problem keeping him in different facilities. . . . A lot of the jails kind of described him as a high-maintenance case. . . . He can be a problem. . . . He would kind of get some of the other detainees going." Bachir "said he would behave himself" in Batavia, Chadbourne said, referring to the upstate New York detention center, but he didn't. Bachir was "kind of sort of an instigator." Before the body could be transferred to any given facility, he explained, the INS would have to explain the prisoner's history; not surprisingly, there were few takers. Eventually, Chadbourne informed the INS Eastern Regional Office, "We're running out of facilities."

The spotlight can work for or against a detainee. It's a window of opportunity experienced by victims of government persecution around the world. A little attention can be worse than none at all by making one a target of retribution without generating enough outside support to influence the persecutors. But once a certain difficult-to-define line is crossed, the attention can become a form of protection. This schema assumes that the "authorities" know who the prisoner is. Were INS officials personally obsessed with Bachir, as Bachir himself believed? Of the thousands of detainees in the system, had he managed to shed anonymity and get onto everyone's radar? Chadbourne said no. "This is not unusual," he told me. "Mr. Bachir is not an unusual case." There have been other INS detainees "that [he] couldn't get into jails." As for whether officials were personally aware of Bachir, Chadbourne said: "I've never met him, never talked to him." He noted that he had a detained population of about 500 in his jurisdiction (as well as another 10,000 nondetained "removal" cases). Chadbourne's denial of Bachir's being on the radar, although logical given the numbers, was unconvincing: he was telling me in the same breath that jails all over the country were refusing to hold him. And a comment by another official in the INS's Eastern Region (one who did not want his name used) seems to indicate that Bachir did indeed have a reputation, even among those who didn't know his case well: "His conduct in every detention center he's been in—he is not a model detainee, and I don't mean that in a flippant sense. . . . I don't have the details, but he's been very difficult. He's been as difficult as he can be."

———

The town of Gadsden is an hour's drive southwest of Birmingham. A quick trip there reveals the combination of diversity and segregation that characterizes much of the country. Not far from the town's Spirit of Citizenship Monument (a diminutive replica of the Washington Monument), a young Palestinian from the West Bank town of Hebron works in a gas station, barely speaks English, and tells me that even though his customers don't understand where the West Bank is, he likes living here. A white woman who grew up here and who runs a downtown café tells me where I can get Mexican food. It's available because of the Mexican farmworkers in the area. She tells me cheerfully that it's so authentic that I won't be able to order unless I speak "Mexican." She assumes I'm in town to write about Etowah County judge Roy Moore, who made national news for posting the Ten Commandments in his courtroom and was later elected chief justice of the State Supreme Court. She's surprised to hear that the nearby county jail houses immigrant prisoners. Later, the jail warden will laugh and tell me that when he and the sheriff were attending community meetings to rally support for a federal contract with the INS, they had to reassure residents who wondered, "You're not going to be turnin' all those Mexicans loose, are you?" At the same time, a correctional officer at the jail tells me she wanted to learn enough Spanish to talk with the INS prisoners, "more than just 'Lay your hands on the counter' or 'I want to search you now.'" Another jail employee says, "The white prisoners are more well thought of than the INS [prisoners] or the colored prisoners."

Just a couple of weeks after I visited, the Etowah County Detention Center announced an $8.4 million expansion. The jail had 376 "fixed beds," and, with the use of plastic "stackable bunks" or "boats"—I had seen INS inmates stacking them as I stood on the tier of their pod with the assistant chief—the population is usually "in the 400 range," according to Chief Wes Williamson. Between 70 and 100 of those beds were contracted by the INS. The assistant chief told me that Etowah County "trustees" are tripled up when bed space is needed for new arrivals, who must be kept alone until the jail personnel get to know them. Once construction was completed, Etowah County would house 324 INS detainees at a rate of $30 to $33 per detainee per day, well below the $55 per "manday" national average. County Sheriff James Hayes told the *Gadsden Times* that the old INS contract had already helped the county pay for new vehicles, training, and equipment.[12] The new, fifteen-year contract, he told me, was expected to raise $120 million in revenue. Local officials in Gadsden were among the great many around the country more than willing to help ease what that INS official Taylor called "significant growing pains." The sheriff explained, "It's sort of like that movie *Field of Dreams*. You build it, and they're going to come."

The INS seemed poised to hold out Etowah County as one of its flagship facilities. Even INS detainees frustrated by their detention had few complaints about conditions per se at Etowah County. The jail opened in 1994 to replace its outdated predecessor across the street. Chief Williamson and his staff spoke convincingly about their dedication to decent jail conditions, and Williamson has a reputation among colleagues and attorneys as well as inmates for his respectful attitude toward the inmates. The new jail's conditions were the direct result of a consent decree that followed a 1988 class-action suit against the old jail,[13] according to Tamara Serwer of Atlanta's Southern Center for Human Rights, though Williamson had not mentioned that. A decent jail is important because much of the criticism of INS detention has focused on local jail conditions, and the prison building boom has certainly not made the problem of overcrowding obsolete. In fact, just three months after my visit a federal judge in Alabama wrote about the "substantial financial incentive" in keeping as many prisoners as possible in the local jails.[14]

At the time the INS was holding over 60 percent of its more than twenty thousand detainees in county jails and had recently announced that most of its long-awaited detention standards would apply to those contracted facilities. These agency standards cover attorney visitation, media interviews, law libraries, detainee grievance procedures, and other crucial aspects of prison life. But as internal agency standards, rather than regulations, they are practically unenforceable. According to Taylor, only two or three of forty local facilities audited in 2000 actually complied with all of the national standards. Etowah County was one of them, and Chief Williamson told me his jail was ready to handle some of the INS's "problem" cases, including hunger strikers as well as long-term or "post-order" detainees, whose deportation cannot be carried out easily if at all. Many of these "problem" cases would also be isolated from potential help. That was not Williamson's point, but neither is it an accident on the part of the INS. The agency refused to adopt a standard that would have prohibited the involuntary transfer of detainees to areas with no pro bono resources, and in Etowah County there is "a complete dearth," according to Chris Nugent of the American Bar Association, the principal organization involved in negotiating with the INS for the adoption of detention standards. Williamson suggested that I take care how I write about Mohammad Bachir to avoid hurting his chances of release by the INS, but he also conveyed his concern that the "end state" of my visit not be that Etowah County and its warden seem to have "buddied up with the media against Uncle Sam."

The Etowah County Detention Center is a generically modern, gray-beige municipal building. The first time I saw Mohammad Bachir was when Chief Williamson, known around the jail as "Chief Wes," escorted me into the booking area where Bachir was being held. Bachir was standing at a long counter, using the phone. He was wearing flip-flops, white "PJ" pants with "Etowah County Jail" stenciled down the leg, and a ratty green T-shirt. He looked up and asked me to wait a moment while he had some documents copied for me. A correctional officer asked him, "How many do you need?"

There were three columns drawn on the dry-marker board behind the main desk going into the booking area.

| NAME | CHARGES | SPECIAL INSTRUCTIONS |
|------|---------|----------------------|
| *Mohammad* | *INS* | *Do Not Move* |

There were no other entries on the chart. The booking area cells were intended for overnight stays, but Bachir had been living in one of them for a full year now. It was a mutually convenient arrangement. The instigator was kept away from the other INS detainees. That made managing him and the others easier. Sympathetic jail officials mentioned that it might also keep Bachir out of trouble; a less sympathetic inmate referred to Bachir as the jailers' pet. Living in booking was lonely and frustrating for Bachir, even while it gave him certain perks that he wouldn't otherwise have had. This was not freedom, but the literal and figurative cages were wider and allowed for more complexity than an outsider might imagine. Bachir had a few quarrels with his Alabama contract jailers, but he was concentrating now on his battle with the INS. Those in direct contact with him had good things to say about him too; it was the bureaucrats who knew only his case history and, to add a further twist, a few of the advocates who had spoken with him who doubted Bachir (though the latter clarified that this did not mean they felt he should be detained).

Even before I visited Bachir in Gadsden, I knew there was something unusual about this incarceration. It is difficult, more often impossible, to contact a prisoner by phone. To reach Bachir, I had only to call a number for the health clinic at the Etowah jail, and someone would hand him the phone. Nurses at the clinic, which was contracted to Healthworks, Inc., even wrote letters to the INS on Bachir's behalf asking for his release. "He has been cooperative, pleasant, friendly, and compliant with the medical staff," reads one memo (it too was handwritten). A typed memo from five clinic workers, all women, calls Bachir "A MODEL DETAINEE" who "HELPS THE OFFICERS AND MEDICAL STAFF IN TRANSLATION WITH FOREIGN LANGUAGES." (Bachir had picked up a lot of Spanish in his years of detention, in addition to his Arabic and English.) Bachir faxed the memo to me from the clinic. One jail employee told me: "He was given a lot of freedom, which is unusual. I think they were afraid he would go to the media."

It was six months before my visit that Bachir had called and left me the message transcribed above. Rose Livingston of the *Birmingham News* had been in touch with Bachir and with Atlanta INS Assistant District Director Tony Campos. "It looks to me like you're getting him away from me . . . because I'm talking to him and I'm about to write something," Livingston had said to Campos. The open channels began to close on her. "I was glad to have a good relationship with INS," she told me. "I don't anymore, but that's okay. . . . [They] have to answer my questions. That's all that matters." Livingston was torn. She didn't want to "aggravate" the situation for Bachir, but she also didn't want Campos to let him languish in jail. She added: "He doesn't like that Mohammad has free access to us." Campos seemed to be taking the whole thing personally. At one point in his "negotiations" with Bachir, according to the prisoner, Campos suddenly flared up about a 1984 ticket for driving without a license, demanding to know why Bachir had not told him about it before.

Yet another ingredient necessary for understanding INS's treatment of Bachir is the agency's institutionalized anti-Arab bias, predating even the first World Trade Center attack. In recommending against Bachir's release from detention in California, an INS attorney had cited "a selection of over 100 pages of documents culled from Respondent's A[lien]-file . . .

[which] demonstrate . . . that [Bachir] has had extensive training in the use of arms and hand to hand combat, and that he may have terrorist connections in the Middle East."[15] Bachir told me he never saw the "over 100 pages," but he thinks he knows where it all started. In 1984, when he was running a video store in Orange County, California, FBI agents arrived one day and told him that someone whose identity they could not reveal had informed them he was a member of the Palestinian Liberation Organization (PLO) before coming to the United States. Bachir does not deny that he was associated with the PLO; he was a resident of a Palestinian refugee camp in south Lebanon, he notes, so "the PLO was the government for us." More to the point, the INS district office not only released Bachir from custody at the time, it proceeded with his green card application. In other words, the allegations were not taken seriously.

Fifteen years later, however, they came back to haunt him. While the INS was justifying its detention of Bachir with its "determination" that he might be dangerous, based on his history of domestic problems, its bureaucrats threw in the old "terrorist" charges for good measure. After all this time, Bachir was told that he must prove that he was not a member of the PLO. At the request of the Arab-American Anti-Discrimination Committee (ADC), Hasan Rahman, chief representative of the PLO to the United States, sent a letter to the INS explaining that the PLO "is not a membership organization." Moreover, the Palestinian bureaucrat wrote to the American bureaucrat, in one of the stranger documents in Bachir's file:

> Even if it were [i.e., a membership organization], it is wrong to criminalize people for their commitment to the principles of the PLO at a time when the PLO is engaged in a partnership for peace with the government of the United States. This cooperation has been going on since the signature of the Oslo Accords on the South Lawn of the White House in September 1993.

The INS was wielding these allegations at a time when the PLO was no longer considered a terrorist organization by the United States. Bachir had not been accused of any violent action, only membership and, in another document, training in hand-to-hand combat. Then the INS "demand[ed] that Mr. Bachir produce a letter written by the State Department stating that the PLO is not on its terrorist list." Bachir's attorney, in a letter to the

INS, is reduced to this: "I was informed by the State Department that the INS has, as does [sic] all other agencies, direct access to the State Department."[16]

Once again, the policy-level racism is enacted more directly between prisoner and jailer. One of the guards administering the welcome beating back at San Pedro had said, according to Bachir, "We want you to suffer the way the hostages in Lebanon suffered a long time ago."

"They took Mohammad from us this morning," said the female correctional officer who answered when I called the jail. He had, in fact, been transferred to the South Carolina hospital to end his hunger strike. "We're all sad." She went on to tell me that since she works the morning shift, she had made Bachir coffee each day. "He was very comical," she said, explaining that Bachir had a knack for mimicking the drunks and crackheads who spent the nights in neighboring cells. On other days, however, he "stresses you to the limit." She had told Bachir her opinion about his criminal history. "I do not agree with what you did, but it's not my job to judge what you did. My job is to keep you secure and safe." She checked the record and told me Bachir had been at the jail for 183 days.

She had been there for ten years. At age forty-five, she, along with thousands of others, was laid off from Gadsden's Goodyear plant, where her father had worked before her. One day while serving jury duty, she ran into the sheriff, whom she knew from high school. He suggested she come to work at the jail. She began that very night, working third shift. There were 78 inmates at the time. She watched from the window as the new jail was built across the street. Now there were 417 inmates, about 50 of them INS detainees. "I dearly love my job," she told me. "I just love to help people."

Bachir was returned to the maternal CO and her colleagues at Gadsden after a relatively short stay in South Carolina's Columbia Care Center (CCC), a private prison-hospital run by the Alabama-based Just Care for the federal government. The prisoners at CCC tend to be those in need of long-term hospice care: AIDS patients, paraplegics, and the mentally ill. And hunger strikers. In early 2000 a couple of frustrated, long-term INS Cuban detainees at CCC took a nurse and an officer hostage for six hours, using a broken fluorescent bulb as a weapon (no one was injured and the prisoners were transferred.)[17] Bachir, during his short stay at the hospital, created his usual multilayered reality. He complied with an intravenous feeding while reminding the medical staff and officers that he was complying and that he could refuse since there was no court order allowing officials to force-feed him. He complained that despite this compliance, he was handcuffed to the bed for the feeding, and he wanted photos taken to document the bruises that resulted. Chief of Security Charles McLendon responded with a personal note on the request form Bachir had filled out: "I will see what can be done to photo your hands. The camera here is not very sensitive, consequently may not pick up or show what you want."

"Let me ask you a question," McLendon said when I called to ask about force-feeding Bachir. He wanted to know whether I would try to convince someone to eat if that person was starving himself. He went on to tell me that hunger-striking South Carolina death row inmate Pee Wee Gaskins had been ordered fed so that he wouldn't die before the state could kill him. Returning to Bachir, McLendon said he tries not to know too much about his prisoners' cases because "it clouds what you know about people." Until given reason to do otherwise, he preferred to treat people the way he wants to be treated himself. At McLendon's facility, Bachir began eating after reportedly going thirty-three days without food.

Tony Campos and George Taylor of the Atlanta INS, which has jurisdiction in South Carolina as well as Atlanta, visited the hospital and spoke to Bachir, who reached me again soon after. Campos had made Bachir confident—not for the first time—that he would soon be released. Livingston told me she believed Campos was angry at Bachir but looking for a way to get him off his hands. "If there's a way to get rid of that man, I will," Livingston paraphrased Campos; but it wasn't so easy, because Campos and Bachir were in a power struggle now, and Campos had to "save face," according to Livingston. Meanwhile, an immigration advocate in Washington, D.C., familiar with the deliberations of INS Headquarters officials over Bachir's case, confirmed that everyone in the INS would be happy to be rid of him. But, the advocate said, even those above the fray of hunger strikes and force-feeding remained wary of releasing Bachir because they did not want the responsibility for what he might do if he got out. "The bottom line," said the advocate, "is they're afraid that if they release this guy he's going to kidnap his child . . . that he's going to do something that really embarrasses the agency. . . . They're really nervous about it because it involves a child." The advocate added, "I think they're afraid of Mohammad" because he's not a "pushover," and added that Atlanta INS was pressuring Bachir not to contact the media. From another office, meanwhile, Bachir's volunteer attorney, one of several along the way, was filing motions with misspellings like "Massechusits" in them and was unaware that the U.S. Supreme Court had agreed to consider cases of indefinite detention like his client's.

There is "the case and the body," and now the body was returned to Etowah County. Bachir was back in the booking cell. He and I had been speaking in one of the visitation rooms, but we had to move when a judge arrived to use the room for bond hearings. A CO allowed us to continue the interview in Bachir's cell with the door open. The cell measured about eight-and-a-half by nine feet. It contained a toilet-sink unit and a steel mirror. Spread out on the floor along the walls were sheets of newspaper, and on top of them were a bottle of skin lotion, a bottle of Coca-Cola, inspirational books, legal documents, and two Styrofoam food containers. There was a calendar on the wall. Bachir and I sat on the very small bed, maybe two and a half feet wide, which seemed to have been built for a child.

In the interview room, I had asked what came into his head the moment he woke up each morning. "When [I] get up, I just feel like I'm lost. I don't know what's happening to me anymore. Then after that, I see I'm still in the same place. Indefinite detention. It's been scary for the last three years. . . . This is not my life. I'm spending the rest of my life in detention. Indefinite. So I feel like sometimes I can't breathe. I just feel like, nothing coming in—no breath, nothing."

When he was at the South Carolina prison hospital, Bachir told me, he had requested oxygen when he felt he couldn't breathe but was told he had to eat first.

"He could breathe," Chief of Security McLendon had said when I asked about the allegation. "Nobody's done anything to his breathing, sir."

Bachir continued: "I get up, I'm scared—that I'm spending the rest of my life in detention because of INS case which is *civil*. I feel like my life is gone. I don't know what's going to happen. I breathe in, then I breathe out, and I pray that one day I'll be with my family."

Bachir had stacks of documents he wanted to show me, notes about other detainees to discuss, and even information about INS detention centers in which he had never been held. "I know everything," he said. "That's why they are going out of their mind." I had to focus to keep him focused, so I hardly noticed the noise in the jail around us. Back in Brooklyn, as I listened to the tape, I was amazed to notice how often we had simply talked through the noise of slamming doors and, much more often than I had remembered, through prolonged screams coming from elsewhere in the jail. Now, from this distance, those screams were chilling.

———

"Everybody's here," Bachir once announced by phone from Gadsden, referring to the INS detainees upstairs, many of whom he knew from jails and detention centers across the country. One unintended consequence of the crisscrossing prisoner transfers in the immigration gulag is the creation of networks of information and, sometimes, solidarity. The transfers are usually unpredictable, so when Bachir briefly met Egyptian Nabil Soliman in the INS Service Processing Center in Batavia, neither man could have known that a year later they would be exchanging hand signals through the narrow windows of the holding cells in the booking area of the Etowah County Jail.

Before I spoke with either Soliman or Bachir, I chatted at the jail with George Taylor. Before becoming the INS Atlanta District's chief of Detention and Removal, Taylor had been a correctional officer for a year and a half at the Bureau of Prisons Terminal Island facility. Before that he was a corrections specialist in the military, running the U.S. Navy's detention center on the island of Diego Garcia in the British Indian Ocean as well as various "afloat facilities." In the INS he made a point of educating himself about the immigration detention system nationwide. In 2001, after five years, he would leave, worn out by his "daily battle" with the bureaucracy at every level of the INS. He had become extremely frustrated with the agency's lack of expertise in corrections and by INS Headquarters officials' lack of responsiveness to detention problems. As an example, he told me how hard he had to fight Washington over its reluctance to pay for TB testing in certain facilities, a health measure necessary for inmates, jailers, and INS officials who visited the jails. He called the INS an "agency that's bankrupt on ethics, morals, and responsibility."

Taylor found the "removal" part of his job taxing too. "It has to be done," he said about deporting people, but "you always wonder what's the fate of that individual when they get back to Lagos, Nigeria, or somewhere in the Middle East." Taylor was willing to talk with me because he trusted the media after an encounter with Sam Donaldson in 1992. In the military he had been granted whistleblower status after facing retaliation for publicly disclosing the misuse of a Bermuda naval base as a vacation spot for military brass and federal officials, and *Prime Time Live* devoted a segment to the incident.[18]

"In the long run, you're a better person for it, and the system is a better system if you do speak out," he told me later. In Gadsden, we were talking about how a new INS director at Krome should handle detainee complaints when Taylor said: "Inmates don't always tell the truth. Inmates don't always lie. You better entertain what's being told."

The following allegations are from another handwritten list that Bachir gave me that day in Gadsden: "7 months pregnant Lebanese woman who has no criminal [record] was isolated for months, they took away her religion 'head cover,' she was crying every day. . . . Iranian woman who begged the officers not to take her 'head cover' religion [off] in front of other people, they start laughing on her, she was crying. . . . Egyptian who they throw him on the floor while he was praying in the holy month of Ramadan and they drag him on the floor, laughing on him—'no criminal record.'" The last example refers to Nabil Soliman. Yet this is not exactly a case of prisoner solidarity; a third detainee told me that Soliman and Bachir disliked each other intensely. They are together in this account because they were both in the Gadsden jail when I visited. It happens that they are also both prisoners of stories practically impossible to unravel from all perspectives at once.

Nabil Soliman entered the United States legally, and he lived in New Jersey for nine years, driving an eighteen-wheeler for a living. He married and later divorced a U.S. citizen. He has five children, two of them U.S. citizens as well. The INS eventually labeled Soliman's marriage fraudulent. When Soliman became impatient one day after waiting more than four hours in line at his local INS office and raised his voice, he was taken aside and soon found himself being questioned by an FBI agent. Promising leads about possible terrorist connections quickly emerged. None of these led to charges against Soliman, but the INS kept him detained.

Soliman's alleged terrorist connections were related to the *first* World

Trade Center attack. When I met him in 2000 he had been detained for about four years, although an immigration judge had already called the terrorist allegations "not sustainable" and "unconvincing." The government itself had admitted in 1997 that it had "abandoned that line of inquiry." Soliman was "never charged with any terrorist activity in the United States," according to the Justice Department. He had never been charged with any other crime in the United States either. Yet the government continued to bundle all these allegations together in its court pleadings, and the INS detained Soliman altogether for five years.[19]

The U.S. government also argued that Soliman was "wanted by the Egyptian authorities" for his alleged connection to a group that is held to be responsible for the 1981 assassination of President Anwar Sadat. Soliman argued that he was a victim of mistaken identity, based on a confusion of names. Egypt had not requested extradition, and the *New York Times* cited documents reportedly showing that Soliman had no criminal record in his country.[20] In May 2000 the Board of Immigration Appeals granted Soliman "deferral of removal" under the Convention Against Torture. This meant that the United States could not return him to Egypt if it was likely that he would be tortured there. An INS official told me that his colleagues "stumbled [and] bumbled" in their testimony about Soliman's identity.

When I spoke with Soliman in Gadsden, where he was engaged in a hunger strike of his own, he did not raise the possibility of anti-Arab bias inside the INS. When I brought it up, he veered back toward the complicated procedural details of his case. A few minutes later, however, he returned to my question, which he justifiably referred to as my "point." Soliman said that after the 1993 World Trade Center bombing convictions, many in New Jersey's Arab community said the evidence must have been fabricated. But he defended the integrity of the American justice system to them. There was a trial, there was evidence, and the defendants were convicted. Now he wonders. From inside INS detention, he said, "I see how the system work. . . . They make me a terrorist."

Soliman also told me that "accepting a tray of food" from his jailers meant accepting what he called his "illegal detention" by the INS. He argued that it was a violation of his First Amendment right to expression and his Fourteenth Amendment right to privacy for jail officials to force-feed him. The INS responded in court pleadings that although Soliman "may have constitutional protections," these are limited when weighed against the government's interest "in preventing hunger strikes and preserving the life of INS detainees."[21] Soliman was just one hunger striker, but his case posed national implications for the INS's management of its ever-increasing, and increasingly frustrated, population of detainees.

Although Soliman had long since agreed to be deported to any available third country and to pay the expenses himself, a Justice Department litigator familiar with the case acknowledged, "We can't find anywhere else to deport him." These were the circumstances that led to what even a district court judge who ruled against Soliman called his "prolonged, and potentially indefinite, detention." The language is significant because in its pleadings to the Supreme Court on the legality of detaining "unremovables" when it seems that no country can be found to take them, the INS emphasized that such detention is not "indefinite" at all.

Soliman had protested with hunger strikes before, including more than a month without food while detained in the INS facility at Batavia, where he had first crossed paths with Bachir. He too was moved to the CCC and on to Etowah County. He began a new hunger strike there and was moved back to Columbia. INS officials tried to win a force-feed order from a district court in South Carolina, and when a judge ruled against the agency, it moved Soliman back to Alabama, where a previous force-feed order was still in effect. (Bachir knew of this litigation when he told CCC officials that they did not have a court order for feeding him.) Soliman had resisted once by biting through a force-feeding tube in the Etowah jail clinic. Jail officials then forcibly sedated him. Because the medication caused him to sleep for some thirteen hours, Soliman complained, he was unable to comply with the Muslim tradition of praying five times each day. On another occasion a correctional officer pulled him off his prayer mat without warning, Soliman alleges, "disrespect[ing] Ramadan"—the same charge recorded by Bachir in his list. Soliman added, however, that officials performed subsequent force-feedings at night in order to respect Ramadan, during which Muslims fast during the day. After he challenged the force-feeding order in federal court in December 2000, Soliman agreed to allow officials to feed him the nutritional supplement Ensure until the judge ruled.

Meanwhile, high-level INS officials had gotten involved. In the internal newsletter of the INS's Office for Immigration Litigation (OIL), an article about strategies for litigating cases of force-feeding focused on Soliman. According to its author, OIL attorney Paul Kovac, the article was prompted by the "increasing number of cases involving detained aliens who conduct hunger strikes." Spread around the country, their protests "left INS officials and Assistant United States Attorneys scrambling for the appropriate response," Kovac wrote. "Detention officials are confronted with a dilemma—do they respect the alien's choice to starve to death or do they abide with their obligation to render medical treatment and prevent suicide by starvation?"[22]

On February 15, 2001, Judge Lynwood Smith of the Northern District of Alabama ruled that the INS has "legitimate penological interests" in force-feeding Nabil Soliman. Smith wrote that Soliman has been "an onerous administrative burden" and also (citing the Justice Department) that the chief of corrections at the Etowah County Jail "overheard that other INS detainees plan to engage in a mass hunger strike if Soliman wins his case."[23] While awaiting the judge's decision, Soliman said his hunger strike was only for himself.

The government was given all the leeway it asked for: in Kovac's words, "substantial deference to the decisions of prison administrators" as well as the "deference [that] courts afford to the Executive Branch in the area of immigration law." Kovac noted that "an alien's status in this country may also dictate the degree of constitutional protections he or she may be afforded." He added ominously: "Perhaps some of these same constitutional principles can be applied to aliens challenging their treatment while in INS detention."

From the high-security unit of the Etowah County Detention Center, Soliman continued to challenge the legality of his detention. He filed a handwritten appeal to the Eleventh Circuit. He was brought to the infirmary each day for the "oral-gastric" force-feeding, according to Chief Williamson. Bachir, who much of the time was allowed to move around in the booking area, was put into his cell whenever Soliman was brought through that area to the clinic. Soliman would soon demand that he not be handcuffed and shackled each day when taken to the clinic, and he would also try to obtain a reasonably priced phone card so that he could make calls to Egypt to continue fighting his case.

"I am not making my detention easy for them," Soliman told me before the district court ruled on force-feeding. When I asked if he might starve himself to death, he compared himself to a soldier who fights "for his right and his people," saying that while it is "not my intention to die," that could be the result. "This is the legal way to fight them," he said.

I put in a call to Chief Williamson to get his side of the latest power struggle with Soliman. He called me back from his cell phone, apologizing for the background noise; he was picking up his children from school. He had smoothly ignored my interest in his private life when I asked about a child's drawing in his office (a small girl and her father in a tent, a bear outside, their guardian angel above), replying only briefly before asking me what exactly my own interests were. Now he simply pointed out that he does not control the price of phone cards sold to the inmates (the jail has a contract with Global Tel-Link). He also said that though he was sympathetic to Soliman's frustrating situation, the inmate "likes to use the 'don't-eat' issue for anything he wants." "I can't let him hold me hostage," he said.

———

Rose Livingston had written about Nabil Soliman after she heard about his case from Mohammad Bachir. She believes that after her story appeared, the INS's Campos may have denied Bachir release to punish him for helping her with the Soliman story. But when Livingston finally met Bachir at the jail, she was surprised to see a man who seemed well fed. "That really threw me," she said. She felt "manipulated" by the prisoner. Perhaps even worse, Bachir was suddenly evasive about putting Livingston in touch with his wife. She left without doing the interview. "I don't have a story," she told me. Livingston added that as she left the jail, a guard told her that Bachir eats "everything he can get his hands on." She contrasted Bachir's hunger strike with Soliman's, which seemed like the real thing. A month later, I would be standing with Bachir in the booking area when Chief Wes good-naturedly patted the prisoner's stomach and said, "Good food, isn't it?" Bachir responded with a smile: "The food is good." A few minutes before, Bachir had been showing me the schedule for "feedings" posted on his door. The COs kept track of what he ate each day. He wanted to emphasize his resistance and the danger he could be in. The hunger strikes were a "controlled reaction," in the words of a psychiatrist who examined Bachir and recommended his release. To make matters more confusing, medical reports from the Etowah clinic indicate that some time before Livingston saw him Bachir was dangerously dehydrated, apparently as a result of his hunger strikes; one report cautions about the possibility of kidney failure.[24]

The maternal CO who was sad to see Bachir leave had said cautiously, "He really knew when and when not to, if you know what I mean." Journalist Livingston said: "I'm not unsympathetic, I just look at him differently."

A day before the town of Gadsden was to celebrate its new contract with INS, Bachir called from the jail again. A special tour of the facility was planned, and Bachir was understandably anxious that he was going to be moved again. "They're going to ship me to some island," he said, sounding melodramatic but genuinely scared. "They're going to ship me some place where I can't speak." Then he laughed. "To Africa, even, or Jamaica." This time he was mistaken. Days later, he got another chance to make his case for release before an INS panel; it was February 2001. In general, detainees held for more than ninety days after they have been ordered deported are entitled to periodic custody reviews by INS officials. As Bachir waited for another decision, Atlanta's Campos cautioned him to "keep a low profile," but the prisoner sounded more defiant than ever. "I let this happen to me," he said, referring to his year in the booking cell, "because they keep telling me: tomorrow, tomorrow, and next week." Then Bachir told me about a Turkish woman who was deported and about a Russian man whom he alleges INS officials threatened to sedate so that they could deport him.

Release was denied. The document, titled "Decision to Continue Detention Following Interview," states in part: "Your extensive criminal record shows that you have a propensity to engage in recidivist criminal activity. . . . You have also failed to clearly establish, that if released from Service custody, that you would not pose a risk to the community. The INS will conduct another review of your custody status in approximately one year of the date of this notice. It is in your best interest to maintain proper behavior while awaiting this review." The document also cites as reason for the denial that Bachir's "institutional history while incarcerated shows that [he] had to be transferred from several detention facilities due to disruptive behavior, which included instigating hunger-strikes, inmate protests and threatening correctional staff officers."

Then, two months later, Bachir was released. Four years of administrative detention ended. Nothing had changed—not his "institutional history" and not his criminal history. Just a few months before, the INS had "determined" that Bachir was dangerous. Now, without explanation, apparently he was not. The old hand-to-hand combat charge had disappeared even earlier. The arbitrariness is so typical of the INS that even to single out these instances of injustice seems, paradoxically, to miss the point: the agency's operation, and the laws behind it, are antithetical to any meaningful notion of liberty.

Yet it must be worse *not* to name those victims of the Justice Department whose names we know. Livingston had written about another Palestinian held at Etowah, Hussein Saker Hassan, a legal resident of the United States who served one year for a drug charge and then was detained by the INS for almost seven years. Then one day the agency released him. "Good behavior while in custody pays off," the INS's Campos told Livingston. The bureaucratic arrogance is almost unbearable. Hassan's brother picked him up on his release and said: "He has turned from a boy into an old man."[25]

After Bachir's February denial, the Arab-American Anti-Discrimination Committee had orchestrated an e-mail barrage to David Venturella, assistant deputy executive associate commissioner at INS Headquarters. Venturella told me that the timing of Bachir's release was coincidental and that the messages had had no influence on the Headquarters decision, which, he said, had not been in his hands anyway. It's hard to know. He has to say that if he is not going to invite letter-writing campaigns from thousands of other prisoners. But more important than the letters may have been the diplomacy of Mohammad Abdrabboh, Bachir's latest attorney. In his twenties and on the case only since the February denial, Abdrabboh was apparently able to speak to the INS bureaucrats without antagonizing them. The bureaucrats, it seems, had indeed wanted to get rid of Bachir as long as they could do it on their terms. One of their terms was this: "You will never discuss the conditions and/or terms of your release with the media. You are not to publish information in any way that relates to the term of your release."[26]

Another condition was this: "You will not violate the Temporary Restraining Order issued by the Superior Court of California, County of Orange . . . filed May 08, 2001." But over the course of several months,

Bachir was arrested and pled guilty to two misdemeanor violations of restraining orders issued by the family court. He paid fines, performed community service, and spent a few weeks in the Orange County Jail. Then, in February 2002, Garden Grove police "made consensual contact" with Bachir in what might have been a post–September 11, ethnic profiling stop; according to Bachir, he and a friend wearing a keffiyeh, or Arab headdress, were standing near his car in a parking lot. No traffic violation was alleged, but police discovered an outstanding warrant, they said. The police contacted the INS, which took Bachir back into custody. About ten months had passed since his release.[27]

"Heads up!!!" exclaimed one INS official in a flurry of agency e-mails about Bachir's return to their detention system. There was no question now about being on the radar. From Headquarters, Venturella wrote: "He will be eligible for a [custody] review. Please ensure he remains in custody. I do not want any one [sic] releasing Mr. Bachir." Venturella also wanted his prisoner transferred from San Pedro to Batavia, where "they are better suited to manage Mr. Bachir." Using a "belly chain," leg shackles, "Service approved wristlock's [sic]," and "a Service Approved C-clamp escort control hold," INS agents put Bachir on board a Northwest Airlines plane. He resisted. INS alleged that Bachir announced he was a "Palestine terrorist" and intended to "blow up" the plane. Yet he was never charged with threatening to blow up the plane. He was, however, indicted for assaulting a federal officer, the usual charge when a prisoner resists or when officers have assaulted the prisoner.[28]

Bachir was placed in Los Angeles's Metropolitan Detention Center, and, since he was criminally charged, a federal public defender was appointed to represent him. He was temporarily denied phone access to his attorney and to his media contacts, according to his public defender, Humberto Diaz. Diaz soon received a letter responding to subpoenas issued to Los Angeles airport police and operations personnel. The city attorney's office wrote that airport police had no records of the alleged incident on the plane. Northwest Airlines also told the city attorney they had no records of such an incident. Bachir pled guilty to lesser charges and was sentenced to eight months time served.[29] He was then successfully moved to INS detention in Batavia.

While he was out of detention on supervised release after the earlier decision, Bachir had left a message one day at the Los Angeles INS office to say he would miss a day of required reporting because of hospitalization. An INS officer confirmed receiving the message. Even though Bachir wasn't picked up by the INS until seven months later, Venturella used the one-day absence to justify the new detention, according to attorney Sophie Feal. Venturella had also spoken directly with Bachir's estranged wife, who reportedly conveyed her fear that her husband would be released again.[30] One of the wife's relatives also tried to contact Venturella and had gone to the INS office in Los Angeles to complain about Bachir's alleged harassment by phone of his wife and her family. That relative warned me not to let Bachir "con you that he's just this poor little lamb being abused by the U.S. government" but added, "If he's supposed to get out, let him out. We'll put it in God's hands and see what happens."

What justified Bachir's detention by the INS at this point? The one-day reporting absence? Immigration agency employees' second-guessing of Orange County family court rulings? Or were these a cover for the continuing power struggle between bureaucrat and prisoner? The INS need not explain. In 2003 the agency unsuccessfully attempted to convince Lebanon to accept Bachir. Then, after seven months' detention in Batavia, it released him onto the street outside the detention center. From a pay phone, Bachir called his latest attorney, who drove him to the train station, and he returned overland to southern California.

—

Nabil Soliman's hunger strike ended on board a chartered plane. When his handwritten appeal reached the Eleventh Circuit, the court appointed Birmingham attorney Elizabeth Barry Johnson to the case. Soliman later wrote to her from Cairo: "There were four guards from the INS to guard me, once I went in the airplane one of them was waiting for me with an injection to make me sleep by the drug. Since there is no chance for rescue [from] this extradition and with this situation, I promise them that I will not make any trouble in change for not taking injection to make me sleep, so they accepted the deal. Two hours later after flying I declared that my hunger strike is over and I request food."

Soliman's case in the Eleventh Circuit had become moot after Justice Department attorneys told the court that the attorney general had received "assurances" from the Egyptian government that Soliman would not be tortured if returned. Soliman's attorney pressed the United States to provide evidence of Egypt's assurances. The U.S. government never did so, but it used the claim of these assurances to withdraw Soliman's protection under the Torture Convention.[31] Four days after Soliman's arrival in Cairo, the U.S. Embassy released a statement:

> U.S. Ambassador David Welch said today that Soliman's removal, coming after successful bilateral discussion, is "another example of the close U.S.– Egyptian cooperation in the war on terror, demonstrating the American commitment to working closely with our friends and allies to eradicate this scourge." Soliman was taken into custody by Egyptian authorities upon arrival at the Cairo international airport.[32]

Then, according to Amnesty International, Soliman was held "incommunicado" for several weeks before being moved to the Tora Prison in Cairo, where his family could bring him food and an attorney could visit. Taken together, the statements from Amnesty International and the U.S. Embassy suggest that the embassy was cooperating with Egyptian authorities during the period in which Soliman was incommunicado.[33] Yet despite the "assurances" that the attorney general had found "sufficiently reliable" to use in court here to justify Soliman's removal, embassy spokesperson Philip Frayne was more cautious: "I can't say with complete confidence that he hasn't been [tortured], but we don't have firsthand evidence to the contrary."[34]

In early 2003, as a national emergency law already in place for years was extended and Egyptian security forces rounded up people suspected of having connections to radical Islamic groups, Nabil Soliman was tried in a state security court.[35] He was sentenced to five years in prison.

# 11 | GOOD AND EVIL IN NEW ENGLAND

At the Etowah County Detention Center in Alabama, Chief Wes Williamson kept pinned to his staff bulletin board an article from *Corrections Technology and Management* about a jail in Manchester, New Hampshire. "Where Did All the Immigrants Go? Jail Profits Leave with INS Detainees"[1] is a true-life parable about allegations of prisoner mistreatment and the resulting revenue losses. The Hillsborough County House of Corrections, the subject of the article, is run by Superintendent James O'Mara, who urges me not to rush when trying to understand his facility and warns me what happens when journalists take immigration lawyers' complaints at face value: "You end up describing the Marquis de Sade's basement when in fact, really, it's more akin to a well-managed kindergarten. . . . You hear more language walking through a mall than you do in this facility."

The formal name of the jail evokes an older era in penology. It is known locally by the even more quaint "Valley Street Jail." The place had become New England's largest immigration detention facility until its lucrative contract with the INS was abruptly terminated in January 2000. Hillsborough had already been attracting intermittent media attention when I first spoke with the superintendent, but within a few months he would be deeply embattled in Justice Department investigations, as well as in Manchester County commissioner squabbles and union-management struggles with his own correctional officers. When two inmate deaths and accusations of sexual assault against women inmates finally put too much heat under the whole arrangement, the federal agency moved its detainees out.

James O'Mara grew up in Dedham, Massachusetts, a working-class town just south of Boston. He wanted to be a policeman but went into corrections instead. "I got bit by a bug that said: you can make a difference." He became a correctional officer in a Massachusetts jail and ten years later was superintendent at Hillsborough. His wife teaches emotionally disturbed children and was training to become a school psychologist. "As far apart as our respective clients are in age, if she's not able to reach these kids, I'm going to get them," O'Mara tells me in a long, unhurried telephone interview. "Isn't that awful?"

He continues: "My neighbors can't believe what I do, because I am extremely active in the community, and they think I have to be a mad dog to be in prison, to be in a corrections setting. I hate to tell you, when I first started I knew more people *in* than wearing a badge. There were kids I grew up with." He laughs. "In the third cell I looked in when I started in corrections was a kid I went to grammar school with.

"I said, 'Hey, Chippy, how you doin'?'

"And he goes, 'Hey, what are you doing here? Hey, pretty good job, huh? Nice benefits.'

"And I said, 'Oh yeah, sure, we're going to see how it works, I'm going to give it a ride.' I found that to be ironic. Yet at a very basic level, it allowed me to succeed in managing these people."

O'Mara is such a skillful manipulator that he tells you what he's doing while he does it. He freely admits how he uses his understanding of inmates to control them. It's his job, after all. "I knew where they came from, I knew the games they played if they were inclined. I'm not able to be conned, so to speak, and more importantly, I'm not a condescending, arrogant, badge-totin' fuck. Many people, when they first get the badge, go through the Wyatt Earp syndrome: 'I have a badge, I'm bad, I can do no wrong.' Whether it's natural or not I won't comment on, but more experience it than they care to admit. Once you get over that, and you realize that not every detainee or inmate is a hunk of garbage, that begins your key to success."

O'Mara tells me a story. One night, while working as a supervisor, he had to talk to the entire shift of fourteen COs about a new prisoner. He needed to rein them in a bit because some of the younger guards were getting cocky with a new inmate sentenced for vehicular homicide. O'Mara told his officers: "I just want to let you know we got this guy in, drunk when he was driving." "Second shift is party shift," he explains to me. "You can still hit those nice joints when you get out at ten or eleven o'clock. And they're going, 'Aw, what a piece of shit he is.'

"You could hear the groundswell. And I just looked at them and said: 'Just to let you know, he is on a leave of absence from the Plymouth County Department of Corrections, where he's a CO.' And they all went, 'Mmmm. Ooohh. Mmmm.' I go: 'Lesson, guys: not everybody's a piece of shit. Don't drink too much tonight.'"

"I do not have an opinion on the rules that the U.S. Congress sets on immigration detention," O'Mara declares, referring to the 1996 mandatory detention laws. Boston attorney Susan Church worked as a public defender before starting to do immigration work, so she is able to see the INS system in the wider context of the criminal justice system. She calls the application of 1996 laws against legal residents with criminal convictions, who previously would have been released back to their lives, "unyielding, harsh, and widespread." The new detentions were so widespread that Boston's local detention facility soon proved inadequate. "Never in its wildest dreams did that agency ever envision itself in the detention business," says O'Mara, and he compares the resulting prison boom to that which followed the harsh drug-sentencing laws of the 1980s.

Hillsborough had some six hundred beds, and within a few years one-third of them would be leased for $65 per detainee per day to the INS. O'Mara is straightforward about his job: "I simply have an opportunity to make use of available beds that exist within my facility to reduce the burden on my local taxpayers by creating a revenue to offset the operating expenses." Even as he speaks openly about his political role, O'Mara shares the defensive posture of many corrections professionals who feel misunderstood. Along with approximately $6 million in annual revenues came the battles with attorneys representing his new detainees. O'Mara believes they "attacked conditions of confinement" as a way of doing battle with immigration policies. Or at least he says he believes that; part of his rhetorical power lay in blurring that distinction. In 1998 O'Mara had denied an intern from Boston College's Immigration and Asylum Project permission to continue making group presentations to INS detainees at the jail, alleging that she had "misrepresented" her intention and was "using housing issues as a way to magnify" her objections to immigration laws.[2] The superintendent acknowledges that his jail is "an environment that's considered probably one of the more stringent in the state—not harsher, not crueler, but stricter. There's not lot of movement." This would certainly be objectionable to "people who believe that people who are here seeking asylum should not be locked up at all," or to "someone [who] in their heart of hearts believes that detention in general, in its most basic form, is the object of disdain."

Often a cultural or social gap between law enforcement personnel and their critics surfaces in their dialogue. O'Mara seemed to have a disdain for the "advocates"; for some of them, he loomed as a larger-than-life villain. A local attorney even commented on his intimidating size. In this case, the bad guy was smarter and more articulate than he was supposed to be, and he was quite conscious of that gap. At one point, O'Mara begins talking about his relationship with inmates and segues into his battle with the advocates: "It really gives you a lot more natural ability to control a situation in a group of people by appearing to be understanding, rather than a superior, up-on-high person—which, by the way, is often an attitude an attorney can start with, until they figure out that you're a human being and you might know what you're talking about."

I have laughed condescendingly a time or two with other journalists about the pleasure of interviewing local sheriffs and wardens who say whatever crosses their minds. It's an experience made even more enjoyable by its contrast to the tight-lipped and unimaginative spokespersons in the INS Public Affairs offices. But James O'Mara is not typical. When he talks to me about "the direct supervision inmate management principle" by which "[the] staff is trained to look at people as rational human beings who make conscious decisions whether or not to violate a rule," he sketches in some corrections history, going back to the Nixon era, and pauses to say, "I don't want to drag you down a big, long road, but it requires architectural support to the thought process." The metaphor is not accidental. Corrections professionals, especially those who know their vocation's history, have an intimate relationship with architecture, and design issues inside the prison contribute to what O'Mara describes as advocate-jailer misunderstandings. Forty-five minutes into our telephone interview, he has a question for me.

"Don't you want to ask me about solitary confinement?"

Well, yeah.

"I don't have a hot-box in the backyard. And there is no 'solitary confinement'" as such. He describes the cell arrangements, which include a "restricted area" where cells are within eyeshot and earshot of each other. His critics, without understanding this, "think of *Cool Hand Luke*." O'Mara does a terrible southern accent, though he adds a deep twang to his Massachusetts brogue: *"What we've got here is a failure to communicate—"* He switches voices again, as crisply as a professional performer, one character interrupting the other: *"Put the boy in the box."*

Local attorneys and their clients also complained about the jail's classification system, which denied INS detainees access to educational and work-release programs. According to O'Mara, this criticism was premised, once again, on ignorance of how jails operate. "It's important for you to know that because INS detainees are contracted inmates for us to manage, they are not allowed to move below general population into what we call at the county level the 'programming mode'—where we'd be looking for employment for them, where we'd be looking for opportunities to put them in the community-based corrections program. They would not be eligible for those because they are being *detained*. . . . Those beds are valued beds in the lower classifications, so we wouldn't want to put someone there who had no hope of getting out, and no hope of going to work soon. So you can see it would actually create a clog."

The underlying problem is simply that INS administrative detainees are in jail. While district INS officials commonly tell advocates that the local jails keep INS prisoners and county inmates separated, this is simply impractical, if not logistically impossible, for the jailers to accomplish. Atlanta INS's George Taylor told me anyone who claims that INS detainees and sentenced inmates are separated in local jails "is full of shit." Advocates' complaints on this score tend to be, word for word, the jailers' defense. Boston attorney Sarah Ignatius: "In general, everyone at Hillsborough is treated the same. Whether you are a criminal inmate or an INS detainee, you are treated like a criminal serving a sentence. . . . The guards didn't care that they are in the U.S. to seek asylum." O'Mara: "I do not run a separate set of rules for INS inmates, for sentenced inmates, or for pretrial inmates."

O'Mara's job is managerial, and his public posture is reflected in his title—"superintendent" rather than "warden." ("*Warden* and *superintendent* are interchangeable," Mississippi warden-turned-death-penalty-abolitionist Donald Cabana once told me. "They mean the same damn thing.")[3] Whatever the terminology, there is no escape from inside the argument and no answer to it from the outside. Once again, the "structure of the system," as the Haitian poet at Krome put it, creates the very problems its apologists claim to solve. The superintendent makes no higher claims for what he is doing, at least not with respect to the INS prisoners. His job is to manage, to supervise, to classify, to control. The INS detainees are not being "corrected" anyway. They "understand," O'Mara says, "we're just keeping them, we're not punishing them." But then the advocates come in and stir them up by telling them, "'You shouldn't be here.'"

O'Mara's bullying and rhetoric dovetail with his insight into the architecture of this policy debate. "I, quite frankly, am not up for, nor am I interested in doing battle with advocates who are seeking to change detention laws by attacking conditions of confinement. If Congress says they can all go out on bail, I really don't care. . . . The [local] taxpayers will have to bear a little bit of that brunt, they won't have that revenue flow. But I don't have people with whips and chains." For its part, because the INS depends on local bed space, it does its best to deflect advocate criticisms while deferring to the local jurisdictions. The two sets of officials are quite clear with each other that the INS is simply not in a position to run the local jails, and as Taylor says, they don't know how to do it anyway. INS Boston Deputy District Director Denis Riordan wrote to O'Mara about a petition of complaints he had received from INS detainees at Hillsborough: "While I am always concerned with issues brought up by those being detained by the Immigration & Naturalization Service in the Boston district, I have no intention of intervening in issues which are solely under your jurisdiction as the superintendent of that facility."

It was O'Mara who faxed me a copy of Riordan's letter when he was getting bad publicity. He knew how to exploit the deniability strategy for his own protection. Here he acknowledges the frustration of INS detainees: "I don't know if there's very much notice provided to detainees when they're moved from facility to facility. I think that bedspace [for the INS] is such a premium, that they need to fill the beds as quickly as possible with whomever they have in their hands at that time. There's not a lot of concern for the individual.

"So given that you have an individual who comes into the Hillsborough

County facility who's not happy, doesn't even know where in the hell he is, first thing he wants is the phone. Well, fortunately, we all know this from the movies. Of course you can use the phone. My goodness, tell people where you are. It helps *us* when you're calmer. But now he goes to a unit and certain things are occurring outside of the facility. His family is no longer being fed—they are trying to get on public assistance but may be reluctant because they don't want to get found [by Immigration]. . . . So pick the worst-case scenario. And the guy turns to a correctional officer and says, 'I fuckin' can't believe I'm here! I hate you! I hate being here!'

"You know what the correctional officer says? 'If you weren't here, I wouldn't have to watch you, either. You're not a county inmate. I'm a county corrections officer.'" O'Mara pauses again. "It's a business decision that we make. I'm just as much a part of this as the county leaders who are responsible for the votes. But I can tell you right now, if you surveyed any one of my corrections officers and asked them, 'Would you prefer to have these detainees gone?' it's a no-brainer. Because it creates fewer people that that person is required to manage. . . . So please bear in mind that the frustration is a pendulum that goes between the keeper and the kept."

The most surprising surprise in O'Mara's performance is his claim that advocates have the immigration agency under their control. He is mightily frustrated by what he perceives, or says he perceives, as the INS's "ever-incessant effort to appease these people."

"Let me try and give you an idea of what I'm up against when I, from Hillsborough County—I'm not going to say, I'm *little* Hillsborough in the *little* state of New Hampshire"—and, of course, he has then said it—"I'm simply going to make a geographic observation that I hope will hammer home the point."

"You're calling from New York," O'Mara continues. "My facility was mentioned at an Amnesty International meeting. Who's there to present *my* point? Who's there to represent *me* when all the advocates are there, bashing INS representatives who know"—he pauses a moment to let diplomacy catch up to his evident anger—"who know *not much* about where they're sending people. They conduct tours, they know the place is clean, that the meals pass the recommended daily allowance for vitamins, the facility is well managed, the staff is well trained. [But] INS is not in a position to describe the day-to-day operation. Yet they're supposed to be there representing their agency—and *my* agency, since I'm the one that's taking the hit."

Insight and blindness are not mutually exclusive, and O'Mara's own deniability zone seems firmly in place. I asked the level-headed Errol Hall, who had been held at Hillsborough, for his take on the superintendent. "Nobody ever saw him. That's just it. This man just hid himself. [He] never came on the pod." O'Mara says, "Quite honestly, I think we do a real good job here." Then he praises the jail building: "It is aesthetically pleasing, and it sets into the modest skyline that the city of Manchester has."

Metal shavings in the food. Maggots in the cereal and rice. A detainee is strapped face-down to a "boogie board" for sixteen hours. Staff ignores a man's complaints about medicine allergies until he passes out in the shower. An HIV-positive inmate taking medication for pneumonia is held naked in an isolation cell for thirty-six hours. A detainee is held in "solitary confinement" because there is no available bed, then held there throughout his proceedings for complaining about it. It "defies logic, therefore, it's not happening," O'Mara says of one allegation that medical treatment had been denied, observing that it wasn't in the accused CO's own interest to have to guard sick prisoners.[4]

Dirty underwear is issued, and one woman receives a disciplinary ticket for washing it herself. "Railroad track" stains are common on underwear, O'Mara observes in our man-to-man interview, adding that detainee laundry complaints are exaggerated. And anyway, if inmates want responses to their grievances, they should go to the proper department. "If you're dissatisfied with the color of our sheets, don't bother the process officer. That's my responsibility because it's my facility." He gets frustrated because "vehicles exist"—he mentions detainee grievance forms—yet he gets calls from attorneys about soiled uniforms and there is no paper trail. He returns to his old theme: "I'm not trying to make us out to be a victim here."

Petty degradations at Hillsborough continued to build. A Haitian woman wrote to attorney Church:

I was told that I could have a clean cotton blanket every three months. I have been here for eight months now. I still have not received a clean blanket. Every CO that I have spoken with has informed me differently of the rules governing a blanket. I am tired of being disrespected and being told different things. . . . They treat me like *menour,* please forgive me for my language. *Menour* means shit. I'm not a piece of shit, and it's not fair to be treated like so. . . .

Most of the COs stand on the upper floor to get a better view of us showering. . . . They call us names, like jail whores, and tell us we're getting deported so get over it. I'm scared being in this jail. . . . As soon as you get this, let me know. The COs told us that they will screen our legal mail and I'm not sure if you'll get this. . . . Please come see me as soon as possible so I can tell you things that I didn't dare put on paper. . . . Most of the other immigrants are afraid to talk because of the treatment they'll receive for doing this. Someone needs to take a stand. I suppose it'll be me! I'm not afraid anymore. Please come see me where-ever I may be.

In August 1999 some thirty legal U.S. residents, among them people whose names were Ouk, Ramos, Pha, Tang, and Escudero, wrote from the Hillsborough jail: "After having completed our sentences in the eyes of justice, we are free men but are treated as animals by the correctional officers here. Verbal abuse and lack of moral respect are issues we face every day." It is just after their hunger strike that I first speak to O'Mara, and his almost clinical explication of this method of protest is seductive in its way. When I ask if he didn't consider such an action "extreme," O'Mara replies, "What's extreme is a Buddhist monk lighting himself on fire." He pauses to let that sink in. "Someone not taking a meal will go unnoticed in a correctional facility unless its done by more than one person and they're letting people know. . . . What I think is trying to be accomplished is a recognition from people outside the facility who are able to identify hunger strikes with a protest of sorts, which prompts further inquiry into the issue that that the person is trying to make.

"Look, I'm not a psychoanalyst. I've just been in corrections for eighteen years, and I've seen it done quite a bit. . . . You and I can identify with someone who is protesting in such a pacifistic manner. I think it is a popular pacifist approach to raising the awareness of others to your plight." As for this particular protest, again: "It began as a . . . result of the detainees being informed by outside advocates that they need to draw attention to their conditions to raise public awareness—[and] it had nothing to do directly or indirectly with the services of this department nor the treatment by this staff."

Church wrote a letter to the Boston INS district director addressing one of O'Mara's countercharges: "Although you may think that defendants always complain about jail conditions, because it is a jail, this is not true. I did not receive the same complaints from any of my public defender clients [at other area jails]." In fact, Church wrote, both of her female INS clients at Hillsborough requested transfer to the women's state prison in Grafton. "Hillsborough is largely renowned as the worst jail in New Hampshire," she noted.

Concord attorney Paul Twomey told the Manchester *Union Leader*'s Pat Grossmith that he had visited many jails and that Hillsborough County had made "conscious decisions to overcrowd." He said the result is "totally degrading conditions. . . . The place is a madhouse." Stealing O'Mara's ace, Twomey described the inmates and the COs as victims: "You have hundreds more people than the facility was built for; you have a staff that is understaffed because of ongoing labor problems," including "mandatory overtime." "Everybody's on edge. Everybody's overworked," Twomey continued, and the INS detainees are, for the most part, locked up "for being poor and from another country." O'Mara tried to dismiss Twomey—"I didn't know he was a corrections expert"—and then tried again to have it both ways. He told the local newspaper: "'If the by-product [of lowering taxes by raising jail revenue] is discomfort with a little bit of crowding— which is not the case; there was a bed for everyone—then that's too bad.'"[5]

When the puzzle pieces are arranged by someone other than O'Mara, the picture looks different. A New Hampshire attorney who confesses to having "the fantasy of taking this place down" told me that the jail has a long history of disgruntled personnel. As O'Mara himself had noted, COs are "resentful" of INS detainees, who make more work for them. They see the detainees bringing in money that they do not get. The Manchester *Union Leader* reported that COs were angry over inequitable pay raises, that O'Mara favored his inner circle over the rank and file. A union representative said: "The sad part of it is there are two James O'Maras—the Jim O'Mara who came from the line staff and knows what corrections is all about and the James O'Mara that is the politician."[6]

Two inmate deaths were reported at the Hillsborough jail in early 2000. A forty-four-year-old Cuban INS detainee had a heart attack; there was no "foul play," according to the medical examiner. Non-INS prisoner Brian Armstrong "hit his head on the floor," according to a U.S. Attorney, was released on bail the next day, and died a few days later. Another inmate would tell the local paper that Armstrong had been beaten while strapped to a chair shortly before he collapsed; jail officials denied this.[7]

Meanwhile, as half a dozen investigations of correctional officers for sexual assault against women inmates began, fourteen INS women were removed from the jail. Then the INS pulled out all its two hundred fifty detainees. O'Mara was reported to have told an INS official to "shove it"—referring to the $6 million per year—when he arrived to transfer the prisoners. There were more ripples through county commission meetings, where O'Mara and the federal contract shared the spotlight. O'Mara defended himself at a public forum in Manchester by saying that what he had really told the INS official was much worse than "shove it." All in all, there seemed some hope that the sparks might cross through what a former immigration judge has called a "disconnect between [INS] Headquarters and the field."

"We're all thinking that these guys are out of control," New Hampshire Assistant U.S. Attorney David Vicinanzo told the *Union Leader.* "We felt if the management of the facility was treating us in this way we were concerned about how low-level employees might be treating inmates who had very little ability to defend themselves." Attorney General Janet Reno was reported to be personally concerned. By late 2001 three COs had been acquitted of allegations for sexual assaults on inmates and three others convicted for nonsexual assaults; all six prosecutions involved non-INS inmates. The federal investigation into the alleged abuses against the INS detainees had "fizzled," according to county officials.[8]

Until the very end, Superintendent O'Mara refined his alliances as circumstances required. He told the *Union Leader* that as the aliens at Hillsborough boarded buses for other jails, "'County inmates could be heard chanting, "USA. USA. USA."'" O' Mara explained: "County inmates consider the INS population to be cry babies and that they brought a lot of difficulties on themselves."[9] At least one veteran INS official felt there should have been more oversight of the Valley Street Jail all along. He told me that he could never say so publicly, however, or his own INS colleagues would "destroy" him.

———

One morning, driving from New Orleans to Jackson, Mississippi, I noticed that I was passing through Amité, Louisiana, so I stopped by the

Tangipahoa Parish Jail to see what had happened to a Pakistani detainee who had been calling me from there. Deputy Sheriff Dean Jensen looked at the records and told me that the man had been "shipped" but that there was no record of his destination. "They scatter 'em to the wind," Jensen said of the federal immigration agency. All the Hillsborough INS detainees were scattered to the New England winds: Lehigh, Niantic, Plymouth, North Dartmouth, Greenfield, and Cranston.

Elizabeth Nabatanzi Luggude-Katwe was one of 1,899 women in INS detention on a given day in 2002,[10] and she was one of the 250 moved out of Hillsborough. She called from the Bristol County Jail in North Dartmouth, Massachusetts. The INS had picked her up one summer day as she returned from an aerobics class, wearing her tights and a sports bra, and took her to jail. Almost three years after leaving Hillsborough, she would be taken from the Bristol County Jail to New York's Kennedy airport with two other women for deportation—Nabatanzi to Uganda and one of the others to Jamaica. Nabatanzi had become "deportable" as the result of a larceny conviction. "I find based on this conviction that she is not a person of good moral character," said the immigration judge.[11] The Jamaican woman taken to the airport that day had become deportable because of a conviction for attempting to steal more than $1 million from a company she worked for.

"You people are so happy. You are going to Europe," Nabatanzi told me she told the INS "escorts" at the airport who had their luggage with them. Then she told them that she was not going anywhere because there was a stay in effect that prohibited her removal. "They said they were going to comatose me," Nabatanzi said. The Jamaican woman also refused to go, though less defiantly. Forty-seven years old and having served her time in the Framingham, Massachusetts, Correctional Facility for Women, Frances had five daughters, all U.S. citizens. The INS escort allowed her to make a call from the airport. Her twenty-three-year-old daughter said she would kill herself when she heard her mother was about to be deported. Frances asked the INS officer to speak to her daughter, and he did. All three women were returned from the airport to detention.

In the jail at Niantic, Connecticut, Frances said, one of the "immigration girls" hanged herself. Other inmates took her down before she died, but the on-duty officer was scared and "wouldn't go near her." The girl was taken to an outside hospital by helicopter and eventually returned to the "population." "They put people right back in the same room," Frances said. "They never gave us therapy. . . . There were girls screaming in their sleep, and I still see it." She and the others were moved out of the Niantic jail when complaints about correctional officers' sexual involvement with the "immigration girls" surfaced too often, she said.

They were moved to Bristol County. According to Rose, a Haitian inmate, the on-site INS counselors there tried to be helpful; the COs referred to the women as "INS whores." The women were regularly strip-searched while they stood over mirrors, even when they were simply being moved from one part of the jail to another and had never been free of handcuffs. Rose had been a legal resident of the United States for two decades and served eleven months for assault with a dangerous weapon. She had hit her daughter with a belt. "If you check my culture," she said by phone, "that's the way I discipline my kid." Her children visit her every couple of weeks but are not permitted contact visits. The visits are by phone, through a window. "We can't even hug them. Some women stay here for five or six months without touching or kissing their husbands or kids . . . or the husbands kiss the glass," she said. "And they end up getting deported."

"They think we are stupid," Elizabeth Nabatanzi told me angrily. "We are very educated. They just want to dehumanize us." An officer in the background said politely; "Elizabeth hang up, it's log time." She said she would call back, but she never did. Her attorney lost track of her. In December 2002 a Dominican woman I didn't know called about Nabatanzi. Gladys was forty-one years old and a legal resident of the United States since age six. She had met Nabatanzi at the York County Prison in Pennsylvania. Gladys had successfully completed an upstate New York "boot camp" following a drug conviction. One day, when she made her semiannual visit to her parole officer, the INS was lying in wait. She was only detained for about two weeks, although in that time she incurred a phone bill of some $600. "You even have to pay for salt and pepper over there," she said, referring to the small packets used by fast-food restaurants. She had lived on a cot in the York County Prison gym along with other women detained by the INS. There were no psychologists, she complained. "If it hadn't been for Elizabeth and other detainees there, I would have gone out of my mind." She spent five sleepless nights while no one responded to her written requests for information about her case. "I really thought I was going out of my mind." Most of all, she wanted to know what would happen to her children, but no one could or would tell her anything. There was a "floor counselor" at the jail, and after a week "he brought some bras and underwear. That's as far as his counseling went."

Gladys was awake at 4:00 A.M. when they came for Nabatanzi. "They told her to pack up her stuff, and she goes." Two days earlier, she continued, York County Prison correctional officers had been passing around a newspaper article about a lawsuit Nabatanzi had filed against the prison.[12] Although Nabatanzi had been ordered deported in 1999, Gladys says of the lawsuit, "I believe that's the reason she was shipped out of there so fast. That's my belief."

—

Across the street from the Adult Correctional Institution (ACI) in Cranston, Rhode Island, a line of green-gray armored vehicles was parked in front of the National Guard Headquarters. It was three weeks after September 11, 2001. From outside, the ACI is colonial brick, slotted windows, and barbed wire on Slate Hill Road, not far from Interstate 95. Inside, Errol Hall and I sat across from each other in the visitation area. A foot and a half to each side of us, other pairs visited. Most were young couples. The modular table-and-chair units (purple metal) were like those I had seen on the exhibition floor of the American Correctional Association convention in Denver two years earlier. The inmates all sat along one side of the units, their visitors along the other. A few babies crawled around underneath. A correctional officer sat at a raised desk at the end of the long room, like an armed high school lunch monitor, with a tiny American flag perched atop his telephone. Above the water fountain, a hand-stenciled sign warned, No Inmate Use, *Solo Para Visitantes* (Only for Visitors).

These were "limited contact visits." The young couples may hold hands. They may not touch each other's faces. They may kiss briefly when the visitor departs. The inmates here are men. Young women visitors lean forward, touching their partners and holding themselves back at the same time. The desire in the room is palpable. So is the desperation, and the resignation. A correctional officer walks by and touches the shoulder of the inmate next to Errol Hall and tells him to get up for a moment. They walk away and whisper. I overhear the word *touching*. Hall tells me that the COs like to mess with the inmates in here. Hall is an INS detainee, but the laminated I.D. card clipped to his blue jumpsuit says "offender" just like everyone else's.

Hall left his native Jamaica for the United Kingdom at the age of seven with his mother. He went to school there and came to the United States in 1973 when he was about twenty-one. His tourist visa soon expired, but he stayed, and he has been in the United States since. His parents and his sisters are here as well. Hall did time in the Massachusetts state prison at Concord for a 1983 armed robbery (two years) and for a 1997 conviction (two years) for "deriving support from prostitution"; he answered calls for an escort service. On completion of that sentence, the INS detained him. He had been in INS custody for two years when I saw him in Cranston, and he was still in INS custody two years after that. He continued his legal battle against deportation because he wanted to see his family again. Acting within its legal authority, the INS refused, not just to set bail, but to grant Hall a hearing in which he could argue that he deserves to be out on bail, under supervision, during the course of his proceedings. It didn't matter that when he was doing criminal time, the Massachusetts Department of Corrections allowed him out on work-release programs and to stay at his parents' home on occasional weekends. After his father had a stroke, Hall tried to get permission from the INS to visit him and then return to custody. He hoped to see his father before he died, but the INS would not allow it.

Hall turned fifty shortly before we met. Throughout our visit, he pressed his fingertips into his temples, saying that he needed therapy but that it was not available here. He kept asking me about myself, about being in New York on September 11, and about the wedding I had just been to in Boston. He told me that he did a thousand push-ups every day. He had a system of sets so that he wouldn't lose count.

I first heard from Errol Hall after Pastor John Rush put us in touch. Rush was doing prison fellowship work in Pennsylvania when he spoke with Hall about a hunger strike among INS detainees at the Lehigh County Jail in eastern Pennsylvania, where they had been transferred from Hillsborough. Hall himself was not participating in the protest, but according to Rush, he was passing along information on behalf of the seven hunger strikers.

"I've never seen anything like it in my life," Hall said of Hillsborough and its "abusive" COs. When I asked what he meant by "abusive," he said he meant verbal abuse and also getting thrown in the hole for thirty and sixty days at a time without a disciplinary hearing. He had been threatened by COs after complaining about inadequate shower opportunities. Hall had tried to contact the family of the Cuban man who died at Hillsborough. He started to keep notes about the inadequate law library, the grievance procedure, and the treatment of other inmates. At first he hid these in a dictionary. Over the next months and years he sent out letters with lists of detainees' signatures to reporters, to the American Bar Association, and to the ACLU. He would take notes and send letters from the Allentown, Lehigh, and Pike County Jails in Pennsylvania, from the Hudson and Passaic County Jails in New Jersey, from ACI Cranston, from the Franklin County House of Corrections in Greenfield, and from Bristol County in North Dartmouth. ("Please come see me where-ever I may be.")

In August 2000 Hall called from New Jersey's Hudson County Jail, where many of the post–September 11 detainees would be held. "This place is getting ready to explode," he said. INS inmates were being put into holding cells "where human waste was clearly visible over the floors and toilets," Hall wrote in a letter signed by thirty-six INS prisoners. "We are given one uniform which we cannot wash because we have nothing else to put on." COs at the jail, Hall added, "sit in a bubble. They sleep, listen to their radios, and look at nudie magazines. . . . We have nobody to reach out to." Jail officials told the detainees to make their complaints to the INS, but there were no INS officials on site. "Our problems go unattended," the letter continued. "This constant movement from jail to jail is causing a great deal of losses for us. Every time we file a petition with the courts, it is always denied either because we cannot meet the court deadlines, or, after being moved, the court lacks jurisdiction to solve our problems. This is causing us reckless infliction of emotional distress." The letter is optimistically addressed, "Attention: Concerned Authority."

Next, Hall called from the Passaic County Jail in Paterson, which would also be used for September 11 detentions. "I don't know what the fuck to do anymore," he said. "They keep moving me." He politely asked, as he always did, if I had any news about changes in the 1996 laws that I could send him. He had been in seven jails in nine months. From Cranston, Hall sent a list of violations signed by twenty-seven detainees to INS Commissioner James Zigler.[13] The complaint mentioned that phone calls from the Cranston jail cost $4.60 for the hookup and $1.69 per minute. One New England immigration advocate told me, with a certain resignation, that no one was pushing the phone issue at the jails because if there were too many detainee calls, the advocacy groups would be overwhelmed. The American Bar Association had visited ACI Cranston, as well as several other jails and detention facilities, to monitor conditions. Part of the group's agreement with the INS was that in exchange for access it would not share any of its findings with the media.

In March 2003 Rhode Island District Court Judge William E. Smith ruled that it was unconstitutional for the INS to deny Hall an individualized bail determination. Judge Smith ordered the agency to "hold a prompt hearing."[14] (He wrote that he could do nothing about Hall's demand that the INS return the legal documents it had confiscated from him.) The next month, Hall went before an immigration judge, who released him on $7,500 bond; this same judge had denied Hall's application for a waiver of deportation, but now Hall would be out of jail while that decision was on appeal. He was taken from the jail at 5:00 P.M. and spent four hours in a Bristol County sheriff's van. Seven other detainees were with him, on their way to lockups in Concord and New Bedford. Hall was driven to the Boston Coast Guard facility, where his family was waiting to meet him. The next morning, he visited his father's grave. Five days after that, the Board of Immigration Appeals denied his appeal. INS agents came to his mother's house in Dorchester and asked for him. Hall's mother asked the agents if she could get his shoes and coat before they took him away, and the agents said they would wait. When she came back out, her son was gone.

A pair of snow skis, a saddle, and a box of ashes are some of the things that have been kept in the property room of the INS's Wackenhut-owned-and-operated detention center in Aurora, Colorado, just east of Denver. The saddle belonged to someone who was apprehended by the Border Patrol while on horseback. The ashes are the remains of a detained Czech woman's husband. I didn't see these things, but INS Assistant District Director for Detention and Removal Douglas Maurer good-naturedly tells me about them—little "human interest" stories, because jail tours quickly become predictable. The tour guides hold up a tray piled with food or gesture toward a pod where a man can walk freely to the bathroom or sit slumped and staring at a television set, and all this is supposed to mean that everything is fine. Maurer says, "You walk back here and you can take a breath of air and it doesn't kill you." People out West often refer to the open air and to the sky, and as you drive around Denver the mountains always seem to be coming into view.

The property room is really an efficiently organized walk-in closet. There are rows on rows of small, mesh hanger bags filled with sneakers and clothing. A tall, wheeled ladder nearby helps to reach the higher bags. There are also rows and rows of shelves for heavier footwear. A small piece of tape labeled "shoes" is affixed to many of the shelves with work boots lined up on them, and often the boot pairs are arranged one shoe on top of the other, with another piece of tape, bearing the prisoner's alien number, on the top shoe's tongue. Some of the work shoes are still covered in dust. A couple of rows of lower shelves are labeled "boots," which in these parts means cowboy boots. Most of the prisoners here are Mexican. The dry-marker board provides the day's tally: 171 are Mexican, and 123 are "OTM," Other Than Mexican; 9 are women.

Facility Administrator Ron Nardolillo, a Wackenhut employee and former New York City police officer, listens as Maurer and his colleague, Supervisory Deportation Officer John Good, chat in an easygoing way about the jail—for my benefit but no less genuine for that. They reminisce about detainees who left an impression. There was the guy from England who stopped eating for thirty-seven days. On the thirty-eighth day he was either force-fed or started eating voluntarily; they each remember it differently. Maurer mentions the depression many suffer from being here: "It's situational, of course." Officer Good clarifies: "I think he means the detainees, not the staff." I can't tell from my notes now if that was a joke.

Abbas Hatami is worried that I won't see what bad shape he is really in. "I'm relaxed today because I took that pill. . . . You should have seen me yesterday." Hatami is intelligent, educated, and in despair. We are speaking in one of the bare, cinderblock visitation rooms of the Aurora Wackenhut. He is a good-looking man, dark curly hair, dark eyes, a prominent nose, and he has a direct and open gaze. A smaller picture of himself laminated onto an I.D. badge with the letters WCC/INS above it is clipped to the pocket of his prison uniform. Here at one of the principal INS detention centers inland from major ports of entry, Hatami feels isolated. As usual, that is no accident. The corporate relations director for Wackenhut Corrections had told me, "We give disguised names to our prisons . . . [so] people don't know it's a prison." The building, like the I.D. badge and the prison uniform itself, bears the letters WCC/INS. Officer Nardolillo said that before working here, he thought this was an insurance company.

Abbas Hatami speaks quietly, and he doesn't fight the same way many advocates and prisoners do, that is, by delving into the procedural details of his case. Instead, he is going through the details of his life, as if he believes that if we simply hear those details, we will understand that he should not be here. He doesn't seem really to believe that himself anymore—he is here, after all—but the details are all he has. He came to the United States from Iran in 1994. The thirty-five-year-old easily received a visa for a six-month stay and a one-year extension: he has master's degrees in electronic and medical engineering. He got married in Portland, Oregon, to a U.S. citizen. She turned out to be an alcoholic, and the marriage was falling apart five years later when Hatami returned to Iran to visit his father, who was dying of cancer. Hatami speaks with dignity, and yet he clearly remains stunned by the breakup and by what he discovered about his wife. These are the details that he cannot let go of, that he needs me to understand. She had told him about her previous drug use, because she was relapsing. She told him about her former boyfriend, because she had started seeing him again. When Hatami returned from visiting his father, he discovered through friends that his wife was in jail. He tried to find her and couldn't. He recalls how bad her drinking had become just before he left to see his father. One night she came into the house, half-crazed, and tried to eat frozen meat straight from the freezer. Hatami asked her, "What is wrong with you?" She told him she was hungry.

Later an INS officer would challenge the validity of their marriage by asking Hatami why they had filed separate tax returns. He had no idea how to answer this. Meanwhile, according to Denver attorney Laura Lichter, the INS examiners contacted Hatami's wife and coerced her into dropping the application for adjusting her husband's status, which had been sitting for eight months unanswered. She withdrew the application without telling Hatami. When he went to the INS office for his scheduled interview, he was detained. "They put me in handcuffs in front of my lawyer," he recalls, referring to a previous attorney who, he says, started shaking when she saw her client get handcuffed. "The officer laugh at me. 'You're going to find out you don't even have bond.' These guys are laughing at me, laughing at me *hard*." Months later, Hatami's wife would leave a message on his answering machine saying, "I'm so sorry."

What part of a man's story is important? How much time do we have to listen to each other? Fauziya Kassindja, in her memoir of detention, recalls how *New York Times* reporter Celia Dugger would ask her a question, scribble furiously in her notebook, and then interrupt when she had heard enough.[1] People need to tell us many things that seem to have no place in a courtroom or a bureaucrat's office or a newspaper article or a book. I interrupt the story of Hatami's broken marriage to ask him about being detained, because that was my subject. His voice cracks. "You don't know how it's hard for me here, to stay here. . . . It's just [a] punishment. . . . What I did wrong?" He can sense that he is deteriorating. "I'm really crazy . . . don't think too much . . . If I [had done] anything, I just say, okay, this is my punishment. But I didn't do nothing wrong." He says he has never even received a traffic ticket. He is sobbing. "For what?"

Nine or ten days after Hatami was locked up, he tripped down some stairs. A nurse gave him Advil. "I'm scared maybe something's happening in my head." He submitted a medical slip to the clinic. Three weeks later he saw the doctor. "'I think you're okay,'" he says he was told.

"Why you say you *think?* I'm not okay. I'm dizzy. . . . I can't even sleep. Why nobody listen to me?" He is speaking softly and slowly now, determined again to tell every detail.

"[The doctor] said, 'You know we can't do nothing else now, but I think you're okay, and I hope you get better.'

"I said, 'That's the only answer?'

"He said, 'Yeah but I can give you more Tylenol, Advil, and some pill to help you sleep.' . . .

"I'm just scared something's happened inside. How can they check?"

It's no accident that Hatami would ask that question; he knows how to fix ultrasound and EKG machines. At the detention center, he fixes things like radios to pass the time. He has told the clinic that he will pay for the test himself if it's a question of money. "But, please, somebody listen. . . . Please help me, somebody. . . . I'm trying to tell them what is happening to me. I always wish to come to America. They put me in jail for nothing."

Trapped in a system designed to be insulated from public scrutiny, detained in a warehouse designed to be hidden from public view, Abbas Hatami and untold others are further trapped inside themselves. Hatami has relatives in Iran, but he gets no comfort or support from them because he is ashamed to tell them where he is. Ashamed that he studied for eighteen years and has no job now. Even his new friends at the detention center think he must have done something wrong, that he must be keeping something from them.

"I'm relaxed today because I took that pill," he says. "You should have seen me yesterday. . . . Today I'm okay. Today I'm really okay."

His voice has become almost inaudible. He has been detained for one month.

———

The view of the Rocky Mountains from the downtown Denver hotel conference room windows made it a little difficult to pay attention at the local American Immigration Lawyers Association lunch meeting featuring guest speakers from the INS. We ate pizza and salad, while a short drive east of the city, at the detention center, a group of Asian detainees was calling off a hunger strike, fearing that even a peaceful protest would prejudice District Director Joseph Greene against them. The detainees understood that Greene, like the thirty-two other INS district directors across the country, through a chain of authority leading up to the attorney general, had too much "discretion"—the word used by the relevant statute—over other people's lives.

Laura Lichter was going to take advantage of the district director's presence at the luncheon to make a case for her client Abbas Hatami. She stood in the back while many of her colleagues finished their lunch. She felt she could win Hatami's release if she filed a plea for habeas corpus in federal district court, but going to court costs time and money, and it would not be necessary if the bureaucrat at the podium would agree to free her client. She believed he had the authority, and she tried to convince him to use his "discretion" to do it. According to the INS, Hatami was not entitled to pay a bond and be released from detention while his case was pending because he had left the United States and returned while his marriage status adjustment was still pending, technically making him an "arriving alien." Oddly, if he had not left but had still been arrested by the INS after they rejected his marital adjustment application, he would have been entitled to a bond.

District Director Greene, who had described himself to his audience as the chief law enforcement officer of the Colorado District of the Immigration and Naturalization Service, told Lichter: "If you believe that there is a legal basis [for your client's release], brief me. If it passes the laugh test, I will pass it on to Headquarters. But that is not the way to effect change." By which he meant, not the way to change the law.

Lichter: "As much as I'd like to effect change, I'd like to get him out before he hangs himself."

Greene: "It's *that* way." His arm was extended, and he was actually point-ing. "District court is that way." It's where Lichter would have to file the habeas petition.

Greene's comment might have been maddening, and it might have seemed flippant, but he was serious. I had spoken to him earlier that day at his office, so I knew that he was a thoughtful man. He also likes to turn a phrase and wrestle with a concept, and he was clearly relishing the intel-lectual encounter with a roomful of lawyers. I took a picture of him on the street after the lunch meeting. He is a man with a middle-aged paunch that he carries lightly. His eyes are in shadow, squinting in the Denver sun (he had pulled off his sunglasses for the picture). He is smiling under his mustache, and he looks like he's having a good time. He had just finished telling the roomful of lawyers that their options are "limited given the stu-pidity of the law which [he is] mandated to enforce . . . and which [they] are mandated to dismantle." Some local attorneys were annoyed that Greene tended to make such a good impression, because they felt that when it came to the bottom line—unchecked power and the willingness to use it—the difference between Greene and the "old school," as one of them put it, was only his "PR savvy." Greene was savvy *and* frank. When the lunch was over, he thanked the group for its willingness to cooperate with him and added, "Damn you for your compelling arguments that continue to saddle me."

"If you can get through a conversation without his using the word *exis-tential,* you've had a pretty strange day." That comment from immigra-tion lawyer Carol Lehman was enough to make me want to interview Joseph Greene. And interviewing him was easy. Whatever his detractors have to say from a policy perspective, he was open to talking. Some dis-trict directors use their public affairs officers to shield them from the pub-lic. Out West, Greene welcomed me into his office.

Two of the photos decorating the wall of that office caught my atten-tion. One shows Bhagwan Rajneesh in the custody of federal agents. The other is an autographed photo of former Attorney General Edwin Meese. The first photo is there because in the mid-1980s, Greene was sent to Portland to supervise the INS investigation of the Bhagwan. He is proud of his role in the Bhagwan indictment, but he is especially eager to tell me about the Meese photo, which was sent to him after he received an award from Meese for his contribution to the Bhagwan case. Greene points out that the photo is warmly inscribed "To Fred." He had apparently received the photo meant for the man behind him in the award recipients' line. His first reaction had been to call Washington and try to get the right photo. Then it occurred to him that this was perfect in its wrongness. "Ed Meese," he tells me, "was by far one of my favorite unindicted co-conspirators. The son of a bitch should have been in jail. . . . What better represents the whole Reagan fucking administration to me than this mistake?" He laughs a hearty and genuine laugh.

Not your typical INS bureaucrat, and no wonder: if the academic job market had not been so tight in the 1970s, Joe Greene would probably be teaching philosophy. A self-described "product of the Jesuit ghetto," he graduated from Loyola College in Baltimore and was working on his Ph.D. at Fordham University when he got married, and realistic job options became a priority. His new father-in-law had worked as an immigration inspector at Kennedy airport and encouraged him to apply. Soon the INS offered him a position. He still figured he would finish his Ph.D. at some point. "That was twenty-five years ago," he laughs.

Joseph Greene explains Colorado's place on the INS map. The Denver District consists of the tristate area of Colorado, Wyoming, and Utah, where Denver is the single major metropolitan area. "Half of Colorado, and most of Utah, are part of the old charters from the Spanish kings. Colorado south of Pueblo was part of Mexico until 1848," he says, dropping into history to make a point about the present. "So there are old Hispanic families in this state that go back to the discovery of the Americas by the Europeans. In many ways, the white bureaucrats that are running the Immigration Service now in Colorado are complete newcomers." Greene is white. Outside, a burrito truck was parked on Paris Street. The proprietor told me he sells the food that his people like—but that he feeds the non-Mexicans too. His customers were waiting for their appointments, sitting on the edge of the lawn and eating outside the Denver INS offices.

Greene adds that Denver's centrality, from its old days as an energy center, persists in its role for INS transport. Meanwhile, traditional smuggling routes from the southern border have shifted to put Denver "in the middle of the flow." In 1994 (the year Abbas Hatami arrived in the United States from Iran), Attorney General Janet Reno announced Operation

Gatekeeper, the goal of which was to "squeeze the balloon," or deter crossing at certain points to force those Mexicans determined to cross to do so through areas remote from major cities.[2] Greene says, "If you look at the map, you can see that El Paso is on a direct route to Denver on I-25, so that that flow of smugglers, who would go up [Interstate] 25, take a right at Albuquerque to go back East, or go up to Denver and then cut across I-76 to go into the Middle West and then on to Chicago, which is a huge magnet—that was kind of closed off." The flow shifted west. "They go right through the Four Corners area into Colorado. They either take this Highway 160, which is a state road that runs right parallel to the New Mexico–Colorado border. Or they go up a little further and pick up I-70 at Grand Junction. So there's a network of roads on the western slope. . . . The most significant strategic shift over that last five years has been Colorado as a pass-through point for smuggling."

The new border strategies forced Mexicans to cross in dangerous areas through the deserts, where many fell prey to rapists, robbers, or the deadly heat. In the late 1990s the Border Patrol's public relations machine was in high gear, and the *New York Times* and National Public Radio repeatedly ran stories set along the Mexico-U.S. border extolling the humanitarian virtues of Border Patrol agents who rescued dehydrated Mexicans by bringing them Gatorade. No doubt many individual agents have struggled to help stranded Mexican travelers. But with rare exception, even the liberal press simply failed to mention that these rescues were necessary because of the strategy premised on pushing the border crossers into terrain that could kill them. "They anticipated all this," San Diego attorney Claudia Smith told me.[3]

When I interviewed the Border Patrol's supervisor in the San Diego sector, he slipped and said "agent" when he meant to say "alien," and he laughed at his mistake. Joseph Nevins has argued that the establishment of the Border Patrol generated the idea of border crossers as aliens—not the other way around—and that Mexicans were considered "alien" whether they had legal crossing documents or not.[4] Unpredictably, the supervisor told me that if there were no wall along the border, movement back and forth might find its own level. He compared the possibility to drug legalization. Speculation aside, he saw himself as a soldier carrying out policies devised in Washington, D.C., and he was glad that this time the troops were being given the means to do their job. That meant more vehicles and more agents. Speaking about the infrastructure of "removal," District Director Greene said: "We have the direct overland route down to El Paso for Mexican nationals, so we can run them down by bus, and then the El Paso people can make arrangements with the Mexican government and have them returned across the border."

Out in the field, the Border Patrol supervisor must also contend with morale problems. He told me that it was a "morale buster" for agents on the incoming shift to find out that it wouldn't do much good to apprehend Mexicans on a particular day because the local detention center was already full. But it was a "morale booster" when aliens were transferred from San Diego, where they had been apprehended, all the way to El Paso before being returned to Mexico. When attorney Smith was tracking the human consequences of Operation Gatekeeper, she noticed that husbands and wives apprehended together were often "released at different border crossings," contrary to the Border Patrol's own policies. Mexican women were flown from San Diego to Las Vegas and back again within two days and held in overcrowded cells; sometimes there wasn't even room for all the women to sleep on the floor. Smith concluded that "the separation of nuclear families" was being done "systematically." If so, the strategy had antecedents. In the 1950s, according to the INS itself, a "major feature" of controlling the border with Mexico was the "rapid expulsion of aliens to points distant from place of employment and apprehension." At the same time, "legal Mexican agricultural workers ('Braceros') were being admitted in growing numbers."[5]

Greene isn't trying to hide anything when he talks about interstate highways instead of foreseeable deaths. The bureaucratic infrastructure supports a gulf—sometimes unavoidable, sometimes exploited—between policy makers and their soldiers. For years, agency officials and immigration attorneys have spoken off the record about the inability of INS Headquarters bureaucrats and Justice Department officials to do anything to change the arbitrariness and even the brutality with which policy is carried out in the field. "When I started out with this agency, say twenty years ago, I think the cultural ethos—if that's a term—of the Immigration Service was that the district director was in fact the potentate," Greene candidly recalls. "The metaphor that I liked was kind of a feudal arrangement. There was a king in Washington, and each district director was like a duke or a baron. You swore fealty to the king, but you also could withdraw fealty if the king was taking you down a path you didn't want to go." He mentions a few of the dukes or barons by name. "These were guys who said, you know, this is my district, I'm responsible for what goes on in it, and I will do what I think is fit and proper—which was possible to do, frankly, because nobody cared about immigration twenty years ago."

The phone rings, and I pause the tape. Then we segue easily from the structure of the agency to the structure of reality. The dissertation Greene never finished was going to be about "William James and the integrity of the real." He explains: "The idea was that in pragmatism, you have a philosophy that respects what I would call the integrity of things, which is not simply their reality but also their value." Philosopher Greene wanted to find a place within the totalizing philosophies for the more intangible aspects of ourselves. "If you wanted to pray or if you wanted to live a life that was guided by values that you couldn't touch . . . then you had to break loose of empiricism. So James . . . said we're entitled to use logic to come to our decisions, but at a certain point in our lives, we come to those choices where logic is insufficient, and in that case we get to rely on something called our passional and volitional nature, which comes about as close as any philosopher has ever come . . . to something like conscience and the human heart. And if you can create a philosophy that allows for those things to have a role in the conduct of our life, then it seems to me that you have come upon a philosophy that respects, more than any other I've ever read, the huge complexity of what it is to be human."

From Washington, Greene would later play a role in Justice Department efforts to assuage public concerns about the post–September 11 dragnet ("No raids, no roundups, none of that").[6] Sometimes the INS hides prisoners intentionally, as it would do then; other times, the gulag and its poorly managed bureaucracy just swallow them. While Greene was still out West, he casually mentioned one of the lost ones. We were discussing long-term detainees. "Our longest case, frankly, is a guy from Poland who's been here for almost five years in our detention. . . . I just found this out a couple of days ago." Greene relished our explorations of the gray areas in philosophy and INS policy, but his view of the "guy from Poland" was black-and-white: "He's a bad guy."

Bogdan Lawniczek was convicted of murder near Chicago in 1991 and sentenced to eight years in prison. He was paroled after serving three years and nine months in Illinois. Lawniczek also had convictions for trafficking cocaine and violating his parole. Three days before his parole date on the murder conviction, he found out that INS had a "hold" on him. That meant he would be deported, except for one thing: because of his criminal past, Poland refused to take him back. He had been in the United States—legally—since 1975. Whether or not he is "a bad guy" is beside the point. The important thing is that he was not a U.S. citizen. Joseph Greene had the authority to keep him detained or to let him go.

"My biggest nightmare, frankly, Mark, is reading in the newspaper that a guy that I released has killed somebody. I mean, not only is that going to be a big letdown for the Immigration Service, but it's going to be very personal for me because I'm the guy who says, yeah, it's all right for him to go. And then if somebody's dead as a result of that, that's going to be real hard to reconcile with. I think what's true is that if the Congress has given us the authority, then they have to give us the means to exercise this authority appropriately. And what I mean by appropriate exercise of authority is, we need to know, and we need to have the means to properly evaluate, whether these people are going to be dangerous to the community or not. We need to be able to provide them with opportunities to turn their lives around." Unfortunately, opportunities for rehabilitation of any kind were practically nonexistent at the nearby detention center. The result was that "it's hard to come to anything like a determination that's fair to [the detainees] or fair to the community I serve." This was just the kind of arm's-length diplomatic position that piqued local advocates.

The more fundamental issue is a blur of legal definitions, identity myths, and power. "Like it or not," Greene continues, "as an exercise of our sovereign authority, we have made the determination that we do not have to deal with all of the criminals of the world. So people who are not citizens of the United States, who have a record, who have committed crimes, who have been convicted by our criminal justice system—they do not have the right to be in this country, or to make demands upon our resources. And to me, that's an essential difference in terms of—I mean, I want these people to be treated fairly. I want them to be given opportunities if they are in some kind of bureaucratic or legal limbo. I want them to have the opportunities . . . to become better people." Yet around the country INS officials regularly deny release to legal permanent residents *after* they have done their time, "justifying" the decision by claiming that the detainees have not shown they are rehabilitated. All the while, the detainees are locked up in jails and converted warehouses where they are lucky if they remain sane.

Setting aside theories of rehabilitation and sovereignty and fairness, Greene says: "Ultimately my job and my duty is to deport these people, and everything that leads up to that is simply like being in a waiting room."

———

Bogdan Lawniczek's waiting room was one of the Aurora Wackenhut prison's twelve disciplinary segregation cells in the Special Management Unit. When Greene told me about him, Lawniczek had already been on INS hold for about five years—longer than he had served for his murder conviction. "Bogie" was living in seg because he wanted to. Fifty-four years old, he compared himself to a mad dog who needed to be away from the noise of other inmates and to be alone so that he could have his few permitted belongings arranged just so. He needed psychiatric care too, but he wasn't getting much of that from Wackenhut or the INS. That wasn't their job.

When Bogie was doing time on the criminal charges at Logan Correctional Center near Springfield, he loved smoking contraband cigars. He laughs when he recalls it as we speak in the echoing visitation room. Then he abruptly returns to the present. "They violate me, the INS. They took my papers away, stripped me, period. I'm illegal now"—meaning that his green card has been revoked. "That's the reason I'm here." Some prisoners survive the deprivation by becoming thinkers; others see their minds destroyed. It is impossible for me to know if Bogie's mind jumped around like this before his decade inside. Pieces of the past and present, without apparent context, surface and spin away. When the manic streams dissipate, it is possible to piece things together by asking him to clarify. His accent remains strong. "They stole my cigars too," he says of INS officers in Illinois, at a jail where he was briefly held. Twenty dollars' worth. He knew because he recognized the smell. Then "they threw me over here."

He liked it here at first. He had been a custom cabinetmaker on the outside, and the Wackenhut administration used to make sure that he had tools so that he could do carpentry and painting around the detention center. He did a lot of cleaning and maintenance work for a while, but it upset him when other detainees messed up his work. When that happened once too often, he went after the other guy "like a pit bull." He tells me he tore some sort of cables off a wall and attacked the prisoner from behind. He is talking fast and laughing, although it's not clear whether he thinks the story is funny or whether he's laughing for some other reason.

There are a number of long-term Southeast Asian detainees in this Wackenhut. Bogie claims that the rules were tightened up because of the Asians' propensity for contraband. "How do you feel about Asians?" he asks himself. "I hate those little bastards, you know, because the little ones cause a lot of problems." One of them was moved into G Dorm, and he had contraband tobacco on him. Detainees would tear pages from Bibles to roll cigarettes. "I don't want nobody smoke in this place," Bogie says, as if he hadn't just told me about the pleasure of smoking cigars in the joint. Now he explains that after twenty years he quit "just like that." Anyway, he likes being in seg because it's more controlled, which means there's less paranoia from the staff about contraband. In the general population the detainees are subjected to strip searches three times a week. That was too much for him.

Then he tells me about a fight during which his leg was injured and which finally drove him to voluntary segregation. One day another detainee walked into the dorm. "He looked at me and smiled and says, 'Hey Bogie, I screwed you again.'" Bogie doesn't explain what the guy was referring to. That's not the point. "I just went, you know, went and grabbed the guy—I didn't want to hurt him, just scare him, because they're little people, you know? Just grab him and shake him, you know?" He chuckles through his heavy breath. "You ever see a dog's fight? That's what they look like, OK? They came for me." A Wackenhut detention officer grabbed him from behind. Bogdan Lawniczek is a large, heavy-set man. Something in his knee snapped, and he went down. He was in medical isolation for three months. When he got out and returned briefly to the dorms, he realized how much better it was to be isolated. A sympathetic Wackenhut officer let him move, with his few belongings, into a segregation cell.

"I want[ed] to go somewhere and be by myself. . . . Nobody got hurt, you know. I went there, and I want to stay there. I don't care. It could be a thousand years . . . I feel very comfortable. I got things where I like. I have a lot of *things*." He pauses. "I'm relaxed. I got *things*. I got a lot of construction books, magazines, you know, that's my favorite thing. . . . It's very comfortable. I'm like a monk, you know. It make me feel good. I got to live. . . . I give five years of my life—I don't even know for what."

Then he says something that makes me understand how little I understand. I try to question him about the Polish embassy's refusal to issue travel documents for him. But Bogie is no longer interested in that problem, because now he wants to go to Afghanistan. He has a friend with connections who can pick him up in Kabul, if he can just make it there. This is in 1999, three years before the attacks that brought Al Qaeda onto our screens. In the concrete interview room inside the WCC/INS Processing Center at 11901 East 30th Avenue in Aurora, talking about Kabul is like talking about the moon. Indeed, for the man who is speaking to me, who says he was willing to swim across the ocean to get there, or to spend a thousand years in an isolation cell to stay out of the general population, "Afghanistan" seems to mean an imaginary sea of tranquillity.

"It's as far and as different—it's like a—" He interrupts himself. "I'm looking for something in life. I'm looking for the *truth*" (in his Polish accent, *truce*). "I get along with Pakistani people, seems to me we always kind of click, you know. . . . So I'm going there. . . . I want to go and touch a tree, you know?" He laughs that he'll have to grow a beard. "At least I'm going to find me peace, you know?" His friend can get him a construction job in Afghanistan. "My friend will be the only one responsible for me there."

The INS contracts with the Wackenhut Corporation, which in turn contracts with a psychiatrist who has prescribed antidepressants for Bogie. But he stopped talking to the psychiatrist after overhearing him laughing with some of the guards about detained Mexicans. The antidepressants help, but they kill his appetite. Guards worried that he was starting a hunger strike. "I just can't eat," he explains. Now when he wakes up, he just drinks coffee and smokes Marlboros. Still he likes taking antidepressants. "I'm like an old dog. I lay down and something bites me and I snap on him, you know. . . . I'm losing it more often, you know, because little things trigger me up, and it scares me because I gotta live, you know."

He remembers a guard who used to tell the detainees, " 'This is not a hotel, this is a jail.' " It's a correctional officer cliché, but it made Bogie angry. "He don't even know what he's talking about. Sure, I have one foot in the electric chair, almost, and he telling me—little guy—a lot of things, all their stuff, they just kind of keep on it. . . . I'll go anywhere. I don't care if you tell me to swim, I'll swim there, you know." He pauses again. "I used to work. It was good for me. Used to get me out of bed." That's when he mentions that the new administration won't let him have his tools, though a friendly officer did once bring him food from a local Polish restaurant. For a moment he is like anyone else recalling a good meal, the cakes, the sausages. But it upsets him when friendly staff members want to chat and joke with him.

"Sometimes they forget I'm a detainee," he says.

Bogie feels there is no one to help him now. A detained kid from Cameroon used to make phone calls for him and would help him photocopy legal documents. The young prisoner was a jailhouse lawyer, so the Wackenhut staff decided to keep them apart. Bogie recalls a Somali prisoner who was chained to the water fixtures in the shower. Then there was the Nigerian who spit on guards, so the SWAT team came in, gagged him, and put him in four-point restraints on a steel table in a room down the hall. (Other detainees noted that the Nigerian became angry and spat after a guard repeatedly refused to let him use the phone to call his lawyer.) As Bogie sees it, the Wackenhut guards are "like little Muppets, to take the heat" off the INS. "Everybody's nervous right now. Everybody's kind of tense, you know." The long-term Southeast Asian prisoners had just called off their hunger strike. Another pause. "It's just, sometimes there's so much things in my mind, you know?" He groans. I ask him whether living in the isolation cell is still helpful.

"I know what I need to survive, you know?" Then another wave of incoherence, though he seems to be choosing his words carefully. "Long as you know you want to have a life, what you want to with the goals, you know, the most important thing, you just got to make it"—his meaning surfaces again—"*wait,* and they will happen. And I wait five years. And I'm telling you, this is *close.* . . . I feel like I'm free—almost."

Days before, one of District Director Greene's subordinates had said matter-of-factly, "[Bogie is] not the kind of guy we're going to cut loose."

———

"However philosophical Joe Greene is, why does this man have this power?" Carol Lehman is a former librarian with a penchant for the right question. She came to this work in her fifties, which might explain why she is able to see it so clearly. After working as a librarian in Wisconsin, Michigan, Arizona, and Colorado, Lehman was waiting for a ride home from a rafting trip when she decided to go to law school. One day her immigration class at the University of Colorado went on a tour of the Wackenhut/INS detention center in Aurora. She stood in the storage room filled with shelves of detainees' clothing and shoes and felt as if she were stuck there. She cried all the way back to Boulder and told her professor, "Teach me what I need to know to get people out of that damned place." During our conversation, she tells me how odd it is to see someone writing down everything she says. But she doesn't stop saying what she thinks. When we first spoke by phone, she said the local chapter of the American Immigration Lawyers Association had "too cozy" a relationship with the district director. "You can definitely quote me on that," she immediately added.

Lehman had an Iraqi client who received two years' probation for an assault conviction. The INS picked him up after the 1996 laws were passed, and he spent three years confined at the Wackenhut facility as the result of a crime for which he had been required to serve no time at all. District Director Greene had the authority to release the Iraqi man from the start, but he refused. Lehman believes that Greene is a "decent" man but says she personally has not seen "the much-vaunted compassion." It is in the context of discussing this client that she asks why he has such power.

When Lehman speaks about detainees, the procedural and emotional abuses emerge as strands in the same fabric. Lack of compassion when it comes to release policies is reenacted in the way the jails are run. Technically, INS Service Processing Centers are not jails, just as, legalistically, neither detention nor deportation is "punishment." But as Lehman observes, "It looks like a prison, it smells like a prison, everybody in it acts like it's a prison." Only INS officials don't like to admit that. "Would you rather be [strip-]searched and hug your wife, or not be searched and talk through glass?" she asks. Lehman tells me carefully that she is "not comfortable" with the use of segregation at the Wackenhut facility. She voices quiet outrage at Wackenhut's use of four-point restraints for inmates who feel suicidal, and she has seen clients deteriorate very quickly there. "I just think it's inappropriate to run that place like a prison." In Lehman's view, INS detention policies are a form of "mind control" that is difficult to fight.

Her theory is not complicated: "People can't stand being there, so they give up rights." Indeed, one advocate reported hearing INS officials describe detention as "the three-sided cell strategy" in which "the fourth side of the cell opens up" into the prisoner's home country.

Lehman offers another example, quickly rattling off the facts. This client was a twenty-six-year-old Mexican man, arrested for possession of marijuana with possible intent to deliver. He was a legal permanent resident of the United States and had not been in Mexico since the age of three. His parents, his children, and his girlfriend were all here. In all likelihood, he would have received a waiver of deportation before the 1996 mandatory detention laws. "People will take a deport just to get out of there," she says, and that's what her Mexican client did. He agreed to leave, avoiding a possible prolonged legal battle with uncertain results. He preferred "to be under the sky instead of in that place." The INS returned him to "his" country.

What strikes Lehman most about the world of immigration law in the United States is that it is "outside everybody's understanding of how the government can treat people." Even the word *unconstitutional* misses the point; Lehman speaks instead about "the *sub*constitutional nature" of this work. Then she asks another question, one she likes to ask her clients: What is the most important thing about becoming a U.S. citizen? Her answer: "They can't make you leave." The Iraqi, the Mexicans, Bogie—all were here legally but had not become citizens. If they had, the INS could not have detained them when they were done with the criminal justice system. Lehman repeats the answer, as much to herself as to me. Or to anyone who might get the message. If you become a citizen, they can't make you leave.

To insist on the inviolability of a line separating citizen from noncitizen, given the fluid nature of things, is akin to building a steel wall—stretches of which are actually topped with greased plastic tubing—that extends beyond the southwestern desert out into the Pacific surf. It was not until 1952, Joseph Nevins reminds us, that Congress "made persons from all 'races' eligible for immigration and citizenship—for the first time since Congress originally restricted citizenship to 'free white persons' in 1790." Persons of African descent and Asians were ineligible for citizenship until 1870 and 1943, respectively. In addition, "U.S. authorities often had great difficulty in deciding who was 'white.' While at one point [a] U.S. court deemed petitioners from Hawaii, Japan, Syria, and the Philippines as non-white, courts ruled that applicants from Mexico and Armenia were, indeed, white." The tides shift. Marian L. Smith of the INS history office and library relates the case of an Egyptian man in Detroit who sued the U.S. government in 1997 "for classifying him as racially white when he was obviously black." Smith notes that the classification was the result of a 1941 standard under which "natives of the cradles of Western Civilization [were considered] to be 'white persons'"—at the time, intended as a progressive change for the purposes of immigrant naturalization. A historical perspective reveals the complexities, but the enforcement mentality staves them off. At a swearing-in ceremony in a Miami civic auditorium, INS District Director Walter Cadman told the new citizens: "Though some of you might have been here for many years, you were nevertheless an alien. . . . You will walk out the same as us."[7]

Lines drawn by even the most dialectically minded bureaucrats tend to remain politics disguised as reason, and all too often, law enforcement trades humanity for power. Durwood Myers has a rare law enforcement mentality, and a brief conversation with him exposes the utter lie of the usual "corrections" logic. Myers is the administrator—he shuns the term "warden"—of the Jefferson County Detention Center in Waurika, Oklahoma, the INS-contracted jail to which Denver would send Bogdan Lawniczek. A local attorney requested medical records in order to look into the allegation that a guard had broken Bogie's leg. The INS "never responded," the lawyer told me, and Bogie "was immediately transferred." Fortunately, he was transferred to the facility run by Myers, who explains his lack of antagonism toward inmates by saying, "I realize that most people on the streets belong in jail and just never got caught."

"My staff is not an authoritarian staff. They're not on a power trip. . . . Most of my officers are gray-headed," says the sixty-five-year-old Myers. Since they are no longer "out to make a mark in the world," they tend to avoid "the authoritarian complex." Myers also adheres to three strict hiring rules: no ex-cops, no ex-Marines, no ex-correctional officers. He himself is all of those. He prefers to hire people who "built fences or cowboyed or farmed." A former cop who helped to integrate the Jackson, Mississippi, police force in the late sixties and early seventies, Myers also makes a point of integrating the dormitories and sports teams at his jail. Ever since the Cubans and Laotians allied themselves against the Vietnamese when the facility first opened, he has realized that "letting them congregate by race" can only lead to trouble. The Waurika jail even sponsors a baseball team of INS detainees. They call themselves the Outsiders. They are the only prison team competing in the statewide league.

Although we spoke more than two years after he had last seen Bogie, Myers still remembered how the Pole was "about as white as a piece of paper" from spending so much time locked inside at Aurora's Wackenhut jail. Myers started taking him to the yard, just a few minutes at a time, so that he could readapt. Bogie was released just a few months later, and already "his social skills were good." When I asked what that meant, Myers said with noticeable pride that it meant Bogie could "communicate in a friendly way with twenty-something other races." He added, "Everybody liked him." I wondered if Myers could speculate on how much of Bogie's poor mental health was the result of being locked up for so long. The man had, after all, shot his fiancée in the face before he went to jail. Myers replied, "I'd say the [prison] environment was about 80 percent of it."

Bogdan Lawniczek works for a Colorado construction company run by the father of a prisoner he met in the Waurika jail. A Nigerian who had been detained in Colorado with him ran into him and told a local attorney that he was doing fine. Abbas Hatami was detained for six months before a federal judge ordered the INS to set a bond for him. Hatami paid the $5,000 and was released. He lives in Denver with his new wife and their son, and he works in an electronics store.

Joseph Greene was transferred to INS Headquarters in Washington. After September 11, 2001, he testified several times before Congress about the INS's role in keeping America safe. Among other assurances, he told representatives that INS and Border Patrol agents had cooperated with local law enforcement agencies along the northern border when "political activists organized protests" related to the Canadian-hosted Summit of the Americas. The immigration agents, according to Greene, helped "to ensure that these protests remained non-violent."[8]

Carol Lehman still practices immigration law in Denver, but she stopped representing detainees because she felt there was little she could do for them. The attorney who requested Bogie's medical records also stopped representing immigration detainees. She said the work broke her heart.

Poet Joseph Brodsky, a survivor of the Soviet gulag, once told an interviewer that prison was preferable to the psychiatric asylum because in the latter one might be subjected to "monstrous experiments . . . no different from opening a clock with a hatchet. . . . Whereas prison—well, what is it, really? A shortage of space compensated for by an excess of time. That's all." Brodsky later extended his space-time ratio to explain why incarceration has been so integral a metaphor to literature. It is because "literature is in the first place a translation of metaphysical truths into any given vernacular."[1] In contrast to the unauthorized vernacular of its prisoners, spokespersons for the INS do what they can to hide the physical and metaphysical truths of the agency's prison world. Often they try to control what prisoners and journalists say. Sometimes, as we have seen, they do it quite explicitly.

The Immigration and Naturalization Service had and now the Bureau of Immigration and Customs Enforcement has the authority to detain an alien who has been ordered deported so that the United States can, in fact, deport him or her. If the detention continues for ninety days after the alien has been ordered removed, the prisoner becomes a "post-order detainee." Long-term detainees whom the agency has been unable to deport were known as "lifers" to advocates, journalists, and prisoners, as well as to government officials. But apparently there was some "guidance," as the bureaucrats say, to change public perceptions. An INS spokesperson in the Central Region suggested that I use the term "unremovable" instead of "lifer": the prisoners could not be removed because the United States did not have the appropriate diplomatic arrangements with their countries, but they were not being held for life. A Washington INS spokesperson actually thanked me for using the term "post-order detainee." "Our critics are legion," the spokesperson said, and INS Public Affairs "urge[s]" reporters to use the technical term. Now that the issue was headed for the Supreme Court, use of the term "unremovable" would tend to undermine the INS's position that the long-term detainees' removal was "foreseeable." "We don't consider anyone unremovable," the spokesperson said.

Jailers sometimes refer to their jail as a house, and the word "vernacular" comes from the word for slaves born in the master's house. So it is fitting that the counterweight to INS "public information" rests in the jailhouse vernacular: "We're doing time here with no numbers," explained a twenty-five-year-old unremovable Laotian. After completing his state sentence for participation in a drive-by shooting, he had been detained in the Aurora Wackenhut/INS detention center for three years, so far. The INS would not release him, and because the United States and Laos do not have a repatriation agreement, he could not be sent back. "We don't know when we're getting out. We're doing dead time."

A U.S. citizen who served time in an Alabama jail and became sympathetic to a number of INS prisoners told me that twenty years earlier, when he first did time, he had wondered about the term "dead time." Another inmate told him it referred to pretrial detention for which one did not receive credit toward a sentence. But in this new era of incarceration, he was seeing something entirely different. "INS is truly dead time," he told me. "That's *dead* dead. They don't ever get to make that up." Disturbed by the fate of immigration prisoners he had met, the U.S. citizen inmate said of INS detention, "It's like out in space—no way home."

———

How much sympathy could you have for a gang member convicted of a drive-by shooting or of "menacing with a firearm"? Imagine that the young man laughs as he waves an imaginary handgun over his head to explain what "menacing with a firearm" means. How much sympathy would you have for him when he complains that the sloppy joes he gets for dinner in prison are watery, or that the Kool-Aid is flavorless, or the meat crusty, or the salad "dead"? How much sympathy would you have if his complaints about the bad food could be used to keep him imprisoned for life, regardless of the original sentence?

There are custody review procedures in place for long-term detainees. After such a review, the INS decides whether a detainee will be released under agency supervision or remain locked up because he is said to be a flight risk or a threat to the community. If the agency decides against releasing someone, even though the criminal justice system has released that person, barring a federal court's intervention, he remains in detention until another custody review ends differently, or until he is "removed."

But what if the United States is unable to deport someone? What if, for example, it lacks diplomatic "repatriation" agreements with a certain country and cannot deport anyone there? Is there any limit on how long the INS can incarcerate such a person? Not surprisingly, the INS has argued that there is no limit. What if "it's certain," as one Supreme Court justice hypothesized, that through no fault of her own, the alien can *never* be deported? Could the INS then hold that person forever?

Government attorney: "That is our position."[2]

Thousands of "lifers"—from Cuba, Iraq, Libya, Laos, Cambodia, Vietnam, and elsewhere—could be affected by the decision in *Zadvydas v. Davis.* The INS lost this case but not before tearing apart the lives and families of a great many people, often using the prisoner's "disciplinary record" of complaints about prison conditions as justification. Kim Ho Ma, a young Cambodian "American" ex-con, whose indefinite detention case would come before the U.S. Supreme Court, went on a hunger strike in the Correctional Service Corporation's Seattle INS detention center. The hunger strike did not last long, perhaps less than a day, in which case it would not even have met the INS definition of a hunger strike. But during two years of litigation, the INS argued from federal district court up to the Supreme Court that Ma's participation in the hunger strike demonstrated his inability to behave and therefore justified his continued and perhaps indefinite detention. A long-term Vietnamese detainee being held for twenty hours a day in a Cranston, Rhode Island, jail cell wrote an open letter:

I realize now that it really doesn't matter if you are cooperative or resist, the outcome is still tragic. . . .

My options are few. If I act out in violence then they will say I am unreformed and will lose all chances of ever seeing my loved ones again. Should

I starve? Will it take my death for people to realize that this is a serious problem that will only grow and should not continued to be *censored*, but instead be resolved?

NO free person shall be punished, imprisoned or deprived of life, liberty and the pursuit of justice without due process of the law???

We are the forgotten ones, lost in the confines of a *Bureaucratic Hypocrisy!*

The government's argument that peaceful protest is a form of misbehavior that justifies continued detention was not the principal argument, but its mere presence in a brief before the Supreme Court is another illustration of government officials' arrogant if often accurate belief that their arbitrary methods are immune to legal argument, or better yet, can defeat any argument. An essential part of the nature of INS repression finds shape in the administrative procedures that fly below the radar of judicial intervention. The real point in the arguments about indefinite detention was, once again, the "climate." Deputy Solicitor General Edwin S. Kneedler used the term "criminal alien" repeatedly in the opening seconds of his statement to the Court. Justice Scalia got the point, and with Hollywood's help, he cut to the legal quick: "So even if you're talking about, you know, a real-life Hannibal-what's-his name, you know, a really wicked, evil person who is going to harm people, there's every reason to believe that this person who's been [ordered] deported because of serial murders, if you can't find a country to send him to, you have to let that person out?"

"That's correct, Your Honor," replied federal public defender Jay Stansell, counsel for Kim Ho Ma.[3]

At the reception in the ACLU office across the street from the Supreme Court building in Washington, one of the participating attorneys declined to give me Kim Ho Ma's phone number, explaining that the legal team was avoiding media interviews with its client. Half an hour later, as the reception thinned, I saw a young man sitting by himself against the wall. He was wearing a ski cap and a leather jacket. He was Asian. He looked out of place and perfectly comfortable. We had a brief and fragmented conversation.

Kim Ho Ma's family fled Cambodia in 1979 when the boy was two. After about five years in refugee camps, they entered the United States as legal refugees, and two years later they were legal permanent residents. In Washington that afternoon, Ma, now twenty-three, told me that growing up in Seattle he was often called "gook" or "chink" on his way to the corner store. Schoolmates taunted him because he ate rice. He and other young Cambodians got together to protect themselves, he said, quickly adding that this does not mean they were a "gang." Ma unhesitatingly revealed that there were problems with the COs, who would lock down the dorms because they were "too loud" or would deride the prisoners by saying, "These guys don't even belong in our country." Ma complained about the COs changing TV channels to "put their little hockey games on. Nobody in there want to watch hockey." Then he said: "Cut out all the legal crap and talk about life in INS detention. I'm from a different country, but I'm as American as anybody. I didn't know I was from Cambodia 'til I went in there." He meant into INS detention.

Ma was not alone in that. A Laotian refugee who grew up in the United States was shocked to discover there was an "immigration hold" on him when he finished a criminal sentence. "I even said the Pledge of Allegiance when I was in school," he told me, though it is impossible to decipher from the poorly taped interview whether he said "*the* Pledge of Allegiance" or "*their* Pledge of Allegiance."

"Our mind is American," another Southeast Asian lifer in Colorado explained. His right arm was tattooed with the word *self-control,* his left with *insane.* Both were adorned with dollar signs.

Kim Ho Ma did join a gang, and in the tenth grade he was convicted of manslaughter after a gang-related shooting. At seventeen, he was tried as an adult. He received credit for good behavior and was released after serving twenty-six months of a thirty-eight-month sentence. But he was only "released" on paper and was transferred into INS custody. "Although the INS repeatedly refers to Ma's criminal record," wrote a California circuit court panel, "this was his only criminal conviction."[4] The INS tried and failed to obtain travel documents from the Consulate General of Cambodia. In May 1999 Ma was given a ninety-day "post-order" custody review. The reviewing officer provided a detailed history of the case. "When given the opportunity to make an oral statement," he wrote, "the Subject along with his attorney Jay Stansell, emphasized the following topics": this was his only conviction; he had done more time in INS custody than he had served for the conviction; he wished to continue studying for his high school diploma, an opportunity that had been interrupted when he was transferred to an

INS facility where such courses were not offered; he wanted to work for his older brother's business; he wanted to help his younger brother grow up; and he wanted to spend time with his seventy-one-year-old father. As for Ma's criminal past and uncertain future, the reviewing officer wrote:

> [Ma] was a member of the Local Asian Boyz (LAB), affiliated in the Seattle area. This gang affiliation provided him feeling of acceptance that he was not obtaining from his community. When he was questioned on his current affiliation with the LAB's he proceeded to affirm that there is "No" affiliation at this time and that there would be no affiliation if released. . . . He would also like to have the opportunity that was never given to him which is to be released from custody to prove that he is not a threat to society.[5]

The reviewer added that he had received letters of support from Ma's family, including an offer of employment from his older brother. Things looked promising.

On the same custody review form, in a box labeled "Institutional History—Positive or Negative," the reviewing officer wrote: "On 10/20/97, the Subject was transferred to King County Jail, Seattle, WA, for his involvement in a planned Hunger Strike that occurred while in Service custody." He elaborated: Ma "was identified as one of the more vocal detainees within the dorms," though he was at the King County jail for over a year with "no record of any behavioral problems." On the page labeled "Action by District Director," there is an X in the box next to "Continue to detain." The form is signed by Assistant District Director George L. Morones, who gave no reasons for the denial in the space provided.

Such are the procedures governing detention that the INS defends in courtrooms around the country as proof that its prisoners get a fair chance. In practice, the administrative custody reviews for long-term detainees are notoriously arbitrary, and there is no appeals process. While *Ma v. Reno* was still pending, the INS shifted decision-making responsibility on these cases to its Washington office, to an entity known as the Headquarters Post-Order Detention Unit (HQPDU). Although the HQPDU signs on to the paperwork, the decision-making power tends to remain in the hands of the district director, who in turn relies on the deportation officer, who might have contact with the actual prisoner. Essentially, a civil service employee is able to decide, based on his or her personal feelings, whether to keep a person locked up.

Immigration detainees are entitled to lawyers if they can get one, but they do not have the right to appointed counsel. Nevertheless, in about 1999, after a surge of INS prisoners with previous criminal records who could not be deported began to file habeas petitions, federal judges in some districts (not immigration judges) began appointing lawyers to represent detainees. Stansell filed a habeas petition for Kim Ho Ma in January 1999, and later that year a district court judge ordered Ma's release, "subject to appropriate conditions." One condition was, "You will abide by all laws." Fourteen months later Ma was arrested for assault and domestic violence. He was released on bond, and he complied with INS requirements to report the arrest. Soon the charges were dismissed. All of this is acknowledged by Assistant District Director Morones in a letter that orders Ma back into INS custody. Why? Apparently because of Morones's personal opinion of Kim Ho Ma. Morone's authority allows him to report his own gut reaction to Ma's police record in a closed case as if it were legal doctrine—which, in a sense, it is:

You have not been convicted of the crime, however no conviction is required. I undertake this revocation [of parole from detention] as a matter of discretion in administrative proceedings. I have examined the police reports, and note that there is a strong testimonial of evidence of the events. That evidence includes an admission from you to a police officer that you did indeed strike your companion. It all supports my conclusion that you are a danger to the public, both those in your immediate circle and the community at large. I come to this conclusion for the two reasons shown below.

First, you deliberately chose to externalize anger and frustration through violence against another person. There is no indication that you were under the influence of either drugs or alcohol—no chemical impaired the control you should maintain over your temper. While neither would justify or excuse your display of rage they might at least explain it. It is clear however, that the manifestation of temper was the pure product of self-indulgence. It can neither be explained nor excused. I believe that there is a strong risk that you will react in similar fashion again should you be thwarted or denied a desire.

Second, your uncontrolled rage imperiled others beyond your immediate companion. By assaulting her while she was driving in traffic, you risked causing her to lose control of the vehicle. That could easily have resulted in an accident, and injury or death to innocent parties. The most charitable interpretation of the event is that your violent temper impaired your ability to foresee that consequence. I believe it more likely though that you simply have no regard for public peace or safety, or the well-being of others. Your actions make it clear that you are either unwilling or unable to subordinate your own desires and impulses to the peace and good order of society. I must therefore conclude that you are a threat to the public safety.

For those reasons I hereby revoke the Order of Supervision under which you were released on October 25, 1999, and order that you be brought back into custody to await deportation.

Perhaps one's political opinion about crime, civil liberties, and government power comes down to this: Are you more disturbed by Kim Ho Ma's alleged violent behavior toward his companion or by George L. Morones's unreviewable "discretion" to imprison Ma, one year at a time, perhaps until he is dead? Ma's action—alleged, but assume that it did occur—was his own. In fact, that is precisely why Morones condemns it: "the pure product of self-indulgence . . . you are either unwilling or unable to subordinate your own desires and impulses to the peace and good order of society." Morones's action is the action of the State. He knows this, which is why his language becomes awkwardly inflated. In the early nineteenth century, one writer coined the term "office tyranny" as a synonym for "bureaucracy."[6]

"It was just a group of guys making a stand because they're facing, quote-unquote, indefinite detention," Ma said of the "hunger strike," as the ACLU reception emptied out. "We call it what they call it. Administrative detention, indefinite detention—in other words, forever. They tell us every day: you're not getting out. I'm nobody to argue with them." About 120 lifers protested at the Seattle detention center that day, and even some of the Mexicans joined in to show their support, despite the "real big racial problems" between the groups. There was no property damage and no violence; the INS does not dispute this. After a brief moment of attention, the INS went back to ignoring the long-term prisoners. The story becomes confusing, though. As Stansell found his way over and listened in, Ma told me that the protest was all over in "a couple of hours." By dinnertime, everybody was eating. "I chose not to eat," he said. He was labeled "a behavioral problem." By the next day, he was eating too. "It was a lost cause."

While the INS regularly denies the existence of prisoner hunger strikes, it may have invented one in this case. The INS does not appear to dispute Ma's version of the abandoned strike. The custody review forms note that Ma was transferred to a different facility "for his involvement in a planned Hunger Strike." According to the Ninth Circuit Court of Appeals opinion affirming the district court order to release Ma, "INS officials found that Ma should remain in detention, based on the seriousness of his conviction, and also on the ground of his threatened participation in a hunger strike." In front of the Supreme Court, the isolated nonincident had shifted slightly but significantly into "disciplinary problems [now plural] while in INS custody."[7] Every little bit helps. "They use the public fear to . . . keep the funding going," the Vietnamese lifer in Rhode Island had explained.

Out West, I had been allowed to speak with a group of seven young lifers in the INS/Wackenhut prison in Colorado. Most of them were from Laos or Vietnam. They were also now from Colorado, Minnesota, California, and Hawaii. All came to the United States legally as young children with their refugee parents. All committed crimes and served their sentences. Now they were doing dead time, and they were trying to convince the Denver INS district director to consider releasing them. When detainees go on a hunger strike, one of them told me, the "goon squad, all in black, and they got this helmet thing," comes in to break up the protest. "They put a stronghold on you." His description of the paramilitary tactics also applies to the administrative "stronghold." Days before we spoke, Wackenhut/INS officials had heard rumors of the impending protest. After recreation, detainees would refuse to come back inside from the fenced-in yard. Supervisory Deportation Officer John Good called them together, according to a twenty-five-year-old Laotian who had been in the warehouse for three years. " 'It's going to effect your review,' " they were told. "It's like a bribe. He's saying we don't want to put this on your record, so when you go to your review you're going to get shot down." Another lifer added: "You know what the funny thing was? The next day an old yellow man, a Chinese dude, come in from out of the blue." A chaplain had come to hear their concerns. "We had to do something to catch their attention in order for them to really pay attention to us."

District Director Joseph Greene once told a Denver reporter that lifers with criminal records needed to prove to him they could behave in a "controlled environment like Wackenhut" before he could let them go.[8] Like so much rhetoric about "criminal aliens," Greene's position seems reasonable at first. In fact, it depends on a willful blindness to daily life in the "controlled environment" under his jurisdiction. One of the Southeast Asian prisoners described that environment:

> You have to get up every day and be around guys all the time. Everybody misses being around women. You miss eating when you want to eat, what you want to eat. And several times a week, officers—I know they're doing their job, but it still messes with the inmates—they come in, they start tearing your stuff apart. They call it shakedown. People in here, especially long-termers like us, we like to live comfortable, you know. We get used to what we're doing. We have two or three blankets, and they come and they take them all [except] one. The dorms is colder than what they feel—they go home every day. They don't understand that we're living here. We talk to them, [but] they always have to back their officers up.

Another young man interrupted: "We're criminals. They don't believe us. We're criminals." The INS prisoner with *self control* and *insane* tattooed on his arms wanted to add something: "Some officers come to work like they didn't get no poonanny, no pussy, and they just have a big old attitude on us. When we come in the door [from one part of the prison to another], they just slam the door on us, and that's when we start getting mad. And then when we get mad, they write us up." The write-ups become part of the inmate's record. "If they don't like you, they can just put all kinds of dirt on your paper."

"Is there any precedent at all," Justice Stephen Breyer asked the government lawyer, "where the Constitution, which says no person shall be deprived of liberty without due process of law, justifies putting a sane human being in the United States [in prison and] depriving him of his liberty forever on the basis of an administrative order, no judge, no jury, no judicial process?" The deputy solicitor general replied that "the basis for the the removal order" and "for the detention" is a criminal conviction.[9] One of the more soft-spoken of the Aurora lifers put it more simply: "We're being punished twice for our crimes."

The Supreme Court consolidated Ma's case with that of Kestutis Zadvydas. The joint decision in June 2001 became known as *Zadvydas*, and these long-term cases are now generally referred to as *Zadvydas* cases. Zadvydas himself was born to Lithuanian refugee parents in a displaced persons camp on German soil after World War II. His parents came to the U.S. legally, bringing Kestutis with them, and he had been here for more than forty years when, after a string of drug-related misdemeanor convictions, the INS attempted to deport him. Neither Germany nor Lithuania would take him. Zadvydas is not a citizen of these or of any other country. He is "stateless." The INS even asked the Dominican Republic to accept him, the logic being that his wife here is Dominican-born; the Domican Republic declined.

In the 5–4 majority opinion in *Zadvydas* Breyer wrote: "Based on our conclusion that indefinite detention of aliens . . . would raise serious constitutional concerns, we construe the [immigration] statute to contain an implicit 'reasonable time' limitation, the application of which is subject to federal court review." Breyer went on to suggest that six months was "reasonable," considering analogous statutes. Ma and Zadvydas had by then been released "under supervision"—Ma after a year and a half in INS detention, Zadvydas after four years.

Justice Anthony Kennedy's dissenting opinion in *Zadvydas* opened with a blunt critique of the majority's "obvious disregard of congressional intent." In proposing the six-month guideline, Kennedy wrote, the majority attempts to "cur[e] the resulting gap by writing a statutory amendment of its own." Whether or not Kennedy was right about that gap, he made a small error of his own that illuminates a different gap. Defending the "fairness and regularity" of INS custody review procedures, Kennedy wrote that if still detained after ninety days, "the alien . . . is transferred to a post-order detention unit at INS headquarters." But Kennedy confused the case and the body; only the former is transferred to headquarters. (The man in charge of the HQPDU, whose stamped signature appears on much of its correspondence, is Michael Rozos, former assistant officer-in-charge at Miami's Krome detention center and on-site official at New Jersey's Esmor detention center at the time detainees rioted to protest conditions there.) The post-order detainee remains in the local jail, the private lockup, or the penitentiary. The often subcontracted deniability gap between government disinformation and the realities of detention is the same one that allows District Director Greene to insist on rehabilitation in a "facility" that makes people worse. The custody review procedures to which Justice Kennedy refers so reassuringly are an extra perimeter around the security fence. As California federal public defender Gillian Black and her colleagues wrote on behalf of a Haitian man whom, for reasons that are unclear, Haiti refused to take back:

> The INS changed its custody review procedure five times during a seven month period. . . . The INS has urged the court to "let the 'process' work." This battle cry suggests that a process exists. . . . The INS has created a fluid process on which neither petitioner or this Court can rely. The INS remains free to implement a new "procedure" in any way it wishes, to disregard the procedure, or to discontinue it entirely. . . . The perfunctory nature of the custody reviews is especially troubling, in light of the fact that *some INS district directors have said they would rather violate INS regulations than release aliens with a criminal history.*[10]

Jean Eddy Le Pen, who had no criminal record, was detained for three years before he received any custody review at all. Even then he "was never notified of a decision." After a fourth year in detention, he was deported and jailed in Port-au-Prince on his return.

———

On a Lerdo (California) Sheriff's Facility form titled "Inmate Written Notice of Intent to Conduct Disciplinary Hearing," an officer writes: "Lying will not be tolerated." On another form, "Facility Rule Violation," the officer details the infraction:

> I was passing out oranges to dorm 8. [The inmate] came up, got his orange and set it on a table. [The inmate], unaware that I was watching, came back to the door stating he wanted an orange because he didn't get one. I told [him] he already received one. [He] stated again that he did not. I refused his request. [He] walk directly to the table, picked his orange up and started to walk to the bunk. I called [him] out of the dorm to ask him why he lied. He stated he wanted another orange. I told [the inmate] he would be written up for lying.

Under "Findings" the officer writes:

> I read the report to the inmate and asked him if the report was true. [He] said "I thought we could have an extra orange." Due to facts in the report the board finds [the inmate] guilty of all charges.

Finally, under "Disciplinary Action Taken," the officer writes: "3 DAYS DIS-CIPLINARY ISOL." It is worth noting among these minutiae that the notice was filed at "0455"—five minutes before five o'clock in the morning. Breakfast in the Lerdo Pretrial Detention Facility in Bakersfield was served at 3:30 A.M., lunch at 9:30 A.M., and dinner at 3:00 P.M. For eleven and a half hours, the choices are overpriced commissary food or maybe an extra orange.

The system is run not only to punish those prisoners who resist it but also to frustrate those who try to accommodate themselves to it. One Laotian man in INS detention at the Kern County Detention Facility knew he was not going anywhere for a while so he tried to make the best of his time there. Request slips, or "kites," are used by prisoners to inquire about an appeal, a classification decision, or an "outdate" ("Que es mi fecha de salida?" What is my release date?). The Laotioan prisoner wrote his own question in the space provided: "Do you offer any vocational programs here?" The slip was returned with an official's handwritten reply: "NO WE DO NOT." The prisoner tried again:

> Since my last request form was never answered and returned to me, I have to ask again. And this will be my fourth attempt since I've been here over the last two year[s], in asking that myself being only an I.N.S. inmate here, is there any way that I maybe allowed to obtain my G.E.D. while I'm here, please? Please answer. Thank you!

The reply: "We don't offer a G.E.D. Program." If active rehabilitation is impossible, one attempts at least to keep intact that bubble Marlon Rajigah handled so delicately in Louisiana. Under the words "To: Commander," the Laotian prisoner tried yet again:

> I am only an I.N.S. detainee, who has been here for two years already and is being kept here indefinately. If we're not even allowed to receive pictures of our own family here in this place. Then can I be allowed to receive a paper print color photo copy of my family, please? Thank you!

The sergeant's response: "At this time, our policy does not allow photocopies."

It is surprising, really, that self-control does not yield to insanity or vio-lence more often that it does; or perhaps what looks like self-control is a form of despair. The Washington Alliance for Immigrant and Refugee Justice received a letter from a group of lifers in the private prison in Seattle where Kim Ho Ma may or may not have participated in a hunger strike:

> Our opinion of this situation.
>
> We, on occasion feel like [we] want to tear up this place (INS dorm) and the county wouldn't want to lease to INS and maybe let us go.
>
> A few have starved themself but only got put into a hospital. We think its a waste of mind for us and money to the tax payer. If there is a real easy way to commit suicide some of us would (including me).
>
> We ask to be sent back to prison (medium custody or minimum) so we can exercise our mind and at least work for 30-dollars a month. Get to walk in the big yard everyday. We don't want much just a release date whether its a year from now or five year from now it doesn't matter, we just want to get out. We are not asking for forgiveness only to ask for the people outside not to forget about us. We are not the best nor are we the worst of criminals. Sometimes we fight among ourselves, because INS we can not touch, we talk to ourselves and think to ourselves everynight realizing that we have gone coo-coo.
>
> Our spirits have shrunk, no emotion what so ever, Frustration becomes a big part of us. . . .
>
> We can say more but we will stop for now. We could go on and on but it could only be heard so far and reach so many people.

"It gave us a chance to be heard," Kim Ho Ma said of the historical argument on indefinite detention, "when back then there wasn't even a single soul that heard the problem. . . . Nobody cared about the guys because the guys didn't exist. . . . They were the scum of society . . . but if you look at it another way, these guys got families."

Ma always knew he would be deported in the end, according to attorney Stansell. In June 2002, a year after the Supreme Court decision, the U.S. government reached a repatriation agreement with Cambodia, and the first group of Cambodians was returned. Of fifteen hundred Cambodians subject to deportation, one hundred were in detention.[11] Ma was among a group of ten sent back a few months later. Cambodian immigration authorities detained him in Phnom Penh for a month but reportedly treated him well. U.S. advocates monitoring the repatriations counseled returnees to take along cash if they could—but not too much, because the more one had, the more one would have to pay Cambodian authorities in bribes to be released from detention there. Returnees took back whatever official paperwork they might have, such as a Washington State driver's license, to begin their new lives. Often the INS confiscated this paperwork during the returns, according to Stansell.

"This to me was do or die," Ma told me after the Supreme Court arguments. "At least I came this far and [was] heard this far." Inside the Supreme Court building, he had recognized some of the Seattle area INS agents seated around him in the audience. When I asked how that felt, Ma put his hand on his chest and said how he imagined *they* felt: "It hurt them to see liberty and justice is served 'cause, quote-unquote, they're the almighty government."

—

Three weeks after the *Zadvydas* ruling, Attorney General John Ashcroft was in Denver. "I came here to discuss the administration's efforts to combat gun violence," he began, "but first I need to address how the Department of Justice is dealing with an emergency situation caused by a recent Supreme Court decision." The attorney general began by unloading some numbers and buzzwords:

> According to Immigration and Naturalization Service statistics there are nearly 3,400 criminal aliens who are or will be subject to release under the Court's order within the next three months. Among these criminal aliens are hundreds of sexual predators, including a rapist and serial child molester, hundreds of drug traffickers, and hundreds of violent criminals including murderers. According to INS statistics, these criminal aliens have 1,851 drug convictions, 772 convictions for assault, 387 convictions for sex offenses, 125 homicides and thousands of other convictions.[12]

In the first seventeen sentences of his prepared remarks that day, Ashcroft used the term "criminal alien" ten times; this does not include the phrase "illegal aliens who have served out criminal sentences" (or "alien" by itself, twice). Lest one get the wrong impression, Ashcroft noted: "I'm especially concerned that these criminal aliens may re-enter [i.e., society, if released from detention] and prey upon immigrant communities within the United States." Ashcroft's use of the term "criminal alien" is not inaccurate, but he could also have referred to the immigrant communities as "alien communities." As the nation's top law enforcement official knows—and as we heard another INS official emphasize at a Miami citizenship ceremony—even legal immigrants are "aliens."

Ashcroft devoted half of his Denver speech to Justice Department policies in the wake of the *Zadvydas* decision. To segue into his original topic ("Project Exile," an initiative for longer prison terms for gun crimes), Ashcroft told his audience that the "guiding principle" for both topics was "public safety." He announced four measures to be taken, each more nebulous than the preceding. First, the Justice Department would make efforts to send some release-eligible aliens back to jail or prison for previously unserved sentences. Second, still working with local authorities, the federal government would bring "additional criminal charges" against detainees "where appropriate." Then Ashcroft referred to the agency's "fluid procedures," which California litigators had unsuccessfully challenged:

> Third, we are also developing procedures to continue to detain aliens where special circumstances may justify continued detention even if their prompt removal is not likely. This includes special risks such as terrorists and especially dangerous criminals. The Supreme Court suggested that such detention might be appropriate under special circumstances.

The mention of terrorists here is notable because the speech preceded the September 11 attacks by two months. The PATRIOT Act, which became law six weeks after the attacks, would give Ashcroft newly broadened authority for indefinite detention. ACLU litigator Judy Rabinovitz observed: "The legislation appears to have been drafted, at least in part, to get around the Supreme Court's decision in *Zadvydas*." Ashcroft continued:

> Fourth, we are developing procedures which will maximize our ability to continue to hold criminal aliens while our diplomatic efforts are underway. These procedures will give the INS, in consultation with the State Department, an opportunity to evaluate the likelihood of repatriation, prior to any decision to release an individual.

Louisiana's New Iberia sheriff, Sid Herbert, told me that shortly after the *Zadvydas* decision, INS officials met with sheriffs from across the state to explain that the boom was over. Louisiana held more than five hundred

INS long-term detainees at one point, and sheriffs there have spoken openly of the resulting economic benefits to their communities. Nationwide there were a few thousand long-term detainees. In the weeks after the June 2001 Supreme Court decision, while immigration lawyers reported varying compliance with the new law around the country, some 800 lifers were released. Releases declined after September 11, 2001, and the INS maintained that some 1,750 Cuban lifers were not covered by the *Zadvydas* decision anyway.[13]

"We will ship no swine before its time," one Justice Department attorney cheerfully told me in a discussion about post-*Zadvydas* custody reviews.

———

Ayub Abukar had been a beneficiary of U.S. immigration policies before he experienced the other side. "I was born in Somalia in 1981," Abukar writes. "I grew up in Barawa (Brava). It's a coastal town of South Somalia, and I inherited a love for sports from my father, a soccer player, and also my older brother who played soccer during his school season." When Abukar was eleven, his father was killed by a rival, majority "clan faction," and one sister was raped by rival clan members. "I hope she is alife and I will see her one day," he writes. The rest of the family fled to Kenya, where they lived in a refugee camp for five years before being granted refugee status and brought to the United States in 1997. Abukar went to high school in Washington, D.C., and then moved with his family to Minnesota's Twin Cities.

"I started drinking and committing simple crimes," Abukar tells me by phone. When I ask "what was going on," he pauses and takes an audible breath. "It was complicated, man. . . . I had a friend, I guess who was a bad friend. He make me lost, man. Make me lost. He make me follow them, drink with them, smoke with them." Abukar was charged with drinking on the street. "It's a petty crime, but it's a crime. Once you become a criminal, that's it." Then he was charged for being a passenger in a stolen car. Then he got drunk and stabbed a friend. "He took my clothes, he took my girl. . . . Somehow—I was protecting myself. I'm not that dangerous, man, and somehow, that happened. I stabbed him."

Abukar does not make excuses. He wrote a few letters from the Minnesota Correctional Facility in Rush City, titling one of them "My

Memory and My Background." His written account of his crimes begins, "The facts of the case are undisputed." He was convicted of misdemeanor third-degree assault and sentenced to two months, with two years' probation. He says his friend later forgave him. He had not become a U.S. citizen, so after the two months he went into INS custody. He argued his case in front of an immigration judge. The INS was represented by its prosecuting attorney, while Abukar represented himself. He lost. The immigration judge found that his crime, although a misdemeanor, was a "crime of moral turpitude" under immigration law.[14] As Abukar explains, "[If] you're an immigrant—they consider like you're a danger to society."

The Rush City jail opened in February 2000, and Abukar was moved there from another in Elk River a month later. An hour's drive north of Minneapolis, it sits in an open landscape of farms, grain silos, and decidous woods, just west of the St. Croix River at the Wisconsin border and adjacent to the Rush City Regional Airport. "It was brand-new, good food, everything was good," Abukar reports. After being held in segregation for three months, the new INS inmates received health clearances and were moved into the general population. As the jail's INS contract expanded, Abukar would be moved to a higher-security unit that held only INS detainees. When I visited the jail held almost 1,000 inmates, 50 of them for the INS. The population of Rush City is 2,101.

The immigration judge had written that Abukar's crime proves that he "lacks good moral character." Abukar writes:

> Has there ever been a time when you didn't quite know what was becoming of your life, yet you knew you had to understand the changes that were taking place and find a way to control them? If you answered "yes," you are not alone. Everyone, rich or poor, free or imprisoned, has at one time felt your life spinning out of control? That's how I felt. I was hopeless, homeless, and very risk to myself, and I couldn't help my self. . . . Losing my loved ones and having to live in a bad environment contributed to the feeling of rolling into the "Down-ward." The perception of successive catastrophe in my life made me violence person and "thoughtless."
>
> When one bad thing after another seems to come upon you without allowing you for a relief period, the chance is to control . . . your behavior. Many people, including myself, have hit bottom of the abyss and survived only to be presented with another challenge, getting out of the situation we found ourselves in.

The situation in which Abukar now finds himself is this: The INS claims he is too dangerous to release and that he should be returned to the country he fled as a boy. He now has attorneys who have asked a federal judge to order the INS either to release or deport him.

Unlike Cubans, Iraqis, Vietnamese, Laotians, and, until late 2002, Cambodians, the problem for detained Somalis is not that the government in their home country refuses to accept them but that there *is* no government in Somalia—a fact the Justice Department has used to justify its deportations there.[15] In early 2003 an unusual issue was addressed by the courts: Are U.S. deportations to the country of Somalia legal under U.S. law? Actually, not everyone agrees on whether "Somalia" *is* a country, but a judge decided that it was not necessary to resolve that question in determining whether Somalis could be sent there.[16]

Federal statutes governing the removal of aliens require that a government agree "to accept" returnees. Whatever "Somalia" is, lawyers for both the Justice Department and detainees agree that it "has no functioning government that could accept" potential returnees. Therefore, according to the Somalis' argument, the absence of a government must mean that they cannot legally be sent there. The U.S. government counters that the successful physical return of the detainees constitutes acceptance, since "there is no . . . government that would be offended." A Minnesota judge responded: "It is difficult for the Court to see how the INS's apparent current practice of dropping off an alien in a territory with no functioning government complies with the statute. In essence, 'acceptance' occurs under this policy when no one returns the deported alien. The silence of a nonfunctioning government in a lawless territory—with grave risks to the deported alien—simply cannot constitute 'acceptance.'"[17]

The Minnesota judge ruled to prohibit deportations to Somalia, but his decision applied only to the particular group of Somalis who had filed suit. Two weeks later, in February 2002, the INS deported about thirty Somalis who had not been named in that lawsuit. INS Public Affairs officer Russell Bergeron told Brian Hutchinson, a Canadian reporter, that he had not heard about the operation but that it sounded "rather routine" (like the Pakistani removals after September 11). A Justice Prisoner and Alien Transport flight gathered Somalis from various parts of the country, along with several from Canada, then flew to upstate New York. The prisoners were transferred to a chartered plane for Amsterdam and then on to the African nation of Djibouti. "They spent one night there, crammed into a single jail cell with no toilet," according to Hutchinson. The INS claimed that the same flight continued to Mogadishu, but Hutchinson wrote that the flight from Djibouti was aboard a Russian aircraft with a Russian crew. The INS admits that chartered flights are necessary because "U.S. government airlines cannot, and do not, fly into Somalia. Additionally, contract security was used as escorts because U.S. government personnel are not allowed to enter the country of Somalia. The contract security was provided by European Union Sky Marshals." Canadian immigration also acknowledged that its personnel do not go to Somalia " 'because of the situation there.' "[18]

The INS "executed the removal orders as efficiently and expeditiously as possible," says its Public Affairs Office. Hutchinson again: "[The prisoners'] last stop was a small airport just outside Mogadishu. The group was herded by Somali soldiers on to a bus and driven into the heart of the city. Trailing them were soldiers driving trucks and 50 caliber machine guns mounted on the roofs. In downtown Mogadishu the prisoners were pulled from the bus, released from their shackles, and abandoned, left to fend for themselves."

When the prisoners were first taken into custody back in the United States in preparation for what one Somali's father called a kidnapping, the INS denied them access to lawyers and refused to let them contact their families, according to Janine DiGiovanni, writing in the *Times* of London. Ayub Abukar's lawyers, citing BBC news reports, wrote that one of the deportees asked for a lawyer and "INS officials responded that there were INS lawyers present." That man was sent off the plane near Mogadishu wearing a prison uniform and no shoes. At least one deportee did not even speak the language. Most had been in the United States for years. DiGiovanni wrote: "En route, the men were shackled. Several say that they were drugged during the flight. Medication, including insulin for one of the deportees, a diabetic, as well as antidepressants, were taken away, their cash was frozen and they were issued with cheques that they are unable to cash."[19]

In November 2002 rumors of more roundups circulated in U.S. Somali communities. The Hate Free Zone Campaign of Washington reported that several Somalis had received phone calls from the Immigration and Naturalization Service asking them to come in to sign papers or to take care of their employment authorization, and then they were detained. In Buffalo a Somali made his required monthly appearance at an INS office and was detained. After his deportation he sent word of the experience back to friends in New York. This time, when the plane stopped in Mogadishu, local authorities reportedly refused to allow the U.S. Somalis to deplane. The plane returned to Djibouti, where some of the deportees were sedated. All were then put onto helicopters, which flew them back to Mogadishu, where authorities "pushed [them] off."[20] In January 2003 Judge Marsha J. Pechman of the Western District of Washington issued an injunction barring Somali deportations nationwide. The judge was unpersuaded by the government's repeated references in oral arguments to Somali "terrorists," since the government declined to provide any evidence, or even any unfounded suspicion, that terrorist charges had anything to do with these detainees. Despite Pechman's ruling, the INS has "refused to provide information about the names and locations" of detainees affected by the court's decision.[21]

The case before Pechman was a class action, and her decision did not apply to Somalis whose cases had already been pending in the courts. Among those was Ayub Abukar.

Before his typewriter broke, Ayub Abukar sent me a five-page commentary in which he strained to fend off his frustration with prison pressures and arbitrary custody procedures by articulating and denouncing them. "In the custody of the INS, if I were asked the single most consistent cause of mental derangement, I can tell you with the utmost confidence that it would be injustice. . . . The injustices of the prison administration could be endured if that were the only injustice. . . . Anyone in INS detention who has faith in retrieving the injustice done him by appealing to American Jurisprudence will go mad unless he abandons it."

Geography and movement are not mysterious to Abukar. He talks about going from Somalia to Kenya to Minnesota the way someone else might talk about going to the corner store. But time is something else. The imprisoned twenty-one-year-old writes: "The mind's relationship to time is fundamental. What can the mind think when the rate of the man has been reduced to such a degree of uncertainty that he cannot predict the next day or the next hour? . . . He could break one of those petty and mean rules of the prison in any moment and upset the balance completely. And also, more importantly, upset the balance of his mind." He has been detained for more than four years so far.

Young Ayub asks: "How do detainees count the time they must serve in custody of the INS when it has no end?"

# 14 | MARIEL CUBANS

*Abandoned, Again and Again*

"He would be the one to talk to," Lieutenant Gary Viator said of Jesus Abreu. "Anything that happens, we look to him for help."

Abreu, forty-four years old, came to the United States from Cuba in 1980. After selling drugs to an undercover police officer, he served three and a half years in an Illinois prison. In 1992 he was convicted of assault on a police officer, and in 1995 he served twenty months in Florida for violating a restraining order against his wife. In December 2000 he was taken into INS custody. In Abreu's INS custody reviews, the immigration officers have asked him repeatedly about the conviction for assault on an officer, even though the judge who heard that case gave him no jail time (he was sentenced to a year's probation).

"Even the ones that murdered," Lieutenant Viator said, have done their time. But Cuba does not have to take them back, and the United States does not have to release them. "INS says, 'Tough, call Castro—he's the one that didn't want you. We don't want you either.'"

Abreu was in charge of the law library at the Calcasieu Parish Jail in Lake Charles, and he also worked as an interpreter between detainees and the jail staff. Viator was in charge of the fifty or so INS detainees at the jail. He and the jail's warden had informed INS officials that Abreu could have a job at the jail after the INS released him. But the INS has denied Abreu's release, saying that the answers he gave during a custody hearing about his prior convictions were not "clear" and that he "tended to blame others for his errors."[1] Viator felt the decision was unfair. So although I had called Lake Charles to set up an interview with someone else, Viator suggested that I speak with Abreu.

"INS always tells you you've got to watch those Cubans," Viator volunteered, "but I ain't had no trouble."

The day before I flew to Louisiana, Lieutenant Viator informed me that the warden had decided I could not interview Jesus Abreu after all. It sounded familiar. There was "a lot going on," and the jail wanted to avoid "controversy." Spinning out justifications, Viator told me that the jail accreditation was in progress and that precisely because Abreu had recently been denied release despite being an exemplary inmate, he might have some complaints. "We can't take that chance," Viator said.

The conversation continued a few days later in the warden's office. Lieutenant Colonel Bruce LaFargue, known as "the Colonel," is a large, affable guy in a suit who, like other wardens I have met, can seem straightforward and calculating at the same time. But there was something else about LaFargue as well. He cultivated a mild eccentricity, and it seemed he would talk to me as long as he felt entertained by having me as an audience. The Cubans are good cooks, the Colonel told me, and they can be loud, but that's just part of their culture. Nothing to worry about. "We don't have no problems with Cubans." Then he took what he said was a Cuban cigar out of his desk drawer.

"They're in captivity here and we make it interesting." For example, he said, they get to wear the purple T-shirts with INS INMATE printed across them rather than the standard-issue prison jumpsuit. They get Spanish-language cable television, computers in the law library, and English as a Second Language and anger management classes. Sixteen months earlier the INS detainees had been in "a warehouse situation," the Colonel explained. Then he came on the job, talked to the inmates about their needs, and, along with Lieutenant Viator, made some changes.

So what about an interview with Jesus Abreu?

"I just want those inmates to understand, this is America but we got structures," the Colonel replied. Acknowledging that Abreu had the right to speak to me if he wanted to, LaFargue looked at me across his desk and said, "We just advised him [not to]. . . . He has a lot of insight into the system, but I think he's also got—"

"—resentment." Lieutenant Viator finished the warden's sentence.

"I don't want him to say anything about INS in general," the Colonel continued. Why protect the INS? I asked, thinking the answer was the jail's contract, the money. Even Viator, sympathetic as he was to the INS prisoners, told me the jail was trying to get more of them.

"I'm not protecting INS," said the Colonel. "I'm protecting him."

"Nobody knows these guys like I do," Viator says. "INS doesn't know these guys"—except for their alien registration numbers, he adds. "They don't *want* to get to know them." Like other lifers, the Cuban detainees are supposed to have one chance each year to convince a panel of INS workers that they should be released. The first time I spoke to Viator, he told me that he had written a letter to the INS complaining about these panel reviews. The detainees are nervous, they have been preparing all year, and then the interviewers rush them through, according to Viator. "To be honest with you, INS don't really care about these people. They couldn't care less."

Viator is not sympathetic to every inmate. "He's an asshole," he says of an INS prisoner who files endless complaints when he's not writing poems. "He wants a special salad with cheese and eggs—we don't do that." As we walk through the housing areas, the lieutenant chats softly with me, and occasionally, without warning, he lets out a call so low and loud and abrupt that it seems to originate from an entirely separate part of him: "Roll C-pod sallyport!" The appropriate doors open to let us through. Viator returns again to Jesus Abreu, telling me that he scored higher than any inmate ever has on a test qualifying him for a welding class. Abreu is a jail trustee, and the warden is willing to send him to the nearby welding school, but the INS refuses to allow it.[2]

A jail tour with Lieutenant Viator is different from any of the others I have been on because Viator stops to talk to the inmates. We stand for a few long minutes at the doorway to "max-max," what Viator calls "smackle," where mentally ill inmates are housed in a row of closed cells. A "Muslim" sits behind the bars of one cell on the floor, staring at us from the dark, across the empty dayroom between us. He smokes and stares. He is allowed out of the cell for one hour each day. Lieutenant Viator tells me that he has called the INS repeatedly to ask that this detainee be moved to a place where he can receive proper psychiatric treatment, but the INS refuses. They give no reason; they don't have to.

Gary Viator was once in the hole himself. He grew up in Louisiana and Mississippi, with a mother and father who were both alcoholics. They were always "dragging us from town to town and bar to bar," he says, adding casually, "I even got locked up in Gulfport." He and his brother were skipping school to beg for food on the street when the local police picked them up. Viator was twelve and his brother was ten. In jail they got into a fight with each other, and Gary was thrown in the hole—nothing but a floor and a drain. He spent three days in there.

That was fifty years ago. Viator has soft eyes behind his glasses, a teddy-bear heft, and a warm though slightly constricted smile. We are standing in the hallway just off the jail lobby, where there is a foil tin with home-made cookies for visitors. A six-pointed sheriff's department star is pinned to Viator's blue uniform shirt; so is a weathered little name tag that doesn't mention his rank but says simply "Gary Viator." In 1966 Viator spent fourteen months as an artillery grunt in Vietnam. "Nobody can imagine it. That's why I never talk about it," he says. I'm not sure how we got on the subject, but he says, "We did a lot of bad things over there. You had to survive." Standing there in the hallway with a sheaf of prison files under his arm, he tells me what it was like—or doesn't quite tell me—to play cards with someone at night and wrap him up in a bag the next day. "That's why it was hard to get close to anybody." Then he smiles and tells me about an exception. *People* magazine ran a story about people who had made the cover of *Life* magazine. One was an unnamed soldier who was quoted as saying, "'I always wanted to find my buddy Gary Viator.'" A friend of Viator's saw that, called him, and Viator called the *People* reporter. Soon he was back in touch with his old buddy. John Wilson had become a cop in Spokane, and two of his four kids had the same names as two of Gary's kids. Their wives hit it off instantly.

His voice changes again. "Some things that you want to forget, you'll never forget." He has never gone to see the Vietnam Memorial in Washington because he wouldn't be able to bear it. "It's just life," he says. "I've been through a lot." Two of his brothers and his mother have died in the last two years. But, he says, "every day I look outside, the sun comes up, the Lord is still in the blessin' business."

Viator shakes his head when we return to the subject of the Cuban detainees. There are tears in his eyes. As for Abreu, "He's got a lot of ideas about Viet—I mean, INS," he says.

———

Here is one of Jesus Abreu's ideas about the INS: "We are completely without protection from their reprisals, and believe you me, they are expert at causing you harm, bodily and mental. They'll just bury you in prison forever." Sally Sandidge, who used to represent Cubans around the country, has written: "If I had to tell what it was like to visit the detainees in one sentence it would be this: It is like visiting people who are buried alive."[3] The warden had decided to let Abreu speak to me, as long as I agreed not to publish his name in a newspaper—in a book would be fine, he said. Apparently he agreed with Jesus himself, who later wrote that he had read somewhere, "if you want to hide knowledge, you put it in a book."

Abreu and the other buried Cuban prisoners were among the 125,000 Cubans who came to the United States from the port city of Mariel in 1980. These Mariel Cubans, often called Marielitos— a term alternatingly descriptive, affectionate, and derogatory—were allowed into the United States on the basis of "parole" by the attorney general. In one of the more esoteric constructions of immigration law, they are not considered to have entered the United States, regardless of how long they have been here. The Mariel Cubans, even while serving as lucrative commodities for communities around the country, "are still technically at our borders . . . [and] are treated as still seeking admission."[4] This so-called entry fiction matters because, according to the law, "excludable" aliens such as the Mariel Cubans are not entitled to the due process guaranteed to all "persons" by the Constitution. In the words of a classic Supreme Court decision: "Whatever the process authorized by Congress is, it is due process as far as an alien denied entry is concerned." One practical consequence of the Mariel Cubans' not having been "admitted" is that they are not entitled to bond hearings to get out of INS detention; the INS has the authority to release them or to lock them up for "almost any reason."[5] According to the Justice Department, because of their unique status, the Mariel Cubans (and certain others) are not covered by the *Zadvydas* decision.[6] A special INS/BICE unit handles the custody reviews of the Mariel Cubans.

"They say legally I'm not in the U.S. Who made the five kids? How come they got my last name? How come I have to pay child support for them?" Abreu understands that he is fighting a legal fiction with his outrage, and he also understands the legal fiction's reality. "It's scary to realize that they can do with you as they please. . . . I wonder how many had they killed and nobody knows about it. Because I don't doubt for a second that they had killed some of us. If they can keep you locked up without having to respond to anyone, if they can pump you full of medication until you lose your mind, what is stopping them from getting rid of whoever they consider a risk to their operation?"

Several Mariel Cuban prisoners told filmmaker Estela Bravo[7] that at the Atlanta penitentiary a Dr. Bolivar Martineau drove inmates "mad," turning them into "vegetables" and "automatons" with injections of Thorazine and other drugs, while the INS justified their continued detention on the basis of their mental illness. Martineau was a deputy warden and the chief medical officer in Atlanta. The prisoners alleged that he forced Thorazine on them when they couldn't sleep, or when they were depressed, or for no reason at all, and that he sometimes hid the medication in their food when they refused it. The doctor responded, "No medication that was given there was for experimental purpose[s]." He also recalled: "The whole prison, as far as I was concerned, was really a psychiatric, social laboratory."

If Mariel Cuban prisoners were not entitled to any more "due process" than the government claims, wrote nine of twelve Sixth Circuit Court justices in 2003, "we do not see why the United States government could not torture or summarily execute them."[8] In a victory for these detainees, the court ruled that indefinitely detained Mariel Cubans are covered by the Supreme Court ruling in *Zadvydas;* that is, despite the "entry fiction" according to which they are not really here, the government cannot detain them forever. The decision applies only to Mariel Cubans detained in the Sixth Circuit, and INS/BICE is free to move them to states not covered by the decision, though some have been released as a result of it.

In the Supreme Court arguments about non–Mariel Cuban indefinite detention, Justice Ginsburg had tried to clarify something: Isn't it the case that "this person has no right to set foot on U.S. land, but we're going to be kind to that person and not dump them in the sea"?

Justice Scalia stepped in to help, rephrasing with an emphasis on the fact that the government could legally do much worse than it was doing: "We're *not* dumping them in the sea, are we?"

The government attorney followed Scalia's lead. "That was exactly the point I was going to make," he said.[9]

"People have killed themselves over this," Abreu tells me. We are sitting in the jail law library. A few rows of computers are behind him. His reading glasses are perched on top of his shaved head, and occasionally he pulls them down to read something from a stack of papers—a relevant statute or a note from his young daughter in Florida. She wrote "I love you" on one side of the paper and "I love me" on the other. "I've heard of people that just hanged themselves. Can you believe having no hope? I'm going to tell you the truth: I know it's the only thing I got, but sometimes I don't even believe in God no more. Because if God exists, what the hell is happening here?"

Abreu has received only one disciplinary write-up in four years of INS custody. He has paid for his criminal convictions. Now he is "doing time for free," no debt left to pay. The review panel recommended denial, and INS Headquarters denied him. There is no appeals process. "I'm the guy they call to stop fights," he tells me almost pleadingly. He was teaching inmate anger management classes. Now he will wait another year for another chance to convince the panel he has changed. He will have about fifteen minutes to do it. The INS officials, Lieutenant Viator told me, arrive at nine and leave by noon after deciding the fate of another half dozen or so persons. "When is it going to end?" Abreu asks.

Between 1983 and 1987, according to attorney Gary Leshaw, who directed the now-dissolved Committee to Support Cuban Detainees, there were about 175 serious suicide attempts by indefinitely detained Mariel Cubans, 9 of them successful. That was just in Atlanta. Today, there are said to be "approximately 1,750 Mariel Cubans" detained in the United States; hundreds more are doing time, after which the INS/BICE can detain them. In addition to being a reliable source of revenue for local governments, the Mariel Cuban detainees have been pawns in U.S.-Cuba diplomatic maneuvering. In 1984 the two countries reached an agreement under which Castro would accept the return of almost 2,746 Mariels with criminal convictions from the United States. A year later, after 201 had been returned, Castro suspended the agreement in retaliation for the Reagan administration's broadcast of CIA-run Voice of America broadcasts, so-called Radio Martí, to the island.[10]

In 1987, near the end of the period for which Leshaw had tallied the

Atlanta penitentiary suicide attempts, the United States and Cuba agreed to begin the deportations again. Within minutes of an announcement on network news, a Mariel Cuban prisoner in Oakdale, Louisiana, threw an empty food tray at a prison employee, according to criminologist Mark Hamm. In the yard the next day, a group of the nine hundred or so Oakdale Cubans "began chanting *somos los abandonados!*"—"We are the abandoned ones." Two days later, 1,394 Mariel Cuban prisoners took over the Atlanta penitentiary, using the PA system to broadcast "Radio Mariel." Hamm argues that the Cubans' "sophisticated organizational structure" along with their "profound sense of spirituality that guided the rebellion" created "the most successful revolt ever undertaken in the annals of American penology, if not world penology." Rather than getting high and losing consciousness after breaking into the prison pharmacy—the downfall of less organized prison uprisings—the Cubans at Atlanta immediately established procedures for dispensing medication. Hamm also writes in his indispensable account, *The Abandoned Ones,* that Atlanta and Oakdale were among "the most non-violent prison riots in American history." In fact, although there were millions of dollars in structural damage, these "were relatively peaceful events."[11]

The Mariel rebels successfully negotiated a moratorium on deportations to Cuba, as well as a system of what Attorney General Edwin Meese repeatedly referred to as "full, fair, and equitable" reviews for each Mariel Cuban prisoner. At a televised press conference during the uprisings, a reporter off-screen asked an interesting question: Did the promise for "full, fair, and equitable," individualized reviews mean that the Cubans were not entitled to such reviews before the uprisings? Associate Attorney General Stephen Trott stood at the podium; alongside him were Attorney General Meese, Federal Bureau of Prisons Director Michael Quinlan, and INS Commissioner Alan Nelson. All declined to answer the question.[12]

The agreements that ended the uprisings "provided generally that all detainees then in custody would receive new reviews," and initial denials would be reviewed by a special Justice Department panel. Two-thirds of those in custody at the time were "approved for release" in the seven months following the uprisings. Today that appeals process no longer exists. A "Cuban Review Plan" remains in place; these are the custody reviews about which Lieutenant Viator complained. According to the plan, a "file review" takes place, and INS officers interview the prisoner. "To recommend release, the panel must conclude the detainee is not a danger to the community and not likely to violate the conditions of release." In practice, detainees are regularly denied access to their own files. They are also regularly prohibited from having legal representation. New Orleans attorney Salvador Longoria reports that law students drive across the state, only to be turned away by the INS representatives, and Viator confirms this practice. When detainees have an attorney or someone else to help, often that person is prohibited from seeing the file.[13]

Jesus Abreu says: "They wipe their behinds with the law here. They do whatever they want, because they can get away with it."

In Louisiana a Mariel Cuban was denied release because he broke the rules of a halfway house by putting his foot on the wall. Another was detained for an additional year because he violated the halfway house curfew one night. These are examples of "halfway house failure," in INS jargon, for which one is sent back into detention to wait another year for another review. Detainee Pedro Prior Rodriguez was living in a halfway house in Rochester when he got mugged. He required treatment for an eye injury. On the grounds of his need for "specialized medical care," the INS revoked his parole and detained him in a mental hospital. When the hospital determined that he was sane, the INS transferred Rodriguez to the Atlanta penitentiary. He had never been charged with a crime.[14]

The examples are scattered, bogged down in bureaucratic secrecy and confusion, and the threads lead into thousands of life stories. "J. H." served five years for drug possession, and then he was detained for ten years (and counting) by the INS. Twenty-three-year-old "W. H." served three years for having sex with his underage girlfriend and for "riding in a stolen car." Then the INS detained him for eight years (and counting). "P. M." was arrested for attempted murder. It turned out to be a case of mistaken identity, and the charges against him were dropped. The INS nevertheless used the arrest to justify his continued detention. Leshaw represented another Cuban whose murder conviction was reversed on appeal, but the "INS refused to accept the verdict" and held him in detention for another four years. It is not surprising the INS does not allow media or, usually, family members to attend the panel reviews. Sally Sandidge writes: "Many of the panelists did this sort of thing: 'What happened in 1981?' 'I was in Fort

Chaffee.' 'Did you have problems?' 'No.' 'Liar, here's a report that said you and others stole food from the cafeteria.'"[15]

Reynero Arteaga Carballo was detained for fifteen years — more than double the length of his criminal sentence—before his release to a halfway house in December 2002. After one panel review, INS officials justified his continued detention by explaining that Carballo showed no remorse for the attempted murder he had committed. At a subsequent review, INS officials justified Carballo's continued detention by explaining that his expression of remorse was "a new tactic of claiming fault" in an effort to get released.[16] As Leshaw and Viator and Abreu all readily concede, many of these prisoners have shown themselves to be dangerous in the past. "The greatest danger however," Leshaw writes, "was the refusal of the U.S. government to establish any type of procedure comporting with due process whereby a detainee could have his or her case heard."[17] He was referring to the 1980s, but that danger persists.

Omar Rodriguez was sentenced to three years' probation for attempted burglary soon after his arrival on the Mariel boatlift. He violated probation by possessing two ounces of marijuana and spent two years in a Texas prison. He was out in 1984 and back in again the same year for another four months on possession. Then he was taken into INS custody. Rodriguez has been in INS custody for twenty years now. On a scrap of paper that looks as if it had been through the laundry, Rodriguez wrote in pencil from the U.S. penitentiary (USP) at Lompoc, California, in 2002: "Where is the civil right and my human right in this free country? . . . It is because I can't defend myself or because everybody quiet before immigration law unjustice?" Rodriguez has written extensively in Spanish about his years of incarceration by the INS, but his writings were destroyed by prison officials when he was moved from a penitentiary in Beaumont, Texas. The last sentence on the faded scrap of paper says, "It's more better to get quiet by now . . ." Rodriguez also sent along a photo of himself dressed in a white T-shirt and khakis. He might be sitting on a park bench on a sunny day in front of a chain-link fence, except for the faint shadow of razor wire loops on the walkway. The photo is attached with a small piece of black electrical tape to a clean sheet of paper with a poem typed on it. On the back of the photo Rodriguez wrote: "This is me. I am fifty years old 1952–03. USP Lompoc CA." It looks like an epitaph.

In Lake Charles, Jesus Abreu says:

Yeah, we might have criminal backgrounds, we might have broken the law.
There are some scumbags in here, but still, we are human beings. At least we
deserve a chance. They are not affecting only us. There's families out there—
there are kids, mothers, wives, sisters. They're suffering, too. They put us
in hell. This is hell. Literal. No hope. No hope. We're fighting Goliath, and
God ain't listening to us. This abuse is twenty years old. Somebody's got to
say something. If they don't want me in this country, send me back. If Cuba
don't want me back, send me to a jungle. I just want to be by myself. Free.
Walk around. Even if I have to hunt the cockroach, raw, with my bare hands.
I'll manage. But don't keep me like cattle. Crushing me here. Not only me—
they're crushing all of us. I don't know what else to say.

Let somebody know. Somebody's got to care, man. If you holler enough,
this is a big country. Not all the people in this country are like INS, I know.
Look at Lieutenant Viator, look at Colonel LeFargue. Maybe this is even
going against them, and they allowing me to talk to you. It's not that everybody's bad. It's just some bad people in charge of INS. There's some officers
here, they look at you with hate, and you never met the guy. There's some
small kid, a young guy, and if he catches you in a cell, handcuffed, he's
gonna beat the dog out of you. For free. Why he hates? I don't even know
the guy. Why INS is like that, I can't understand.

I would like INS to get me in a plane, give me a parachute, and drop me
in the jungle. Somewhere. I'll survive. I'd rather be in a jungle, in the desert,
in the middle of the ocean, than be locked up. You know how much suffering you see here? You know what it is like to sit in here and you see your life
waste away? Just doing nothing. Being fed like a cow. Because that's what we
are—cattle. We are cattle here. They're using us for money.

The relative peacefulness of the 1987 riots was not only because of prisoner tactics, Mark Hamm argues, but also because of BOP Director
Quinlan's self-described strategy of "endless patience," to which Meese also
adhered. But Justice Department foot soldiers were standing by, anxious
"to go in and kick some Cuban ass." This was among the candid comments captured in a home video made for the archive of the Border Patrol
Tactical Team (BORTAC) at Oakdale and Atlanta. The video shows damage to prison infrastructure and BORTAC members practicing maneu-
vers in empty fields. In a caricatured Spanish accent, one team member

tells of a Cuban prisoner's graffiti, "liberty or die." From behind the camera, the agency's narrator mockingly reads more graffiti from an abandoned section of the prison: "'We are not criminals, we are humans'—that's one of my favorites," he says.[18]

Border Patrol officials often serve as panel members at custody review hearings. Attorney Longoria described the situation of the prisoner who sits opposite them: "absolutely no resources, [and he] has been moved from state facility to state facility—without, of course, letting anybody know—their family or their lawyer or anybody that cares about them." Unrepresented, and perhaps speaking no English, Longoria continued, "this person . . . is supposed to face these INS people at this panel review, and somehow or another prove that he is worthy of release, that he's not going to become a violent offender and that he does have support—a job waiting, a home, or whatever."

In 2001 at least 160 Mariel Cubans had been detained by the INS for a decade or more.[19] But some get out. Miguel Lopez Bignotte got out. He served ninety days on a misdemeanor cocaine possession charge after several previous misdemeanors. Then the INS detained him for fifteen years. Suddenly one day in 2002, he was no longer considered a danger to society and was released. Lopez was sent from the Beaumont penitentiary to a local halfway house to start his life again. His mother, who had come from Cuba two years earlier so that she might visit him (and was allowed to be present at a panel review hearing), had moved into an old age home in Miami. She later returned to Cuba.

———

A young black man on his way into the Calcasieu jail raises both arms toward the sky and shouts, "What's up!" He doesn't bother looking around, because the disembodied voice that had greeted him a moment before came from behind one of the slotted windows of the low brick building. A large yellow sign warns in red letters against "unauthorized communication with inmates." A couple of women on their way inside ignore catcalls from the slots. An attorney with his sleeves rolled up stands chatting with the voice of an inmate he cannot see.

I was watching all this from a rented car in the parking lot, waiting for an INS detainee and an INS agent to walk out of the jail. Lieutenant Viator had told me that a Mariel Cuban woman was being released and put on a bus that afternoon. Though I didn't know what either agent or inmate looked like, it was obvious when they appeared. He was a balding, mustached, heavy-set, white man wearing a plaid sport shirt and carrying a stack of paperwork; she was also large, dark-skinned next to him, wearing a baggy white T-shirt and blue denim shorts and carrying a large duffel bag. All the dollars, all the infrastructure, all the statutes and suffering and lies, all of the 200,000 stories of persons detained last year by the INS, and here were one man and one woman, the keeper and the kept, walking out of a jail and through a parking lot in Lake Charles to his car. Her bag went into the trunk of the white sedan, and they headed out. Soon they stopped and went inside a bank. Barbara Perera would tell me later that when the bank refused to cash the check for $201.35 from her mother, the INS officer, Brian Gueringer, vouched for her. Then he drove her to the Greyhound station.

Gueringer briefly chatted with me about the Mariel review process as we stood beside his white Mitsubishi in the Greyhound lot. Based in nearby Oakdale, Gueringer himself sometimes served on the review panels. He asked me if I knew why he never told anyone whether he recommended denial or release. Then he answered the question himself: "Because I don't have to." He never felt a conflict between his personal feelings and the requirements of the law, he said, because as a panel member he only made recommendations; someone in Washington made the final decision. "The rule of Nobody," writes Hannah Arendt, "is what the political form known as bureau-cracy truly is." In the parking lot of the small Greyhound station just off I-10, from which buses would soon be heading west to El Paso and east to Jacksonville, our brief conversation came to a close.[20]

Barbara Perera had a couple of hours before her bus left. Sitting in my rental car, she cried and told me why jail visitation days were so painful. She used to try to sleep through the weekend visitation, but the humidity and lack of air-conditioning kept her awake. She wanted to sleep so that she would not see other prisoners visiting with their families. Perera's mother was seventy-two and recovering from heart surgery in Miami. Her own twenty-one-year-old son and seven-year-old daughter were in Miami as well. Perera, thirty-nine, had been locked up for six years. She served three years for shoplifting after she stole $1,100 worth of clothing while working at a low-paying cashier job. When her sentence was completed, the INS held her for another three years. She had not seen her daughter in the last two years, since being moved from Miami's Krome detention center to a series of Louisiana jails.

"It's not their fault," she said of the other inmates. "They don't know what I was going through. They come and say, 'You see my baby' and I say, 'Yeah it's pretty.' But I hurt inside because I want to see mine, and then they only allow me two phone calls a week."

Perera said she feels like she's on "a different planet" all of a sudden. They had not given her much advance warning of her release, and jail officials were ready to handcuff her for the last walk out of custody. "I wish you would," she told me she said to them. Then simply: "No. And I kept on walking." A second CO told the first to back off. The next minute, Perera was telling me she will be "righteous," that she'll make better choices next time, and that she has paid her debt now. Of course, her debt was paid halfway through the six years and surely overpaid even then. Later she will say, "I paid twice for one crime."

The lanky Greyhound driver—gray shirt, gray pants, cowboy buckle, slow cigarette—was stowing luggage, but Perera wanted to keep her bulky duffel bag with her. "I was so afraid," she told me four months later in Miami. "I didn't even get off the bus but one time, because I was scared of the bus leaving me stranded." Finally, at one rest stop, the driver told her to get something to eat. She bought some junk food and quickly got back on. "When we did a transfer in Jacksonville, he got to tell me to get off the bus. He said, 'Go up to that bus right there, and you're going to get in that bus right there and show him your paper'"—the ticket. "And I didn't come out one time."

The damage detention does to a person does not end when she is released. Former Krome guard Eddie Calejo had served less than a year in federal prison, and when he got out it was hard for him to get up in the morning or go shopping. "You just feel like people are looking at you differently," he said. "They really don't, but you feel like they do, because you feel branded." Barbara Perera was at her mother's apartment, a few miles east of Calejo's southwest Miami home, when we met for the second time. "I don't sleep," she said. "All I do is eat and eat. I can't take too much noise. I don't like to be around people. I just want to stay in the house." She had found a job driving the elderly to medical appointments. She spoke a lot about her "nerves." She still carries her confinement inside her, and she still remembers others who have not gotten out.

> They are really messing with people's mind. And it hurt me. Julia is still out there, and she got a nerve problem too. Her nerves got bad. Then she went without her medication for a while, because the psychiatrist didn't come see her. You have to get the okay from INS before they come see you, and that takes time. Wait, wait, wait. She even did some crazy stuff like swallow razors. She tried to hang herself. When you're in a place like that, crazy stuff coming through your head, because I can tell you, I was frustrated myself. When is my day going to come? And you didn't see no days. You don't see no day. Many times I wake up in the morning and I don't know if I'm going to make it through the next day. It's not right. And I fear for her, because she's still there.

Julia Gomez said she knows it's "against God" to try to kill herself, but she preferred that to living the rest of her life in detention. Gomez was twenty-one when she left Cuba on the Mariel boatlift. Like other Mariel Cubans, she spent a few months at relocation centers in the United States. In 1997 Gomez was sentenced to fourteen months for misdemeanor crack cocaine possession after a string of other misdemeanors. She served her time at the Broward Correctional Institute in Ft. Lauderdale, and she completed a drug treatment program there. According to Gomez, the INS has failed to provide her with the antidepressant medication she had been taking before she was locked up. The INS has refused to release Gomez because she is suicidal. Character references from the Cottonport jail warden and other correctional officials did her no good; instead, INS panel members also used the fact that Gomez didn't know where she would live if released as a justification for keeping her imprisoned.[21]

Barbara Perera and Julia Gomez met in Louisiana's New Iberia Parish Jail, southwest of New Orleans, in the midst of acres of sugarcane fields. Gomez too thinks about her fellow prisoners, and she used to write letters to them, even while incarcerated herself, because she knew they had no one. "I just had to keep telling them, everything is going to be alright. You just hang in there. We're all going through the same thing. At least I drop them a letter, and they drop me one." Jailhouse attorney and mediator Abreu told me how he kept himself from losing his mind: "I keep myself busy. I take care of everybody else's problems, because I cannot take care of mine."

Like many young Cubans who left the island in 1980, Gomez did so to escape police harassment. "I didn't want to come to the U.S. My daddy and my mommy begged me not to. But there was a police officer who always bothered me. He told me if I didn't come over here he would lock me down forever. So I got scared and I came." She had asked her INS deportation officer to ship her back, but that didn't happen. Now the INS— and later the Department of Homeland Security—had the legal authority to lock her down forever. In early 2003 Gomez was in a federal penitentiary in Dublin, California, waiting for transfer to a halfway house. The INS said it was simply waiting for a bed to become available; the single federally funded release program for long-term INS detainees, which was cheaper than detention, had been defunded.[22] Gomez had been detained for four years since completing her sentence.

> The last thing they have to do is just kill us, but see, they can't do that, though. It's going to be a little bit too much. But they do it mentally. . . . No way out. Die. That's how it seems sometimes. Your only way out is dying. . . . Sometimes I go so low that I believe that God is not helping me. But then I pick up again, and I keep going, and I keep going. Because there's a God. Because he's the one that keeps me talking right now.

Sometimes, Gomez said, before going to sleep, she prays that she will not wake up. "I'm talking to you, but I need somebody to speak back to me."[23]

"Julia gone," Barbara Perera told me in her own mother's apartment. "Julia's not the same Julia."

Perera believes that she herself survived detention by finding activities to keep her occupied. In New Iberia she was not permitted to work, so she read and wrote and played cards. In Cottonport she gave the other inmates manicures and pedicures. In Lake Charles she would sit up all night sewing for the officers—not their uniforms but their "free world clothes." It was voluntary work, and she made a few tips. "It stopped my mind," she says. "It keep me off thinking a lot."

Perera and her seven-year-old daughter are both in therapy now. "She can't get used to me," Perera explains. Her plan had been to return home briefly to see her family and then go back to Louisiana for an offshore oil job. All that changed when she saw her young daughter. Her daughter didn't want to stay with Barbara at first; her mother had been away for six of her seven years. Perera understands that it will take time. She hugs her daughter, who is crying, until the girl begins to smile. She holds her for a while. Then she sends her off to spend the night with the godmother she has grown close to. Perera watches her daughter, accompanied by her grandmother's husband, walk out the door with her small backpack. From the street in front of their apartment building, you can see the Miami River, where stowaways in cargo ships sometimes come ashore and where small boats are piled with stolen and discarded merchandise to be resold in the Caribbean.

———

In Havana there was little to say to Jesus Abreu's grown nephew. I sat with him and his wife and their young son in the same small apartment where Jesus had grown up. The nephew told me what he remembered about his uncle. Jesus Abreu had gone to officer training school and become disenchanted by the hypocrisy of the revolution when he saw the way high-ranking officers lived. The neighborhood police used to harass him for approaching tourists to earn dollars, and other young men in the neighborhood resented him for his light skin and his intelligence.

The nephew's wife had turned down the volume but left the television on. The sound of the program we were watching was audible from neighboring apartments. It was a musical variety show, with regular shots of Castro, who was in the audience and seemed to be enjoying himself. The nephew wanted to understand his uncle's situation. Explaining it here in the old section of Havana, some distance from the legal details, it seemed simple and stark. No one could say when his uncle would be released. Under the law, the U.S. government could hold him until he was dead.[24]

Thinking back to the year of the boatlift, Jesus Abreu's nephew told me that many people had left this neighborhood for the port of Mariel and, ultimately, the United States. He recalled individuals one by one, building by building, block by block. Then I walked back to my hotel through the largely empty nighttime streets, past those same buildings, along those blocks. Miami was a short flight away.

I could not have written this book without the help of more people than I can name here.

First, I thank the prisoners and former prisoners who spoke with me or wrote to me. Most were or remain immigration "detainees," though a few were U.S. citizen prisoners doing time. Some are named here, and many others are not. Because our conversations were usually one-sided, few of them may realize how much they taught me.

I am also indebted to INS, Justice Department, and correctional officials who spoke with me. Of the few I have already named, special thanks to Edward Calejo, Richard Franklin, Judith Marty, and George Taylor. I also thank Bureau of Prisons Public Affairs officials, clerks at various courts and at the Merits Systems Protection Board, and those INS spokespersons who responded honestly to my questions. Marian L. Smith, Crystal Williams, and Zack Wilske of the INS Historical Reference Library in Washington, D.C., were extremely helpful and patient.

Journalists can be unresponsive, but Elise Ackerman, Susana Barciela, Aldrin Brown, Robert Kahn, Rose Livingston, Elizabeth Llorente, Dan Malone, Teresa Mears, Alexandra Polier, Alisa Solomon, and Steven Rubin have all been generous.

Rachel Schuder's fastidious work transcribing taped interviews made her indispensable; her observations along the way often helped me to notice things I had missed. Pimpila Thanaporn and Rylan Morrison also provided valuable help with transcriptions.

I have been extremely fortunate over the past decade or so to have had contact with a wide-ranging group of attorneys, activists, and others who work on behalf of immigrants in the United States, even though I have never met some of them in person. Inevitably, I have omitted names, for which I apologize, but among those who have provided information, ideas, explanations, or inspiration by their example are Eleanor Acer, Abira Ashfaq, Jane Bai, Gillian Black, Thomas Brannen, Karol Brown, Miranda Brown, David Cole, Will Coley, Erin Corcoran, Rita Dave, Christina DeConcini, Sophie Feal, Regis Fernandez, Bill Frelick, Niels Frenzen, Joan Friedland, Liliana Garces, Jane Guskin, the late Arthur Helton, Alisha Horowitz, Anwen Hughes, Sarah Ignatius, Leticia Jimenez, María Jimenez, Barry Johnson, D'Ann Johnson, Laurie Joyce, Dan Kowalski, Laurie Kozuba, Carol Lehman, David Leopold, Salvador Longoria, Kathleen Lucas, Joan Maruskin, Nancy Morawetz, Melanie Nezer, Christopher Nugent, Karen Pennington, Ai-Jen Poo, Nick Rizza, Oren Root, Hussein Sadruddin, Jim Salvatore, MacDonald Scott, Rebecca Sharpless, Andrea Siemens, Jay Stansell, Martin Stolar, Alicia Triche, Tara Urs, Allison Wannamaker, Matt Wilch, and Wendy Young. I am also grateful to a variety of staff members of the American Civil Liberties Union Immigrant Rights' Project, the Florida Immigrant Advocacy Center, the Catholic Legal Immigration Network, the Coalition for the Human Rights of Immigrants, Desis Rising Up and Moving, the Lutheran Immigration and Refugee Service, Human Rights Watch, the Lawyers Committee for Human Rights, Amnesty International, and the American Bar Association.

I offer special thanks and my respect to Miami's Haitian Refugee Center staff of the early 1990s, where in some ways this began. Since then, Esther Olavarría's quiet and continuing dedication and Cheryl Little's determination and laughter have helped to keep me going. Sharon Ginter's patient assistance has been invaluable.

Allyson Collins kindly read early chapters, and Margaret Taylor generously read the manuscript and provided valuable suggestions and legal expertise. Judy Greene was continuously helpful with information and encouragement. In the early stages of the project, Simon Lipskar, Joe Sharkey, and John Brehm provided generous suggestions and assistance.

Will Ferroggiaro of the National Security Archive advised me on Freedom of Information Act requests.

I gratefully acknowledge the editors of publications where the germs of parts of this book first appeared: *CovertAction Quarterly, Haïti Progrès, Index on Censorship, Nieman Reports, Prison Legal News,* the *Miami Herald,* and the *Texas Observer.*

I am more than appreciative for the support that my editor, Naomi Schneider, has given this project. My thanks also to Sierra Filucci, to editor Sue Heinemann and copy editor Sheila Berg for their keen eyes and deft pencils, and to others at the University of California Press.

This book has been more a part of my life than I could have imagined, and many friends have provided encouragement, support, criticism, editing, and love in inseparable combinations. I am deeply grateful to David R. Dow, Gina Cunningham, Peter Eves, Holly Wolf, Byron Kim, Joshua Levinson, Kevin Pask, Tom Perrotta, and Lisa Sigal. Danielle Webb has helped me to know what I could do. Gregg Ellis helped me to finish it, and this book could not have come to exist as it does without the friendship and detail-oriented gifts of Judy Rabinovitz and Miraan Moon Sa.

I remain saddened by the death of my friend Julie Jacobson, coeditor of *New Politics,* to whom I would so much have liked to hand a copy.

This book is also dedicated with love to my parents, Frieda and Melvin Dow.

Responsibility for any mistakes here is mine.

# NOTES

The identities of some of the people in this book have been disguised. Unless otherwise indicated, quotations for which no source is cited are from interviews or correspondence with the author.

Quotations from court proceedings are from the author's notes unless official transcripts are cited. Copies of unpublished sources cited (e.g., e-mails, memoranda, and typescripts) are on file with the author.

## CHAPTER 1: INVISIBILITY, INTIMIDATION, AND THE INS

1.  The poem, titled "Krome," reads:

    Lieu où je connais pour la première fois
    Là où j'endure toute sorte de souffrance
    Mais ce lieu presque me rend fou
    Parce que j'ai trop pensé à ma vie

    Lieu où je n'ai pas de liberté
    Et j'aime beaucoup la liberté
    Et j'ai une uniforme de mépris
    Oh! Je ne connais que fais-je?

    J'ai encore jeune pour souffrir
    Cette peine là est trop dur pour moi
    Parfois je pense à suicider
    Mais la nature n'a pas encore voulu

Ce lieu m'a fait connaître
Toute sorte de souffrance
Ça m'a fait pleurer parfois
Mais sans une consolation

Place that I know for the first time/Where I endure all kinds of suffering/
This place almost makes me crazy/Because I think too much about my
life // Place where I have no freedom/And I love freedom very much/And
I wear this uniform of contempt/Oh! I don't know what I will do // I'm
still too young to suffer/The pain here is too much for me/Sometimes I
think of killing myself/But Nature would not want that // This place has
shown me/All kinds of suffering/It has made me cry sometimes/Without
consolation.

2.    Debbie Sontag, "Krome: Stories of Despair," *Miami Herald,* April 11,
      1990, A1. Todaro later said: "The INS has followed me around the camp
      since I spoke to the *Herald,* watching everyone I talk to. The INS really
      thinks they're above the law, and who is going to make them account-
      able?" Affidavit, Haitian Refugee Center, 1990.
3.    Detaining minors with adults became a violation of INS policy and the
      law as a result of the 1997 settlement in *Flores v. Reno,* 113 S.Ct. 1429. Also
      see Human Rights Watch, *Slipping through the Cracks: Unaccompanied
      Children Detained by the U.S. Immigration and Naturalization Service*
      (New York, April 1997).
          In 2000 an INS assessment team visited Krome. Team member Kim
      W. Porter, San Diego INS deputy assistant district director, noted, "Gen-
      eral policies were difficult to locate." However, two policies were "found"
      concerning the detention of juveniles at Krome (dated 1996 and 1998);
      both made clear that minors should not be held with adults. Porter
      wrote: "The existing design of the facility prohibits enforcement of
      these policies." John J. Pogash, INS Headquarters juvenile coordinator,
      who also participated in the assessment, wrote: "When questioned about
      juvenile policy, [Krome] SPC [Service Processing Center] staff seemed
      unaware as to whether it existed or if it did, where it could be found."
      "Krome SPC Back-up Material" (2000), at Tabs 3 and 4.
4.    For "stashed out of sight": e-mail message from Weiss, quoted in U.S.
      Department of Justice, Office of the Inspector General, *Alleged Decep-
      tion of Congress: The Congressional Task Force on Immigration Reform's
      Fact-finding Visit to the Miami District of INS in June 1995* (June 1996).
          Weiss was "demoted and reassigned" to a lower-paying job in Dallas;

the INS argued that her "reassignment was 'logistical rather than disciplinary'" (essentially the same claim the agency makes when it transfers detainees who protest detention conditions). Weiss subsequently won an appeal through the U.S. Merit Protection Board and was awarded back pay and returned to what her attorney called a "better job" in the Miami District office; the government paid her legal fees. In the decision on her appeal, the administrative judge wrote that Weiss was "obeying the orders of her superiors" when she reduced the population of Krome before the congressional delegation arrived, which is "an exculpatory explanation for her alleged misconduct." "A contrary finding would require the Board to hold that an agency may discipline an employee for carrying out an order, and also discipline her for refusing to carry out the same order." (U.S. Merit Protection Board, Central Regional Office, *Constance K. Weiss v. Department of Justice*, AT-0752–97–0417-I-1, Initial Decision of Administrative Judge Jeremiah J. Cassidy, September 4, 1997; author interview with Weiss's former attorney Peter A. Quinter, May 29, 2003.) Also see OIG, *Follow-up Report* (September 1997); Carol Rosenberg, "A Dozen Punished in Krome Scandal," *Miami Herald*, February 22, 1997, 1A; [no author], "INS Workers Appeal Demotion, Transfer," *Miami Herald*, March 11, 1997; U.S. Merit Protection Board, *Valerie M. Blake v. Department of Justice*, CH-0752–97–0402-I-1; and chap. 3, note 8.

On Krome storage room: Chief Detention Officer Walter Le Roy of San Pedro, California, participated in an INS assessment of Krome and wrote: "I recommend that periodic audits conducted by a disinterested party take place unannounced at least once a month. . . . [A] large amount of detainee property remains in the storage area for detainees who have either been deported, bonded out, transferred or released. The facility lacks procedures for the proper disposal of such property. Detention Officers advised that excess property is donated to Goodwill Industries without attempts to contact the detainee and either allowing them to come back to the facility and pick it up or mailing it to them being made" ("Krome SPC Back-up Material" [2000], at Tab 8).

Le Roy does not address the intentional disposal of prisoners' property—which in at least one case included an account of life at Krome. In 1996 a Nigerian detainee, Theophilus Adebise-Ayodele, collapsed on the soccer field at Krome and later died. His fiancée told me that when she visited him he had shown her "a whole stack" of his writing about what went on at Krome; when she went to pick up his property after his death, Krome officials gave her photographs and other belongings, but his writings were gone. "They got rid of that one box," she said. Elsewhere, a Mariel Cuban detainee told me his writings about INS detention and prison conditions were destroyed before one of his transfers, and many detainees have complained of guards throwing away their paperwork, so we can assume that many accounts of INS and non-INS prison life have been destroyed.

5. Todaro's and my dismissals were reported in Debbie Sontag, "Krome Teachers Link Firings, Criticism," *Miami Herald,* May 8, 1990, 1B; Ardy Friedberg, "Krome Teachers Blame Firings on Disclosure about Abuses," Ft. Lauderdale *Sun-Sentinel,* May 8, 1990; Charisse L. Grant, "Schools Try to Rehire Teacher Dismissed from Krome," *Miami Herald,* May 9, 1990, 1B (concerning school board's discussion of finding employment for Todaro somewhere other than Krome); James Lemoyne, "Florida Center Holding Aliens Is under Inquiry," *New York Times,* May 16, 1990, A8.

6. Quotations from William S. Bernard, "A History of U.S. Immigration Policy," in *Immigration: Dimensions of Ethnicity,* ed. Richard A. Easterlin, David Ward, et al. (Cambridge, Mass.: Belknap Press, 1992), 87; Shawn P. Aubitz, Introduction to Records of the Special Boards of Inquiry, District No. 4 (Philadelphia), Immigration and Naturalization Service, 1893–1909, National Archives Microfilm Publications, Pamphlet Describing M15000 (Washington, D.C., 1987), 4. On rareness of deportations, see U.S. Department of Justice, Immigration and Naturalization Service, *An Immigrant Nation: United States Regulation of Immigration, 1798–1991* (Washington, D.C.: U.S. Government Printing Office, 1991), 11–12.

7. U.S. Department of Justice, Immigration and Naturalization Service, *Isle of Hope, Isle of Tears,* prepared by Kathleen Barry, typescript, no date [probably 1986]. Quotation regarding "island prison": from Justice Robert Jackson's dissent in *Shaughnessy v. United States ex. rel. Mezei* (1953). The prisoner, Ignatz Mezei, was born in either Hungary or Gibraltar, apparently to Romanian parents, and lived in New York State for twenty-five years. He traveled to Hungary to visit his dying mother and remained there for nineteen months because of difficulty securing a visa for his return. Mezei was held on Ellis Island when he returned in 1950 and was detained there for more than twenty-one months without a hearing. The stated reason for Mezei's detention was that he was a "national security threat," but the basis for that determination was kept secret from him. Mezei's limbo status was the result of a provision of the immigration law according to which he had not made an "entry" into

the United States and therefore had limited rights to oppose U.S. authority to detain him on U.S. soil; he was considered an "excludable alien." This landmark case is used today to justify the government's indefinite detention of Mariel Cubans who have been here for decades but whose "parole" into the country from a port of entry has been revoked by the INS, usually as a result of their criminal convictions (see chap. 14).

8. Arthur C. Helton, "The Legality of Detaining Refugees in the United States," (New York University) *Review of Law and Social Change* 14.2 (1986): 355. Remark regarding "needless confinement": quoted in Timothy J. Dunn, *The Militarization of the U.S.-Mexican Border, 1978–1992: Low-Intensity Conflict Doctrine Comes Home* (Austin: Center for Mexican American Studies, University of Texas at Austin, 1996), 46. On "average detained alien of the 1970s": U.S. General Accounting Office, *Criminal Aliens: INS's Detention and Deportation Activities in the New York City Area*, GAO/GGD-87-19BR (December 1986), 10. On "the Service's concentrated effort": INS Authorization and Budget Request to Congress, 1968 (INS Historical Reference Library, Washington, D.C.).

9. For "tended to be casual": Bernard, "History of U.S. Immigration Policy," 82; "brutal": author interview with former Los Angeles Asylum Office supervisor, Judith Marty. William French Smith quoted in Dunn, *The Militarization of the U.S.-Mexican Border*, 46. Helton, "The Legality of Detaining Refugees in the United States," 367. On continuation of Haitian detention today, see U.S. Department of Justice, Office of the Attorney General, *In re D-J-, Respondent*, 23 I&N Dec. 572 (A.G. 2003), Interim Decision #3488, April 17, 2003; Associated Press, "Ashcroft Rules on Immigrants' Detention," April 24, 2003; "DHS to Detain Asylum Seekers under 'Operation Liberty Shield,'" *Refugee Reports* (Washington, D.C.: Immigration and Refugee Services of America March–April 2003), 5; American Immigration Lawyers Association, "Is There Rule of Law in Immigration?" Press Release, April 24, 2003.

10. On "the detention of hundreds of thousands": Gelbspan, *Break-ins, Death Threats, and the FBI: The Covert War against the Central America Movement* (Boston: South End Press, 1991), 184; on "alien activists": Memorandum to Alan C. Nelson, INS Commissioner, from Deputy Attorney General D. Lowell Jensen, Subject: Formation of Alien Border Control Committee, June 27, 1986. I am grateful to James X. Dempsey of the Center for Democracy and Technology for providing me with copies of documents related to the 1986 ABC Plan. Also see James X. Dempsey and David Cole, *Terrorism and the Constitution: Sacrificing*

*Civil Liberties in the Name of National Security* (Washington, D.C.: First Amendment Foundation, 2002), 39 ff.

11. Figures from 1973 through 1980: INS Authorization and Budget Request to Congress, 1976–1980 (INS Historical Reference Library, Washington, D.C.).

12. The report continues intriguingly: "Alien criminality has many phases not generally understood. Perhaps the majority of the so-called crimes committed are not crimes at all, but offenses which are offenses only because committed by aliens. Then, in many communities, the immigrant is frequently recorded as a criminal by reason of a most discreditable system of exploitation, which exists for the profit of officials rather than for the protection of the community. Nevertheless, there is a dangerous and apparently growing criminal element in the country due to immigration, and it is this element to which the attention of the commission is especially directed." "Statement Relevant to the Work and Expenditures of the Immigration Commission Created under Section 39 of the Immigration Act of February 20, 1907," H.R. Doc. 1489 (Washington, D.C.: U.S. Government Printing Office, February 7, 1909).

13. "Since 1986, the INS has had in place the Alien Criminal Apprehension Program (ACAP), which has one objective—to locate, apprehend, and remove criminal aliens from the community, and ultimately, from the United States, in as expeditious a manner as possible" (Testimony of Joseph R. Greene, Acting Executive Associate Commissioner for Field Operations, Immigration and Naturalization Service, Before the House Committee on Government Reform, Subcommittees on Government Efficiency, Financial Management and Intergovernmental Relations; Criminal Justice, Drug Policy and Human Resources; and National Security, Veterans Affairs and International Relations on INS's Relationship with State and Local Law Enforcement, November 13, 2001).

In 1988 the INS began its Institutional Removal Program (IRP) in cooperation with the Executive Office for Immigration Review and state and local correctional authorities. "The IRP process ideally begins with the identification of potentially deportable foreign-born inmates as they enter the correctional system and culminates in a hearing before an immigration judge at a designated hearing site within the federal, state, or local prison system" (U.S. Department of Justice, Office of the Inspector General, Audit Division, *Audit Report: Immigration and Naturalization Service Institutional Removal Program,* September 2002 [02-41], i). In the 1990s the INS referred to its program of "criminal alien centralization" (U.S. INS, "Immigration and Naturalization Service Detention and Deportation Program," January 26, 1996). In the late 1990s the Bureau of Prisons contracted with the Corrections Corporation of America to operate facilities especially for noncitizens serving criminal sentences. Justice policy analyst Judith Greene has called the arrangement a bailout of the nation's leading private prison company. See Judith Greene, "Bailing Out Private Jails," in *Prison Nation: The Warehousing of America's Poor,* ed. Tara Herivel and Paul Wright (New York: Routledge, 2003), 139 ff.

INS officials' 1934 lecture to colleagues about deportation and arrest procedures contained only a brief reference to custody issues: "It is necessary at times to conduct hearings at prisons, jails, alms houses, and hospitals. It has been held [by courts] that a hearing held in prison while an alien is an inmate thereof does not render the hearing unfair" (U.S. Department of Labor, Immigration and Naturalization Service, Lecture #22 [2d ser.]: "Warrant and Deportation Procedure," by W. W. Brown, Chief Administrative Officer, INS, and R. M. Charles, Examiner, INS, November 12, 1934, 7).

14. Joseph Nevins, *Operation Gatekeeper: The Rise of the "Illegal Alien" and the Making of the U.S.-Mexico Boundary* (New York: Routledge, 2002), 88. For "while it pursue[d] a reversal": Women's Commission for Refugee Women and Children, *A Cry for Help: Chinese Women in INS Detention—Delegation to Visit Asylum Seekers Held in York and Berks County Prisons, Pennsylvania* (New York, March 2–5, 1996).

15. According to INS/BICE public affairs spokespersons, the agency does not track the number of asylum seekers in detention (author e-mail correspondence with BICE spokespersons, 2003). Eleanor Acer of the Lawyers Committee for Human Rights writes: "At any time, the U.S. government detains about 22,000 non-citizens in INS detention facilities and jails, and it has been estimated that several thousand of those detainees are asylum seekers. Precise statistical information about asylum seekers, including the number of asylum seekers in detention, has long been difficult to obtain from the INS. For years, in fact, the INS has been unable to regularly provide statistical information relating to detained asylum seekers—even in the face of a federal statute requiring the INS to report these numbers to Congress" (Acer, "Living Up to America's Values: Reforming the U.S. Detention System for Asylum Seekers," *Refuge* 20.3 [May 2002]: 46). Also see Lawyers Committee for Human Rights, *Refugees behind Bars: The Imprisonment of Asylum Seekers in the Wake of the 1996 Immigration Act* [New York, August 1999], 33). In 2003, according to Senator Edward Kennedy's office, a DHS official

said that from 1999 to 2002 approximately 13 percent of the total detained population (of some 22,000) were asylum seekers.

For "eliminated the INS's discretion" and 1994–2001 figures: "Statement of Joseph Greene, Acting Deputy Executive Associate Commissioner and Edward McElroy, District Director, U.S. INS, Before the House Committee on the Judiciary, Subcommittee on Immigration and Claims, Regarding a Review of Department of Justice Immigration Detention Policies," December 19, 2001. On "the world's largest agency": "INS: Smuggling, Foreigners' Rights," *Migration News* 6.1 (January 1999): www.migration.ucdavis.edu. On INS Atlanta District Chief of Detention and Removals George Taylor: author interviews.

16. According to the Office of Immigration Statistics, there were 22,716 detainees in INS custody at the end of February 2003. "As early as 1935": "Judge Sorry Alien Women Placed in County Jail Tanks," *El Paso Times,* February 6, 1935. Approximately 60 percent in jails and private facilities: e-mail correspondence from INS spokespersons Kerry Gill and Karen Kraushaar, April 2003.

17. *Harrisburg Patriot,* June 22, 1993, and York County detention costs quoted in Joan Maruskin, "Voices from around the Country Call for INS Detention Reform," *Migrationworld* 23.4 (1995). At the time the *Golden Venture* refugees were being held in these communities, it happened that local demolition work involving asbestos was necessary; a York County commissioner commented, "We've got the labor force to do it in prison"; another added, "You're thinking of those Asian guys." (Elizabeth Cummings, "Commissioners' Comments Anger Attorney of Refugee," *York Daily Record,* August 31, 1993, 1B.)

18. Mississippi sheriff quoted in Dianne Klein, "INS 'Lifers' Locked Up in Limbo," *Los Angeles Times,* February 6, 1994. Miami INS official: Deposition of Kenneth Powers, Assistant District Director for Detention and Deportation, *Haitian Refugee Center, Inc. v. Reno,* No. 93-0080-CIV-DAVIS, S.D. Fl., July 30, 1993. Nigerian detainee: author interview, 1996.

19. Quotation from Steve Logan, chair and CEO of Cornell: Cornell Earnings Conference Call, Third Quarter 2001; on-line broadcast transcribed by justice policy analyst Judith Greene (unpublished). Quotation from George Zoley, CEO of Wackenhut: Greene, "Bailing Out Private Jails," 145. "If there has ever been a time" and "Nowhere is this evident": quoted in former Justice Department attorney Joseph Summerill, "Homeland Security: The Challenge of Finding Jail Space," *American Jails* (January–February 2003): 6.

20. U.S. Department of Justice, Immigration and Naturalization Service, *An*

*Immigrant Nation,* 5, 15. Also see U.S. Department of Justice, Immigration and Naturalization Service, *Extension Training Program, Lesson 1.2: History and Organization of the INS,* October 1984. In addition to BICE, the new agencies are Bureau of Citizenship and Immigration Services and the Bureau of Customs and Border Protection.

21. American Civil Liberties Union Immigrants' Rights Project, *Justice Detained: Conditions at the Varick Street Immigration Detention Center* (New York, 1993), 32–33.

22. U.S. Department of Justice, Immigration and Naturalization Service, "FY 1995 Implementation Strategy: Justice Prisoner and Alien Transportation System, March 1, 1995," draft typescript, 11.

23. Aleksandr I. Solzhenitsyn, *The Gulag Archipelago, 1918–1956: An Experiment in Literary Investigation,* trans. Thomas P. Whitney (New York: Harper & Row, 1973), 616 (Translator's Notes), 4.

24. The INS/BICE detention standards are available at www.immigration.gov/graphics/lawsregs/guidance.htm.

25. David Cole, "National Security State," *Nation,* December 17, 2001.

26. U.S. Department of Justice, Office of the Inspector General, *The September 11 Detainees: A Review of the Treatment of Aliens Held on Immigration Charges in Connection with the Investigation of the September 11 Attacks,* April 2003. Nat Hentoff notes that Glenn A. Fine, the inspector general responsible for this report, is a Clinton appointee ("Justice Denied at the Source," *Village Voice,* June 25–July 1, 2003, 29).

27. Richard Cohen, "Ashcroft's Attitude Problem," *Washington Post,* June 10, 2003, A21. In an earlier defense of the administration's policy, Jeffrey Toobin wrote that "the detention of a thousand or so people in the initial dragnet after September 11th has produced few stories of true government abuses" ("Ashcroft's Ascent," *New Yorker,* April 15, 2002, 61).

28. Deposition of Kenneth Powers, Miami INS Assistant District Director for Detention and Deportation, *Haitian Refugee Center, Inc. v. Reno,* No. 93–0080-CIV-DAVIS, S.D. Fl., July 30, 1993.

29. Nancy Morawetz, "Understanding the Impact of the 1996 Deportation Laws and the Limited Scope of Proposed Reforms," *Harvard Law Review* 113.8 (June 2000): 1943, 1945.

30. See Seán McConville, "Local Justice: The Jail," in *The Oxford History of the Prison: The Practice of Punishment in Western Society,* ed. Norval Morris and David J. Rothman (New York: Oxford University Press, 1998), 267 ff.

31. In at least one case, the INS's terminology backfired. An INS detainee in a privately operated Florida county jail escaped. The INS charged him

criminally. The "detainee" argued that the relevant statute making escape a crime applied to "prisoners," not administrative "detainees." On that basis, a court threw out the charge. (*Gilberto Villegas-Alen v. Florida,* First District Court of Appeal, No. 1D98–3771, November 9, 2000.)

32.  According to the INS, detention is not "punishment" but rather a means "to effect deportation"; "I feel like I don't even exist": Vietnamese detainee Loi Nguyen. Both quoted in Tony Perez-Giese, "Waiting to Exile," Denver *Westword,* January 21, 1999.

33.  Walt Whitman, *An American Primer,* ed. Horace Traubel (San Francisco: City Lights Books, 1970; first published 1904), 6.


## CHAPTER 2: SEPTEMBER 11

1.  *Oren Behr and Yaniv Hani v. Ashcroft et al.,* U.S. District Court, Northern District of Ohio, 1:2001cv02847.

2.  Leopold quoted in Tamar Lewin and Alison Leigh Cowan, "Dozens of Israeli Jews Are Being Kept in Federal Detention," *New York Times,* November 21, 2001, B7.

3.  Declaration of Michael E. Rolince, Section Chief, International Terrorism Operations Section, Counterterrorism Operations Section, Federal Bureau of Investigation. This so-called mosaic theory affidavit was submitted by the government in the proceedings of many September 11 detainees.

4.  Zurofsky then filed an amicus brief in *North Jersey Media Group v. Ashcroft,* U.S. Court of Appeals for the Third Circuit, No. 02-2524. Also see Human Rights Watch, *Presumption of Guilt: Human Rights Abuses of Post–September 11 Detainees,* New York, August 2000, 12.

5.  Memorandum from Chief Immigration Judge Michael Creppy to All Immigration Judges; Court Administrators; Subject: Cases requiring special procedures, September 21, 2001.

6.  Robert S. Kahn, *Other People's Blood: U.S. Immigration Prisons in the Reagan Decade* (Boulder, Colo.: Westview Press, 1996), 87. Kahn writes that the Department of Justice created the Executive Office for Immigration Review "in 1983 in response to criticism from human rights advocates who pointed out that immigration judges work for the same agency as do INS deportation officers, prosecuting attorneys, and prison guards." "On paper," he writes, "the EOIR becomes a separate branch from the INS"—just as the Border Patrol is—"though most immigration judges were drawn from the ranks of INS trial attorneys, and both

branches answer to the U.S. attorney general. Creation of the EOIR did not change any immigration policies" (95 n. 47).

7. Stephen Reinhardt, "Judicial Independence and Asylum Law: Remarks Prepared for Delivery . . . at the Annual Conference of the International Conference of the International Association of Refugee Law Judges," Wellington, New Zealand, October 24, 2002.

8. Nancy Chang and the Center for Constitutional Rights, *Silencing Political Dissent: How Post–September 11 Anti-Terrorism Measures Threaten Our Civil Liberties* (New York: Seven Stories Press, 2002), 72. Ron Klain quoted in Philip Shenon and Robin Toner, "U.S. Widens Policy on Detaining Suspects," *New York Times,* September 19, 2001, B7.

9. Jake Bernstein, "An Anti-War Republican! An Interview with Congressman Ron Paul," *Texas Observer,* January 31, 2003. Also see James X. Dempsey and David Cole, *Terrorism and the Constitution: Sacrificing Civil Liberties in the Name of National Security* (Washington, D.C.: First Amendment Foundation, 2002), 157; the new indefinite detention authority depends on the attorney general's certification of the prisoner as a "suspected terrorist," with "terrorism" defined broadly enough to include a "barroom brawl" or financial support to a "disfavored" organization (156).

10. David Cole, "Terrorizing Immigrants in the Name of Fighting Terrorism," *Human Rights* (American Bar Association) 29.1 (winter 2002): 11.

11. Quotation from INS counsels: T. Alexander Aleinikoff and David Martin, "Ashcroft's Immigration Threat," *Washington Post,* February 26, 2002, A21. Prepared Remarks of Attorney General John Ashcroft, International Association of Chiefs of Police Conference, Minneapolis, October 7, 2002.

12. William Glaberson, "Detainees' Accounts Are at Odds with Official Reports of an Orderly Investigation," *New York Times,* September 29, 2001, B2.

13. Department of Justice Transcript, "Attorney General Ashcroft Outlines Foreign Terrorist Tracking Task Force," October 31, 2001.

14. For "dream world": Department of Justice Transcript, "Testimony of Attorney General John Ashcroft: Senate Committee on the Judiciary," December 6, 2001. For "a preventative campaign": Department of Justice Transcript, "Attorney General Ashcroft Announces the Appointment of the Special Master to Administer the September 11 Victim Compensation Fund," November 26, 2001. For "honest, reasoned debate": Attorney General Transcript, Senate Judiciary Committee, "DOJ Oversight:

Preserving Our Freedoms While Defending against Terrorism," December 6, 2001.

15.    Assistant Commissioner for Investigations Joseph Greene quoted in Somini Sengupta and Christopher Drew, "A Nation Challenged: The Immigration Agency; Effort to Discover Terrorists among Illegal Aliens Makes Glacial Progress, Critics Say," *New York Times,* November 12, 2001. On Absconder Apprehension Initiative (AAI) detentions: Statement of Michael T. Dougherty, Director of Operations of the Bureau of Immigration and Customs Enforcement, Regarding a Hearing on "The War on Terrorism: Immigration Enforcement Since September 11, 2001," Before the House Judiciary Subcommittee on Immigration, Border Security and Claims, May 8, 2003. On special registration detentions: there were 2,781 detentions in connection with National Security Entry-Exit Registration System (NSEERS), as of May 25, 2003, according to BICE spokesperson Nancy Cohen. (Despite Dougherty's release of AAI detention numbers to Congress, Cohen told me that these numbers are not released.)

16.    For Malkin: Michelle Malkin, *Invasion: How America Still Welcomes Terrorists, Criminals, and Other Foreign Menaces to Our Shores* (Washington, D.C.: Regnery, 2002), xiv, 205. For "Each action taken": Attorney General Transcript, Senate Judiciary Committee, "DOJ Oversight: Preserving Our Freedoms While Defending against Terrorism," December 6, 2001. For Rowley: "Full Text of FBI Agent's Letter to Director Mueller," *New York Times,* On-line edition, March 6, 2003.

17.    According to David Cole, "Of the more than 1,500 people arrested since September 11 in the dragnet investigation of that day's crimes, not one has been charged with any involvement in the crimes under investigation" ("Operation Enduring Liberty," *Nation,* June 3, 2002). According to Human Rights Watch, "As of July 2002, none of the 'special interest' detainees has been indicted for terrorist activity; most had been deported for visa violations" (*Presumption of Guilt,* p. 3).

In 2003 three men apprehended in the post–September 11 roundups were on trial in Detroit for allegedly supporting terrorism. Ashcroft had said that the men "were suspected of having knowledge of the Sept. 11 attacks," but the Justice Department itself later reversed this position, stating, "At this time, the Department of Justice does not take the position that the three Michigan men had knowledge of the Sept. 11 events" (quoted in Don Van Natta Jr., "Justice Dept. Alters Stand on 3 Detained," *New York Times,* November 3, 2001, B5). Zacarias Moussaoui, the alleged twentieth hijacker, was already in custody at the time of the September 11 attacks.

18. Ben Tinsley, "INS Detainee Apparently Hangs Self in Cell," *Fort Worth Star-Telegram,* September 29, 2002; Ben Tinsley and Diane Smith, "INS Detainee Hanged Self While on Suicide Watch," *Fort Worth Star-Telegram,* October 8, 2002. The former article quotes INS headquarters public information officer William Strassberger saying that the INS was conducting its own investigation of the death of detainee Amos G. Williams, age forty; despite repeated requests in 2003 to Strassberger and other INS/BICE officials for the results of the supposed investigation, no results were ever provided to me.

19. Lisa Schroeder Al Shihri, "Life without Majid: The Wife of a Post 9–11 Detainee Weathers Separation," *Dallas Peace Times,* April–May 2002.

20. Daniel Patrick Moynihan, *Secrecy: The American Experience* (New Haven: Yale University Press, 1998), 168.

21. "Special interest" detainees at the Passaic County Jail, for example, were reportedly allowed to make only one phone call per week (Lawyers Committee for Human Rights, *A Year of Loss: Reexamining Civil Liberties since September 11,* New York, 2002, 32).

22. Chertoff quoted in Human Rights Watch, *Presumption of Guilt,* 41. Bergeron quoted in Human Rights Watch, *Presumption of Guilt,* 41, citing Jim Edwards, "Attorneys Face Hidden Hurdles in September 11 Detainee Cases," *New Jersey Law Journal,* December 5, 2001. Ashcroft quoted in Richard A. Serrano, "Ashcroft Denies Wide Detainee Abuse," *Los Angles Times,* October 17, 2001.

    Also see Department of Justice, Office of the Inspector General, *The September 11 Detainees: A Review of the Treatment of Aliens Held on Immigration Charges in Connection with the Investigation of the September 11 Attacks,* April 2003. This chapter was written before the OIG report was issued.

23. In subsequent chapters, we will see examples of the INS's double standard on detainees' privacy. On February 27, 2002, INS spokesperson Karen Kraushaar gave me detailed information on Mohammad Bachir's case after Bachir was rearrested. I had contacted INS Headquarters official David Venturella about Bachir; Venturella did not respond, but Kraushaar did, and provided me with a detailed version of the government's allegations against Bachir (see chap. 10). The INS provided details about the case of Tony Ebibillo after the *Washington Post* reported on the agency's attempts to forcibly sedate him (see chap. 4). To portray a Somali in a different light than the press had, INS Public Affairs provided me with a written statement that included personal information about the detainee (see chap. 13, note 18). The privacy issue in these cases

is arguably a different matter from the government simply withholding the names of detainees. But whatever the legitimacy of the INS/BICE's commenting on the cases mentioned here, it is clear that the government "protects" detainee privacy when its own interests are served by doing so. Also, although refusing to release the names of September 11 "special interest" detainees publicly, the Justice Department provided these names to the detainees' respective embassies, according to Human Rights Watch (*Presumption of Guilt,* 29–30).

24.    On Salvadorans: Robert Kahn, "Under Surveillance: The FBI Exposed in the Valley," *Texas Observer,* March 13, 1992. Also see Gelbspan, *Break-ins, Death Threats and the FBI: The Covert War against the Central America Movement* (Boston: South End Press, 1991), 132 ff., 218–19. On Iranians: Najeeb Hasan, "Unsafe Asylum," *Metro Silicon Valley,* www.alternet.org, April 21, 2003.

    In another case, an asylum applicant from Guinea alleged that INS officials provided his name and information to the government he was fleeing in order to investigate the validity of his asylum claim. *Malik Jarno v. Warren Lewis, INS, et al.,* U.S. District Court for the Eastern District of Virginia, Alexandria Division, October 31, 2002.

25.    See Dan Malone, "INS Faulted for Secret Detentions," *Dallas Morning News,* December 12, 1999; "851 Detained for Years in INS Centers," *Dallas Morning News,* April 1, 2001. The lawsuit is *Dan Malone, The Dallas Morning News, L.P. v. U.S. Department of Justice, Immigration & Naturalization Service,* U.S. District Court, Northern District of Texas, Ft. Worth Division, No. 400-CV-0060-Y, January 25, 2000.

    The 851 did not include long-term Cuban detainees who were said to be tracked in a distinct category.

26.    *ACLU of New Jersey v. County of Hudson,* Superior Court of New Jersey, No. A-4100-01T5, January 22, 2002.

27.    Quoted in ACLU of New Jersey, "ACLU of New Jersey Files Lawsuit Seeking Information on Post–September 11 Detainees," January 22, 2002.

28.    The United States opposed the UN prison monitoring plan "because of potential demands for access to the detention camp at the United States naval base in Guantanamo Bay, Cuba, where more than 500 detainees [were said to be] suspected of being Al Queda members. . . . American officials have told United Nations human rights committees and monitors that the federal government cannot force states to open their prisons" (Barbara Crossette, "U.S. Fails in Effort to Block Vote on U.N. Convention on Torture," *New York Times,* July 25, 2002, A7).

29.    Interim rule, 8 CFR 236 and 241, "Release of Information Regarding

Immigration & Naturalization Service Detainees in Non-Federal Facilities," April 17, 2002. Department of Justice, News Release, "INS Issues Rule Governing Release of Detainee Information," April 18, 2002.

30. Before long, the new rule would be used in Florida to prevent detainees from seeing their lawyers. Bulletin Broadfaxing Network, Henry Pierson Curtis, "Jail Cites INS Secrecy Rule in Denying Attorney Access," *Orlando Sentinel*, July 2, 2002 (reprinted by Bulletin Broadfaxing Network).

31. Declaration of James Reynolds; and Memorandum Opinion, *Center for National Security Studies v. Department of Justice*, U.S. District Court for the District of Columbia, Civil Action No. 01-2500. Reynolds's fear of reprisals against detainees may in some cases have been realized, although unrelated to the release of their names here. The *New Jersey Law Journal* attempted to follow some of the deportations. Reliable information about returnees' treatment in their home countries is difficult to obtain, cautions Jim Edwards. "But in 14 cases, the *Law Journal* identified men who had been re-imprisoned in foreign countries, sometimes for months, and re-interrogated about their links to terrorism, simply because they stepped off a plane under supervision of the Immigration and Naturalization Service. The men were generally held incommunicado." Jim Edwards, "Sept. 11 Detainees Fear Abuse in Their Homelands after Deportation," *New Jersey Law Journal*, December 12, 2002.

32. Judge Gladys Kessler, Memorandum Opinion, *Center for National Security Studies v. Department of Justice*, Civil Action No. 01-2500.

33. Letter from Newark INS District Director Andrea J. Quarantillo to the author, July 15, 2002.

Early in 2003 BICE Headquarters spokesperson Karen Kraushaar informed me through Gill that my request to interview another Pakistani detainee was denied. The reason given was that all detention facilities were off-limits due to the status "orange" national security alert as the war with Iraq began. Gill told me I could resubmit the request in ten days, which I did. The alert status was now "yellow," but my request was again denied. When I asked the reason for this, Gill referred me to the agency's media detention standards on its Web site. I, in turn, e-mailed to ask which standard explained the interview denial, and Gill suggested that I call him. When I called, I told him that I was recording our conversation. He put me on hold for several minutes, then said I should put my question in writing to Deputy Director of Public Affairs John Shewairy. I did so, and a year later, despite additional requests, Shewairy had not explained the reasons for the denial.

34. Elizabeth Llorente, "INS Denounced for Pulling out of Public Forum," Bergen *Record,* May 8, 2002; Gill's explanation continued: "Our district director agreed to participate in a community meeting, not a media event." For "a law student who was investigating INS compliance with Freedom of Information Act regulations": "Note: The Secret Law of the Immigration and Naturalization Service," *Iowa Law Review* 56 (1970).

35. For "presumption of disclosure" see U.S. Department of Justice, "Government Adopts New Standard for Openness," October 4, 1993. For "effectively reversed": Lawyers Committee for Human Rights, *Year of Loss,* 11. For "to withhold records": John Ashcroft, Attorney General, "Memorandum for Heads of All Federal Departments and Agencies," October 12, 2001. For "secretly drafted . . . making it easier": Jack M. Balkin, "A Dreadful Act II," *Los Angeles Times,* February 13, 2003.

36. Examples are innumerable, but just two more illustrate the range of absurdity and obfuscation at work here. When Tucson attorney Vikran Badrinanth tried to obtain a copy of an Indian client's file, the INS FOIA office denied his request, stating that his client was "a fugitive from justice" who "has not made his whereabouts known to the INS" and is "therefore not entitled" to his own file. The "fugitive" was in INS custody at the Florence, Arizona, Service Processing Center, according to Badrinanth. The attorney won an appeal of the FOIA denial, but, Badrinanth told me, the agency never produced the file.

Arizona journalist Scott Stanley had to go to court to force the release of photographs of illegal immigrants who died trying to cross the U.S.-Mexico border. The published photographs included two of men shot in the back by Border Patrol agents. One agent was "acquitted of assault and murder"; the other shooting occurred when "the Border Patrol's surveillance camera was not running." Although this case did not involve a FOIA request, it fits the pattern of secrecy that the Bush administration has sought to legitimate. Tim Vanderpool, "Shot at the Border," *Mother Jones,* January–February 2000.

37. See Jana Mason, "Where America's Day Begins: Chinese Asylum Seekers on Guam," *Refugee Reports* (Washington, D.C.: U.S. Committee for Refugees) 20:8, August–September 1999. Mason notes that the United States has held some of the Chinese near Guam on Tinian Island— "where U.S. immigration laws do not apply." She writes that cells designed for two prisoners often held five Chinese women and that a U.S. detention official said, "'It's a good thing these women are small.'"

38. Andrew Cockburn and Patrick Cockburn, *Out of the Ashes: The Resurrection of Saddam Hussein* (New York: HarperCollins, 1999), 248. On Ali,

see Martin Lasden, "Under Suspicion," *California Lawyer,* November 1999.

39. Dempsey and Cole, *Terrorism and the Constitution,* 140, 127.

40. Martha L. Willman, "Nine Inmates Hurt in Mira Loma Protest," *Los Angeles Times,* September 18, 1999, B3. "Deputies Quell Disturbance at INS Facility in High Desert," *City News Service,* September 17, 1999.

41. Statement of R. James Woolsey, Senate Judiciary Committee, Subcommittee on Technology, Terrorism, and Government Information, October 8, 1998.

42. Even in "secret evidence" cases, the government will sometimes produce a summary of the classified evidence. In this case, newly declassified documents revealed that an INS agent had lied when she claimed to have asked and been refused permission by the FBI and the CIA to prepare such a summary, according to Woolsey Statement, and *In the Matters of Mohammad Jwer Al-Ammary et al.,* Los Angeles, Appellants' Reply Brief in Support of Appeal from the Decision of the Immigration Judge; U.S. Dept. of Justice, Executive Office for Immigration Review, the Board of Immigration Appeals, March 25, 1999.

43. Lasden, "Under Suspicion." On Hawley, see Woolsey Statement; Cockburn and Cockburn, *Out of the Ashes,* 249.

44. Woolsey Statement, attachments; Cockburn and Cockburn, *Out of the Ashes,* 250; *In the Matters of Mohammad Jwer Al-Ammary et al.*

45. *In the Matters of Mohammad Jwer Al-Ammary et al.,* Agreement entered into with the Immigration & Naturalization Service on June 9, 1999 and modified on January 23, 2001.

46. U.S. Department of Homeland Security, Immigration and Customs Enforcement Statement, March 20, 2003. Numbers of detained Iraqis cannot be released: author interview with INS public affairs spokesperson Karen Kraushaar, March 23, 2003.

47. *Shaughnessy v. United States ex. rel. Mezei* (1953); Mezei's origin was uncertain.

48. Jim Edwards, "Anatomy of a 'Special Interest' Case," *New Jersey Law Journal,* May 20, 2002.

   Mehmoud's case was also reported by several other sources, both here and abroad. In one year after the attacks, 39,842 box cutters were confiscated from travelers by airport security personnel. The number reflects the period between February 17, 2002, and February 28, 2003, according to the Transportation Security Administration (Press Release, March 10, 2003).

49. David Rohde, "U.S.-Deported Pakistanis: Outcasts in 2 Lands," *New York Times,* January 20, 2003.

50. Human Rights Watch, *Presumption of Guilt,* 23. Letter from Dennis W. Hasty, Warden, Metropolitan Detention Center (MDC), Brooklyn, to Rachel Ward, Amnesty International USA, New York, January 31, 2002.

51. On sixty detainee cases, see Amnesty International, "Concerns regarding Post September 11 Detentions in the USA" (March 2002), 31 n. 42. The Nepalese man's case is also mentioned in this report (32); my account of it is based on an interview with attorney Olivia Cassin.

52. Benjamin Weiser, "Jordanian Student Held in U.S. Says Police Abused Him in Jail," *New York Times,* December 5, 2001, B8. Benjamin Weiser, "Judge Rules against U.S. on Material-Witness Law," *New York Times,* May 1, 2002, A10. Benjamin Weiser, "Manhattan: Jordanian Sues U.S. in False Arrest," Metro Briefing, *New York Times,* September 13, 2002, B8. William Glaberson, "Jail Warden Is Summoned on Treatment of Peter Gotti," *New York Times,* September 13, 2002, B6.

53. Human Rights Watch, *Presumption of Guilt,* 24 n. 67.

54. Steve Fainaru, "U.S. Deported 131 Pakistanis in Secret Air Lift," *Washington Post,* July 10, 2002, A1. Michael Higgins, "Ottawa Issues Rare U.S. Travel Advisory," *National Post* (Montreal), October 30, 2002, A1. "Hundreds of Pakistanis Still in U.S. Prisons: Fallout of Sept. 11 Attacks," *Dawn* (Karachi) Internet edition, February 12, 2002. Jane Standley, "America's 11 September Detainees," *BBC News* On-line, February 7, 2002. Herbert A. Sample, "Man Blames 9/11 Backlash for Deportation," *Sacramento Bee,* August 27, 2002. Amran Abocar, "U.S. Security Measures Drive Asylum Seekers to Canada," *Reuters,* April 1, 2003.

Of some 120,000 Pakistanis who lived in a Brooklyn neighborhood, "15,000, maybe more, have left for Canada, Europe or Pakistan, according to Pakistani government estimates. . . . The immigration bureau acknowledges that more than 83,000 males have registered and that 2,747 are currently detained, but refuses to specify the number of Pakistanis" (Michael Powell, "An Exodus Grows in Brooklyn," *Washington Post,* May 29, 2003, A1).

55. MDC windows painted: author interview. California prison: Office of the Inspector General, *Report to Congress on Implementation of Section 1001 of the USA Patriot Act,* January 22, 2003.

CHAPTER 3: ANOTHER WORLD, ANOTHER NATION

1. U.S. Department of Justice, United States Attorney, Southern District of Florida, Miami, "NEWS RELEASE: FORMER KROME GUARD BEATING DETAINEE," January 4, 1996.

2. "Morning Report," Krome Service Processing Center, Miami, Florida, April 17, 1990.

3. Rape and "consensual" sex in exchange for release or the promise of release were commonplace at Krome, according to Calejo. His descriptions of these practices at Krome are practically identical to those given by former contract guard Tony Hefner of the INS Port Isabel Processing Center in Harlingen, Texas, in Tony Hefner and Jacalyn McLeod, *Between the Fences: Inside a U.S. Immigration Camp* (Bloomington, Ind.: First Books Library, 2002).

4. See, for example, Human Rights Watch, *All Too Familiar: Sexual Abuse of Women in U.S. State Prisons* (New York, December 1996).

5. U.S. Department of Justice, Civil Rights Division, "Notice to Close File," File No. DJ 144-18-2967, May 18, 1993.

6. "MEMORANDUM FOR SDEO [Supervisory Detention Enforcement Officer] AND THRU CHAIN OF COMMAND. FROM: Detention Enforcement Officers, Krome SPC Miami, Florida. SUBJECT: Women and Minors Housed in Processing," August 9, 1998.

7. Meissner said that the INS "lacked the capability needed to be certain that our staff implement policies and procedures at a field level and adhere to rules and regulations properly." Testimony of Commissioner Doris Meissner, Immigration & Naturalization Service before the Committee on the Judiciary, Subcommittee on Immigration, Concerning Oversight of the INS, October 2, 1996.

8. On "voluntary change," see Carol Rosenberg, "Congressman: 'Kromegate' Punishments Are Too Light," *Miami Herald,* February 27, 1997. On "deception of Congress": U.S. Department of Justice, Office of the Inspector General, *Alleged Deception of Congress: The Congressional Taskforce on Immigration's Fact-finding Visit to the Miami District of INS in June 1995* (June 1996). On Cadman's role: ibid., 180 ff. Also see OIG, *Follow-up Report: Alleged Deception of Congress* (September 1997). After the Krome deception, Cadman was temporarily assigned to a Border Patrol station in Pembroke Pines, Florida, where he answered phones: "Asked to describe his current responsibilities, Cadman says bitterly, 'I'm still the incumbent district director'" (Elise Ackerman, "Agents of Deception," Miami *New Times,* September 12–18, 1996, 28). On Cadman's job on and after September 11, 2001: CBS *60 Minutes,* "Immigration & Naturalization Service," March 10, 2002. "Plum job": author interview with anonymous INS official. INS/BICE public affairs spokesperson Nancy Cohen confirmed that Cadman was the agency's officer-in-charge in Madrid. On the Krome deception, see also Mark Dow, "Deception,

Dehumanization, and the INS," three-part series in *Haïti Progrès*, July 24, July 31, August 6, 1996; and Michelle Malkin, *Invasion: How America Still Welcomes Terrorists, Criminals, and Other Foreign Menaces to Our Shores* (Washington, D.C.: Regnery, 2002), 169 ff.

9.  Tom Vanderbilt, "When Nike Meant More than 'Just Do It': Desolate Missile Sites Recall the Days of 'Duck and Cover,'" *New York Times*, March 5, 2000, CY3.

10. U.S. Immigration and Naturalization Service, Southern Regional Office, "Survey and Recommendations on the Functions, Mission, and Resources of the Krome North Service Processing Center—Miami, Florida, December 31, 1981," 1, 3 (typescript).

11. On Salvadorans and Guatemalans, see Robert S. Kahn, *Other People's Blood: U.S. Immigration Prisons in the Reagan Decade* (Boulder, Colo.: Westview Press, 1996). On Haitians, see Paul Farmer, *The Uses of Haiti* (Monroe, Me.: Common Courage Press, 1994). Also: Mark Dow, "U.S. Savagery in Haiti," *New Politics* 4.4 (winter 1994); "A Refugee Policy to Support Haiti's Killers," *New Politics* 5.1 (summer 1994); and "Occupying and Obscuring Haiti," *New Politics* 5.2 (winter 1995). Some Haitian democratic activists in the 1990s felt that one goal of U.S. refugee policy was to *remove* influential Haitian activists from their country at a time when the United States was supporting antidemocratic forces; see "Reflections on the Fifth Anniversary of the U.S. Occupation," *Haiti Info*, October 2, 1996.

12. Carol Huang, "Haitian Refugees Detained; Protest," *Laredo Morning Times*, November 17, 1992, 1A.

13. For "a program at work" see Judge James Lawrence King, *Haitian Refugee Center v. Civiletti*, 503 F. Supp. 442 (S.D. Fla., 1980), 519; quoted in Cheryl Little, "United States Haitian Policy: A History of Discrimination," *New York Law School Journal of Human Rights* 10 (spring 1993): note 21. For "never designed for detention": Miami INS District Director Robert Wallis, as quoted in Miami District INS's notes of a December 12, 2000, "Krome Stakeholders" meeting between INS and local advocacy groups; the notes were shared with the meeting participants and are reproduced in Florida Immigrant Advocacy Center, *INS Detainees in Florida: A Double Standard of Treatment* (Miami, December 2001), 302.

14. U.S. INS, Southern Regional Office, "Survey and Recommendations," 6, 38.

15. Deposition of Dr. Aida Rivera, Public Health Service, Krome North Ser-

vice Processing Center, Miami; *Haitian Refugee Center, Inc. v. Reno,* No. 93-0080-CIV-DAVIS, S.D. Fla., July 29, 1993. Rivera said there were almost daily complaints about the water, which, in her words, "is yellow" and "has a metallic taste." Detainees complained "that the water gives them skin conditions and stomach problems and things like that."

16. U.S. INS, Southern Regional Office, "Survey and Recommendations," 9.

17. Ibid., 6; emphasis added.

18. Affidavit of unnamed Haitian woman detained at Krome; Haitian Refugee Center, 1990.

19. Gary Monroe, *Detention at Krome: Photographs of Haitian Refugees* (Miami: The Gallery, Miami-Dade Community College North Campus, 1982).

20. U.S. Department of Justice, Immigration and Naturalization Service, National Firearms Unit (Altoona, Pa.), *Annual Report of Shooting Incidents for Calendar Year 2000.*

21. There are exceptions. See, for example, Elizabeth Llorente, "Dreams Turn to Despair," Bergen *Record,* May 24, 1999; and Rachel L. Swarns, "Asylum Seekers Suffer Psychological Setbacks, Study Says," *New York Times,* June 17, 2003. In contrast to Llorente's article, the *Times* article relies on a human rights report to legitimize the topic of psychological trauma and depression caused by incarceration. See Physicians for Human Rights and Bellevue/NYU Program for Survivors of Torture, *From Persecution to Prison: The Health Consequences of Detention for Asylum Seekers* (Boston and New York, June 2003).

Though misused in describing the Calejo-Bernard incident, *torture* is sometimes the right word. At Florida's Jackson County Jail in 1998, INS inmates described the regular use of "shock shields" against INS and state prisoners. According to one inmate witness, they would be tied down

in the position of a crucifix. After an inmate was tied, he would be left in that position for over nine hours with no food or drink. The inmate[s] . . . would be forced to dirty themselves. They were sometimes tied without any clothes. . . . The guards would administer electric shocks to the inmates while they were tied with an electric shield and a stun gun. . . . The guards would also give electric shocks and spray pepper spray at inmates who were handcuffed. The inmates were completely helpless and not fighting with the guards.

(Affidavit taken by Florida Immigrant Advocacy Center [FIAC], June 1988)

Cuban inmate Jose Mestre Dorticos described a concrete slab with steel rings at the corners:

Handcuffs were placed on my hands and my feet were shackled and then the handcuffs were attached to each of these rings. . . . After they tied me down [an officer] brought in a large shield, placed it over me and shocked me once with it. When the electricity ran through my body, I felt paralyzed. I'm not sure how long it lasted. . . . After shocking me, [the officer] hit me and called me a "fucking bitch," I cussed him back. [He] placed his boot on my left temple and pushed my head down to the bench. The bench cut a deep gash on my eyebrow and it began to bleed profusely. The only attention I received was the following day when [someone] gave me a bag of ice for the wound.

(FIAC affidavit, July 14, 1998)

Mestre's drawings of the concrete slab and shock shield were reproduced in Andres Viglucci, "Immigrants Allege Abuse at Jail in N. Florida," *Miami Herald,* July 30, 1998, 1A.

Bahamian detainee Patrick Johnson said, "They do things to us like it's fun to them, probably because we are foreign people. They figure immigration ain't going to do nothing. They make you believe INS is along with them"; Placido Pacheco of the Miami INS district office said, "We cannot dictate to the county or the State of Florida what standards they should have in their facilities" (Teresa Mears, "A Shock to the System," Miami *New Times,* July 30, 1998). Johnson was held for eleven months at Jackson County. Later, at Krome, he told me:

It was like a nightmare. It was hell. One morning I wake up, they was changing the uniforms, and the lady there she give me a big shirt, right? So I told her that it was too big, and she said the nigger word to me. You know, like "Nigger, get from the door." . . . And next thing again that I know, they pulled me out of the cell, and they started beating me, and they take that shield and put it on my chest, and they shock me. . . . She put it on my chest, and it knocked me out and a current run through my body. . . . When they hit me the first time, it knocked me to the ground, and I started to get back up, and she put it on my chest again. And I saw colors and stars and everything, running through my whole body. You know, my whole body, my brains and everything. I even couldn't remember nothing then. That's how terrible it was. And they was calling me "nigger." . . . They was saying, "Nigger, we gonna kill you, nigger." And so I say, "I'm gonna call INS." "Nigger, if you call INS, INS know anyway—they bring you here to us. We do whatever we want to do with you."

Johnson also described the slab to which inmates were tied with leather straps:

Concrete. Cold, cold, cold, cold. And they'll cut the AC up high, high, high, and you'll be butt-naked. . . . You're on your belly. . . . And when time to eat, they loose one hand. So you eat, and they strap you back. It's torture, man. . . . It was like a nightmare there. I never know people could live like that. See, because I growed up in my life, I never see color 'cause I think that God created all men as one, you know? You and me, as one. 'Cause God created one man, 'cause he was one God. And when a person could do that to a person, there is—of the devil. There is evil. But right now I'm still sitting in jail.

As a result of complaints filed by FIAC, the Civil Rights Division of the Justice Department investigated and concluded that the Jackson County Jail was violating the Constitution through its use of excessive force as well as its denial to prisoners of access to courts. It also noted the "startling blue arc of electricity" across the face of the activated electronic shield (letter from Bill Lann Lee, Acting Assistant Attorney General to J. Milton Pittman, Chair, Board of County Commissioners, Jackson County, Marianna, Florida, March 30, 2000). The INS inmates were transferred out of the jail.

After describing these practices at Jackson County, a Cuban man told me, "I would love for you to use my name." But when he realized that I was writing about the INS, he changed his mind immediately, fearing retribution from the agency.

22. United Nations Convention Against Torture and Other Cruel, Inhuman, or Degrading Treatment or Punishment, *Consideration of Reports Submitted by States Parties under Article 19 of the Convention*, February 9, 2000.

23. U.S. Immigration and Naturalization Service, Eastern Region, Detention and Deportation Division, "Krome SPC Back-up Material" (August 2000), Tab 6.

24. The original Chinese and the translation are both included in Haitian Refugee Center, "Conditions at Krome North Service Processing Center," Miami, June 1991. A month before the letter was written, Miami INS District Director Richard Smith publicly used the term "Chinaman" and subsequently apologized: "I didn't know it was inappropriate. . . . My exposure to the Asiatic culture has been extremely limited." Alfonso Chardy, "INS Official Apologizes for Remark," *Miami Herald*, May 8, 1991.

25. The memo released to me was written by a special agent whose name was blacked out to Assistant Director, Internal Investigations, Stephen Schenk, March 26, 1996.

On whistleblowers, retaliation, and the OIA, see Joe Cantlupe, "Does the INS Culture Shield Misconduct?" *San Diego Union Tribune,* May 7, 2000; and Cantlupe, "Watchdog or Attack Dog?" *San Diego Union Tribune,* May 7, 2000. On OIG complaints and whistleblowers, also see Denise Hamilton, "Immigration and Molestation Service," *New Times L.A.*, March 14, 2002. These articles mention allegations of mistreatment of undocumented persons.

Two months after the attacks on New York and Washington, the U.S. Senate Committee on Governmental Affairs, Permanent Subcommittee on Investigations, held hearings on the "INS Policy on Releasing Illegal Aliens Pending Deportation Hearing" (November 13, 2001). The main topic was apprehension and release of aliens on the U.S.-Canada border. Testimony from several Border Patrol agents emphasized the need for more funding and detention space if the "catch and release" policy were to be overcome. But there was an important secondary theme. Border Patrol agent and union president Mark Hall had been threatened with unpaid suspension and demotion for speaking without permission to the media. In his testimony, Hall criticized management for proposals to dismantle the union, for failing to provide security against terrorists, and for threatening reprisals because he was saying these things.

26. Alisa Solomon, "Exiled from the Promised Land," *Village Voice,* March 10, 1998, 55.

27. Alisa Solomon, "The Prison on Varick Street," *New York Times,* Op-Ed, June 11, 1994.

28. U.S. Immigration and Naturalization Service, Eastern Region, Detention and Deportation Division, "Krome SPC Back-up Material," Tab 9.

29. Ibid., Tab 5.

30. "You have no rights . . .": quoted in Louis J. Salome and Paul Lomartire, "Krome as Much a Prison as It Is a Processing Center," *Palm Beach Post,* January 28, 2002. On continuing sexual abuse allegations, see Florida Immigrant Advocacy Center, *INS Detainees in Florida: A Double Standard of Treatment* (December 2001); *INS Detainees in Florida: A Double Standard of Treatment—Supplement* (January–April 2002); and Women's Commission for Refugee Women and Children, *Behind Locked Doors: Abuse of Refugee Women at the Krome Detention Center* (October 2000).

31. American Friends Service Committee, "Where Destiny Takes Me: Story of a Salvadoran Exile" (Philadelphia, May 1991), 21.

1. Affidavit of INS deportation officer Kimberly Boulia, attached to the indictment in *United States of America v. Tony Ebibillo-Epken* [sic], U.S. District Court, Southern District of Florida, 91-0914-Cr-Nesbitt, December 17, 1991.

2. Interviews with American Airlines employees were conducted by the federal public defender's (PD's) office in Miami after Ebibillo was indicted on trumped-up criminal charges. Summaries of and quotations from interviews with airline employees are taken from memoranda written by Carlos Fernandez to Lori Barrist of the PD's office. See below.

3. " 'This is not the creme de la creme,' [Rozos] says of Krome's residents. 'You have got scumbuckets here'" (Jeanne DeQuine, "Critics Call for Closure of Immigration Center," *USA Today,* June 14, 1991, 6A). The Haitian Refugee Center, where I worked at the time, sent letters of concern to INS officials and congressional representatives. The *Miami Herald* responded with an editorial expressing its own concerns in extreme terms: "For the Third Reich's ideologues, Jews, Gypsies, blacks, and other 'vermin' weren't the *crème de la crème* either" ("Bucketful of Bigotry," *Miami Herald,* July 5, 1991, 12A). Joan C. Higgins, INS assistant commissioner for detention and deportation, wrote to me at the Haitian Refugee Center that INS Headquarters had requested Miami District Director Richard Smith "to furnish this office with a complete report on this matter" (July 24, 1991). A month later Smith wrote to U.S. Representative Ileana Ros-Lehtinen:

Mr. Rozos' remarks, while not felicitously phrased, were taken out of context. He was discussing the fact that there are among Krome's detainees persons of uncertain background, including admitted Tonton Macoutes, aliens with criminal charges pending but who have not been convicted, and other aliens convicted of crimes classified as misdemeanors. His comments were not directed at Krome's general population or at any specific nationality . . .

Smith continued: "Mr. Rozos has always discharged his duties with the highest regard for the safety and well-being of all detainees. . . . One unfortunate misquote should not be allowed to destroy his reputation and career." More than ten years after the "scumbucket" remark, former Krome officer Nestor Meiggs told me that the negative publicity had led to Rozos's transfer from Krome. Meiggs said that Rozos had tears in his eyes when they shook hands and said good-bye.

When Amnesty International (AI) visited Krome in 1991, a delegation member asked about allegations that a detention officer had raped a Haitian detainee. (On the allegation itself, see Lizette Alvarez, "Guard Accused of Rape," *Miami Herald,* March 28, 1991, 1B.) According to a confidential AI memo provided to me, Rozos reportedly said, "This so-called rape . . . this woman says she was raped and you ask her how long did it last and she says one minute. Well, personally, I would have been embarrassed." While Rozos apparently enjoyed being provocative—and, according to Tony Ebibillo, allegedly threatened detainees—former Krome officer Eddie Calejo told me he never saw Rozos physically abuse a detainee. After his Krome job, Rozos was assigned to the INS's Esmor detention center in Elizabeth, New Jersey; during his term there, in 1995, detainees rioted to protest inhumane conditions. He currently works as head of the Post-Order Detention Unit at INS/BICE Headquarters in Washington, which reviews custody release decisions on long-term detainees.

4. See note 1 above.

5. Americas Watch [now called Human Rights Watch/Americas], *Frontier Injustice: Human Rights Abuses along the U.S. Border with Mexico Persist Amid Climate of Impunity,* May 13, 1993, 33; and *Brutality Unchecked: Human Rights Abuses Along the U.S. Border with Mexico,* May 1992, 31.

6. U.S. Immigration and Naturalization Service, Eastern Region, Detention and Deportation Division, "Krome SPC Back-up Material," Miami [?], August 2000, 14. The observation about transfers was made by a BOP warden acting as part of the INS assessment team.

7. Andres Viglucci, "Inmates Complain of Crush at Krome," *Miami Herald,* February 16, 1996.

8. Concerning the final appeal: in August 1993, while in the Ft. Lauderdale jail, Ebibillo received news that his Petition for Review of an Order of the INS had been dismissed by the Eleventh Circuit Court of Appeals in Atlanta.

Much if not most of the information about Ebibillo's situation was collected and circulated by Cheryl Little, then supervising attorney of the Haitian Refugee Center, and by me. Thus much of the information in letters expressing concern from human rights groups, including the one from Americas Watch cited below, also came from Little and me. See: Nwachukwu Ezem, "Nigerian Arrested after 10 Years in Miami Accuses INS of Mistreatment," *Miami Times,* December 19, 1991; William Booth, "U.S. Accused of Sedating Deportees," *Washington Post,* October 7, 1993, 1A; Andres Viglucci, "INS Deports Nigerian without Telling Lawyers," *Miami Herald,* January 12, 1994; and [no author], "Our Failed Immigration Policy: Turnstile on Our Border," *Miami Her-*

*ald,* December 14, 1993. The latter story wryly concluded its short account of Ebibillo's situation with the words, "No one knows when he will leave"; the story appeared on the day he was deported.

The INS's internal report on the case is "Summary of Case of Tony EBIBILLO Ekpen, Case File A29 392 576, Prepared by Immigration and Naturalization Service/Detention and Deportation Division," October 12, 1993. The *Miami Herald* had reported on January 12, 1994, that the INS and the PHS "ordered a review of the drugging" after the earlier *Washington Post* article had appeared.

9.  While examples of alleged forced sedation of detainees have been difficult to document in detail, among those that have surfaced are the following.

In a report on detained asylum seekers, the Lawyers Committee for Human Rights has noted, "Some . . . have complained of the use of forced sedation" (*Refugees behind Bars,* 15). Llorente has reported that Steve Townsend, former assistant warden of the CCA's INS detention center in Elizabeth, New Jersey, filed a lawsuit "claiming that he was fired by [CCA] after alerting the INS that detainees were being forcibly sedated and improperly restrained. . . . INS at first denied the sedations, agency officials and advocates recalled. But shortly afterward, they confirmed the incidents after the advocates returned with medical records. The INS said the sedations were justified because the inmates had posed a danger" (Llorente, "New Concerns about INS Detention Center," Bergen *Record,* May 25, 1998).

While denying allegations of a forced sedation at a CCA/INS detention center in Laredo, CCA legal representative Richard Crane "explained [that] on a one-time basis, to control a detainee or prisoner, it is not illegal to administer sedatives without consent. Repeated drugging, according to Crane, requires a court order" (Diana Claitorr and Louis Dubose, "In Jail in Laredo," *Texas Observer,* August 14, 1987).

In California, an attorney for the INS told a judge, "'Sometimes it is necessary to sedate an alien, but we always obtain a court order first.'" He made the statement in the context of a hearing on the threatened sedation of Bao Dong, a detained Chinese woman who was reportedly resisting deportation. According to a paralegal in the federal public defender's office, an INS deportation officer said that if the detainee did not cooperate next time, "'the INS officers would bring a doctor with them to forcibly sedate her'" (T. T. Nhu and Hallye Jordan, "Suit Seeks to Block INS from Sedating Deportee," *San Jose Mercury News,* May 4, 2001; "Court Halts INS Plan," May 8, 2001).

In Florida, a detained woman from St. Kitts was transferred from Krome to the Ft. Lauderdale jail. According to her affidavit, guards there refused to give her maxi pads when she began menstruating: "I didn't know what to do. I felt desperate. . . . So I took some of my own blood and wrote the word HELP on the wall using my blood. The officers took pictures of me and took pictures of the wall. They started making fun of me, telling me I was crazy." She was finally given two pads. When she needed more, guards refused again. "They put me in the . . . black restraining chair. I was strapped down in the chair and handcuffed for sixteen hours. . . . I wasn't allowed to use the bathroom or get a pad. . . . I went to the bathroom on myself and was bleeding on my clothes." The next day the woman was sent to a hospital. "[Jail officers] told the hospital I was hallucinating and seeing things. They also showed the doctor the pictures they took of me when I wrote HELP on the wall. The doctor asked me if I was acting that way so that I wouldn't get deported. I told him no. I told him I was there [at the hospital] because of the bad treatment I got at the jail. He asked me how I felt at the hospital. I told him I felt so relieved." Four days later, a nurse gave her an injection. The woman reported, "[The nurse] said the doctor ordered it. I fell right back asleep. The next thing I remember is some-body telling me it was time to go. It was somebody in a uniform. I think it was the same officer who brought me to the hospital." The woman was taken back to Krome for her luggage. "[Then] I was taken to the airport and boarded a plane. I fell asleep again. I don't remember everything about that morning after I got the shot." On arrival in St. Kitts, she said, "I felt weak and dizzy. . . . My speech was slurred. I was talking very slow and my jaw felt heavy." (Personal Statement of _____, Ft. Laud-erdale, June 13, 2001; in Florida Immigrant Advocacy Center, *INS Detainees in Florida: A Double Standard of Treatment,* Miami, December 2001, 204–5.)

In 1992 Chinese asylum seeker Ho Guo Xiang was detained at Krome. "The day before his scheduled hearing, the INS mistakenly informed him that the United States would be sending him back to Ecuador." Ho had come to the United States via Panama and Ecuador. "Believing that his transport to Ecuador would mean his eventual deportation to China, Ho attempted suicide by slashing his left wrist. He yelled and caused a disturbance, requiring six officers to restrain him. He then received treatment in the form of fifty milligrams each of thorazine and benedryl, and remained in four-point, then two-point restraints as he slept, for nearly all of the twenty-four hours before his hearing. Forty-five minutes before his hearing, attendants woke Ho and transported him to the hearing site. Ho's lawyer and the IJ [immigration judge] learned of the suicide attempt from an agent only moments before the hearing. The agent did not notify them of the medication given Ho or his confinement prior to the hearing. The IJ did not continue the hearing or inquire into Ho's ability to proceed." The judge denied Ho's application for asylum; the Board of Immigration Appeals upheld the denial, despite claims that the hearing had been unfair because of Ho's medical condition. Joan Friedland filed a motion in federal court asking for a new hearing for Ho, based on his condition and other issues; the motion was granted. (Summary and quotation from Memorandum Opinion and Order of Judge Edward B. Davis, *Ho Guo Xiang v. Walter Cadman,* U.S. District Court, Southern District of Florida, Case. No. 93–640-CIV-Davis, April 20, 1993.)

In 1985 "INS agents forced [a Salvadoran asylum seeker] to swallow Valium. Then they guided her hand as she made a mark on a form. The mark gave INS permission to deport her," which it did; a federal judge then ordered the INS to bring her back (Lizette Alvarez and Lisa Getterr, "Asylum: The Magic Key," *Miami Herald,* December 15, 1993). Robert S. Kahn reports that in the 1980s INS detainees at FDC Oakdale (Louisiana) were "drugged . . . on the steel bed in the solitary confinement room" (*Other People's Blood: U.S. Immigration Prisons in the Reagan Decade* [Boulder, Colo.: Westview Press, 1996], 158).

In "My Experiences with INS Officials," a four-page typed account, detained Nigerian asylum seeker Jerry Jide Okey wrote that on September 9, 1997, he was "accosted" by an INS deportation officer (whom he names) at the Berks County, Pennsylvania, jail. Okey gave me a copy of his report when we met in York, Pennsylvania, after he was released. Okey wrote: "[The officer] drove me to JFK Airport, New York. He pushed me around, threatened to inject me to sleep, or to blow up my head with a pistol. He put heavy duty shackles on my legs. He armed himself with pistol, injection, and all kinds of dangerous weapons. He used the f**k and profane words on me, and called me nigger. He also invited the Ghana Airways Manager to also threaten me to board the plane." Allen Erenbaum, INS director of congressional relations, wrote to Pennsylvania Senator Arlen Specter that Okey's "allegations of physical abuse were not substantiated" but that the deportation officer "was found to have violated Service policy regarding his handling and transportation of Mr. Okey" (January 6, 1999).

"I suspected the reason why the INS was so ferociously against me,"

Okey wrote, "was because I was responsible for producing and disseminating newsletters [i.e., from inside the jails], which were written and printed by me, to expose the activities of the INS in the prolonged incarceration of refugees in various county prisons. Some of these newsletters were confiscated during a search into my legal mail, to halt its further circulation. I was warned of the consequences of my action, as the newsletters carried my name and alien information."

10. Emphasis "added," though the quotation is from Bergeron's comments in a telephone interview with the author and not from written material.

11. Memorandum from Nestor E. Meiggs, Lieutenant, to Mr. Joseph Kennedy, Captain, November 20, 1991, Krome SPC, Miami, Florida.

12. "Routine Memorandum Prepared on Form G-2," in Immigration and Naturalization Service, Office of Information Systems, Records Systems Division, Records Management Branch, Mail and Correspondence Section, *Correspondence Manual,* Revised October 1985, 73.

13. Mark Dow, "No Exit: Detained at Export Plaza," *Texas Observer,* May 12, 2000, 12–15.

14. Dianne Klein, "INS 'Lifers' Locked Up in Limbo," *Los Angeles Times,* February 6, 1994.

15. Receipt of my FOIA request for information on this flight, dated December 22, 1999, was acknowledged by the INS FOIA Unit on February 23, 2000. On June 26, 2001, a FOIA specialist called to ask if I was still interested in the requested information. I told her on the phone and in writing that I remained interested. I did not receive any further response.

16. Balogun's attorney submitted United Nations documents citing the Civil Liberties Organization, a nongovernmental organization in Nigeria that investigated the return of Nigerian asylum seekers from Germany in 1998. The group reported: "Nigeria Immigration Service (NIS) and the National Drug Law Enforcement Agency (NDLEA) officials are usually in charge of taking custody of the deportees and sorting them out. . . . Those who carried documents indicating that they are Nigerians were detained upon arrival [in Lagos]. The German authorities who deported them labeled some of them as having been involved in various unspecified criminal activities, which is the reason given by the security agencies for their continued detention. They are detained at various centers in Lagos, including four illegal airport detention centres. . . . There detainees are said to be ofen suspended upside down and tortured overnight. Others are detained at the N[ational] D[rug] L[aw] E[nforcement A[gency] cells at the Nigerian Cargo Handling Company (NAHCO) facility, and

at the Hadj camp . . . near the airport. Visitors are barred from approaching these areas. Detainees who have money to pay are freed, while those who do not remain in detention indefinitely without charge or trial."

17. Klein, "INS 'Lifers' Locked Up in Limbo." The Nigerian aviation reporter's account is Isiaka Aliagan, "US Deports Billy Eko, 77 Others," *The Guardian,* December 17, 1993.

18. The INS official was referring to Celia W. Dugger, "After a 'Kafkaesque' Ordeal, Seeker of Asylum Presses Case," *New York Times,* April 1, 1997, A1; see also two letters to the editor responding to the article: Adam S. Keller, M.D., "Tortured Immigrants Edure a Catch-22," *New York Times,* April 8, 1997, A14; and C. O. Awani, Acting Consul General of Nigeria, "Nigerian Asylum Seeker Claimed False Identity," *New York Times,* May 12, 1997, A14.

Prejudice can be hard to pin down and yet impossible to deny. After the world-renowned Ogoni activist Ken Saro-Wiwa was executed by the dictatorship of General Sani Abacha in 1995, his widow, Hauwa Saro-Wiwa, fled Nigeria with their one-year-old son. She was granted political asylum in the United States. Then, in September 1999, she was stopped for a routine traffic violation in San Pablo, California, and local police handed her over to the INS. She was detained in the Marin County Jail for six days. It turned out to be an administrative mixup, but for days the INS refused to explain why it was holding her. She was freed through the intervention of attorney Sarah Jones and Representative Tom Lantos but only after she agreed to sign an order of supervision. Saro-Wiwa noted on the form that she was signing under duress and that she had been refused access to her attorney. Jones told me later that based on her conversations with jail officials and her attempt to meet Saro-Wiwa outside the jail, she is convinced that jail and INS officials timed her client's release so as to make sure that she would not be present.

When Saro-Wiwa told an INS officer that she worked as a teacher, "he was a little taken aback." The officer seemed to have "a perception of me being a criminal or . . . a layabout," she told me. Jones added that the case was plagued by "the assumption that because [Saro-Wiwa] was from Nigeria, that she was lying about everything." Not surprisingly, prejudice and ignorance go hand in hand. Most of Sarah Jones's clients are Central and South Americans, but when she represents Africans, she takes a map of the continent with her to the INS office. Jones is African American. "Africa is not a country, it's a continent, and I have to explain this every time," she told me. INS officials in San Francisco were "gung ho" to deport Saro-Wiwa, she continued, and because they had never heard of her husband they had no idea why so many people were volunteering to help her. "They thought it was just another African—why is the media involved?"

19. See, for example, Statement of Thomas J. Kneir, Deputy Assistant Director, Criminal Investigative Division, Federal Bureau of Investigation, "On Combating International African Crime," Before the Committee on International Relations, U.S. House of Representatives, July 15, 1998.

20. Carol Harvey, "Why SES Mobility? Why Not! An Interview with Chris Sale, Office of Management and Budget," *OPM Message to the Senior Executive Service,* winter–spring 1999. Available at www.opm.gov/ses/newsletters/ws99/ses5-99.pdf.

21. Border Patrol supervisor interview in Dow, "Alien Watch," *Index on Censorship,* March 1996. On "immigration inspectors on horseback": Nevins, *Operation Gatekeeper: The Rise of the "Illegal Alien" and the Making of the U.S.-Mexico Boundary* (New York: Routledge, 2002), 26.

22. For "a formidable army": Anthony DePalma, "'A Tyrannical Situation': Farmers Caught in Conflict over Illegal Migrant Workers," *New York Times,* October 3, 2000, C1. For "detained in empty grain warehouses" and "The almond-eyed Mongolian": Alexander Saxton, *The Indispensable Enemy: Labor and the Anti-Chinese Movement in California* (Berkeley: University of California Press, 1971), 243–44. For "Abroad, the country": "Here's hoping," *Economist,* January 15, 2000.

   Obviously these prejudices are not limited to the United States; as I was writing this chapter, an article appeared explaining that in Switzerland foreign residents can apply for Swiss nationality "as long as they are integrated into Swiss society. . . ." "As part of what some media have dubbed the 'fondue test,' local officials usually stop by the applicant's house to check on how the family lives, the level of cleanliness, and, some say, even what they eat. [A Bosnian applicant said,] 'Whether our house is clean or not does not indicate whether we are fit to be citizens'" (Elizabeth Olson, "Swiss Refusal of Citizenship to Immigrants Raises Debate," *New York Times,* May 5, 2000).

23. Ebibillo alleged that the bloodstains were the result of beatings he received from immigration officers. I saw the clothing when it was delivered from the federal Metropolitan Correctional Center to the Haitian Refugee Center after Ebibillo had been deported. The prison staff—this is not an INS facility—was professional and cooperative in returning Ebibillo's money to him through me, at his request.

   The INS claims it delayed Ebibillo's scheduled deportation in order to investigate the procedures used to drug him. The timing suggests the possibility that the agency wanted to deport him before an attorney contacted by Amnesty International could reopen his case (he had filed his original political asylum application without the help of an attorney). The associate director of Human Rights Watch wrote, "While the INS was not legally bound to reconsider Ebibillo's case, the extenuating circumstances called for a favorable exercise of discretion, rather than a special effort to send him back to possible persecution" (Letter from Gara LaMarche, Associate Director, Human Rights Watch, to INS Commissioner Doris Meissner, April 29, 1994).

## CHAPTER 5: THE WORLD'S FIRST PRIVATE PRISON

1.   Prison Realty, *Letter to Shareholders and Annual Report on Form 10-K*, 1998. CCA is the primary tenant of Prison Realty.
2.   Wackenhut's facility in Jena, Louisiana, was not an INS detention center. On nurse who "jacks offenders": a February 2000 Justice Department report, as quoted in "I Know Why the Cajun Bird Sings," *Harper's*, July 2000, 29.
3.   Kenneth Efe says that his father was chairman of the Social Democratic Party (SDF) in Nigeria's Edo state. In 1997 Efe himself joined the SDP's youth division. In June of that year Efe attended an SPD-organized rally marking the anniversary of the annulled 1993 elections. Police officers began firing on the crowd and beating participants, including Efe. According to documents Efe's attorneys filed with the Board of Immigration Appeals, "Bleeding profusely from a head wound, he managed to escape into a nearby apartment building where he grabbed a knife to defend himself." He was accosted by the same officers, who again began beating him. Efe stabbed one of them in the stomach and escaped again. The officer later died. Efe fled to his uncle's house in Kastina state and then to Lagos, where he soon learned that police had arrested and beaten his father "for refusing to disclose his whereabouts." In December 1997 Efe stowed away on the ship that took him to Galveston. On arrival he asked to apply for political asylum, and he was detained at the Houston Processing Center, an adult facility. He was also held at a county jail.

When he arrived here, Efe claimed to be thirteen years old. According to the INS, he was at least eighteen. The agency based its findings on dental exams. Efe's attorneys, Jennifer Reynolds of Houston and Morton Sklar of the Washington-based World Organization Against Torture, countered with evidence that includes a journal article titled

"Eruption Times of Third Molars in Young Rural Nigerians." The attorneys argued that the dental exam used by the INS is unreliable. In addition, guidelines of the United Nations High Commissioner for Refugees, the lawyers argued, call for a "margin of error" in borderline age determinations. Sklar and Reynolds complained that the INS was violating its own guidelines on the treatment of juveniles. They wanted Efe removed from the adult facility in Houston and detained appropriately or placed in foster care. See Mark Dow, "No Exit: Detained at Export Plaza," *Texas Observer*, May 12, 2000, 12–15. Also see Deborah Tedford, "Is Teen a Juvenile or Adult?" *Houston Chronicle*, June 25, 2000, 31A.

Efe was detained at the Houston Processing Center until August 2002, when he was deported to Nigeria.

4. "Answering the Billion Dollar Question," pamphlet prefacing Prison Realty's 1998 *Letter to Shareholders and Annual Report on Form 10-K*, 3.

5. Allegations of the mistreatment of prisoners and detainees in private facilities are certainly not limited to CCA facilities, but those concerning CCA have been extensively documented. See, for example, Greg Jaffe and Rick Brooks, "Violence at Prison Run by Corrections Corp. Irks Youngstown, Ohio," *Wall Street Journal*, August 5, 1998, A1; Eric Bates, "Private Prisons," *Nation*, January 5, 1998; Bates, "*Prisons for Profit, cont.,*" *Nation*, May 4, 1998 (reprinted by *Corporate Watch*, www.corpwatch.org); Bates, "CCA, the Sequel," *Nation*, June 7, 1999; "US: Asylum Seekers Allege CCA Abuse," *Prison Privatisation Report International* (London: Prison Reform Trust, April–May 1999); Associated Press, "Prison Company Settles Lawsuit by Inmates," *New York Times*, March 4, 1999, A22; Richard P. Jones, "Prison Firm Accused of Ongoing Inmate Abuse," *Milwaukee Journal Sentinel*, July 24, 1999 (reprinted by Media Awareness Project, www.mapinc.org); Eric Friedmann, "Prison Privatization: The Bottom Line," *Corporate Watch* (www.corpwatch.org), August 21, 1999; Jake Adelstein, "Whither American Dominance? Merits of Privately Run Prisons under Debate," *Yomiuri Shimbun* (Japan; English on-line edition), February 22, 2000; Barry Yeoman, "Steel Town Lockdown," *Mother Jones*, May–June 2000; Judith Greene, "Bailing Out Private Jails," in *Prison Nation: The Warehousing of America's Poor,* ed. Tara Herivel and Paul Wright (New York: Routledge, 2003), 139 ff. Also see Christian Parenti, "Privatized Problems"; Judith Greene, "Lack of Correctional Services"; and Elizabeth Alexander, "Private Prisons and Health Care," in *Capitalist Punishment: Prison Privatization and Human Rights,* ed. Andrew Coyle et al. (Atlanta: Clarity Press, 2003), 33, 34, 65,

72. On allegations of CCA abuses in its Elizabeth, New Jersey, INS detention center, see chap. 7, note 7.

6. "CCA: A Quality, Cost-Effective Solution," pamphlet, January 1996.

7. Markup on sneakers: justice policy analyst Judith Greene quoted in Eric Sullivan, "Jail Sell," *Metroland,* May 15, 2000 (reprinted at www.alternet.org). Markup on radio and "prohibiting inmates' families": Amy Roe, "Life Pricey inside Bay County Jail," *News Herald,* July 25, 1999; in Florida, public prison commissary prices tend to be inflated, but less drastically, according to Roe.

Inmates are not the only victims of privatization. A Florida government study also notes that a major source of savings to the state from private prisons results from the private companies' ability to reduce employee retirement and health benefits; the study refers to a Wackenhut-operated prison. (Office of Program Policy Analysis and Government Accountability, *Private Prison Review: South Bay Correctional Facility Provides Savings and Success: Room for Improvement,* No. 99-39, March 2000, 7.)

8. When I sent a copy of the *Texas Observer* with my article on the Houston Processing Center (see note 3) to detainee Olu Balogun, Warden Martin apparently intercepted it; Balogun did not receive it, but he says he heard Martin discussing it with Assistant Warden Cook.

9. The Cuban detainees were being held indefinitely by the INS. In a widely covered story, several of them took hostages at the St. Martinville Parish Jail in Louisiana in December 1999.

10. The group of about thirty CCA/INS Houston detainees, referring to themselves as "Africa Black Nationals," wrote a letter to the National Association for Blacks in Criminal Justice (with copies to the ACLU, Barbara Walters, and others) asking to be deported immediately:

It is difficult to fight a case here because the Library is Outdated. . . . We have been physically and emotionally attacked on many occasions by Mexican Inmates. . . . We have been beaten up by the CCA guards and Captains on many occasions in trying to seek for our rights. . . . We have been physically and emotionally abused by the [INS] Deportation Officers. . . . They harass us with threats of deportation . . . and when the case is over, they never call us for the information needed to expedite our deportability. . . . The Africa Black Nationals (especially Nigerians and Jamaicans) have been the main target for inhumane treatment. . . . Some of us have spent at least 2 years now in the INS custody here at the Corrections Corporation of America waiting to be deported. . . . We do not know if there are Kickbacks being served to some of the INS Officials, or an agreement between the INS Officials and the CCA officials, because this depends on how long we have been detained, is how much money they make out of us from the Federal Government. It is difficult to determine because of the condition we are in, but there is a very strong feeling of detention fraud. . . . If there is anybody sensible reading this complaint, she or he will at least get an expanded understanding. We think that Americans need to know where and how their tax dollars are being spent and the attendant results. (January 22, 1996)

11. Promotional material from Prison Realty, 1998. Lobbyist's remark: Mark Silva, "Guards to Protest Privatizing Prisons," *Miami Herald,* February 5, 1999, B1. TransCor president quoted in Vince Beiser, "Interstate Inmates," *Mother Jones,* May–June 2000. Corrections officer quoted in Bates, "CCA, the Sequel" (citing *Cleveland Plain Dealer*).

12. On first two privatized prisons: "CCA opened for business in 1983, locking up its first inmate the following year. Wackenhut Corrections began in 1984 as a division of Wackenhut Corp.—it's now a separately traded subsidiary—and won its first contract two years later" (David Sedore, "Private Prisons Don't Lock in Savings," *Daily Business Review,* May 2, 1997). Statement of Congressman Ted Strickland Before the House Subcommittee on Appropriations for the Department of Commerce, Justice, and State, the Judiciary, and Related Agencies, March 23, 2000. For "Faced with empty beds": Eric Schlosser, "The Prison-Industrial Complex," *Atlantic Monthly,* December 1998 (on-line version, pt. 2). On "behind the backs of local officials": S. K. Bardwell, "Neighborhood, Officials Find Double Shock in Jail Escape," *Houston Chronicle,* August 9, 1996; Bardwell, "Local Private Jail Begins Moving Oregon Inmates: Officials Unaware Offenders Housed Here," *Houston Chronicle,* August 10, 1996. Friedmann, "Prison Privatization."

13. Geoff Davidian, "Hunger Strike Here Fells Romanian Refugee Seeking Asylum," *Houston Chronicle,* October 8, 1992.

14. On "in Texas": e-mail correspondence with Carl Reynolds, General Counsel, Texas Department of Criminal Justice, May 26, 2000.

15. This paragraph is based on a letter from ninety-five El Paso detainees to Amnesty International; the letter was "adapted" and reprinted in the Lutheran Immigration and Refugee Service's "Detention Watch Network News," October 1997.

16. Robert S. Kahn, *Other People's Blood: U.S. Immigration Prisons in the Reagan Decade* (Boulder, Colo.: Westview Press, 1996), 151 ff.

17. INS, "Record of Sworn Statement in Proceedings," March 31, 1998.

18. CCA, Annual Report, 1995, 10.

19. U.S. Government Procurements (Modification) for Transportation, Travel, and Relocation Services; Subject: Nigeria Mission; Sol. HQ-2-R-00017. *Commerce Business Daily,* posted in CBDNet on December 13, 2001.

20. Author interviews with Gaston Fairey. Fairey told a reporter, "There's a [CCA] corporate policy encouraging a kind of use of force that's illegal under American law," and added, "I'm not talking about a written policy." He also said, "It appears that more and more private correctional systems use excessive force as control techniques. . . . The private prison business is a competitive market where companies cut costs by cutting corners on salaries and training" (Elizabeth Llorente, "Asylum Seekers Sue Elizabeth Jailers," Bergen *Record,* February 25, 2000). Years before, South Texas attorney Patrick Hughes said that the purpose of strip-searches at a CCA/INS detention center in Laredo, filled with Central American asylum seekers, "was to create an atmosphere of fear and repression and they discourage [detainees] from seeing their attorneys," that is, because detainees were strip-searched after attorney visits (Diana Claitorr and Louis Dubose, "In Jail in Laredo," *Texas Observer,* August 14, 1987).

21. See Amnesty International, *India: Punjab Police: Beyond the Bounds of the Law,* May 1995; and *India: Determining the Fate of the 'Disappeared' in Punjab,* October 1995.

22. Corrections Corporation of America, Houston Processing Center, Memorandum to All Houston Processing Center Staff, from Pamela Fugazzi, Warden; re: Milissa Grace, December 8, 1995.

23. Corrections Corporation of America, Problem Solving Notice, "Confidential: Not to be released outside corporation," Date of Notice 12/12/95.

## CHAPTER 6: "KEEPING QUIET MEANS DENY"

1. Nationwide, Wackenhut Correction Corp.'s fourth-quarter 1999 per diem averaged $48.79; the figure for the Queens facility is higher than that average, according to Patrick Cannan, director of corporate relations.

2. Robert H. Bork Jr., "Big George Wackenhut," *Forbes,* no. 132, November 12, 1983; "Company Interview: Richard R. Wackenhut," *Wall Street Transcript,* June 1999 (rpt.); Wackenhut Corporation, 1998 Annual

Report, and 1998 Form 10-K filed with the Securities and Exchange Commission. Number of prisons operated includes projected openings through 2000. On strikebreaking, see Ken Silverstein and Alexander Cockburn, "America's Private Gulag," *Counterpunch* 4.1 (January 1–15, 1997). On British Petroleum, see Gregory Palast, "Ten Years After—But Who Was to Blame?" *Manchester Guardian,* March 21, 1999.

3. See note 14 below.

4. Somini Sengupta, "Limits on Parole Dash Refugees's Hopes," *New York Times,* November 2, 1998, B3.

5. These are my tabulations from the INS's "daily count" sheets of June 2, 1999. I have followed their breakdown in listing Congo and Zaire separately, Kosovo as a country, and so on. Lengths of detention are conservative estimates as the "date detained" entry does not necessarily represent the earliest day of detention—in cases, for example, when someone is transferred from another facility or sent to a hospital and then returned to the detention center.

6. See chap. 2, note 23.

7. Solomon, "Wackenhut Detention Ordeal," *Village Voice,* September 7, 1999. I once asked INS Baltimore District Director Benedict Ferro when his office had last inspected a particular county jail used to hold INS detainees, and he responded: "I don't know, but I believe it's an annual requirement, and it has been done within the past year." Note his progression toward certainty. See Mark Dow, "'INS Females': Haitian Women Detained in Maryland," *Haïti Progrès,* March 12, 1997.

8. Nationwide, only 20 percent of all INS detainees were represented in their immigration court proceedings in FY 1999, according to an unpublished statistic provided by the Executive Office for Immigration Review to the Committee on Administrative Law of the Association of the Bar of the City of New York for a forum, "Due Process and Immigration Law," March 27, 2000. (Author interview with forum moderator Arthur Helton, Senior Fellow for Refugee Studies and Preventive Action, Council on Foreign Relations). Not surprisingly, detained asylum seekers are less likely than nondetained asylum seekers to have attorneys; see Andy Schoenholtz and Jonathan Jacobs, "The State of Asylum Representation: Ideas for Change," *Georgetown Immigration Law Journal* 16 (summer 2002): 766, 772.

9. Berlitz earns $9 million to $12 million per year from contracts with the Justice Department's Executive Office for Immigration Review for immigration court interpretation nationwide, according to Susan Gryder, senior manager, Quality Assurance, Berlitz International.

10. Phares Mutibwa, *Uganda since Independence: A Story of Unfulfilled Hopes* (Trenton, N.J.: Africa World Press, 1992), 134, quoted in Human Rights Watch, *Hostile to Democracy: The Movement System and Political Repression in Uganda,* New York, August 1999, 33.

11. Author interview with Arthur Helton, Senior Fellow for Refugee Studies and Preventive Action, Council on Foreign Relations.

12. U.S. Committee for Refugees, *World Refugee Survey* (Washington, D.C., 1999), 80.

13. My retelling of Kutesa's story is based on his courtroom testimony on September 20, 1999, the INS APSO interview transcript of March 23, 1998, and my interviews with Kutesa and his attorney.

14. Lawyers Committee for Human Rights, *Refugees behind Bars: The Imprisonment of Asylum Seekers in the Wake of the 1996 Immigration Act,* New York, August 1999, 12, 9. According to the report, the New York INS in various parole denials has "implied that Congressional intent somehow weighed against release stating that 'it is Service policy that [parole] authority is carefully and narrowly exercised to be in conformity with statutory purpose and legislative intent'" (12). Also: "New York parole denial letters have implied that the fact that an asylum seeker has passed the credible fear process is not even relevant to parole eligibility. Instead, these denial letters imply that granting parole requests is somehow contrary to 'congressional intent.' Meanwhile, it is asylum seekers . . . who suffer because of failures to follow the parole guidelines" (29).

15. Human Rights Watch, *Hostile to Democracy.*

16. Letter from McElroy to Nicholas J. Rizza, Amnesty International USA, San Francisco, Calif., February 12, 1999; emphasis added.

17. Miguel Garcilazo, "INS Detention Center Planned Near Airport," *New York Daily News,* January 20, 1997; letter from McElroy to Jane Sung-ee Bai, Executive Director, Committee Against Anti-Asian Violence, August 20, 1999.

## CHAPTER 7: THE ART OF JAILING

1. U.S. Immigration and Naturalization Service, Headquarters Detention and Deportation Division, "The Elizabeth, New Jersey Contract Detention Facility Operated by ESMOR Inc.: Interim Report," July 20, 1995.

2. Esmor Inc., A Corrections Services Company, "Technical Proposal to U.S. Department of Justice for RFP CO-22–88 San Diego, California,"

August 1988. Barbara Muller quoted in Viejas Cultural Integrity Fund, "INS Detention Center/Viejas Indian Reservation—San Diego County," undated press release.

3. Jennifer Peltz, "Pahokee Youth Jail Gets Seven Weeks to Clean Up Act," *Palm Beach Post,* July 16, 1999, 1B.

4. Sam Scolnik, "Tacoma to Have New INS Building," Seattle *Post-Intelligencer Reporter,* September 24, 2002.

5. Molly Gordy, "INS Mgrs. Demand the Ax for Boss," *New York Daily News,* December 3, 1996. William Branigi, "Field Managers Accuse INS Operations Director of Cronyism, Seek His Ouster," *Washington Post,* December 6, 1996. On "LaGuardia taught a course . . . was later convicted": Transcript of *60 Minutes,* "I.N.S.," March 10, 2002 (CBS Worldwide, Inc.); author interview with anonymous INS headquarters official.

6. Matthew Purdy and Celia W. Dugger, "Legacy of Immigrants' Uprising: New Jail Operator, Little Change," *New York Times,* July 7, 1996, A1. John Tierney, "Accountability at Prisons Run Privately," *New York Times,* August 15, 2000, 1B.

7. On "risk of public scrutiny": see chap. 5, note 1. *Oluwole Aboyade and Salah Dafali v. Corrections Corporation of America, Prison Realty Trust, Inc. et al.,* U.S. District Court for the District of New Jersey, Newark, no. cv-00-2067, February 2000. Concerning events described in the lawsuit, see also Elizabeth Llorente, "Asylum Seekers Sue Elizabeth Jailers," Bergen *Record,* February 25, 2000. On the incident that led to the suit, see Elizabeth Llorente, "INS Moves Outspoken Asylum Seeker," Bergen *Record,* April 15, 1999; [editorial], "A Suspicious Transfer," Bergen *Record,* April 16, 1999; Elizabeth Llorente, "Beating of Asylum Seeker Described," Bergen *Record,* April 19, 1999; [editorial], "A Beating or an Injury?" Bergen *Record,* April 29, 1999; Monique El-Faizy, "INS Defend Discipline of Jailed Asylum-Seeker," Bergen *Record,* April 30, 1999. J. Scott Blackman, INS acting eastern regional director, wrote to the paper "to underscore [the INS's] commitment to proper and humane treatment of all detainees in INS custody"; "On Elizabeth Detention Center," Letters, Bergen *Record,* May 2, 1999.

In September 2003 a jury found in favor of CCA on the charges concerning Aboyade; it found CCA guilty of both assault and battery against Dafali—but not guilty of infliction of emotional distress—and awarded Dafali $1 (one dollar). The plaintiffs have filed a motion for a new trial.

In his closing argument, CCA's lead counsel Brad Simon made repeated, sarcastic references to the plaintiffs' "wild conspiracy theories about retaliation" and asked jurors to rely on their "common sense" rather than "fantasies" that guards would beat and isolate frustrated detainees. He also argued (more plausibly) that the plaintiffs were suing the company rather than individual officers or the INS because they wanted money—and then he told the jury that CCA "has the right not to be extorted." Finally, he made sure to mention that the plaintiffs were "illegal immigrants" (the same tactic used by correctional officers' defense counsel in *New Jersey v. Rice,* as we will see).

Aboyade and Dafali were detained at the INS/CCA Elizabeth detention center in 1998. Aboyade alleged that after his name appeared in the Bergen *Record* and other papers—where he was surprised to find himself described as a leader—he was put into a segregation cell that had been covered with human feces by another hunger striker and was told by a CCA official to eat the other protester's shit. CCA officers allegedly roughed him up, but a former CCA officer actually testified that Aboyade "ran into the supervisor's hand." All this came in tandem with other CCA taunts—the usual remarks about fucking his mother and Africans eating like monkeys. From seg, Aboyade filed numerous complaints—directed to the INS, but which must go through CCA—yet these went unanswered. A CCA officer noted in the seg logbook that Aboyade was "very verbal." He continued working on his asylum appeal while denied access to the law library; he attempted to submit the appeal from segregation, but it never reached the Board of Immigration Appeals. (He would later be granted political asylum.) After about a week, Aboyade was moved to another isolation cell and held there for three more weeks. Former CCA/Elizabeth warden Chris Brogna testified that CCA headquarters had been notified of the hunger strike "because this is a high profile facility," but he acknowledged that the protest for which participants were put into isolation was completely nonviolent. Aboyade testified that when detainees chanted, "No food! No food! No food!" CCA officers told them that they were "making the company to lose money." When Aboyade was put into segregation, CCA officials confiscated and never returned a diary he had kept about his first four months in detention. Early in the trial Aboyade told me that neither the jury's decision nor the possible financial award were important to him. What mattered was "that I was able to bring my experience, what happened to me at Elizabeth, into this court."

Salah Dafali arrived in the United States as a stowaway—but only because he thought the ship he took from Italy was headed for Canada. INS detained him in Elizabeth, refusing to deport him, as he requested.

CCA officers allegedly threatened to send Dafali to a county jail to be sexually assaulted by other inmates. They also sexually threatened him themselves. Dafali met INS detainees who had been held at Elizabeth for two and three years, so he believed it when officers threatened to keep him there for fifteen. He finally cut his wrists and began having "tantrums," according to Brogna. Dafali also began a hunger strike. He was forced into four-point restraints. While he was restrained, the CCA chief of security allegedly hit him in the face. The water to Dafali's isolation cell was cut off, according to CCA's own records. A former employee of TransCor America—CCA's subsidiary prisoner transportation company—testified that he saw "a bootprint" on Dafali's face shortly after Dafali was "tagged up" or assaulted; CCA records called the wound "self-inflicted." A CCA videotape of the assault on Dafali ends abruptly. A CCA official testified that the battery had run out. Aboyade, who had been in a nearby cell, testified that the security chief ordered the camera off of Dafali, who was begging officers to stop. A CCA shift supervisor took Polaroids of the injured Dafali; court documents note that CCA failed to produce these in the course of litigation and provided no explanation. (Polaroids of Dafali taken by an INS official were in evidence, however.) "They beat me on the 28th," Dafali told me; "they transferred me on the 29th." He was detained for a total of forty-one months and remains subject to detention and deportation at the agency's discretion.

8. Quarantillo's remark "It was understood by all parties": quoted in Steve Chambers, "INS Embroiled in New Dispute over Cutoff of Detainee Programs," Newark *Star-Ledger*, December 22, 1999; Quarantillo continued: "The reason for the suspension is because Jesuit Refugee Service broke the covenant that had been reached with the INS"—that is, not to discuss detention with the detainees.

Quarantillo's comment "INS has no objection to Matthew 25": quoted in Patricia Zapor, "Radical Reading: Detention References Kill Bible, English Classes," Catholic News Service, January 7, 2000. The problematic passage in Matthew 25:35–36 reads: "I was a stranger and you took me in: Naked, and ye clothed me: I was sick, and ye visited me: I was in prison, and ye came unto me." Will Coley of the Jesuit Refugee Service said he heard that INS monitors enjoyed the Bible class; then they reported on it to INS officials in the district office (Elizabeth Llorente, "Asylum Seekers' Classes Halted; Policy Breach Cited," Bergen *Record*, December 22, 1999).

On suicide attempts: Elizabeth Llorente, "Lacking Liberty, Some Detainees Attempt Death," Bergen *Record*, May 24, 1999.

9. Wole Soyinka, *The Open Sore of a Continent: A Personal Narrative of the Nigerian Crisis* (New York: Oxford University Press, 1996), 65, 75. Soyinka continues: "Let us face it, as many Nigerians themselves and visitors to Nigeria do concede, Nigerians appear at times to require a coercive hand in directing their social awareness. There is something about my fellow nationals that requires that their sense of egoistic mindlessness be drastically pruned, that they be made to recognize the rights of others. As a former and still enthusiastic enforcer of road safety culture in Nigeria, I not only testify to this but confess that I took particular satisfaction in training our corps to crush the egos of that arrogant breed of drivers, the civilian elite and military officers especially, who felt that they were above the law and could kill and maim with impunity" (77–78).

10. *The State of New Jersey v. James Rice, Charles Popovic, Michael Sica, et al.,* Superior Court of New Jersey, Law Division—Union County, Criminal, Indictment No. 96–01–00104I.

11. Smishkewych gave me a list titled "Languages Appearing in the New Jersey Superior Court" in 1996. Spanish was by far the most common, followed by Portuguese, American Sign Language, and Polish. These were followed by Vietnamese, Haitian Creole, Korean, Mandarin, Arabic, Italian, Russian, Greek, Serbo-Croatian, Gujarati, Cantonese, Khmer, Urdu, French, Romanian, Farsi, Turkish, Hungarian, Hindi, Albanian, Panjabi *[sic]*, Tagalog, Hebrew, Macedonian, Ukrainian, Czech, Foo Chow, German, Armenian, Japanese, Pashto, Slovak, Bengali, Bulgarian, Min Nan, Amharic, Malinke, Nepali, and Thai.

12. I was not in the courtroom on the day the verdicts were read. See Ronald Smothers, "3 Prison Guards Guilty of Abuse of Immigrants," *New York Times,* March 7, 1998, A1; MaryAnn Spoto, "From a Jail to Prison for 3 Involved in 'Brute' Force," Newark *Star-Ledger,* May 2, 1998.


CHAPTER 8: "CRIMINAL ALIENS" AND CRIMINAL AGENTS

1. Minnie-Lou Lynch, "A Short History of Oakdale, Louisiana and Surrounding Areas," 1997. Typescript in Oakdale Public Library.

2. Minnesota Lawyers International Human Rights Committee, *Oakdale Detention Center: The First Year of Operation,* Minneapolis, July 1987. Robert S. Kahn, *Other People's Blood: U.S. Immigration Prisons in the Reagan Decade* (Boulder, Colo.: Westview Press, 1996), 151–52.

3. *McFarlane et al. v. INS,* Civil Action No. 92-0709, Sect. K Mag. 6, U.S. District Court, Western District of La.; the suit was transferred to the

Lake Charles Division, where it became Civil Action No. 92-1201. I am very grateful to the district court clerk in Shreveport for finding and sending me the pleadings.

4. Here is the INS boilerplate: "The Service makes a priority of ensuring safe and humane treatment for INS detainees, and we act swiftly upon finding merit in any allegation of improper treatment. Mistreatment of an INS detainee is not tolerated under any circumstances." This was the response when I asked INS public affairs officer Karen Kraushaar which local jail contracts the INS had terminated as a result of allegations of mistreatment (I was not asking about FDC Oakdale); she replied that such information could not be made public and provided the quoted statement instead (e-mail correspondence, October 15, 2002).

5. U.S. Department of Justice, Bureau of Justice Statistics, "Key Facts at a Glance: Correctional Populations," August 25, 2002. In 1980 the jail population was 183,988, and the prison population was 319,598. In 2001 the jail population was 631,240, and the prison population was 1,330,980. These numbers do not include INS detainees.

6. Ofra Bikel, *Snitch,* a Frontline Co. Production with Ofra Bikel Productions, Corp. Boston, WGBH, 1999.

7. Alan C. Nelson, "A Governor's Brave Stand on Illegal Aliens," *New York Times,* August 23, 1993.

8. U.S. Immigration and Naturalization Service, Investigations Division, "The Newest Criminals: The Emergence of Non-Traditional Organized Ethnic Crime Groups and INS' Role in Combatting Them," October 8, 1986. Typescript.

9. U.S. Department of Justice, Drug Enforcement Administration, Border Patrol, and I&NS, "El Paso Intelligence Center Special Report: Rastafarian Movement," April 25, 1975. Typescript.

10. "Immigration Act of 1990: Report on Criminal Aliens," April 1992, 6, 7, 9. The report's mention of the Oakdale prison refers to what was then called the Federal Correctional Institution in Oakdale, or "Oakdale I." Videotape of Oakdale opening ceremony, March 21, 1986; INS Historical Reference Library, Washington, D.C.

11. Deborah Sontag, "Black Officers in I.N.S. Push Racial Boundaries," *New York Times,* October 30, 1994; emphasis added.

12. For Carlson: recorded on videotape, see note 10. Carlson's words are quoted here to contrast his political rhetoric with Franklin's observations of life inside the Oakdale prison; the use of this quotation is not intended to link Carlson directly with any of the allegations made in this chapter.

1.  E-mail from Donald B. Looney to Dennis C. Riordan and Bruce Chadbourne, "Subject: Trip Report—County Jails," March 5, 1999.

2.  See Randall McGowen, "The Well-Ordered Prison: England, 1780–1865"; and John Hirst, "The Australian Experience: The Convict Colony," in *The Oxford History of the Prison: The Practice of Punishment in Western Society,* ed. Norval Morris and David J. Rothman (New York: Oxford University Press, 1998), 87, 245.

3.  McGowen, "The Well-Ordered Prison: England, 1780–1865," 83. McGowen does not put "reform" in quotation marks; Foucault, however, writes: "The movement for reforming the prisons, for controlling their functioning is not a recent phenomenon. It does not even seem to have originated in a recognition of failure. Prison 'reform' is virtually contemporary with the prison itself: it constitutes, as it were, its programme" (*Discipline and Punish: The Birth of the Prison,* trans. Alan Sheridan [New York: Vintage Books, 1977], 234; also see 81–82).

4.  Jean Genet, *A Thief's Journal,* trans. Bernard Frechtman (Toronto: Bantam Books, 1964), 5.

5.  Edward M. Peters, "Prison before the Prison: The Ancient and Medieval Worlds," in Morris and Rothman, eds., *The Oxford History of the Prison,* 5.

6.  Both women were deported. On Yvenie, see Mark Dow "'INS Females': Haitian Women Detained in Maryland," *Haïti Progrès,* March 12–18, 1997; and Women's Commission for Refugee Women and Children, *Liberty Denied: Women Seeking Asylum Imprisoned in the United States* (New York, April 1997), 20–21.

    In 1999 a United Nations "fact-finder" criticized the use of shackles in the United States on asylum seekers in airports and on women prisoners in labor and during childbirth (Elizabeth Olson, "U.N. Panel Is Told of Rights Violations at U.S. Women's Prisons," *New York Times,* March 31, 1999, A16). In the same year, Amnesty International and the Prisoners' Rights Project of the Legal Aid Society in New York criticized the routine use of shackles by the New York City Department of Correction on women "after giving birth and, in some cases, during delivery, in violation" of a previous federal court order; prison officials disputed the reports (Nina Siegal, "Inmates Again Shackled during Birth, Critics Say," *New York Times,* April 11, 1999, Metro, 33). The New York Police Department issued a memo instructing officers to use plastic rather than metal handcuffs when cuffing prisoners to metal hospital bed frames; the policy change was intended to protect the police officers from possible electrocution when the prisoners were defibrillated ("Plastic Cuffs for Prisoners in Hospital," *New York Times,* June 10, 1999, Metro, 7). Also see Amnesty International, *Not Part of My Sentence: Violations of the Human Rights of Women in Custody* (March 1999).

When Iranian filmmaker Jafar Panahi's *The Circle* was opening in the United States—the film's ad read, "Her only crime was being a woman"—Panahi himself was at Kennedy airport, chained for ten hours to a bench and to people from around the world. Panahi later said of his film: "Being in this circle doesn't mean we have to sit and wait. We have to struggle and widen this circle, in order to survive." He said of being chained up at JFK: "Every time I moved my legs, the cuffs got tighter" (quoted in Jonathan Curiel, "A Filmmaker Feels the Circle Tighten," *San Francisco Chronicle,* May 8, 2001, E1; also see Lance Lattig, "Jafar Panahi's INS Trial," *Village Voice,* May 16–22, 2001).

Panahi had been chained to the bench when he protested INS attempts to photograph and fingerprint him after he was unable to produce the required transit visa. Scrutiny of Iranian travelers had increased under the Bush administration at the time. Panahi intended to be at the New York airport only for a couple of hours, en route from Hong Kong to South America. U.S. authorities returned him to Tehran. From there Panahi wrote an open letter to the National Board of Review of Motion Pictures (distributed by the Human Rights Watch Film Festival):

They chained my feet and locked my chain to the others, all locked to a very dirty bench. For 10 hours, no questions and answers, I was forced to sit on that bench, pressed to the others. I could not move. I was suffering from an old illness, however, nobody noticed. Again, I requested them to let me call someone in New York, but they refused. They not only ignored my request but also to a boy from Sri Lanka who wanted to call his mom. Everybody was moved by the crying of the boy, people from Mexico, Peru, Eastern Europe, India, Pakistan, Bangladesh and . . . I was thinking that any country has its own law but I could not just understand those inhuman acts. . . .

I knew my film, The Circle, was released there for two days and I was told the film was very well received too. However, the audiences would understand my film better if they could know that the director of the film was chained at the same time. They would accept my beliefs that the circles of human limits do exist in any part of this world but with different ratios. I saw the Statue of Liberty in the waters and I unconsciously smiled. I tried to draw the curtain and there were scars of the chain on my hand. I could not stand the other travelers gazing at me and I just wanted to stand up and cry that I'm not a thief! I'm not a murderer! I'm not a drug dealer! I . . . I am just an Iranian, a filmmaker. But how I could tell this, what language? In Chinese, Japanese or to the mother tongues of those people from Mexico, Peru, Russia, India, Pakistan, and Bangladesh . . . or in the language of the young boy from Sri Lanka? Really in what language? I had not slept for 16 hours and I had to spend another 15 hours on my way back to Hong Kong. It was just a torture among all these watching eyes. I closed my eyes and tried to sleep. But I could not. I could just see the images of those sleepless women and men who were still chained.

7.    Nancy Morawetz, "Understanding the Impact of the 1996 Deportation Laws and the Limited Scope of Proposed Reforms," *Harvard Law Review* 113.8 (June 2000): 1939.

8.    *Demore v. Kim,* No. 01-1491, Transcript of Oral Argument, January 15, 2003.

9.    Justice Stevens's majority opinion in *INS v. St. Cyr* (June 25, 2001), footnote 51; citing 1999 U.S. Bureau of Justice Statistics figures.

10.    Immigration and Naturalization Service, Atlanta District Office, "Immigration & Naturalization Service Update: Removal of Criminal Aliens" [no date]. Also see Mark Bixler, "INS Memo to Prosecutors Called 'Despicable,'" *Atlanta Journal-Constitution,* May 25, 2000.

11.    In 1996, when Copes was warden of the jail in Tensas (owned but not operated by Louisiana Corrections Services), officers systematically beat a group of Cuban men detained there by the INS. The following recitation of events is excerpted from a lawsuit brought five years later by the Southern Center for Human Rights to oppose the transfer of Alabama state inmates to jails run by Louisiana Corrections Services and Warden Copes (*John Spellman v. Don Siegelman,* Circuit Court of Montgomery County, Alabama, August 2001):

> 23.    Gary Copes is currently the regional warden in charge of both the South Louisiana Correctional Center and the Pine Prairie Correctional Center.

> 24.    On July 22, 1999, Copes was indicted in federal court on 7 counts of violation of prisoners' civil rights for his participation in and cover-up of the beating and intimidation of six prisoners.

> 25.    Copes was the warden in charge of the Tensas Parish Detention Center, a private facility owned and operated by LCS, on October 31, 1996, when a disturbance resulted in a general lock-down of the facility. Six prisoners, identified by jail officials as the ringleaders in the disturbance, were stripped naked, placed together into a cell, and

sprayed with pepper spray. The six prisoners were then each taken into a storage room, one at a time, where each one was beaten by three jail deputies using their fists, boots, and a 24 inch metal baton.

26. At trial, Copes admitted in sworn testimony that he was present during the beatings and did nothing to stop them. At trial, Copes further admitted under sworn testimony that he approached each prisoner as he was led back to his cell, and told each one, "If this happens again, you're going to have to deal with me."

27. Despite severe and extensive injuries, the six prisoners were kept in the 2-bunk cell for one week to 10 days following the beatings. Despite severe injuries caused by the beatings, including broken bones, the prisoners were not taken to medical services until on or about November 7.

28. Copes did not report the disturbance or the beatings until two weeks later, when he spoke with a friend at the Immigration and Naturalization Service. An INS Special Agent immediately investigated and removed all INS prisoners held at the detention center the day after his investigation.

29. After a hung jury and mistrial, Copes was promoted by LCS to regional warden, where he currently oversees the two private facilities in Louisiana where Defendants may transfer Plaintiff and 500 other Alabama prisoners. . . .

As noted, Copes himself was acquitted in the Tensas beatings trial. At Pine Prairie, when I asked him what happened, he said this: "Were they beaten? Yes, they were beaten. That's in the court records. They were beaten. Was I indicted? Yes, I was indicted. Was I acquitted? Yes, I was acquitted."

He continued: "I never laid a hand. I did not give the order. I tried to talk the sheriff out of what he did. He did not listen. He was the boss. His chief deputy was there. The two guys that were over me, neither one of them would listen. No, I did not stand there and witness the beatings. I knew they were going on. You can hear them all over the place. The other people were found guilty—they pled guilty. I chose not to [plead] because I did not participate. I am even the person who notified the INS people that it happened." Later he added: "The sheriff ordered it, and they [the outside deputies with the chief of security] carried it out, and I called INS and reported it, because I didn't want any part of it."

According to Copes, the local fire marshal had made a visit to the jail and said that prisoners' lockers could not be left in the middle of the floor.

"We tell the inmates, from this point forward you pull them out, you get what you want, then you push them back under your bunks," Copes said. When inmates did not comply with the new system, he and his staff became frustrated: "We had rules that had to be followed. The fire marshal was telling us what to do." So they decided to start turning off the inmates' television set as a punishment whenever lockers were left out. The first time, it was turned off for thirty minutes; the second time, for an hour. "Then they started hoopin' and hollerin' and carrying on and throwing things. [Officers] ran and got me. By the time I got there, [the inmates] [had] set a fire inside. They were throwing footlockers."

Copes paused to gather his thoughts as the narrative becomes a bit more complicated.

So I—prior to me—just when I'm getting there, anyway, one of our chiefs of security went in to try to talk to them. One of [the inmates] punched him in the face. So he pepper-sprayed him, and backed out. I hollered at him to back out. "Just give him the door. . . . Everybody back out of there. Everybody. Every officer." My decision was, we were going to wait ten minutes, and we were going to let it calm down, see what happened. If we could, anyway. But in the process of waiting, the order was that the sheriff had to be notified about everything. And I agreed with that the order. . . .

By the time the sheriff got there, I had already gone into the dormitory and told the [inmates] if they would be quiet, I would listen to them. But I would only talk to one individual. And he came up to the front. He was a Mariel Cuban. He spoke very good English. They put the fire out. He walked out of the dorm with me. We started talking. He apologized for punching the captain. He said he lost his temper. I mean he was very nice, very polite—he made a mistake. I said, "That's going to cost you a little bit now." He said, "I understand that." Everything was calm. Everything was quiet. I said, "Here's the deal I'll make you. Go back in there, clean the place up, get everything put back like it was. You and your representatives come out, and we will all sit down and talk about this." Okay.

Then the sheriff showed up. It wasn't my ballgame after that. He's the boss. He's in charge. He took over. That's when I went to my office. And if you want that spelled out: I didn't like the way he handled it. So that's pretty much where it was.

Copes said that the sheriff called in about three hundred deputies from outside the jail. They filled the dorms with gas and administered systematic beatings with metal batons.

I'll be quite honest with you—they did use nightsticks or batons . . . metal batons. There's no question that they did that, or they couldn't have broken bones, 'cause they broke some bones. By the time I saw, two of them had already been done . . . By the time I can get to the sheriff, to try to *find* the sheriff, hell, they'd already beat two or three more.

Finally, Copes wanted to return to the indictment. It ruined his career, he told me. He felt he had had a future as warden of a large state penitentiary. "I'm lucky that I work for a real good company. I'm lucky that INS understood—they looked at it and saw it, you know. When you put something like that on your record, if you want to call it that, it don't go away. It does not go away." All this took a toll on his family too, especially his wife: "Those three years [of litigation] probably added a good fifteen years to her life. You can see it. But she knew I didn't do anything wrong. She knows I'm not that kind of person, and it was terrible."

12. Associated Press, "Three Seamen Caught after Fleeing Ship in La."; "Earthweek: A Diary of the Planet," distributed by Los Angeles Times Syndicate; Associated Press; "2 Caucasian Inmates Indicted in Prisoner's Death," Baton Rouge *State-Times/Morning Advocate,* August 17, 2002, 6B.

13. Quotations here and below from Transcript of Oral Argument, *Calcano-Martinez v. INS,* No. 00–1011, April 24, 2001; and Transcript of Oral Argument, *INS v. St Cyr,* No. 00–767, April 24, 2001.

14. Emphasis added.

15. INS, "Statement: Keeping Our Communities Safe Is INS's Top Priority" [undated; probably May 2000].

16. Margaret H. Taylor, "Behind the Scenes of *St. Cyr* and *Zadvydas:* Making Policy in the Midst of Litigation," *Georgetown Immigration Law Journal* 16.2 (winter 2002): 278–79.

17. Philip G. Schrag, *A Well-Founded Fear: The Congressional Battle to Save Political Asylum in America* (New York: Routledge, 2000), 152, 153, 150. Taylor, "Behind the Scenes of *St. Cyr* and *Zadvydas,*" 278.

18. These profiles are taken from CIEJ literature, except for Dawlett, which is in Brief *Amici Curiae* of Florida Immigrant Advocacy Center et al., *INS v. St. Cyr,* 7–8.

19. Jake Bernstein, "Lamar's Alien Agenda," *Texas Observer,* October 25, 2002.

20. Criminal alien figures from INS spokesperson Karen Kraushaar, e-mail correspondence with the author, October 15, 2002. Smith quoted in Eric

Schmitt, "Court to Take Up Deportation Rules," *New York Times*, April 22, 2001.

## CHAPTER 10: "SPEAK TO EVERY MEDIA"

1. Jennifer Gonnerman, "Inside Rikers Island: A Portrait of the Nation's Largest Penal Colony," *Village Voice*, December 19, 2000.
2. My thanks to reporter Kim Alphandary for providing me with a tape of her interview.
3. This account of the March riot is based on Ben Ehrenreich, "Black and Blue on the Border," *LA Weekly*, March 27–April 2, 1998.
4. Los Angeles INS's Leonardo Kovensky quoted in Lillian de la Torre-Jimenez, "Inmigrante acusa al INS de maltratado," *La Opinión*, July 17, 1998, 1B (my translation).
5. Lillian de la Torre-Jimenez, "Huelga de hambre en carcel del INS," *La Opinión*, July 9, 1998; Ehrenreich, "Black and Blue on the Border"; author interview with the AFSC's Roberto Martinez.
6. Former INS general counsel David Martin and unnamed Senate source quoted in Sam Skolnik, "New Law, Overcrowded Facilities Exacerbate INS's Difficulties," *Texas Lawyer*, October 12, 1998, 7.
7. It's no accident that the expanding notions of illegality (i.e., the 1996 laws) and of extralegal rightness (i.e., we are not citizens, but it's unfair to apply these laws to us) coincide. Saskia Sassen writes: "When the objects of stronger police action include an ever-expanding spectrum of people—immigrant women, men and children—sooner or later the state will get caught in the expanding web of civil and human rights. It will then violate those rights, interfering with the functioning of civil society" (*Guests and Aliens* [New York: New Press, 1999], xix); she also argues that "immigration policy making can no longer be confined to national governments" (153).
8. Bachir gave the Amnesty International Refugee Office permission to share these notes with me.
9. Ben Ehrenreich, "Hunger Strikes and Body Blows," *LA Weekly*, July 24–30, 1998; AFSC U.S./Mexico Border Program, "Update: El Centro Hunger Strike," San Diego, July 15, 1998.
10. Ann S. Kim, "Detainee: Feds Failed to Stop Hunger Strike," Associated Press, August 24, 1999. County corrections official Marc Cusson acknowledges in this article that the INS moved some prisoners "'because some of them were identified as inmate leaders, which is not

a good thing to allow to continue in any correctional facility.'" Kim's article also notes that detainees had been calling the Associated Press from the Hillsborough County jail until "officials began preventing outgoing calls to the media. After phone calls with the detainees were blocked, officials said the hunger strike was over."

11. Michael Beebe, "Nondeportable Detainees Spend Years of Confinement in Legal Limbo," *Buffalo News,* February 6, 2000.

12. Lisa Rogers, "INS Officials in Gadsden to Make Official Announcement of Jail Expansion Contract," *Gadsden Times,* March 6, 2001.

13. *Rogers et al. v. Etowah County,* 717 F.Supp. 778, N.D. Ala. 1989.

14. Judge U. W. Clemon was referring to Morgan County, not to Etowah County, but his words provide vivid context: "The sardine-can appearance of its cell units more nearly resemble the holding units of slave ships during the Middle Passage of the 18th century than anything in the 21st century." Quoted in David Firestone, "Packed Alabama Jails Draw Ire of Courts Again," *New York Times,* May 1, 2001, A1.

15. United States Government Memorandum from Richard G. Vinet, General Attorney, INS, San Pedro, Calif.; to Rosemary Melville, INS Deputy District Director, Los Angeles, March 25, 1998.

16. Letter from attorney Kamal Nawash to INS, March 12, 1999; letter from Hasan Rahman, Chief Representative of PLO to U.S., to Richard G. Vinet, General Attorney, INS, San Pedro, Calif., November 3, 1998.

17. John Allard, "Inmates Hold Prison Guard, Nurse Hostage," *The State,* January 17, 2000.

18. Taylor spoke to Donaldson on ABC's *Prime Time Live* in December 1992. Also see Scott Hadly, "Navy Reassigns Case Involving 3 Officers," *Los Angeles Times,* March 27, 1994; "San Diego Officer to Review Navy Whistle-Blower Case," *Los Angeles Daily News,* April 2, 1994; "Navy Abandons Charges against Whistle-Blower," *Orlando Sentinel,* March 29, 1994.

19. See *Nabil Ahmed Soliman v. United States,* U.S. Court of Appeals for the Eleventh Circuit, No. 01–11313-FF.

20. Nina Siegal, "After 2 Years in Deportation Fight, a Hunger Strike," *New York Times,* January 31, 2000, B5. Although the U.S. Attorney's Office in Birmingham repeatedly declined my requests for specific documents it cited in its case against Soliman, it did send me a copy of one decision favorable to the government, which I had not requested.

21. Government's Memorandum in Support of Nabil Soliman's Civil Immigration Detention and Force feeding Order, *In Re: Nabil Ahmed Soliman,* 134 F. Supp. 2d 1238, N.D. Ala. 2001.

22.  Paul Kovac, "Force feeding of Detained Aliens," in U.S. Department of Justice, *Immigration Litigation Bulletin* 5.1 (January 31, 2001).

23.  Memorandum Opinion of Judge Lynwood Smith, *In Re: Nabil Ahmed Soliman.*

24.  On "controlled reaction": Letter from G. Michael Shehi, M.D., to George Taylor, INS, January 20, 2001; Medical Supervisor's notes on Bachir from Healthworks, Inc., Etowah Co. Detention Center, July 4, August 11, and August 16, 2000.

25.  Rose Livingston, "Palestinian Can't Go Home, but Will Leave Etowah Jail," *Birmingham News,* February 2, 2000. Livingston's other articles on Hassan in the *Birmingham News* are "Palestinian in Limbo Sits in Gadsden Jail," January 9, 2000; "Palestinian Man's Case Reviewed," January 27, 2000; and "Palestinian Savors Freedom," February 3, 2000.

26.  INS, "Conditions of Release under an Order of Supervision—Additional Conditions," April 2001. Bachir did not provide me with a copy of the release conditions. According to attorney Sophie Feal, these conditions became obsolete with Bachir's rearrest. His subsequent release conditions did not include the ban on media contact, according to attorney Joanne Macri.

27.  INS, "Order of Supervision," May 29, 2001. Author interviews with Lt. Paul Prince, Garden Grove Police Department; receptionist in North (Orange County) Judicial District Court; and Anaheim City Attorney (Family Court) Mark Logan, February 27, 2002. Bachir's violations of the restraining orders in June 2001 and September 2001 were phone calls to the house of the protected parties, according to Anaheim Police Department Lieutenant Joe Vargas (author interview, July 11, 2003).

28.  For "Heads up!!!": e-mail message from INS official Ruben A. Cortina [to INS officials], Re: Bachir, February 8, 2002. Venturella e-mails, February 8, 2002. Description of restraints and alleged plane incident: INS San Pedro SPC, Use of Force Report, from Jerry L. Petrey Jr, Detention Enforcement Officer, to Officer in Charge, February 15, 2002. INS spokesperson Karen Kraushaar read to me from an account giving essentially this INS version of the alleged plane incident; interview, February 27, 2002. The criminal indictment was *United States v. Mohammad Mahmoud Bachir,* CR 02–0335-LGB, Central District of Calif., Los Angeles. Bachir alleges injuries at the hands of the officers, but even aside from that, see chap. 4, note 5, on this INS and Border Patrol practice.

29.  Interviews and e-mail correspondence with federal public defender Humberto Diaz. Letter from Los Angeles Deputy City Attorney Dikran H. Sassounian to Diaz, July 8, 2002. Before Bachir's plea agreement,

Diaz asked me to testify about the INS's targeting of Bachir while he was in detention, and Diaz provided the judge and government attorneys with an earlier version of this chapter; the judge declined to allow such testimony.

30. On Bachir's reporting absence and wife's contact with Venturella: author interviews and e-mail correspondence with Sophie Feal, Volunteers Lawyers Project, Buffalo, N.Y. INS/BICE's detention of Bachir was now in apparent violation of the Supreme Court ruling in *Zadvydas v. Davis,* which held that detention must generally be limited to six months beyond the date of a removal order when there is no reasonably fore-seeable chance of actually removing the alien.

31. Office of the Attorney General, Memorandum for James W. Ziglar, Commmissioner, Immigration and Naturalization Service, from John Ashcroft, Subject: Nabil Ahmed Soliman, June 7, 2002. This memo was attached to the government's motion in the Eleventh Circuit to dismiss the case as moot. In it, Ashcroft states: "The Secretary of State has obtained, and forwarded to me, assurances from the government of Egypt that Mr. Soliman would not be tortured if he were removed there. . . . After consulting with the Secretary of State and taking into account all relevant considerations, including human rights practices in Egypt, I have determined that these assurances are sufficiently reliable to allow Mr. Soliman's removal to Egypt." In early 2003, however, the State Department reported that accounts of torture by Egyptian security serv-ices in 2002 were "numerous" and "credible" (U.S. Department of State, Bureau of Democracy, Human Rights and Labor, *Country Reports on Human Rights Practices—2002—Egypt,* March 31, 2003).

32. U.S. Embassy, Public Affairs Section, Cairo, "The United States Returns Egyptian Accused of Conspiracy in Sadat Assassination," July 5, 2002. Muntasir al-Zayat, Soliman's attorney back in Cairo, "told the BBC that Mr Soliman was no[t] in fact convicted of participation in the assassination of Sadat," as claimed by the U.S. Embassy's statement, "but of being an Islamic Jihad member in mass trials that followed Sadat's killing. Mr Zayat was himself a defendant in these mass trials" ("U.S. Hands over Egyptian Militant," *BBC News* On-line, June 16, 2002).

33. Amnesty International, "Forcible Return/Fear of Torture or Ill Treat-ment: Egypt/USA: Nabil Ahmad Soliman," AI Index: MDI 12/032/2002, September 18, 2002. Because it appears that Soliman's incommunicado custody immediately followed the U.S. Embassy's announcement of his arrival in Cairo, I asked U.S. embassy spokesperson Philip Frayne several times (via e-mail and phone messages) whether the embassy knew where

Soliman was imprisoned at the time Amnesty International described him as being incommunicado; Frayne did not reply, though he had promptly answered my other questions about the case.

34. On "reliable" assurances: see note 31 above. Frayne, "I can't say": e-mail correspondence with the author, March 2003. Frayne also wrote that "[Soliman] has not complained to us about having been tortured"; and, later, that the assurances from Egypt were in writing but that he could not "release that document."

35. Egyptian Organization for Human Rights, "At the First Day of 2003: Members of 'Muslim Brotherhood' Have Been Arrested," January 8, 2003. Also see BBC News, "U.S. Hands over Egyptian Militant."


## CHAPTER 11: GOOD AND EVIL IN NEW ENGLAND

1. Bill Pomerleau, "Where Did All the Immigrants Go? Jail Profits Leave with INS Detainees," *Corrections Technology and Management,* July–August 2000, 56–59.

2. Associated Press, "Legal Aide Accused of Inciting Immigrants; Access Limited," *Boston Globe,* February 16, 1998, B3.

3. David R. Dow and Mark Dow, eds., *Machinery of Death: The Reality of America's Death Penalty Regime* (New York: Routledge, 2002), 179.

4. Unless otherwise noted, these allegations are taken from numerous letters sent to INS officials by lawyers and detainees. Copies were later included in a packet of materials sent by Boston's Political Asylum/ Immigration Representation Project to David Vincinanzo in the U.S. Attorney's Office in Concord, once the Justice Department had begun its own investigation of the Hillsborough jail. The "boogie board" allegation was made by Armand Trudeau, a former Hillsborough jail correctional officer; Pat Grossmith, "Crisis at the County Jail: Mother: Daughter, 19, Denied Medicine and Ogled in Shower," Manchester *Union Leader,* February 7, 2000. Solitary confinement because of overcrowding: interview with Susan Church. "It defies logic": quoted in Pat Grossmith, "Crisis at the County Jail: Inmates Tell Disturbing Jail Tales," Manchester *Union Leader,* February 7, 2000.

5. Pat Grossmith, "Valley St. Jail Called State's Worst," Manchester *Union Leader,* January 29, 2000.

6. Nancy West, "Hillsborough County Jail Chief Praised, Knocked," Manchester *Union Leader,* March 5, 2000.

7. Nancy West, "Inmate Says Man Who Died Was Beaten in Jail," Manchester *Union Leader,* March 5, 2000.

8.    Pat Grossmith, "County Jail Boss on Hot Spot for Probe Comments," Manchester *Union Leader,* February 3, 2000. Immigration advocates had been making INS officials aware of allegations of abuse at Hillsborough for some time, as we have seen. Nevertheless, it was only when U.S. Attorney Paul Gagnon warned the INS that its detainees might be in danger at Hillsborough that the agency removed them (author interview with Assistant U.S. Attorney Dan Feith, June 18, 2003).

9.    Grossmith, "Valley St. Jail Called State's Worst."

10.   In August 2002 the INS held 21,087 detainees; 19,184 were men, 1,899 were women, and 4 were categorized as "unknown." One detainee (female) was under a year old; five women and seventy-six men were over sixty-five years old. U.S. Department of Justice, Immigration and Naturalization Service, Office of Policy and Planning, *Monthly Detention Report,* August 2002.

11.   Transcript of Oral Decision of the Immigration Judge (Patricia Sheppard), Executive Office for Immigration Review, Boston, *In the Matter of Elizabeth Nabatanzi,* September 10, 1999.

12.   John Hope, "INS Detainee Files Suit," *York Daily Record,* December 6, 2002, 4C. Nabatanzi's handwritten complaint, *Elizabeth Nabatanzi v. Warden Thomas Hogan et al.,* was filed at the Harrisburg courthouse on November 26, 2003. John Hope kindly provided me with a copy.

13.   In yet another example of the INS's reflexive secrecy, its spokesperson Karen Kraushaar refused to comment on rumors that it had ended its relationship with ACI Cranston, saying that the agency does not "discuss contractual matters publicly"; the assistant to the director at the jail, however, confirmed that the INS still had a contract there. (Author interviews, 2003.)

14.   *Hall v. INS,* Decision and Order, U.S. District Court for the District of Rhode Island, C.A. No. 02-1038.


CHAPTER 12: OUT WEST

1.    Fauziya Kassindja and Layli Miller Bashir, *Do They Hear You When You Cry* (New York: Delacorte Press, 1998), 462.

2.    The image of "squeezing the balloon" has been used informally to describe the border strategy, but I have not found it in any official description.

3.    In a review of border strategy, the General Accounting Office stated: "The [INS] strategy to strengthen the border called for 'prevention through deterrence,' that is raising the risk of apprehension for illegal aliens to

'make it so difficult and so costly to enter this country illegally that fewer individuals even try.' The objectives of the strategy were to close off the routes most frequently used by smugglers and illegal aliens (generally through urban areas) and shift traffic through the ports of entry that inspect travelers or over areas that were more remote and difficult to cross. *With the traditional routes disrupted, INS expected that illegal alien traffic would either be deterred or forced over terrain less suited for crossing,* where INS believed it would have the tactical advantage." Despite that summary, the report continues: "Some data indicate that . . . shifting illegal alien traffic to areas that are more remote and difficult to cross has resulted in *an unanticipated effect*—that is, a change in the causes and locations of the deaths of some illegal aliens who attempt to cross the border at these remote border areas." (U.S. General Accounting Office, *Illegal Immigration: Status of Southwest Border Strategy Implementation,* May 1999, GAO/GGD-99-44, 3, 21; emphasis added.)

4.  Joseph Nevins, *Operation Gatekeeper: The Rise of the "Illegal Alien" and the Making of the U.S.-Mexico Boundary* (New York: Routledge, 2002), 53–54.

5.  Claudia Smith, California Rural Legal Assistance, Letters to Mark Reed, INS District Director, San Diego (December 29, 1995) and to Chief Border Patrol Agent Johnny Williams, San Diego (March 27, 1996). Richard C. Hoy, Regional Counsel, Southwest Region, "Regional Concept—Part Two," *I&N Reporter* [a newsletter of the INS], April 1956.

6.  Greene quoted in Somini Sengupta and Christopher Drew, "A Nation Challenged: The Immigration Agency; Effort to Discover Terrorists among Illegal Aliens Makes Glacial Progress, Critics Say," *New York Times,* November 12, 2001.

7.  Nevins, *Operation Gatekeeper,* 102, 224 n. 58. Marian L. Smith, "Race, Nationality, and Reality: INS Administration of Racial Provisions in U.S. Immigration and Nationality Law Since 1898," *Prologue,* Quarterly of the National Archives and Records Administrative, 34.2 (summer 2002): 104. Cadman, "Though some of you": I heard this myself at the Knight Center ceremony in Miami when Haitian-born Gaston Jolicoeur and several hundred others became U.S. citizens on January 25, 1994.

8.  Testimony of Joseph R. Greene, Acting Executive Associate Commissioner for Field Operations, Immigration & Naturalization Service, Before the House Committee on Government Reform, Subcommittees on Government Efficiency, Financial Management and Intergovernmental Relations; Criminal Justice, Drug Policy and Human Resources;

and National Security, Veterans Affairs and International Relations on INS's Relationship with State and Local Law Enforcement, November 13, 2001.

CHAPTER 13: DEAD TIME

1.  Solomon Volkov, *Conversations with Joseph Brodsky: A Poet's Journey through the Twentieth Century,* trans. Marian Schwartz (New York: Free Press, 1998), 69. Siobhan Dowd, ed., *This Prison Where I Live: The PEN Anthology of Imprisoned Writers* (London: Cassell, 1996), xi.
2.  Transcript of Oral Argument, *Ma v. Reno,* No. 99–7791, 43.
3.  Ibid., 7.
4.  *Ma v. Ashcroft,* U.S. Court of Appeals for the Ninth Circuit, No. 99–35976, D.C. No. CV-99-00151-RSL, Opinion on Remand and Opinion, July 27, 2001.
5.  Custody determination documents are included as exhibits in the pleadings of *Ma v. Reno,* No. 99-7791.
6.  Raymond Williams, *Keywords: A Vocabulary of Culture and Society* (New York: Oxford University Press, 1983), 49.
7.  *Ma v. Reno,* U.S. District Court, Western District of Washington, Respondents' Motion for Stay Pending Appeal, U.S. District Court for the Western District of Washington, 2.
8.  Tony Perez-Giese, "Waiting to Exile," Denver *Westword,* January 21, 1999.
9.  Transcript of Oral Argument, *Ma v. Reno,* No. 99-7791, 53–54.
10. *Jean Eddy Le Pen v. INS,* U.S. District Court, Eastern District of California, No. CV-F-99-5098 AWI HGB P, Petitioner's Response to Respondent INS's Answer to the April 11, 2000, Order to Show Cause/ Petitioner's Brief in Support of Petition for Writ of Habeas Corpus, Motion for Release, 40, 42. Emphasis added.
11. Lourdes Medrano Leslie, "Cambodian Immigrants Who Broke Laws Fear Deportation under New Treaty," Minneapolis *Star Tribune,* September 16, 2002.
12. U.S. Department of Justice, Attorney General Prepared Remarks, "Long-Term INS Detainees/Colorado Safe Neighborhoods Event," July 19, 2001.
13. On 510 lifers in Louisiana: New Orleans *Times-Picayune* May 25, 2001. The numbers are confusing, in part because the INS itself determines which detainees are eligible for review under *Zadvydas* in the first place. According to the Catholic Legal Immigration Network (CLINIC), the

INS reported in October 2001 that of 1,800 cases identified for *Zadvydas* review, 830 persons had been released. Five months later the INS released figures showing that 950 persons "with removal orders of six months or older, remained detained." Laurie Joyce, "INS Detention Post-*Zadvydas v. Davis*, Feb. 2002–Aug. 2002," CLINIC (Los Angeles). Almost two years after the Supreme Court ruling, of 2,067 *Zadvydas* cases reviewed, "just under half" remained detained, according to Michael Riley, "Lawsuits Decry 'Indefinite' Detentions," *Denver Post*, March 20, 2003.

On 1,750 Cuban lifers: U.S. Department of Justice, Petition for a Write of Certiorari, U.S. Supreme Court, *Snyder v. Rosales-Garcia*, No. 02-1464, April 2003. Also see chap. 14, note 10.

One victim lucky enough to surface through the new "developing procedures" and to find representation was Donald Seretse-Khama. District of Columbia District Court Judge John D. Bates's decision in *Seretse-Khama v. Ashcroft* (No. 02-0955) is devoted to a review of the INS's reviews of the detainee, and it illustrates not the "hollow nature" of the review process, as is so often the case, but rather the black hole of unmonitored INS custody even when the review itself is fair.

Seretse-Khama was born in Liberia and came to the United States when he was eight; he has lived here ever since. In 1990 he became a legal permanent resident and three years later was convicted of possession with intent to distribute cocaine. He was sentenced to eight years in the Virginia Department of Corrections. After early release, Seretse-Khama was transferred to INS custody in 1998 and held without bond. As part of the deportation process, the detainee submitted to an interview with the Liberian consulate in order to arrange travel documents, without which the deportation cannot legally be carried out. "Petitioner truthfully answered [the consulate's] questions," a judge later wrote, "and correctly stated the capital of Liberia and the president's name. . . . He also stated that he did not have any family in Liberia." His sister, stepfather, and stepmother lived in Virginia.

"More than three months after" Seretse-Khama's first custody review, Liberia had not issued travel documents to take him back. INS deportation officer Ashly Ocasio "recommended petitioner's release from INS custody, stating that petitioner would not pose a threat to the community." But "the supervisory detention officer did not concur" with the release decision, and Seretse-Khama remained in custody. Two and half months later there was another review. This time the INS officer wrote: "I have spoken with the detainee on numerous occasions. I have concluded that he literally has no family in Liberia. The Liberia Embassy does not want to send back. Unfortunately, without the endorsement of the Liberia Embassy, getting a document is impossible."

Again Ocasio recommended release, and this time the supervisor agreed. Seretse-Khama was to be let go "under an order of supervision," but he wasn't. *"There is nothing in the record explaining why [he] remains detained and was not released at that time,"* the judge wrote.

Three months later Seretse-Khama was charged with and pled guilty to attempting to injure a jail employee and destroying property. He received an effective sentence of six months, for the course of which he was transferred to U.S. Marshal custody. Then, when he was back in INS custody, officer Ocasio once again interviewed him and once more recommended supervised release, this time with $12,000 bond. She explained:

The Liberian Consulate verified that the subject is Liberian, however, will not issue a travel document. . . . The Embassy is of the belief that the subject really has no ties to Liberia. He came to the US as a child and does not speak the language. The Embassy is of the opinion that the subject will become a public charge because there is absolutely no family in Liberia.

He was not released.

Continuing his chronology, Judge Bates makes note of the *Zadvydas* decision in June 2001. Four months later the INS notified Seretse-Khama that his detention would continue. Supervisory deportation officer Neil Acui soon wrote to the still unresponsive Liberian Consulate: "It is now incumbent upon the [INS] to carry out this deportation order," apparently taking note of the new law that it was now necessary to flout. "Without explanation, that decision informed him that '[t]he INS is pending receipt of your travel document and you will be removed in the reasonably foreseeable future.'" This statement, the judge wrote, "was simply and blatantly false." Seretse-Khama had now been detained for about three years, not including the six-month sentence for his frustrated explosion.

Another seven months passed, and Seretse-Khama filed suit in Bates's court. The INS's initial response was an effort to use its relationship with the local jail as a loophole to escape accountability. Prisoners' habeas corpus petitions typically name as defendants a variety of officials who play a role in their incarceration. Seretse-Khama originally sued the INS but failed to name as a codefendant Edward L. Crosley, superintendent of the Central Virginia Regional Jail in Orange, where he was being held.

The INS argued that the judge must dismiss the case because the unnamed warden "is the true custodian." Later the government tried another tactic, arguing that INS District Director Warren Lewis, whom the suit named, was in fact "the proper respondent and custodian" but that Judge Bates had no jurisdiction over the detention; the judge presided in the District of Columbia, went this argument, and although INS official Lewis's office was in Arlington—within the judge's jurisdiction—"his actions . . . all occurred in the Western district of Virginia" where the jail is, outside the court's jurisdiction. "The government has taken this Court and petitioner on a very troubling procedural ride," the judge wrote.

Two weeks after the prisoner filed suit, the INS conducted another review. This time the officer recommended his continued detention, writing that Seretse-Khama "has not made an attempt to find an alternate country to be removed to. In addition, he still remains positioned on not returning to Liberia." Officer Ocasio further explained:

The Service needs to vigorously pursue the issuance of a travel document and seek more assistance from HQ. The last attempt was approximately 8 months ago. Several major issues concerning foreign nationals has arisen over the last eight months and I believe that the Service (HQ) will be successful in obtaining a travel document. . . . Based on the subject's behavior while in Service custody and the belief that a document is still obtainable with the assistance of HQ, it is my recommendation that he remain in custody.

In a letter to Seretse-Khama, the INS added:

After both interviews and the most recent request, the consulate informed the [INS] that you are in fact a citizen of Liberia. However, they were not willing to issue a travel document because you told the consulate that you did not want to go back to Liberia. By this action, you have actively worked to prevent your own departure from the United States.

This was apparently a direct attempt to use the loophole in *Zadvydas,* which says that if the detainee is responsible for preventing the diplomatic arrangements for deportation, then his detention may continue. Judge Bates disapprovingly noted the timing of this new logic:

The recent assertion of this additional explanation for petitioner's detention pending removal is not credible. Moreover . . . petitioner's simple and honest explanation that he did not want to return to a country to which he had no ties, without any accompanying affirmative lack of cooperation, is not a refusal to cooperate that supports an extension of detention.

The judge ordered Seretse-Khama's supervised release on bond. "There is little doubt that the public interest would be better served here by protecting the petitioner's liberty interest," he wrote. Seretse-Khama was freed after four years in INS custody.

14. Written Decision of the Immigration Judge (Kristin W. Olmanson), U.S. Department of Justice, Executive Office for Immigration Review, Bloomington, Minn., *In the Matter of Ayub Haji Abukar,* in Removal Proceedings, March 7, 2000. Abukar's appeal to the BIA was dismissed.

15. As of December 2003 the United States was still not carrying out deportations to Iraq, according to a BICE spokesperson.

16. On "whether 'Somalia' *is* a country": see U.S. Magistrate Judge Arthur J. Boylan, Report and Recommendation, *Jama v. INS,* U.S. District Court, District of Minnesota, Civ. No. 01-1172 JRT/AJB, note 7.

17. For "there is no . . . government that would be offended": government brief as quoted in *Abukar v. Ashcroft,* U.S. District Court, District of Minnesota, Civ. No. 01-242 JRT/AJB, Petitioner's Memorandum in Support of Amended Habeas Corpus and Opposition to Respondent's Return, Motion to Dismiss, and Memorandum in Support. For "It is difficult for the Court to see": U.S. District Judge John R. Tunheim, Memorandum Opinion and Order Adopting the Report and Recommendation of the Magistrate Judge, *Jama v. INS,* U.S. District Court, District of Minnesota, Civ. No. 01-1172 JRT/AJB.

18. Brian Hutchinson, "Snatched," *Seattle Weekly,* March 21–27, 2002; INS statement e-mailed from INS Public Affairs officer Karen Kraushaar, February 27, 2002. The INS statement explicitly responds to the *Times* of London account of the deportations; see note 19, below.

19. Janine DiGiovanni, "How American Dream Faded in Downtown Mogadishu," *Times Online,* February 26, 2002.

20. Hate Free Zone Campaign of Washington, "INS Detaining Somalis for Deportation to Somalia," November 13, 2002. On Somali in Buffalo: Author interview with attorney Bonnie Crogan Mazur, April 2003.

21. See Judge Marsha J. Pechman's Order Granting Injunction and Certifying Class, *Yusuf Ali Ali v. Ashcroft,* U.S. District Court, Western District of Washington at Seattle, No. CO2-2304P, January 17, 2003. According to Seattle attorney Karol Brown, "The government made no attempt to link any detained or deportable Somali to terrorism. Their only argument was that the AG needed the 'tool' of deportation to fight terrorism, and

some allegations that there were terrorist activities occurring within Somalia." The INS's Office of Immigration Litigation and its Public Affairs office refused to clarify their terrorist allusions when I asked. For "refused to provide": Brown, e-mail correspondence, October 2003.

## CHAPTER 14: MARIEL CUBANS

1. Notification of Parole Denial (Aviso Final de Denegación de la Libertad Condicional), May 30, 2002 (author's translation from Spanish). These same reasons for denial are routinely given in other Mariel cases, according to ACLU Immigrants' Rights Project attorney Judy Rabinovitz.

2. INS (now Bureau of Immigration and Customs Enforcement) Public Affairs officer Temple Black of New Orleans disputes this account. Without mentioning specific detainee names, I asked him why the INS prohibits detainees from participating in programs at county jails even when the jail itself would allow it; this is a practice reported by other Louisiana jails as well. Black replied:

We do not prohibit detainees in parish jails from doing anything. What detainees can or cannot do while in a parish jail is the decision of the sheriff or jailer running that particular jail. Many of them have policies restricting the activities of detainees they are holding for other entities (in this case, they are holding them for us—they are not state prisoners) for liability and security reasons.

Regardless, it would be ridiculous to state that we would prohibit a detainee from participating in an educational program. There may be state or parish rules that prohibit them from spending state funding for certain programs on non-state detainees. As far as outside activities, it is a security matter. I'm sure they don't prohibit them from "outside activities" such as exercising in a secure area. Certainly, they are not going to allow them "trustee" status that would allow them to go outside a secure area of the facility unguarded. They are responsible for making sure that the detainee doesn't escape.

(E-mail correspondence, April 22, 2003)

When I summarized INS spokesperson Black's response to Lt. Col. Bruce LaFargue, warden of the Calcasieu Parish Jail, LaFargue said: "He knows better than that." According to LaFargue, jail personnel provided security at the welding class—sufficient security to satisfy the warden—but the INS still refused to allow Abreu to attend.

3.  Sally Sandidge, "On the Road Again," *Atlanta Lawyer,* Fourth Quarter 1992, 9.

4.  Statement of Joseph Greene, Acting Deputy Executive Associate Commissioner, Before the House Committee on the Judiciary, Subcommittee on Immigration and Claims, Regarding a Review of Department of Justice Immigration Detention Policies, December 19, 2001.

5.  Quoted from the decision in *Rosales-Garcia v. Holland* and *Carballo v. Luttrell,* Nos. 99-5683/5698, U.S. Court of Appeals for the Sixth Circuit, March 5, 2003.

6.  *Zadvydas v. Davis,* No. 99-7791.

7.  Estela Bravo, *The Cuban Excludables* (Prodoc, 1995).

8.  *Rosales-Garcia v. Holland* and *Carballo v. Luttrell,* Nos. 99-5683/5698, U.S. Court of Appeals for the Sixth Circuit, March 5, 2003.

9.  Transcript of Oral Argument, *Zadvydas v. Davis,* 52–53. Justice Ginsburg's question about "dumping" someone in the sea is an allusion to Justice Robert Jackson's dissenting opinion in *Mezei.*

10. On Atlanta suicide attempts: Gary Leshaw, "Atlanta's Cuban Detainees: A Retrospective," *Atlanta Lawyer,* Fourth Quarter 1992, 12.

    On "approximately 1,750 Mariel Cubans" detained: quoted from the Department of Justice's April 2003 Petition for a Writ of Certiori, U.S. Supreme Court, *Snyder v. Rosales-Garcia.* Four years earlier, INS Public Affairs spokesperson Karen Kraushaar provided the same figure to Dan Malone, then a reporter for the *Dallas Morning News.* (E-mail correspondence from Kraushaar to Malone, November 16, 1999; citing detention figures as of September 1999.) In November 2003, according to BICE Public Affairs, there were 1,100 Mariel Cubans in detention nationwide.

    Regarding hundreds more doing time: As of April 3, 2003, there were 366 Mariel Cubans and 337 other Cubans serving criminal sentences in BOP facilities, according to BOP spokesperson Carla Wilson. The INS/BICE also has the authority to detain Cubans who may be doing time in state prisons or local jails.

    On agreement to return almost 2,746 Mariels: Alfonso Chardy and Paul Anderson, "1500 Mariel Felons to Be Sent Back," *Miami Herald,* September 29, 1993. On suspension a year later: Mark S. Hamm, *The Abandoned Ones: The Imprisonment and Uprising of the Mariel Boat People* (Boston: Northeastern University Press, 1995), 222, 223.

11. Hamm, *The Abandoned Ones,* 21, 15, 40, 34, 36, 31.

12. Trott said: "We'd rather not get into the details of that." CNN *NewsDay* broadcast, November 23, 1987.

13. For "provided generally that all detainees": Leshaw, "Atlanta's Cuban Detainees," 15. For "To recommend release": Karla Harr, "Mariel Cubans: The Forgotten Lifers," *Migration World* 27.5 (1999). "Procedures" written by the Cuban Review Panel specify that nonlawyers may represent detainees in these hearings. The procedures also specify that Mariel Cuban prisoners should not have to go through the often time-consuming process of obtaining their own files through FOIA requests, a process especially frustrating if not futile since detainees are regularly transferred between facilities. (INS Central Office, Detention and Deportation Division, "The Cuban Review Plan Process" [typescript with attachments; undated, ca. 1989]). Nevertheless, Mariel Cuban detainees are forced to use the FOIA to obtain their own files. (Author correspondence with Mariel Cuban detainee; Helen Morris, "Detention Reviews for Long-Term Detainees," *Bender's Immigration Bulletin*, June 15, 1999, 611.)

14. The term "halfway house failure" is from the INS's "Cuban Review Plan Process." These "failures" not only send one back to prison or jail but also apparently reset the clock on detention length and skew the already scant government information available. The Rodriguez story is from Daniel Golden, "U.S. No Haven for These Cuban Refugees," *Boston Globe,* March 29, 1987, A23. The other halfway house anecdotes were told to me by Mariel Cubans.

15. Initialed examples are from Harr, "Mariel Cubans: The Forgotten Lifers"; Leshaw, "Atlanta's Cuban Detainees," 15; Sandidge, "On the Road Again," 8.

   In August 2003 I requested permission to observe a certain Mariel Cuban detainee's panel review, but the INS denied it on the basis that these hearings are not open to the public.

16. INS official(s) quoted in Supplemental Brief for the Petitioner-Appellant, *Reynero Arteaga Carballo v. Mark Luttrell and INS,* Sixth Circuit Court of Appeals, No. 99-5698, January 16, 2002.

17. Leshaw, "Atlanta's Cuban Detainees," 9.

18. BORTAC, untitled videotape of Atlanta and Oakdale uprisings (November 1987), INS Historical Reference Library, Washington, D.C.

19. On at least 160 Mariels detained: Dan Malone, "851 Detained for Years in INS Centers," *Dallas Morning News,* April 1, 2001, A1.

20. Hannah Arendt, *Eichmann in Jerusalem: A Report on the Banality of Evil* (New York: Viking Press, 1963), 289. The next day, the INS's Gueringer would tell a Louisiana warden not to speak with me. In 1999 St. Martinville Parish Jail warden Todd Louviere was held hostage by Mariel

Cuban detainees, yet he was reportedly sympathetic to their cause. (Some of the Cubans were returned to Cuba, as they demanded; others were kept here and charged with kidnapping.) Louvierre had agreed to an interview, but in St. Martinville he told me by phone that he had changed his mind because Gueringer had advised him not to do it.

Meanwhile, some 130 Pakistanis rounded up after September 11 were being moved from New Jersey jails to a detention center in Waterproof, Louisiana, on the Mississippi border, for easy transfer to an airbase near Alexandria for deportation. An INS official in Waterproof reportedly told a Florida attorney that he had been instructed not to confirm the presence of the Pakistanis.

21. On Gomez's swallowing razor blades as one reason for continuing her detention: Cuban Review Summary Sheet, April 23, 2001; Final Notice of Parole Denial, June 26, 2001. On character references and Gomez's not knowing where she would live if released: Cuban Review Summary Sheet, March 16, 2000.

22. Catholic Legal Immigration Network, *The Needless Detention of Immigrants in the United States* (Washington, D.C., August 2000), 27.

23. Gomez was speaking here to Judy Rabinovitz. Some of Gomez's words are quoted from this taped interview with Rabinovitz and are used here with the permission of both women. (Rabinovitz spoke to Gomez at the New Iberia jail in 2002. As Rabinovitz was speaking with Cuban detainee Barbara Perera there, the warden forced Rabinovitz to leave.) Other Gomez quotations are taken from a written account of her experiences that she submitted with a habeas corpus petition and sent to me.

24. Jesus Abreu was released in spring 2003. The INS/BICE retains the authority to take him back into custody "at any time for almost any reason. . . . [He] need not do anything for the INS to revoke his parole" (see note 5 above).

# SELECTED BIBLIOGRAPHY

Abramsky, Sasha. *Hard Time Blues.* New York: St. Martin's Press, 2002.

American Civil Liberties Union Immigrants' Rights Project. *Justice Detained: Conditions at the Varick Street Immigration Detention Center.* New York, 1993.

Amnesty International. *Concerns Regarding Post-September 11 Detentions in the USA.* New York, 2002.

——. *Detention of Asylum Seekers in the United States.* New York, n.d.

——. *Lost in the Labyrinth: Detention of Asylum-Seekers.* New York, September 1999.

——. *"Not part of my sentence": Violations of the Human Rights of Women in Custody.* New York, March 1999.

Anderson, Benedict. *Imagined Communities: Reflections on the Origin and Spread of Nationalism.* New York: Verso, 1991.

Anderson, Lloyd C. *Voices from a Southern Prison.* Athens: University of Georgia Press, 2000.

Andreas, Peter. *Border Games: Policing the U.S.-Mexico Divide.* Ithaca: Cornell University Press, 2000.

Arendt, Hannah. *Eichmann in Jerusalem: A Report on the Banality of Evil.* New York: Viking Press, 1963.

Belle, David, and Nicholas Wrathall. *Abandoned: The Betrayal of America's Immigrants.* Crowing Rooster Arts, New York, 2000. Documentary film.

Bravo, Estela. *The Cuban Excludables.* Prodoc, 1995. Documentary film.

Burnham, David. *Above the Law: Secret Deals, Political Fixes and Other Misadventures of the U.S. Department of Justice.* New York: Scribner, 1996.

Burton-Rose, Daniel, and Paul Wright, eds. *The Celling of America: An Inside Look at the U.S. Prison Industry.* Monroe, Me.: Common Courage Press, 1998.

Calavita, Kitty. *Inside the State: The Bracero Program, Immigration, and the I.N.S.* New York: Routledge, 1992.

Catholic Legal Immigration Network. *The Needless Detention of Immigrants in the United States: Why Are We Locking Up Asylum-Seekers, Children, Stateless Persons, Long-Term Permanent Residents, and Petty Offenders?* Washington, D.C., August 2000.

Chang, Nancy, and the Center for Constitutional Rights. *Silencing Political Dissent: How Post–September 11 Anti-Terrorism Measures Threaten Our Civil Liberties.* New York: Seven Stories Press and Open Media, 2002.

Chevigny, Bell Gale, ed. *Doing Time: 25 Years of Prison Writing.* New York: Arcade, 1999.

Chin, Ko-lin. *Smuggled Chinese: Clandestine Immigration to the United States.* Philadelphia: Temple University Press, 1999.

Cobb, Richard. *The Police and the People: French Popular Protest, 1789–1820.* London: Oxford University Press, 1970.

Cole, David. *No Equal Justice: Race and Class in the American Criminal Justice System.* New York: New Press, 1999.

Conroy, John. *Unspeakable Acts, Ordinary People: The Dynamics of Torture.* New York: Alfred A. Knopf, 2000.

Dempsey, James X., and David Cole. *Terrorism and the Constitution: Sacrificing Civil Liberties in the Name of National Security.* Washington, D.C.: First Amendment Foundation, 2002.

Dickens, Charles. *American Notes.* Centennial Edition. Geneva: Edito-Service S.A., n.d. [1942].

Dow, Mark. "Alien Watch." *Index on Censorship.* March, 1996.

———. "'Ambassadors and Assassins': Polishing the Image of Krome." *Haïti Progrès,* February 24, 1999.

———. "Behind the Razor Wire: Inside INS Detention Centers." *Covert Action Quarterly* 57 (summer 1996). Summarized with additional comments in "Inside INS Detention Centers: Racism, Abuse, and No Accountability," in Peter Phillips and Project Censored, *Censored 1997: The News That Didn't Make the News—The Year's Top 25 Censored News Stories.* New York: Seven Stories Press, 1997.

———. "Challenging the Limits Imposed by the INS on Reporting." *Nieman Reports,* 56.4 (winter 2002).

———. "Deception, Dehumanization, and the INS" (3 parts). *Haïti Progrès,* July 24, July 31, August 7, 1996.

———. "Des détenus africains à Krome: Les dernières victims de la discrimina-cion." *Haïti Progrès,* March 6, 1996.

———. "Enforcement Means You're Brutal." *Index on Censorship,* January 21, 2001 (on-line edition).

———. "FIX '96: New Laws Rip Families and Lives Apart." *Haïti Progrès,* June 21, 2000.

———. "'Freedom without Conditions': Resistance at Krome." *Haiti Insight* (National Coalition for Haitian Refugees) (winter 1993). Reprinted as "Lib-erté sans conditions: Résistance à Krome." *Haïti Progrès,* April 14, 1993.

———. "Hunger Strike at Immigration Detention Center in Queens." *Haïti Progrès,* September 8, 1999.

———. "'INS Females': Haitian Women Detained in Maryland." *Haïti Progrès,* March 12, 1997.

———. "L'INS organise une tournée de propagande au center de Krome." *Haïti Progrès,* May 8, 1996.

———. "Just Another African." *Index on Censorship.* May 8, 2000 (on-line edi-tion).

———. "The New Secret War against Immigrants." *Haïti Progrès,* January 30, 2002.

———. "No Exit: Detained at 'Export Plaza.'" *Texas Observer,* May 12, 2000.

———. "'Our Daily Ordeal Is Going Unnoticed': Cries for Help from Krome." *Haïti Progrès,* August 12, 1998.

———. "Secrecy, Power, Indefinite Detention" and "'Make It Hard for Them': A Hunger Strike against the INS." In *Prison Nation: The Warehousing of America's Poor,* ed. Tara Herivel and Paul Wright, 93–99, 269–73. New York: Routledge, 2003. (First published in *Index on Censorship,* March 2001; and *Prison Legal News,* August 2001, respectively.)

———. "We Know What INS Is Hiding." *Miami Herald,* November 11, 2001.

Dow, Mark, and Judy Greene. "Protest against a Prison in Kendal." *Miami Her-ald,* February 5, 2001.

Dowd, Siobhan, ed. *This Prison Where I Live: The PEN Anthology of Imprisoned Writers.* London: Cassell, 1996.

Dunn, Timothy J. *The Militarization of the U.S.-Mexican Border, 1978–1992: Low-Intensity Conflict Doctrine Comes Home.* Austin: Center for Mexican American Studies, University of Texas at Austin, 1996.

Dyer, Joel. *The Perpetual Prisoner Machine: How America Profits from Crime.* Boulder, Colo.: Westview Press, 2000.

Easterlin, Richard A., David Ward, et al. *Immigration: Dimensions of Ethnicity—Selections from the Harvard Encyclopedia of American Ethnic Groups.* Cam-bridge, Mass.: Belknap Press, 1982.

Einolf, Christopher J. *The Mercy Factory: Refugees and the American Asylum System.* Chicago: Ivan R. Dee, 2001.

Eves, Peter, and Gina Cunningham. *Mothers for Freedom: Hunger Strike at Krome Detention Center.* Ynot Productions, Miami, 1999. Short documentary film.

Farmer, Paul. *AIDS and Accusation: Haiti and the Geography of Blame.* Berkeley: University of California Press, 1992.

———. *The Uses of Haiti.* Monroe, Me.: Common Courage Press, 1994.

Florida Immigrant Advocacy Center. *Cries for Help: Medical Care at Krome Service Processing Center and in Florida's County Jails.* Miami, December 1999.

———. *Florida County Jails: INS's Secret Detention World.* Miami, November 1997.

———. *INS Detainees in Florida: A Double Standard of Treatment.* Miami, December 2001.

———. *INS Detainees in Florida: A Double Standard of Treatment—Supplement.* Miami, January–April 2002.

———. *Krome's Invisible Prisoners: Cycles of Abuse and Neglect.* Miami, July 1996.

Foucault, Michel. *Discipline and Punish: The Birth of the Prison.* Trans. Alan Sheridan. New York: Vintage Books, 1977.

Gallagher, Mary. *¿De dónde?* New York: Dramatists Play Service, 1991.

Gelbspan, Ross. *Break-ins, Death Threats and the FBI: The Covert War against the Central America Movement.* Boston: South End Press, 1991.

Genet, Jean. *The Thief's Journal.* Trans. Bernard Frechtman. Toronto: Bantam Books, 1964.

Griswold, Erwin N. *The Fifth Amendment Today.* Cambridge, Mass.: Harvard University Press, 1955.

Haitian Refugee Center. "Conditions at Krome North Service Processing Center." Miami, June 1991.

Hamm, Mark S. *The Abandoned Ones: The Imprisonment and Uprising of the Mariel Boat People.* Boston: Northeastern University Press, 1995.

Hefner, Tony, and Jacalyn McLeod. *Between the Fences: Inside a U.S. Immigration Camp.* Bloomington, Ind.: First Books Library, 2002.

Herman, Judith. *Trauma and Recovery: The Aftermath of Violence—From Domestic Abuse to Political Terror.* New York: Basic Books, 1997.

Human Rights Watch. *All Too Familiar: Sexual Abuse of Women in U.S. State Prisons.* New York, December 1996.

———. *Cold Storage: Super-Maximum Security Confinement in Indiana.* New York, October 1997.

———. *Detained and Deprived of Rights: Children in the Custody of the U.S. Immigration and Naturalization Service.* New York, December 1998.

———. *The Human Rights Watch Global Report on Prisons.* New York, June 1993.

———. *Presumption of Guilt: Human Rights Abuses of Post–September 11 Detainees.* New York, August 2002.

———. *Locked Away: Immigration Detainees in Jails in the United States.* New York, September 1998.

———. *Prison Conditions in the United States.* New York, November 1991.

———. *Slipping through the Cracks: Unaccompanied Children Detained by the U.S. Immigration and Naturalization Service.* New York, April 1997.

Immigration Law Enforcement Monitoring Project of the Rio Grande Valley. "Abuse Will Not Be Tolerated!—A Call for Accountability Amid Increasing Human Rights Abuses along the South Texas/Mexico Border." Harlingen, Tex., May 1998.

Kahn, Robert S. *Other People's Blood: U.S. Immigration Prisons in the Reagan Decade.* Boulder, Colo.: Westview Press, 1996.

Kassindja, Fauziya, and Layli Miller Bashir. *Do They Hear You When You Cry.* New York: Delacorte Press, 1998.

Kerwin, Donald. *Migrants, Borders, and National Security: USA Immigration Policy since September 11, 2001.* New York: Center for Migration Studies, 2002.

Kurzban, Kurzban, and Weinger. "Report on Laredo and Port Isabel Detention Centers." Miami, 1993.

Kwong, Peter. *Forbidden Workers: Illegal Chinese Immigrants and American Labor.* New York: New Press, 1997.

Lawless, Robert. *Haiti's Bad Press.* Rochester, Vt.: Schenkman Books, 1992.

Lawyers Committee for Human Rights. *The Detention of Asylum Seekers in the United States: A Cruel and Questionable Policy.* New York, December 1989.

———. *Interim Report on the Pilot Parole Project of the Immigration and Naturalization Service.* New York, November 1990.

———. *Is This America? The Denial of Due Process to Asylum Seekers in the United States.* New York, October 2000.

———. *Refugees behind Bars: The Imprisonment of Asylum Seekers in the Wake of the 1996 Immigration Act.* New York, August 1999.

———. *Slamming "The Golden Door": A Year of Expedited Removal.* New York, March 1998.

———. *A Year of Loss: Reexamining Civil Liberties since September 11.* New York, 2002.

Lutheran Immigration and Refugee Service. *Detention Watch Network News.* Baltimore, Md., 1997–2001.

Malcolm, Janet. *The Crime of Sheila McGough.* New York: Vintage Books, 1999.

————. *The Journalist and the Murderer*. New York: Vintage Books, 1990.

Malkin, Michelle. *Invasion: How America Still Welcomes Terrorists, Criminals, and Other Foreign Menaces to Our Shores*. Washington, D.C.: Regnery, 2002.

McElrath, Karen. *Unsafe Haven: The United States, the IRA and Political Prisoners*. London: Pluto Press, 2000.

Minnesota Lawyers International Human Rights Committee, and Physicians for Human Rights. *Hidden from View: Human Rights Conditions in the Krome Detention Center*. Minneapolis, Minn., and Somerville, Mass., April 1991.

Morris, Norval, and David J. Rothman, eds. *The Oxford History of the Prison: The Practice of Punishment in Western Society*. New York: Oxford University Press, 1998.

Moynihan, Daniel Patrick. *Secrecy: The American Experience*. New Haven: Yale University Press, 1998.

Musalo, Karen, Deborah Anker, et al. "The Expedited Removal Study: Report on the First Year of Implementation of Expedited Removal." International Human Rights and Migration Project, Markkula Center for Applied Ethics, Santa Clara University. Santa Clara, Calif., May 1998.

Musalo, Karen, Lauren Gibson, et al. "The Expedited Removal Study: Report on the First Three Years of Implementation of Expedited Removal." Center for Human Rights and International Justice, University of California, Hastings College of the Law. San Francisco, May 2000.

————. "The Expedited Removal Study: Report on the Second Year of Implementation of Expedited Removal." Center for Human Rights and International Justice, University of California, Hastings College of the Law. San Francisco, May 1999.

Nevins, Joseph. *Operation Gatekeeper: The Rise of the "Illegal Alien" and the Making of the U.S.-Mexico Boundary*. New York: Routledge, 2002.

Oshinsky, David M. *"Worse than Slavery": Parchman Farm and the Ordeal of Jim Crow Justice*. New York: Free Press, 1996.

People of the Golden Vision. *The Golden Vision: A Newsletter in Support of the Men and Women of the Golden Venture*. York, Pa., 1993–97.

————. *The Plight of Chinese Refugees in America*. York, Pa., n.d. [1994?]. Short documentary film.

Robertson, Shari, and Michael Camerini. *Well-Founded Fear*. Epidavros Project, New York, 2000. Documentary film.

Robinson, Greg. *By Order of the President: FDR and the Internment of Japanese Americans*. Cambridge, Mass.: Harvard University Press, 2001.

Sassen, Saskia. *Guests and Aliens*. New York: New Press, 1999.

Saxton, Alexander. *The Indispensable Enemy: Labor and the Anti-Chinese Movement in California*. Berkeley: University of California Press, 1971.

Scarry, Elaine. *The Body in Pain: The Making and Unmaking of the World.* New York: Oxford University Press, 1985.

Schrag, Philip G. *A Well-Founded Fear: The Congressional Battle to Save Political Asylum in America.* New York: Routledge, 2000.

Solzhenitsyn, Aleksandr I. *The Gulag Archipelago, 1918–1956: An Experiment in Literary Investigation, I–II.* Trans. Thomas P. Whitney. New York: Harper & Row, 1973.

Stephan, Alexander. *"Communazis": FBI Surveillance of German Emigré Writers.* Trans. Jan van Heurck. New Haven: Yale University Press, 2000.

Theoharis, Athan, G., ed. *A Culture of Secrecy: The Government versus the People's Right to Know.* Lawrence: University Press of Kansas, 1998.

Trilling, Lionel. *The Opposing Self: Nine Essays in Criticism.* New York: Viking Press, 1955.

U.S. Commission on Immigration Reform. *Legal Immigration: Setting Priorities.* Report to Congress. Washington, D.C.: U.S. Government Printing Office, 1995.

———. *U.S. Immigration Policy: Restoring Credibility.* Report to Congress. Washington, D.C.: U.S. Government Printing Office, 1994.

U.S. Committee for Refugees. *Refugees at Our Border: The U.S. Response to Asylum Seekers.* Washington, D.C., September 1989.

U.S. Department of Justice, Office of the Inspector General. *Alleged Deception of Congress: The Congressional Task Force on Immigration Reform's Fact-finding Visit to the Miami District of INS in June 1995.* June 1996.

———. *Management Assistance Review of the Miami District Office of the Immigration and Naturalization Service.* February 1990. Report no. I-90-03.

———. *The September 11 Detainees: A Review of the Treatment of Aliens Held on Immigration Charges in Connection with the Investigation of the September 11 Attacks.* April 2003.

———, Audit Division. *Audit Report: Immigration and Naturalization Service Institutional Removal Program.* 02-41. September 2002.

U.S. Department of Justice, Office of Justice Programs, Bureau of Justice Statistics. *Immigration Offenders in the Federal Criminal Justice System, 2000.* NCJ 191745. August 2002.

U.S. General Accounting Office. *Alien Smuggling: Management and Operational Improvements Needed to Address Growing Problem.* May 2000. GAO/GGD-00-103.

———. *Criminal Aliens: INS's Detention and Deportation Efforts in the New York City Area.* December 1986. GAO/GGD-87-19BR.

———. *Criminal Aliens: INS's Efforts to Identify and Remove Imprisoned Aliens Need to be Improved.* July 15, 1997. GAO/T-GGD-97-154.

——. *Criminal Aliens: INS's Efforts to Remove Imprisoned Aliens Continue to Need Improvement.* October 1998. GAO/GGD-99-3.

——. *Detention Policies Affecting Haitian Nationals.* June 16, 1983. GAO/GGD-83-68.

——. *Immigration and Naturalization Service: Overview of Management and Program Challenges.* July 29, 1999. GAO/T-GGD-99-148.

——. *Immigration Enforcement: Challenges to Implementing the INS Interior Enforcement Strategy.* June 19, 2002. GAO-02-861T.

——. *Immigration Management: Strong Leadership and Management Reforms Needed to Address Serious Problems.* January 1991. GAO/GGD-91-28.

U.S. Immigration and Naturalization Service. "FY 1995 Implementation Strategy: Justice Prisoner and Alien Transportation System." Draft typescript. Washington, D.C., March 1, 1995.

——. *Statistical Yearbook of the Immigration and Naturalization Service, 2000.* Washington, D.C.: U.S. Government Printing Office, 2002.

——. Eastern Region, Detention and Deportation Division. "Krome SPC Back-up Material." Miami, August 2000.

——. Headquarters Detention and Deportation Division. "The Elizabeth, New Jersey Contract Detention Facility Operated by ESMOR Inc.: Interim Report, July 20, 1995."

——. Southern Regional Office. "Survey and Recommendations on the Functions, Mission, and Resources of the Krome North Service Processing Center—Miami, Florida, December 31, 1981." Typescript.

Vera Institute of Justice and Appearance Assistance Program. *Testing Community Supervision for the INS: An Evaluation of the Appearance Assistance Program. Volume I—Final Report to the Immigration and Naturalization Service, Prepared under INS Contract #COW-6-C-0038 for an Appearance Assistance Program.* New York, August 1, 2000.

Welch, Michael. *Detained: Immigration Laws and the Expanding I.N.S. Jail Complex.* Philadelphia: Temple University Press, 2002.

Wiener, Jon. *Gimme Some Truth: The John Lennon FBI Files.* Berkeley: University of California Press, 1999.

Williams, Raymond. *Keywords: A Vocabulary of Culture and Society.* New York: Oxford University Press, 1976.

Women's Commission for Refugee Women and Children. "Behind Locked Doors: Abuse of Refugee Women at the Krome Detention Center." New York, October 2000.

——. "A Cry for Help: Chinese Women in INS Detention—Delegation to Visit Asylum Seekers Held in New Orleans Parish Prison and Hancock County Justice Facility." New York, March 2–5, 1995.

———. "Forgotten Prisoners: A Follow-up Report on Refugee Women Incarcerated in York County, Pennsylvania." New York, July 1998.

———. "Liberty Denied: Women Seeking Asylum Imprisoned in the United States." New York, April 1997.

———. "An Uncertain Future, a Cruel Present: Women in INS Detention—Delegation to Visit Asylum Seekers Held in York and Berks County Prisons, Pennsylvania." New York, September 24–26, 1995.

Zepeda, Fabiola. "Castigo sin Culpa: Penalty without a Crime." Manuscript.

Arab-American Anti-Discrimination Committee (ADC), 205, 212, 223

Arabs: bias against, 26, 38–39, 86, 211, 218. *See also* Middle East

Arendt, Hannah, 297

Armstrong, Brian, 236–37

Army Corps of Engineers, 54

asbestos, 314n17

Ashcroft, John: evasiveness of, 201; forty-eight-hour rule of, 23; immigration hearings closed by, 20; preventive detention policy of, 45–46; priorities of, 25; on right to counsel, 29; secrecy under, 22–23, 35–36, 316n4; on Soliman's deportation, 360n31; on *Zadvydas* cases, 277–78

Asian asylum seekers and detainees: on "controlled environment," 272; hunger strikes of, 248; length of detention of, 16, 267; Polish detainee on, 256. *See also* Cambodian "American" detainee; Chinese asylum seekers and detainees; Laotian detainees; Vietnamese detainees

asylum seekers: detention of, 7, 9, 337–38n18; differential treatment of, 54–55; fears of, 134; home countries of, 119–20; moved from jail to jail, 29, 76; number of detained, 313–14n15; privacy of, 30–31, 114, 320n24; racism against, 68–69; sexual advances toward, 53; strategies to discourage, 98–99, 121; torture of, 120–21, 131; treated as animals, ix–xiii; treated as inmates, 231; unreported by INS, 313–14n15; violence against, 140, 162–63. *See also* deportation; detainees; political asylum; *specific people*

Atlanta (Ga.) detention center: drugs forced on detainees in, 290; officers' attitudes in, 295–96; suicide attempts in, 291–92, 370n10

Atlanta (Ga.) District (INS): Bachir's case in, 206–7, 211, 214–15

attorneys: Correctional officers' differences with, 230; denial of access to, 29, 282, 293, 321n30; disruption of relationship with, 181; files kept from, 293; frustrations of, 262; INS staff on, 132; limited access to, 43, 337–38n18; percentage of detainees represented by, 344n8; right to, 29, 31–34, 269

Aubitz, Shawn P., 6

Aurora (Colo.) Service Processing Center: abuse reported in, 258, 259–60; appearance of, 110–11; hunger strikes in, 135, 248; long-term detainees in, 271; opening of, 97; property room in, 244–45; segregation cells in, 255–57; strip searches in, 256; tours of, 129–30, 259; unremovable detainees in, 264; visitation rooms in, 245

automatic stay order: rationale for, 23

Avoyelles Parish Jail (Marksville, La.), 77, 96

Bachir, Mohammad: accusations against, 211–13; attitudes toward, 210–11, 359–60n29; beating of, 204, 213; concerns about releasing, 214–15; criminal sentences served by, 197–98, 224, 359n27; detained again, post-9/11, 224–25, 359n28;

CCA. *See* Corrections Corporation of America

CCC (Columbia, S.C., Care Center), 213–14, 219

Central Virginia Regional Jail (Orange), 366–67n13

CFR (Code of Federal Regulations), 35

Chadbourne, Bruce, 206–7

Chang, Nancy, 23

Chertoff, Michael, 29

Chinese asylum seekers and detainees: advocacy group for, 63; Calejo on, 50; circumstances of, 8; on discrimination, 60–61; held in Guam, 36, 322n37; history of, 86, 87; hunger strike of, 205; labor of, 314n17; profits from, 10; sedation used on, 333–35n9; stereotypes of, 329n24. See also *Golden Venture*

Church, Susan, 229, 234–36

CIEJ. *See* Citizens and Immigrants for Equal Justice

*Circle, The* (film), 352–53n6

Cisneros, Robert, 132

Citizens and Immigrants for Equal Justice (CIEJ): origins of, 173–74; rally of, 175, 187, 192–93

citizenship: detainees on, 202, 260; eligibility for, 260–61; swearing in for, 261, 363n7

Civil Liberties Organization (Nigeria), 336–37n16

Clemon, U. W., 358n14

Cliff, Jimmy, 195

CLINIC (Catholic Legal Immigration Network), 52, 364–65n13

clink (sound), 177

Clinton, Bill, 8, 9, 117, 173, 192

Coalition for the Human Rights of Immigrants, 40

Cockburn, Andrew, 36

Cockburn, Patrick, 36

Code of Federal Regulations (CFR), 35

Cohen, Nancy, 318n15, 325–26n8

Cole, David, 13, 23–24, 318n17

Coley, Will, 348n8

Colombian detainee: complaints of, 203; on fear of retaliation, 204

Colorado District (INS), 248–53. *See also* Aurora (Colo.) Service Processing Center

Columbia (S.C.) Care Center (CCC), 213–14, 219

commissioner, INS. *See specific commissioners:* Meissner, Doris; Nelson, Alan C.; Zigler, James

Committee Against Anti-Asian Violence (CAAAV), 114, 129

Committee to Support Cuban Detainees, 291–92

Community Relations (INS), 99, 112

Connecticut prisons, 188, 238–39

contract security, 283. *See also* private prison companies

Convention Against Torture (CAT): asylum claim based on, 100–101; "deferral of removal" of deportation under, 218; "withholding" of deportation under, 124–25, 134

Cook, Jimmy: on attempted suicides, 98; mentioned, 89, 97, 341n8; on working in detention, 89–92

*Cool Hand Luke* (film), 231

Copes, Gary: on brutality, 184–85, 186; treatment by, 177, 182–83, 187; trial and acquittal of, 184, 353–56n11

Cuban asylum seekers *(continued)*
remembered, 301; suicide attempts
of, 291–92, 370n10; on survival,
300–301; treatment of, 182–83;
uniforms for, 17
Cusson, Marc, 357–58n10
custody reviews: appeals process absent for, 291; arbitrariness of, 223,
268–70, 294; Border Patrol officers
at, 296; changing process of, 274;
detainees eligible for, under *Zadvydas* cases, 364–65n13; Kennedy's
defense of, 273–74; for lifers, 265–
66; for Mariel Cuban detainees,
287, 292–93, 371n13; positive points
in, 267–68; schedule for, 222, 224;
secrecy of, 293–94

Dafali, Salah, 140, 346–48n7
*Dallas Morning News,* 30–31
*Dateline,* 159
Dave, Rita, 175–76, 181
Dawlett, Ihsan Elias, 193
dead time: uncertainty of, 283–84;
use of term, 264. *See also* long-
term detainees
DeKalb County (Ala.) Jail, 205
Del Rosso, Pete, 40–41
democracy, 24, 172
Denton County (Texas) Jail, 28–29
Denver (Colo.): as central for INS
transport, 250–51. *See also* Aurora
(Colo.) Service Processing Center;
Colorado District (INS)
deportation: alternatives to, 74–75;
as cost-cutting method, 103–4;
expedited removal in, 9; federal
requirements in, 281–83; home
countries' reprisals after, 33,
321n31; imprisonment following,

226, 274, 276–77; of legal permanent resident, 171–74, 260; none
sent to Iraq, 368n15; petty crimes
as justification of, 179–81; process
of, 83–84, 87–88; program for,
312–13n13; requests for, 96, 135,
341–42n10, 347n7; resistance to,
70, 73–74, 238, 292–93; results of,
83–84, 336–37n16; as retaliation
for lawsuit, 240; third country for,
219, 273; as threat, 52, 115–16;
timing of, 167, 338–39n23; U.S.-
Cuba negotiations on, 291–92;
"withholding" of, 124–25. *See also*
custody reviews; repatriation
agreements; sedation, forced
Desis Rising Up and Moving
(DRUM), 40
detainee numbers: asylum seekers,
313–14n15; detention enforcement
officers and, 130; registration, x,
131–32; in year 2002, 362n10; in
year 2003, 314n16; in years 1973–
1980, 8; in years 1994–2001, 9,
30–31, 320n25
detainees: "administrative," 9, 16, 74,
111, 270, 315–16n31; communication of, 131, 133, 203, 216, 296 *(see
also* telephone calls); counting of,
50–51, 135; death of, 236–37, 242,
251, 362–63n3 *(see also* suicides);
definition of, 14–15, 16–17, 32;
depression of, 327n21; despair of,
97–98, 101–4, 125–28, 176, 248,
258, 276, 291, 295; fears of, 134,
204, 215–16; hiding/losing of,
253–54; as manipulative, 93, 101;
mistreatment of, 1–4 *(see also*
abuse; sedation, forced; torture);
names of, 23, 29, 30–34; nation-

alities of, 50–51, 96, 113, 200, 245;
overcrowding of, 4; "problem"
cases of, 209–10; profits through,
9–11, 97, 111, 196, 208, 229,
342n12; release as option for,
111; treated as prisoners, 231;
as victims, 15–16, 236; vulner-
ability of, 52. *See also* asylum
seekers; long-term detainees;
*specific countries* (e.g., Nigerian
asylum seekers and detainees)
detention: assumptions in, 162–63;
automatic stay order in, 23; damage of, 298–300; detainees' complaints as justifying, 265–66; as
deterrent, 7, 45–46; fraud suspected in, 96, 341–42n10; history
of policy on, 6–7; induced mental
illness as reason for, 290; infrastructure for, 25–26, 55, 232, 252–
53; public awareness of, 12–13;
restrictions on discussing, 34–35,
98–99, 129–30, 140, 321n33,
348n8; slavery compared with, 10,
358n14. *See also* custody reviews;
length of detention; release from
detention
detention enforcement officers
(DEOs): advocates' differences
with, 230; attitudes of, 57–58, 65;
brutality of, 87, 167, 184–86; on
challenges of job, 89–90; conditioning of, 162–63; on control
tactics, 148–52; counter-charges
used by, 74–75; on detainees'
rights, 91–92; INS treatment of,
169; morale of, 44–45, 64; number
per detainee (1997), 130; prosecution of, 48–50, 144–47, 151–52,
353–56n11; report filed by, 52–53;

suicides of, 58, 97–98; on "three-
sided cell" strategy, 260; training
of, 56–57, 105; vacations for, 73,
238. *See also* correctional officers
(COs); racism; *specific people*
detention facilities: beat and greet
reception in, 142–44; cell dimensions in, 41–42, 322n37; commissary in, 95, 341n7; fencing at, 56;
hearings in, 91; inside and outside
of, 18; inspection of, 344n7; invisi-
bility of, 2; local jails as, 9, 209–
10, 231, 232; locations of, 11–12;
prisons compared with, 16–17, 94,
259; proprietary attitudes toward,
129–30; as "recession proof" industry, 156–57; shortage of, 8;
windows covered in, 47, 128. *See
also* prisons; private prison companies; *specific facilities*
Detroit (Mich.): detainees' trial in,
318n17
Dhine, Lulseged, 63–64
Diamant, Leran, 19–21
*Diario/La Prensa* (newspaper), 133
Diaz, Humberto, 224, 359–60n29
DiGiovanni, Janine, 282
Dinkins, David, 118
dissidents, 14, 70
district directors, INS. *See specific
district directors:* Cadman, Walter
"Dan"; Ferro, Benedict; Greene,
Joseph; Lewis, Warren; McElroy,
Edward J.; Quarantillo, Andrea;
Slattery, William; Smith, Richard;
Wallis, Robert
Djibouti: Somalis transported to,
282, 283
Domestic Security Enhancement Act
(2003), 35

Hungarian detainee, 39–40
hunger strikers: attitudes toward, 101; correctional officer on, 235–36; by death row inmate, 214; demands of, 57, 70; of El Centro detainees, 201–4; force-feeding of, 213–14, 218–20; hospital care for, 213–14; INS invention of, 270–72; interview during, 198–99; medical care for, 127, 132, 133–34, 186, 213–14; as misbehavior justifying detention, 265–66, 268, 271; motivation of, 111–14, 125–28, 130–33; nonviolence emphasized in, 203; as opposition to "illegal detention," 218–19; psychological warfare in, 106–8; restraints during, 348n7; retaliation against, 98, 135; transfer of leaders of, 204
Hurricane Andrew, 65, 76–77
Hutchinson, Brian, 282–83

Ignatius, Sarah, 231
illegal immigrants: deaths of, 251, 322n36, 362–63n3; definition of, 13–14; extremist attitudes toward, 86–87; media coverage of, 26–27. *See also* aliens; borders
Illegal Immigration Reform and Immigrant Responsibility Act (IIRIRA, 1996): complexity of, 187–90; implications of, 9, 15–16, 173; INS criticism of, 190–92, 249; mandatory detention in, 198, 201–2, 229–30; in Mariel Cubans' case, 289–91; passage of, 9, 173, 192; public misunderstanding of, 179–81; reform efforts on, 174; retroactive implementation of, 173, 188–90; as "subconstitutional," 260

illegality: definitions of, 357n7
Illinois prisons, 255
immigration: debate on, 14–15; history of, 6–9
Immigration and Asylum Project (Boston College), 229–30
Immigration and Naturalization Service (INS): accountability lacking for, 11, 13–14, 90, 139–40, 225, 294, 365–67n13; arrogance of, 266; asylum seekers treated as animals by, ix–xiii; biases in, 68–69, 86–87, 162, 211–13, 218; branches of, 316–17n6; complaints to, 52–53, 115–16, 137, 201–3; criticism of, 217; culture of, 14, 85–86; deniability strategy of, 232–33, 369n2; history of, 6–9; hopelessness exploited by, 101–4; humanity glimpsed in, 129–30; immigration laws (1996) criticized by, 190–92; as inhumane, 158, 161, 204, 351–53n6; injustice of, 283–84; media access restricted by, 30–31, 34–35, 61–62, 99, 129–30; media's relation to, 2, 83–84, 95; on mistreatment of detainees, 161, 350n4; on numbers of detainees, 30, 313n15, 314n16, 318n15, 370n10; oversight absent for, 53, 325n7; power of, 248–49, 252–53, 289–90, 293, 294; reorganization after 9/11, 85–87; targets of, 26; terminology of, 17–18, 263–64, 315–16n31; transferred to Homeland Security Department, 11. *See also* detention; Justice Department; policy and guidelines (INS); secrecy; transfers and transport; *specific INS officials*

immigration courts and judges: asylum hearing in, 116–25; attitudes of, 84, 279–81, 337–38n18; bureaucratic proceedings in, 14; closed in special interest cases, 20, 22; description of, 116–17; history lesson in, 119–20; incomplete information for, 334–35n9; Justice Department's control of, 23, 116–17, 316–17n6; languages appearing in, 349n11; lawsuit on access to, 22–23, 316n4; location of, 313n13; names removed from court dockets for, 23, 29; order to hold, 243; positive signs for, 172; refusal to hold, 241; small talk in, 118–19; on terrorist allegations, 218. *See also* Board of Immigration Appeals (BIA)

Immigration Law Enforcement Review Committee (proposed), 73

India: persecution of Sikhs in, 105–6

Indian asylum seekers and detainees: beatings of, 144–45; hunger strikes of Sikh, 105–9; request for files of, 322n36

inmate: use of term, 32, 82. *See also* detainees; prisoners

INS. *See* Immigration and Naturalization Service

Institutional Removal Program (IRP), 312–13n13

*INS v. Enrico St. Cyr,* 187–90

*Iowa Law Review,* 35–36

Iqbal, Zafar, 193

Iran: public misunderstanding of, 38

Iranian detainees: abuse of, 216; at airport, 352–53n6; circumstances of, 245–46, 259; despair of, 248; medical care for, 247; privacy of, violated, 31

Iraq: conference on, 36; no deportations to, 368n15

Iraqi detainees: complaints of, 203; held in Guam, 36–37; number of, 39, 323n46; racism against, 38–39; secret evidence on, 204–5

IRP (Institutional Removal Program), 312–13n13

Islamic Jihad, 360n32

isolation: humiliation and, 169–70; purpose of, 127, 181, 248; as threat, 59; uses of, 58, 70. *See also* segregation cells

Israeli detainees: circumstances of, 19–20; courtroom proceedings and, 20, 22–23; families of, 24; INS and FBI interviews of, 21–22; release of, 20–21

Jackson, Robert, 39–40, 310–11n7, 370n9

Jackson County (Fla.) Jail, 327–29n21

jail: as house, 264. *See also* detention facilities; prisons

Jamaican detainees: beatings of, 164–67; Calejo on, 50; circumstances of, 240–41; complaints of, 203; deportation of, 238; "rushing" of, 167–68; slapping of, 65; stereotypes of, 164

James, Rossi, 72

James, William, 253

Jaramillo, "Charlie," 193

Jefferson County (Okla.) Detention Center, 261–62

Jena Juvenile Justice Center (La.), 92, 339n2

Jensen, Dean, 238

Jesuit Refugee Service, 140, 348n8

on interviews with detainees, 198; on memo preparation, 80, 166–67; as mind control, 259–60; on minors, 308n3; on mistreatment of detainees, 350n4; on monitoring hunger strikers, 127; on parole, 111, 122, 345n14; on privacy, 31, 319–20n23; racism in, 211–13; reality vs., 252–53; repression in, 266; on restraints, 178–79; on sedation, 77–81, 80–81; on transfer of protest leaders, 114–15; violation of, 165

Polish detainee: circumstances of, 255–57; criminal conviction of, 253–54; "hold" on, 254–55; release of, 262; on survival, 257–58; transfer of, 261

political asylum: denial of, 7, 8; detention despite, 8; differential treatment in granting, 54–55; Ebibillo's request for, 73–74; execution and, 337–38n18; hearings for, 110–11; protected categories in, 124. *See also* asylum seekers; Convention Against Torture (CAT)

politics: of mandatory sentences, 163–64; of secrecy, 36–37

Pope, Anthony, 144–46

Popovic, Charles, 144, 152

Porter, Kim W., 308n3

Port Isabel (Texas) Processing Center, 325n3

*Prime Time Live,* 217

prisoners: death of, 236–37; definition of, 14–15, 16–17; detainees compared with, 235–36; number of (1980–2001), 163, 350n5

Prisoners' Rights Project (Legal Aid Society, New York), 351–52n6

prison mentality, 154–55, 228–29, 261–62

Prison Moratorium Project, 40

Prison Realty, 97

prisons: accountability of, 11; counting inmates in, 50–51; detention facilities compared with, 16–17, 94, 259; longing for, xii–xiii; noise in, 160, 216; physical structure of, 176–77, 230; problems created by, 186, 232; psychiatric asylum compared with, 263; racial politics in, 66–67; reform of, 351n3; reporting on, 197; visitation facilities in, 240. *See also* detention facilities; private prison companies; *specific prisons and locations*

private prison companies: bailout of, 312–13n13; cost-cutting by, 103–5; employee benefits in, 104–5, 341n7; escapes from, 315–16n31; financial arrangements of, 96–97; low profiles of, 90, 110–11; mistreatment and violence reported in, 104–5, 340–41n5, 343n20; profits of, 9–11, 97, 342n12; secrecy of, 90; as shield for INS, 14, 138. *See also* Correctional Services Corporation (CSC); Corrections Corporation of America (CCA); Esmor Corporation; Louisiana Corrections Service (LCS); Wackenhut Corrections Corporation (WCC)

processing centers: use of term, 55. *See also specific processing centers*

Project Exile, 278

property, personal. *See* belongings of detainees

protests and demonstrations: of Chinese asylum seekers, 60–61; description of, 37; by Haitian community, 4–5; by Mariel detainees, of Cuban deportations, 292; as negotiation, 126–27; nonviolent, 54–55, 61, 199–200, 203; officials' response to, 54–55, 114–15; outside detention centers, 4–5, 41–42, 106; outside INS offices, 112, 129; strategy to break up, 127; in Union Square (N.Y.C.), 40. *See also* hunger strikers

Public Affairs (INS): on privacy, 319–20n23; on terminology, 263–64. *See also* secrecy; *specific INS spokespersons:* Aquino, Luisa; Bergeron, Russell; Black, Temple; Cohen, Nancy; Gill, Kerry; Kraushaar, Karen; Strassberger, William; Thorn, Mark; Wooley, Lamar

Public Health Service (PHS): Ebibillo's sedation and, 72, 73, 77–78; INS policy on sedation and, 80–81. *See also* medical care; nurses

public safety, 278

punishment: doubled for criminal aliens, 272–73; medical care as, 92; rejection of term, 17, 316n32. *See also* custody reviews; sedation, forced; segregation cells; shackles and restraints

Quality Sales (company), 19

Quarantillo, Andrea, 34–35, 140, 348n8

Queens (N.Y.) detention center: beating in, 134–35; courtroom in, 116; description of, 110, 134; hunger strikes in, 111–14, 125–29, 130–33; media interviews discouraged at, 98–99; power struggle in, 133–34; violence in, 112–15

Quinlan, Michael, 292, 295

Rabinovitz, Judy, 13, 180, 278, 369n1, 372n23

racism: among correctional officers, 152–53, 161, 166; institutionalization of, 38–39; investigation of, 168–69; persistence of, 86–87; rejection of, 261–62; as widespread, 68–70, 158

Radio Martí, 291

Rafael, Sally Jesse, 159

Rahman, Hasan Abdel, 212

Rajigah, Marlon: on beatings, 181; detention of, 174–76, 275; on immigration laws, 179, 180–81; on jailers, 186; on profits, 196; on segregation, 194–95; warden on, 182–83

Rajneesh (Bhagwan), 249

Ramirez, John, 99

rape: complaints about, 62, 331–32n3; frequency of, 52, 325n3. *See also* sexual abuse; sodomy

Rastafarians, 164

Reagan, Ronald: attorney general under, 249–50; Castro and, 291–92; Haitians detained under, 7; militarization of borders under, 8

refugees: detention of, 63–64, 265–68. *See also* asylum seekers; political asylum

Regis, Teresa, 126

regulations: American obsession with, 20; appropriateness standard as, 34–35; on detainees' names, 33, 34; standards vs., 13. *See also* policy and guidelines (INS)

rehabilitation, 254–55, 273

Rehnquist, William, 179–80

Reinhardt, Stephen, 23

release from detention: arbitrariness of, 223; conditions for, 223–25; decline of, post-9/11, 279; denial of, 254–55, 285–86; difficulty in adjustment after, xii–xiii, 298; husbands and wives separated in, 252; of Mariel Cuban detainees, 296, 297; questions about, 275; recommendation for, ignored, 365–67n13; revocation of, 269–70; under *Zadvydas* cases, 364–65n13. *See also* custody reviews; deportation; *specific people*

religion: as comfort, 45; disallowing traditions of, 216, 219; failure to understand, 21; hunger strikes and, 105–7; Rastafarian, 164; threat to Saudi detainee concerning, 27. *See also* Muslim detainees

Reno, Janet, 35, 237, 250–52

repatriation agreements: absent for some countries, 264, 265–68; with Cambodia, 276–77; Somalia situation in, 281–83

Reynolds, James, 33

Reynolds, Jennifer, 339–40n3

Rhode Island prisons, 240–43, 362n13

Rice, Jimmy: conviction of, 144, 147, 149, 151; description of, 151–52, 154

right to counsel, 29, 31–34, 269. *See also* attorneys

Rikers Island, 174, 197

Riordan, Denis, 232

Rivera, Aida, 71, 327n15

Rivera, Anthony, 4

Rivera, Lupe (Guadalupe): on cost-cutting, 104; departure of, 105; on hunger strike, 106–7; on sedation, 81–82; on segregation cells, 91; sympathy of, 102–4; on violent tactics, 104–5

Robinson, Craig, 176

Robinson, Evaristo, 126

Rockingham County (N.H.) Jail, 205

Rodriguez, Omar, 294

Rodriguez, Pedro Prior, 293

Roe, Amy, 341n7

Romanian asylum seekers, 98

Roosevelt, Franklin D., 11

Rowley, Coleen, 26–27

Rozos, Michael: Ebibillo threatened by, 74–75; on Krome detainees, 331–32n3; positions of, 65, 138, 273, 331–32n3; on visitation requirements, 5

Rush, John, 241

Rush City (Minn.) jail, 280

Russian detainee, 222

Rwanda: genocide and war in, 119–20, 123–24

Sabah, Rachel, 21

Sadat, Anwar, 218, 360n32

St. Cyr, Enrico, 187–90

St. Kitts: woman deported to, 334n9

Sale, Chris, 85

Salvadoran asylum seekers: lawsuit concerning, 199–200; moved from jail to jail, 29; privacy of, violated, 30–31; sedation of, 335n9; on slaps and blows, 65

WCC. *See* Wackenhut Corrections Corporation (WCC)

Weiss, Constance "Kathy": on confiscated belongings, 3; legal assistance denied by, 5; positions of, 2, 4, 308–9n4; relief efforts and, 65

Welch, David, 226

Welch, John, 178

Westphal, Amy, 33

whistleblowers, 62–63, 217

white: definition of, 260–61

Whitman, Walt, 17

Whitney, Thomas P., 12

Whonder, Derrick, 158

Wicomico (Md.) jail, 178

Williams, Amos G., 319n18

Williamson, Wes: on Bachir's case, 221; on Etowah jail, 208–9; interests of, 227; on "problem" cases, 209–10; on Soliman's case, 220, 221

Wilson, Carla, 370n10

Wilson, John, 288

Wilson, Pete, 164

women detainees: abuse of, 216, 237; conditions for, 9, 52–53, 252; correctional officers' watching of, 235; on Krome, 56; menstruation of, 334n9; miscarriage of, 178; number of (2002), 362n10; shackling of, 178–79, 351–52n6; strip searches of, 239; transferred from Hillsborough, 238–40. *See also* rape; sexual abuse

Wooley, Lamar, 61

Woolsey, James, 37–38, 323n42

work-release programs, 16–17, 231, 241

*World Press,* 133

World Trade Center bombing (1993), 8, 173, 217–18. *See also* terrorist attacks (2001)

writings: despair in, 294, 307–8n1; destruction of, 294, 309–10n4; hopes in, 195; materials for, denied, 70. See also poetry

Wynn, Dougie, 152

York County (Pa.) Prison, 10, 115, 239–40

*Yusuf Ali Ali v. Ashcroft,* 368–69n21

Yvenie, Emmanuel, 178, 351–52n6

Zadvydas, Kestutis, 272–73

*Zadvydas* cases: Ashcroft on, 277–78; detainees eligible for review under, 364–66n13; on length of detention, 265, 273–74, 360n30; loophole in, 367–68n13; Mariel Cubans and, 289–91; origins of, 272–73; timing of, 278–79

*Zadvydas v. Davis. See Ma v. Reno; Zadvydas* cases

Zapata, Emilio, 102

Zayat, Muntasir al-, 360n32

Zeidan, Malek, 22–23

Zigler, James, 242

Zurofsky, Bennet D., 22–23

| | |
|---:|:---|
| Indexer: | Margie Towery |
| Compositor: | BookMatters, Berkeley |
| Text: | 11/14 Adobe Garamond |
| Display: | Knockout, Gill Sans Book, Adobe Garamond |
| Printer and binder: | Maple-Vail Manufacturing Group |